"Benevolent Assimilation"

Finally, it should be the earnest and paramount aim of the military administration to win the confidence, respect, and affection of the inhabitants of the Philippines by assuring them in every possible way that full measure of individual rights and liberties which is the heritage of a free people, and by proving to them that the mission of the United States is one of benevolent assimilation, substituting the mild sway of justice and right for arbitrary rule.

FROM PRESIDENT MCKINLEY'S "BENEVOLENT ASSIMILATION" PROCLAMATION DECEMBER 21, 1898

"BENEVOLENT ASSIMILATION"

The American Conquest of the Philippines, 1899–1903

STUART CREIGHTON MILLER

YALE UNIVERSITY PRESS

NEW HAVEN AND LONDON

Designed by James J. Johnson
and set in Caledonia Roman by G & S Typesetters, Inc.
Printed in the United States of America by
The Murray Printing Co., Westford, Mass.

Library of Congress Cataloging in Publication Data

Miller, Stuart Creighton, 1927–
    "Benevolent assimilation."

    Bibliography: p.
    Includes index.
    1. Philippines—History—Insurrection, 1899–1901.
2. Philippines—History—1898–1946.   I. Title.
DS679.M59   959.9'03   82–1957
ISBN 0–300–02697–8   AACR2
ISBN 0–300–03081–9 (pbk)

10 9 8 7 6 5 4 3

IN MEMORY OF MY PARENTS

Stewart Gillespie Millar   AND   *Susanna Morrow Dunleavy*

of Dromadarragh, Augher, Tyrone   *of Derrylagham, Kilcar, Donegal*

Contents

Illustrations

between pages 128 and 129

"Saved from the Cruel Spaniard." (*The Chronicle, Chicago*)
"The White Man's Burden." (*The Journal, Detroit*)
General Emilio Aguinaldo (*National Archives*)
General Arthur MacArthur (*National Archives*)
General Adna Chaffee (*U.S. Army Military History Institute*)
General Henry W. Lawton (*U.S. Army Military History Institute*)
Filipino victims of American bombardment on the first day of the war (*National Archives*)
Filipino prisoners at the Rio Grande in Pampanga (*U.S. Army Military History Institute*)
Filipino officers posing before the war (*Library of Congress*)
Macabebe scouts in formation, Pampanga (*U.S. Army Military History Institute*)
The Filipino leaders (*Library of Congress*)
General Elwell S. Otis and his aides (*U.S. Army Military History Institute*)
Aguinaldo saluting as he boards the U.S.S. *Vicksburg* (*National Archives*)
General Frederick Funston aboard the *Vicksburg* with his prize (*National Archives*)
"Did He Do It?" (*The St. Paul Dispatch*)
"February 12—'Lest We Forget.'" (*The New York World*)
"Bryan's Road to the White House." (*The Chicago Inter-Ocean*)
"Trade Follows the Flag." (*The New York World*)
"'Kill Every One over Ten.'—Gen. Jacob H. Smith." (*The Evening Journal, New York*)

ix

MAPS

Acknowledgments

I am deeply indebted to many scholars who have read this manuscript, or portions of it, and have provided me with crucial corrections and valuable suggestions. Peter Stanley, to whom I am particularly grateful, not only read the entire manuscript carefully, but also invited me to participate in the Philippine-American History Project sponsored by the Harvard University–Henry R. Luce Foundation over a number of summers. This provided me the opportunity to work with Theodore Friend, Richard Welch, Frank Golay, John Larkin, Bonifacio Salamanca, Michael Onorato, Michael Cullinane, Norman Owen, Bernardita Reyes Churchill, Glenn May, Kenton Clymer, Reynaldo Ileto, Ronald Egerton, and, of course, the project director, Peter Stanley. Most of these scholars read a shorter version of the chapter on the American soldiers and the war in the Philippines and responded with enthusiasm. Glenn May generously shared with me some of his own research on the pacification of Batangas, at that time not yet published. Dick Welch, who has been mining this and related fields for years, provided stimulating and humorous commentary on our overlapping research interests.

A number of scholars in my own university, San Francisco State, read the sections of the manuscript that touched on their areas of expertise. Robert Cherny read the chapters on anti-imperialism and the election of 1900, and Philip Siegelman the introductory chapter on American imperialism. John Curtin read the entire work. All of them provided corrections, suggestions, and encouragement. Stanley Bailis, Donald Barnhart, Marshall Windmiller, and Devere Pentony convinced me to retain the epilogue with minor changes just as I was about to delete it. Needless to say, none of the above scholars shares any responsibility for errors that may remain in this work.

The burden of research would have been impossible without the unstinting aid of many librarians and archivists, too numerous to list here. I would like to thank Dr. Richard Sommers of the United States Army Military History Research Center at Carlisle Barracks, Carlisle, Pennsylvania, for his effective help during two visits to his impressive archives and for his prompt replies by mail to many subsequent inquiries on my part. I am grateful to the staffs at the university libraries at Harvard, Berkeley, Stanford, Columbia, Yale, the Missionary Research Library at the Union Theological Seminary, and those at the Library of Congress, the National Archives, the American Antiquarian Society, the Boston Athenaeum, the public libraries of New York City, Boston, and San Francisco, and the historical societies of New York, Massachusetts, Pennsylvania, and California.

Friends and relatives lent assistance in many ways. Bill Broder, novelist, playwright, historical fiction writer, Sausalito neighbor, friend, and tennis foe, was delighted with the work and kept me going with warm enthusiasm. My wife, Naomi, spent many hours working on too many drafts with a discerning eye and a ruthless blue pencil. My son, Peter Isaac, chipped in with some proofreading chores. Roberto Susanna lent me his Calabrian villa at Copenello where I worked on the first rough draft in spite of such distractions as a turquoise Ionian Sea at my feet and encircling vistas of the coastal mountains of "Italy's California." Giovanni Gatti and the charming Rosetta Stranges contributed in myriad ways to make my family's stay there infinitely more pleasant. On the outer reach of Cape Cod, where most of this work was subsequently written over many summers, an adequate research library and decent copying machine were out of reach. My sister, Olive Keeler, and a friend, Dan Sanders, saved me countless miles of travel doing errands for me in Boston and Hartford. For such personal touches, I am at a loss for words to express accurately the depth of my gratitude.

Finally, I would like to thank Lorraine Whittemore of my school's Faculty Manuscript Service for directing so efficiently the production of a final draft, and Dean Devere Pentony for continuing to fund this service in the face of budget squeezes. I am also grateful to Margaret Rice of my school's Cartography Laboratory for her skillful work on the maps.

Truro, Massachusetts   S.C.M.

American Imperialism:
Aberration or Historical Continuity?

The question of American imperialism has been subject to agonizing debate ever since the United States acquired a formal empire at the end of the nineteenth century. In part, the agony stems from America's exaggerated sense of innocence, produced by a kind of "immaculate conception" view of this country's origins. The first settlers sought to escape the political and social sins of Europe, as did subsequent waves of immigrants over the next three centuries; they were not likely to reproduce a system from which they had fled in protest. In some mysterious manner, therefore, they left behind their old ways, or shed them upon arrival in the New World, as one might discard old clothing, and fashioned new cultural garments based solely on experiences in a new and vastly different environment. At least it is possible to infer as much from the school texts and patriotic speeches on which so many Americans have been reared. America's cultural antecedents in western civilization are not stressed in these sources, and it is difficult to learn from them that the American Revolution was largely an English affair; that the United States Constitution owes its structure as much to the ideas of John Calvin and Thomas Hobbes as to the experiences of the Founding Fathers; that Jeffersonian thought to a great extent paraphrases the ideas of earlier Scottish philosophers; and that even the allegedly unique experiment of frontier egalitarianism has deep roots in seventeenth-century English radical traditions.

The notion of such a cultural metamorphosis is entirely romantic, but the concept of a totally unique social system fashioned solely by the experiences of colonial Americans is in harmony with the prevailing pragmatic style of America. It also makes it difficult for many Americans to come to grips with social flaws associated with the "Old World," such as militarism, imperialism, inequality, and the misuse of power. The tendency of highly patriotic Americans is to deny such abuses and even to assert that they could never exist in their country. At the other end of the scale, overly self-critical Americans tend to exaggerate the nation's flaws, failing to place them in historical or worldwide contexts. The application of criteria for America different from the rest of the world is another expression of this sense of uniqueness, one which has affected the American debate over imperialism.

One patriotic school of writers has generally denied that American imperialism ever existed. As Albert Beveridge, historian and senator from Indiana, once explained, "To have an empire one must have a monarchy."[1] Americans altruistically went to war with Spain to liberate Cubans, Puerto Ricans, and Filipinos from their tyrannical yoke. If they lingered on too long in the Philippines, it was to protect the Filipinos from European predators waiting in the wings for an American withdrawal and to tutor them in American-style democracy. The task was complicated by ethnic and class divisions and the alleged need to protect Ilocanos, Visayans, and others against the dominant Tagalogs. If the Yankee presence was bloody initially, it was, in the end, ephemeral and supposedly most beneficial to the Filipinos, leaving behind better transportation, mosquito control, the work ethic, the seed of Protestantism, and that perfect symbol of American beneficence, the ubiquitous schoolhouse. In short, these writers accept the official version of the American conquest of the Philippines, one that is not totally without supportive evidence. The Germans certainly made their intentions clear through aggressive naval maneuvers on Manila Bay as America debated the fate of the Philippines in 1898. American rule was short (as compared with the colonial histories of European powers) and did leave many benefits behind, but it did not end the internal class, ethnic, and religious strife, which persists to this day. Needless to say, this patriotic interpretation is no longer heard very often, although a small academic circle is attempting to salvage portions of it.[2]

In the highly self-critical mood of the post–World War II era, the tendency has been to exaggerate American imperialism and the injustices created by it. Marxist historians and writers of the New Left find it difficult, if not impossible, to perceive any benefits flowing from American imperialism; it was, ipso facto, an unmitigated evil. Moreover, American imperialism, in their view, did not begin with the Philippines but with Jefferson's purchase of the Louisiana Territory and continues to this day. American history is one of continuous expansion that left behind a long string of nonwhite victims. The driving force behind the expansion across the continent and out into the Pacific was, and still is, capitalist greed. Its rationalization was, and still is, the racist creed. For these writers, capitalism is the root of all evil, a role similar to that played by monarchy for nineteenth-century Americans. Socialist imperialism is to them an impossible contradiction in terms.

Between these two positions, another point of view recognizes American expansion overseas as imperialistic but perceives it as a corruption of the traditional American sense of mission to serve as an example to others, a beacon on a hill that would eventually light up a world in political darkness. At the end of the nineteenth century, this noble tradition became a more aggressive missionary impulse to carry the American way of life to others whether they liked it or not. But the corruption was short-lived and by the Wilsonian era America had rejected a formal empire. In the words of Samuel Flagg Bemis, intellectual mentor to a generation of diplomatic historians, this ephemeral imperialistic impulse was "a great aberration in American history."

Pervading all three schools of thought is considerable semantic confusion. Expansion across the underpopulated American continent was a less conscious, perhaps "natural," act as settlers climbed the next hill or forded an adjacent river until they reached such "natural" boundaries as the Pacific or Caribbean. Crossing an ocean, however, was a more conscious act of will to expand beyond contiguous areas. Moreover, as Professor A. P. Thornton has pointed out, expansion into the American West was not met with effective resistance by the sparse and scattered native population and permitted Americans to extend democracy in the process, an option not open to the Dutch in Indonesia or to the English in India. It was this link between the extension of democracy and the westward march that made it easier for Americans to view innocently their bloody conquest of the Philippines as a continuation of the western expansion of democracy.[3]

But "natural" defies precise meaning. John Quincy Adams once argued that Cuba and Santo Domingo were "natural appendages" to the United States. Some Americans extended the meaning of "natural boundaries" to include a "natural defense perimeter," thus justifying the annexation of Hawaii. One of the most effective anti-imperialists during the war in the Philippines, Senator George Frisbee Hoar of Massachusetts, had no qualms over annexing Hawaii because it was underpopulated and part of America's outer defense network. To him, Hawaii differed little from Texas or California.

The term "imperialism" is no more precise, and its overuse and recent abuse is making it nearly meaningless as an analytical concept. In a brilliant attempt to penetrate this confusion, Professor Thornton concluded that "imperialism" is "more often the name of the emotion that reacts to a series of events than a definition of the events themselves. Where colonization finds its analysts and analogists, imperialism must contend with crusaders for and against." Thus, many scholars of late have used the term pejoratively to cover any social injustice, domestic or abroad, and to mean any kind of nefarious influence. In 1935, W. L. Langer complained that "if imperialism is to mean any vague interference of traders and bankers in the affairs of other countries, you may well extend it to cover any form of influence. You will have to admit cultural imperialism; religious imperialism, and what not. Personally, I prefer to stick by a measurable, manageable concept." Little did Langer dream that he had predicted exactly what would happen over the next few decades.[4]

On the American scene, some scholars have not only refused to differentiate between continental and overseas expansion, but also make no distinction between formal empire and the more informal one involving indirect, largely economic, controls that the United States has long exercised in Latin America and over much of the world since the Second World War. There is no little irony in this, as some of the more prominent anti-imperialists during the Philippine war proposed just this sort of arrangement as an alternative to formal empire. For example, Andrew Carnegie, the leading "angel" for the anti-imperialist cause, and Edward Atkinson, the movement's most notorious spokesman, believed that the economic power of the United States would soon bring most of the globe under American domination without the burdens of military conquest and colonial management.[5]

If the definition of imperialism is to be broadened to include the informal arrangements labeled "neocolonialism," then its origin for America would be in China, rather than in the Louisiana Territory. From the beginning of the China trade in 1785, the United States increasingly became England's junior partner, lending moral support to gunboat diplomacy and reaping treaty benefits after each British assault. Isolationism did not apply to the Pacific, and it was no accident that the first formal American military venture with European allies since the Revolutionary War alliance with France was in China during the Boxer Crisis of 1900.[6] Indeed, all of the early plans for a formal empire focused on the China trade. Hawaii, Midway, and Pago Pago were pictured as stepping-stones to China. The acquisition of Alaska and the Aleutians was rationalized as providing a northern outpost to tap the elusive wealth of Old Cathay. Once plans were discussed for an isthmian canal in the postbellum period, such Caribbean isles as the Danish Virgin Islands, Cuba, and Santo Domingo took on new significance as part of the East Coast's path to the Pacific and China.

Opposition to expansion, continental or overseas, is at least as old as the Hartford Convention in 1814. Because the demands for expansion were often sounded in the accents of Dixie, Free-Soilers in the North opposed such activity as a proslavery conspiracy. After the Civil War, some of the strongest opposition to overseas expansion came from the South, due to racial fears of incorporating into the body politic more "unassimilable" types. Contrary to left-wing theory, it would appear that business leaders were also opposed to the creation of a formal empire. They welcomed commercial expansion but took their cues from England's laissez-faire policy in the middle of the nineteenth century and viewed colonies as expensive and unnecessary. While the unification of Germany and Italy led to a more intensive scramble for any unclaimed real estate after 1870, forcing England to reverse her colonial policy, American businessmen continued to be indifferent, if not opposed, to overseas expansion for another three decades. It was this conservative opposition that stymied ambitious imperialist schemes by President Grant and later by Secretary of State James G. Blaine. Nevertheless, some steps toward a formal empire were taken during the first three decades after the Civil War. Whereas Alaska and the Aleutians could be tied conceptually to the continent, an 1878 treaty strengthened ties to Samoa with American rights to a coaling station at Pago Pago. Blaine followed up a reciprocity treaty with Hawaii with a declaration in 1881 that these islands were within the "American system," which may have accomplished little in a legal sense, but it did put the major powers on notice that this archipelago was an American plum to be picked at its own choosing. In renewing the treaty in 1887, an amendment was added to give the United States exclusive rights to build a naval base at Pearl Harbor.[7]

An American empire would have made little sense without a creditable global navy to replace the obsolete one largely of Civil War vintage. In 1883, Congress allocated the funds to construct a new navy. With great fanfare, blaring headlines, and front-page illustrations, the public over the next decade followed one fast, lightly armored cruiser after another down the ways, out to sea trials, and on to fleet assignments. In 1890, attention shifted to newly built battleships as each in turn became a journalistic celebrity. A Naval War College was founded in 1884 at Newport, Rhode Island, to teach naval officers the latest in seaborne weaponry and tactics.[8]

While this modern fleet was being assembled, a rationale to justify imperial ambitions was allegedly being put together. The maturing industrial economy needed outlets for surplus goods and capital. A particularly severe depression between 1893 and 1897 may have enhanced the importance of securing these outlets. There was also the fear that trade and investment barriers would be raised around the world as the major powers intensified their scramble for colonies. At the same time, historians have argued, Americans were made uneasy by the official declaration following the 1890 census that the frontier no longer existed and by Frederick Jackson Turner's contention that "the first period of American history is over." For some the new frontier would be an industrial one, while others looked beyond the nation's boundaries for its replacement. "It is to the oceans that our children must look as we once looked to the boundless west," Senator Orville Platt advised.[9]

Some Americans also believed that England's power had peaked and urged that the United States pick up the reins of international leadership from her. Some reasoned that historical inertia made this inevitable: from the cradle of civilization in Mesopotamia to the Nile valley, Crete, Greece, Rome, Spain, France, and finally England, the course of imperial power had been relentlessly westward. Brooks Adams, however, warned that this course could be halted in London, before drifting eastward to Berlin or, worse, to Moscow. Added to such romantic notions was a good deal of Anglo-Saxon nonsense that envisioned American world leadership as somehow racially inevitable—the nation's "manifest destiny," as Harvard's Professor John Fiske called it in his celebrated lecture published in *Harper's* in 1885. That same year, the home missionary Josiah Strong published a popular book in which he asked rhetorically: "Does it not look as if God were not only preparing in our Anglo-Saxon civilization the die with which to stamp the peoples of the earth, but as if he were massing behind that die the mighty power with which to press it?" Editors of the German and Catholic press denounced such "Anglo-Maniacs," while in Chicago Finley Peter Dunne's "Mr. Dooley" poked fun at all the "blarney":

> You an' me Hinnissy, has got to bring on this here Anglo-Saxon alliance. They're a lot iv Anglo-Saxons in this country, Hinnissy. There must be as manny as two in Boston. They'se wan up in Maine. Teddy Rosenfelt is an Anglo-Saxon. An' I'm an Anglo-Saxon. Th' name iv Dooley has been the proudest Anglo-Saxon name in th' county Roscommon f'r manny years. Me ol' friend Domingo will march at the head of the Eyetalian Anglo-Saxons whin th' time comes. There ar-re twinty thousan' Rooshian Jews in th' Sivinth Ward. They'd be a turrible thing f'r anny inimy iv th' Anglo-Saxon alliance to face. I tell ye, Hinnissy, whin th' Sons iv Sweden, and th' Circle Francaize, an' th' Polacky Binivolent Society, an' th' Benny Brith, an' th' Afro-Americans an' th' other Anglo-Saxons begin f'r to raise their Anglo-Saxon battle cry, it'll be all day with th' eight or nine people in th' wurruld that has th' misfortune iv not bein brought up Anglo-Saxons.[10]

It is, of course, impossible to ascertain how many Americans were affected by such rhetoric. Although businessmen were interested in markets, raw materials, and investment opportunities overseas, few seemed to think that a formal empire was necessary. As it turned out, most exports and surplus capital went to Mexico, Canada, and Europe after the creation of an American empire. Very few politicians called for an empire before the war presented America with potential colonies. Two anti-imperialist editors did worry as early as 1897 about "a growing 'empire doctrine,' or the doctrine that it is the duty of our country to increase its domain," but it is difficult to find much evidence to support such a fear before the war with Spain.[11]

It is also possible to interpret such writers as Strong or Fiske very differently, that is, as calling for no more than an Anglo-Saxon alliance, or for a cultural, rather than a military, conquest. Missionaries were fond of using military metaphors and were forever envisioning themselves as Christ's warriors storming the ramparts of Satan for worldwide, evangelical victory. More appropriately perhaps, America's foremost naval strategist, Captain Alfred Thayer Mahan, also used military metaphors to describe commercial expansion, from which later historians inferred demands for more sweeping imperialist ventures and a preoccupation with social Darwinian survival. "All around us now is strife; 'the struggle of life,' 'the race of life' are phrases so familiar that we do not feel their significance until we stop to think about them," Mahan wrote. But the rest of the article makes it clear that the captain had a very limited imperial appetite, calling only for strategically located coaling stations and naval bases to support expanded commerce and missionary activity. But he described American industry as an "ironclad" that was "mighty for defense, weak for offense" and warned: "Within, the home market is secured; but outside, beyond the broad seas, there are the markets of the world, that can be entered and controlled only by a vigorous contest, to which the habit of trusting to protection by statute does not conduce." His emphasis on a large merchant marine, "the link that joins the products and the markets," and on the commercial value of Hawaii, "the great central station of the Pacific, equidistant from San Francisco, Samoa, and the Marquesas, and an important post on our lines of communication with both Australia and China," indicate that his concern was at least as commercial as it was military. Like so many of his contemporaries, he also anticipated "conflict between German control and American interests in the islands of the Western Pacific," in which Hawaii would play a decisive role.[12]

Recently, one historian has taken to task the widely accepted interpretation of American imperialism that maintains that events follow the philosophical and strategic utterances of a handful of spokesmen for imperialism, whose influence has never been demonstrated. He argues that this popular view is much too rational. Indeed, the nation's almost exclusive focus on the Atlantic and Europe indicates that the effect of a Pacific "lobby" could not have been very great before the war with Spain. Less than five percent of the nation's exports left from Pacific ports, and much of that was grain bound for Europe via the Horn. The highly touted new navy was concentrated defensively along the Atlantic coast. Potential naval bases at Pearl Harbor and Pago Pago remained undeveloped until the twentieth century. The network of submarine cables, with all its commercial and military value, was ignored in the Pacific in favor of the Atlantic and Caribbean. Even the Protestant missionary movement concentrated its efforts more in the Near East and India than in China. According to this interpretation, the acquisition of a formal empire was essentially a historical accident rather than the product of a small cabal of imperialist plotters. Not until the destruction of the U.S.S. *Maine* in Havana and the subsequent victory over Spain was there an avalanche of demands for a Pacific empire.[13]

This revisionist challenge was long overdue, but possibly it is overstated. China always loomed larger in America's imagination than it did in the reality of the statistics on trade and Protestant conversions. Its huge population offered enormous potential in the minds of traders, missionaries, and some statesmen, but economic and evangelical success proved to be an elusive phantom for more than a century. Yet, China's lure never died in American hopes and anticipation. It played into the hands of American imperialists when the war with Spain presented an easy opportunity to create a formal empire in the Pacific.[14]

If calls for an empire were rare and inconsequential before 1898, the belligerent cries for a crusade against Spain were not. In part, a crusade may have represented a convenient escape from the malaise that seemed to afflict the nation during the final decade of the century, induced by the economic crisis and by the less desirable results of industrialization (such as corruption, mismanagement, waste, health hazards, slums, and human suffering), exposed by muckraking journalists. Cities seemed clogged with disparate groups that threatened to convert them into modern Towers of Babel. As Populist Mary Lease had once suggested, staple growers were "raising hell," and Coxey's army of broken farmers and unemployed workers marched on Washington. A series of bloody strikes and racial riots resembled open warfare before troops were called in to restore order. Some Americans went on nativistic rampages against Negroes, Mexicans, Chinese, Italians, and Catholics. An oath of allegiance was created to test the loyalty of "subversives," while private armies drilled in preparation for an anticipated "papist" uprising. Even the sacred gold standard was challenged, and many Americans agreed with Secretary of State Walter Gresham that "symptoms of revolution" were omnipresent in 1895. The bleak pessimism of Brooks Adams, the implied foreboding in Turner's essay, and the popular anxiety over America's future were reflected in the works of Hamlin Garland, Edward Bellamy, William Dean Howells, Frank Norris, Upton Sinclair, and Edgar Watson Howe. Henry Adams beat a quick retreat to a more stable medieval civilization.[15]

It is not surprising that the nation might have sought escape in an orgy of jingoism to distract itself from the very real, as well as imagined, problems at home. A war might heal the internal divisiveness; it might bring together at last the blue and the gray while obfuscating the class antagonisms enhanced by industrialization and fusing the new ethnoracial and religious divisions wrought by shifting immigration patterns. President Grover Cleveland's bellicose stance against the British in the 1895 Venezuelan boundary dispute only provided a temporary elixir for the people, and even then, it offended some Anglo-Saxon sensibilities in the ruling elite. That same year another rebellion broke out in Cuba against Spanish rule, the specter of a cruel, oppressive, and decadent Catholic monarchy primed the nation for a crusade. The yellow press went to work, fomenting a state of frenzied moral indignation. As Senator Hoar complained, every congressman had two or three newspapers in his district "printed in red ink shouting for blood."[16]

But Cleveland was jealous of his prerogative to make foreign policy and was not going to allow hysterical editors to do it for him. Approaching the end of his term and having no intention of seeking reelection, the president could better afford to resist popular pressures. Three years earlier he had refused to recognize a rebellion in Hawaii engineered by Americans and settled by U.S. Marines. Now he warned Congress that, if it allowed the "rascally Cubans" to stampede it into declaring war, he would refuse to move the army. Nevertheless, Cleveland did quietly escalate diplomatic pressure on Madrid to institute reforms in Cuba or risk exhausting "American patience." Ironically, this merely encouraged the Spanish to adopt more Draconian measures in the hope of ending the rebellion more swiftly. To this end a new commander, General Valeriano Weyler, instituted concentration camps and began a campaign of systematic torture and murder, winning him infamy in American headlines, which referred to him as "the Butcher," a "Human Hyena," or a "mad dog." One editor explained that "there is nothing to prevent his carnal animal brain from running riot with itself in inventing tortures and infamies of bloody debauchery." Another newspaper chanted mindlessly: "Blood on the roadsides, blood on the fields, blood on the doorsteps, blood, blood, blood."[17]

McKinley essentially continued Cleveland's policy of publicly insisting that he was opposed to intervention in Cuba, assuring Senator Carl Schurz that he would tolerate "no jingoistic nonsense" in his Administration but at the same time quietly increasing diplomatic pressure on Spain. He also appointed Senator John Sherman secretary of state in order to make room in the Senate for his campaign manager, Mark Hanna. Two years earlier, Sherman had vowed that "no earthly power" could keep the United States out of Cuba. As chief diplomat, he dashed off impulsive, belligerent messages to Madrid. Spain did not help matters by comparing Weyler's tactics to those of General William Tecumseh Sherman, who happened to have been the secretary's brother. McKinley also kept at his post Cleveland's consul-general in Havana, Fitzhugh Lee. This flamboyant descendant of the Confederate hero not only openly sympathized with the Cuban rebels, but also was instrumental in convincing the president that a warship was necessary to protect American nationals in Havana. Because Lee was so partisan, McKinley sent a close friend, William J. Calhoun, on a fact-finding mission to Cuba. His bleak report and recommendation of intervention prompted a strongly worded ultimatum from the president to Madrid, warning that reforms leading to pacification had to be carried out with sufficient speed to avoid a rupture between the two countries.[18]

Actually, McKinley's warning was not much different from Cleveland's final message to Madrid, but Spain enhanced its seriousness by delaying an answer for two months and then responding in language that was haughty and insolent by diplomatic standards. This pushed the two nations to the brink of war at the end of the summer of 1897, and only the assassination of Spain's Prime Minister Casanovas rescued the situation, by paving the way for a more liberal cabinet that removed Weyler and proposed reforms leading to greater Cuban autonomy. McKinley was then able to claim a diplomatic victory and momentarily allay his jingoistic critics.

McKinley's taciturn style still baffles historians in their attempts to discern his real intentions, but even if he genuinely wanted to avoid a war, a series of events early in 1898 made this option humanely impossible. In mid-January, Spanish colons and former soldiers of Weyler demonstrated against Madrid's proposed reforms and wrecked the offices of Cuban newspapers and businesses that had endorsed the proposals. These incidents convinced McKinley to comply with Lee's request for a battleship. In the wake of the riots, the Spanish minister in Washington, Enriqué Dupuy de Lôme, wrote privately to a friend ridiculing the proposed reforms and describing McKinley as "weak and a bidder for the admiration of the crowd, besides being a would-be politician who tries to leave a door open behind himself while keeping on good terms with the jingoes of his own party." A Cuban secretary sympathetic to the rebels leaked the comments to the Cuban junta in Washington, which passed it on to William Randolph Hearst. Although de Lôme's characterization of McKinley was not all that different from domestic criticisms of him, the *New York Journal* revealed it under the headline, "Worst Insult to the United States in Its History."[19]

Again, Madrid exacerbated the matter by delaying an apology and finally delivering one in insolent language that merely magnified the effect of de Lôme's original comments. By then, however, Spanish officialdom had much more to contend with than the indiscreet remarks of a diplomat. On February 15, the U.S.S. *Maine* blew up in Havana Harbor and went to the bottom. Although the captain, one of the few survivors, warned against hasty judgments before a thorough investigation, the yellow press accused Spain of murdering the crew "in cold blood" with "a secret infernal machine." The president maintained a scrupulous silence, but his assistant secretary of the navy, Theodore Roosevelt, showed no such restraint, openly accusing Spain of "an act of dirty treachery."[20]

Almost every segment of American society clamored for intervention. The business community had risked jingoistic wrath by counseling the president not to be emotionally stampeded into intervening in Cuba. "If popular passion is permitted to force the administration into war, what is the conclusion suggested to our masses?" asked the *Journal of Commerce* in New York. "Simply that they may have whatever mad follies they hanker after provided that they raise their clamor to the requisite pitch." Such advice to the president provoked the *Sacramento Bee* to denounce Wall Street as the "colossal and aggregate Benedict Arnold of the Union, and the syndicated Judas Iscariot of humanity." By March 1898, however, the business community appeared to have joined the majority except for one maverick Chicago stockbroker who still argued that the Cubans were "nothing but mongrels not fit for self government." Even McKinley's defeated opponent, William Jennings Bryan, declared that "the time for intervention has arrived." Only the German-language and Catholic press held steadfast for neutrality.[21]

In spite of the enormous pressure to intervene, McKinley maintained his silence except to plead for "deliberate consideration" on the Cuban issue, which only fanned the flames of popular moral indignation. Mobs in Virginia and Colorado burned the president in effigy. Others hissed at his picture in theaters or defaced it at other public locations. Republican editors cautioned McKinley that "the people want no disgraceful negotiations with Spain." The *Chicago Tribune* pleaded with him to intervene immediately, warning him that "an administration that stains the national honor will never be forgiven." Meanwhile, spectators packed the galleries of Congress—some wrapped in American flags—to urge on their favorite jingoistic orators. The French ambassador advised his government that a "sort of bellicose fury has seized the American nation." Clearly America wanted its crusade and negotiation was out of the question.[22]

As if McKinley needed another shove into war, Senator Redfield Proctor of Vermont, a Republican advocate of peaceful negotiation with Spain, delivered a three-hour speech on the horrors of the *concentrados* and the widespread starvation in Cuba before concluding that only American intervention could alter the situation. Only hours later, McKinley sent his final ultimatum to Madrid, demanding Cuban independence by April 15, or "the President, having exhausted diplomatic agencies to secure peace in Cuba, will lay the whole matter before Congress." To convince Spain that he meant business, he asked Congress for a fifty-million-dollar military appropriation.

A last-minute papal offer to arbitrate was ignored, and war was declared on April 25 as having existed since April 21. Congressmen literally danced through the Capitol singing "hang General Weyler to a sour apple tree as we go marching on." Young men stampeded to enlist; lusty cheers emanated from pulpits, lecterns, editorial pages, and other public forums. A few feeble protests were all but lost in the surge of patriotism. Everyone wanted to get into the act, from young Teddy Roosevelt to aging Civil War heroes pleading for an opportunity to swish swords in the air one more time and bellow "charge." General Lee's old cavalry chief, "Fighting Joe" Wheeler, resigned from Congress to lead dismounted cavalry in Cuba. He was an important symbol for the argument that the war with Spain would at long last heal the sectional breach (although this was lost on one incorrigible soul, who shouted to his men charging a retreating Spanish line, "We've got the damn Yankees on the run!").[23]

John Hay called it "a splendid little war," but in reality it was not much more than the two overly glamorized naval victories at Santiago Bay in Cuba in July and at Manila in May. Marines landed at the mouth of Guantánamo Bay and gallantly held off Spanish counterattacks, but the army's only significant land campaign was a disaster that merely demonstrated the ineptness of its commander, General William Shafter, and of the War Department in procuring and transporting supplies. After some initial victories at El Caney and San Juan Hill on the outskirts of Santiago—which produced a couple of heroes in General Henry Lawton and Colonel Theodore Roosevelt—Shafter decided to wait for Santiago's surrender; meanwhile, disease began to decimate his army. This sorry episode produced a national scapegoat in Secretary of War Russell Alger.

In spite of these military realities, however, the war helped the country to forget its domestic troubles and partially alleviated its anxiety over the future. The next stage in the nation's history, in answer to Professor Turner's concern, would be that of world power status. For many Americans, the new "frontier" would be a formal empire captured from Spain. If many Europeans were surprised at the easy victory, few Americans were. Senator Chandler had predicted that the war would last anywhere from fifteen minutes to ninety days. It lasted one hundred days. Tropical diseases struck down many more Americans than did Spanish bullets.[24]

2

Enter the Philippines

A tenacious myth, created and nurtured by two generations of historians, is that Admiral George Dewey's victory at Manila Bay in 1898 came as a stunning surprise to American political leaders and average citizens alike, none of whom had even heard of the Philippines. As Mr. Dooley put it, no one was sure if they were "islands or canned goods." According to legend, President McKinley was forced to consult a globe to ascertain the location of those "darned islands." Yet American firms had been engaged in the Philippine abaca trade long before Dewey arrived there. Economic intelligence pertaining to the archipelago appeared sporadically in the commercial press, and the most valued fiber for cordage was Manila hemp. Once the Philippine Insurrection began in 1896, one year after the start of Cuba's revolution, there was a dramatic increase in the press's coverage of the Philippines. Editors obsessed with Spanish oppression in Cuba found it only natural to turn their attention to additional evidence of tyranny in Spain's far-flung empire. No one mentioned the Philippines as a potential American colony at that early date, but several editors were aware of the interest of Japan and England in these islands should Spain lose control over them. Two California editors expressed concern over Spain's Asian squadron at Manila in the event of war. Weeks before the Battle of Manila, headlines predicted that Spain's Pacific fleet based in the Philippines would be Dewey's target. It is difficult to believe that many American leaders were much surprised by Dewey's action or that they were so ignorant of the Philippines.[1]

Of course, the war had scarcely begun and the country needed a hero quickly, so all the hoopla about "America's Lord Nelson" having "totally eclipsed Trafalgar" may reenforce the impression that Dewey caught the press and political leadership unprepared. The real surprise was the sudden need to make a decision about the fate of the Philippines. American imperialists did not wish to repeat England's mistake in India by colonizing a large, densely populated area. They were interested in pinpoint, strategically located colonies to provide communication links and logistic support for commercial and missionary enterprises. Dewey himself made it clear that it would be a mistake to keep anything except Manila and the naval base at Cavite.[2]

During the summer of 1898, imperialist expectations for a Philippine base escalated to the retention of all of Luzon, and finally to the annexation of the entire archipelago. Military reasoning seems to have motivated this change: It would be difficult to defend part of the area should an unfriendly power colonize another portion of the Philippines. Senator Henry Cabot Lodge set about to convert the president to "the large policy" that summer. McKinley, however, was a reluctant imperialist, agreeing with his new secretary of state, John Hay, that the islands should be returned to Spain after "ceding a port and the necessary appurtenances selected by the United States." The president's confession that "the truth is I didn't want the Philippines and when they came to us as a gift from the Gods, I did not know what to do with them" has been dismissed as hypocrisy after the fact. But this quandary was reflected editorially across the nation immediately following the news of Dewey's victory.[3]

Before July, very few editors advocated keeping all of the Philippines. The influential Republican organ *Inter-Ocean* recommended that America retain no more than a naval base and a coaling station and return the rest of the archipelago to Spain. Not until August did this editor change his mind and advise the president that to keep only a part of the Philippines would be "a great blunder." Even those editors strongly opposed to any overseas expansion were at a loss initially over the ultimate fate of the islands. The *Republican* in Springfield, Massachusetts, suggested selling the islands to England, or possibly to Japan, provided that such a sale did not "disturb the balance of power." The *Journal* in Boston declared that there was nothing morally reprehensible about selling or giving the Philippines to "a friendly colonizing power," since the Constitution would not allow an American colony. One anti-imperialist editor even suggested an international auction. "For so rich a prize," and with "every power" viewing "with jealous eyes its acquisition by any other," the bidding would have to be "very lively." The *Boston Herald*, however, protested against selling Filipinos "like so many serfs," and insisted that the "only moral course" was to return the islands to Spain.[4]

Such callous reasoning was by no means restricted to anti-imperialists. While the nation pondered the fate of the Philippines, imperialist editors insisted that any decision should rest on practical considerations alone. "The whole surface of the earth has been stolen and restolen . . . and the process will be repeated," observed the *Detroit Tribune*. "This is not said in cold cynicism. It is merely cold fact," so the president should keep in mind that "profits and not prophets" determine "morality." Military needs must be paramount, the *Argonaut* in San Francisco advised. "Moral force is all very well, but it does not check hostile fleets or invading armies." There was but "one broad, sweeping, irrefutable answer" to the growing debate, declared the *Baltimore American*. "It is the same old law of the survival of the fittest. The weak must bend to the strong and today the American race is the sturdiest, the noblest on earth."[5]

Only when imperialist editors came out in favor of retaining the entire archipelago did they use higher-sounding justifications related to the "white man's burden." Although the underlying assumption of both (imperialists and anti-imperialists) was that the Filipinos were not capable of governing themselves, the unctuous paternalism of editors favoring annexation lent them the appearance of having a moral edge in the debate. The *Indianapolis Journal* scoffed at all the sudden talk of "uplifting savages" and opposed annexation precisely because the "inhabitants resist the civilization of the temperate zones instinctively, because they have not the mental and moral fiber to uphold it. Therefore why talk of carrying civilization to these islands?" Other anti-imperialists catered more frankly to the nation's racial fears. An imperial policy would bring in via the back door those kept out by the exclusion laws, a mass of "Asiatic hybrids," warned the *Pilot* in Boston. Even the usually loftier *Republican* warned that annexing the Philippines would not only "plunge us head, neck and breeches into world affairs, but it would bring into the American system a lot of Malays, Chinese Mestizos," and others of "inferior race."[6]

In Congress, the debate over imperialism began in earnest with the bill to annex the Hawaiian Islands. Western congressmen recycled the specter of the Asian menace, used to secure passage of the exclusion laws. Once again, steak-and-potato-eating American workers would be in "deadly competition with those who live on a bowl of rice and a rat a day," prophesied Nebraska's Senator William Allen. California's Representative Johnson, warning over and over again of "the immoralities unmentionable" and the "nameless contagions" spawned by "Asiatics," read into the *Congressional Record* an article entitled "Shall We Annex Leprosy?" "Honey Fitz" Fitzgerald, grandfather of John Fitzgerald Kennedy, demanded of his fellow congressmen, "Are we to have a Mongolian state in this union?" Champ Clark mined the same vein, but with more humor, asking the House to imagine a pigtailed senator from Hawaii seated in that "august chamber chopping logic" with an erudite Hoar or Lodge. The Speaker of the House, Thomas Brackett Reed, tried his hand at logic, using a string on a globe to demonstrate that the Aleutians were closer to China than were the Hawaiian Islands. But this debate took place in the midst of the war—weeks after the first troops had landed in Cuba—and neither fear, humor, nor logic could stem the emotional tide of a bumptious nationalism. Hawaii was formally annexed on June 15, 1898. The big fight would be over the Philippines, which was too distant to be part of a "natural" defense perimeter, too densely populated, and climatically unsuitable for American settlement.[7]

McKinley never made public his views on the Hawaiian question. He continued to mask them during the Philippine debate, playing his cards so close to his chest that his real intentions continue to baffle historians to this day. His enigmatic style once provoked the *Washington Post* to label him "a Chinese statesman." If McKinley was inscrutable, John Hay was downright deceitful. By praising Andrew Carnegie's anti-imperialist articles in the *North American Review*, Hay gave the steel magnate the distinct impression that he intended to keep "the American 'empire' within the continent, especially keeping it out of the vortex of militarism," or so Carnegie reported jubilantly to his friends. Of course, Carnegie had a tendency to understand what he wanted to hear. At any rate, Hay was at that moment trying to persuade the president to keep more of Spain's Pacific possessions. He complained to McKinley that "so many men among us do not, or cannot believe in the American people and their glorious destiny."[8]

At what point McKinley altered his position on the Philippines is impossible to say. His authorization of troops to be sent there in early summer does not necessarily contradict his public position that he was uninterested in anything more than a base, or possibly the city of Manila. He had to land troops to establish a claim to any portion of the Philippines in future peace negotiations with Spain. From limited evidence it is possible to infer that not until August did he decide to keep all of Luzon, and in October the entire archipelago. These decisions may have had more to do with a shift of popular opinion as reflected in the press than with the counsel of Lodge or Hay.

The *Literary Digest* polled 192 editors in September and reported that a solid majority favored retention of all the Philippines. One-third of the editors preferred to limit American acquisition to a port, base, or, at most, the island of Luzon; only one-sixth wanted the president to get out altogether and recommended that the islands be either left in Spanish possession or sold to a friendly power. Only three editors recommended independence for the Philippines.[9]

A September editorial in *Inter-Ocean* noted a commensurate swing in the business world, which was just "waking up to the opportunities the war has brought at a moment when the immense increase of our manufacturing capacity has rendered foreign markets necessary for us." The *Literary Digest* corroborated this impression and reported that the fate of the Philippines was the "liveliest topic" in commercial circles. "While many leading trade journals enthusiastically favor a policy of retaining all territory which fortune of war has thrown under our control, yet the trade press is not by any means a unit in this demand." For obvious reasons the leaders of businesses requiring heavy capital investment, and the financiers likely to underwrite it, favored permanent control. But some manufacturers and traders and all agricultural interests remained uneasy over potential competition from cheap labor. Thus the *Railway Road* declared that "one way of opening up a market is to conquer it," while the *Call*, representing California-Hawaii sugar interests, wanted no competition from the Philippines. Moreover, the *Call*'s editor shared his state's Sinophobia and feared militarism as well. Labor unions and the military were, in his opinion, not only economic parasites, but political threats; strikes promised "mob-rule," while colonial adventures would produce a "man-on-horseback" to return and threaten a popular political coup against democracy.[10]

There was far less discord in the endorsement for keeping all of the Philippines from the Protestant religious establishment, particularly from its missionary wing. Spain had long banned Protestant missionaries from her possessions, and to the missionaries Dewey's victory was nothing other than "God's vengeance." Cast as a Biblical hero, either as David or sometimes as Joshua, Dewey arrived off Manila and "the Spanish fleet went down as miraculously as the walls of Jericho." The admiral's guns were "God's own trumpet-tones summoning his people out of their isolation into the broad arena of the world's great life." The *Woman's Evangel* rhapsodized, "Manila, Santiago, Puerto Rico—Old Glory everywhere afloat . . . the quick tread of armies and the rapid rush of hosts and the roar of guns. Prompt obedience . . . prompt action everywhere and 'victory' is shouted all the world around." Almost in unison, religious editors across the nation immediately following the news of Manila asked what God intended "by laying these naked foundlings at our door." Clearly, to them, "the American Republic" was "on the way to a larger ministry in world affairs." Any talk of getting out of the Philippines or elsewhere enraged these editors. "What folly to conquer territory and then turn it over to the possession of another power." Worse than folly, it was "utter blasphemy" to another editor:

> The acquiring of the Ladrone, the Caroline, and the Philippine islands, and even Cuba, Porto Rico, and the Canaries, *as a result of the war in which Spain, by her barbarities in Cuba forced us*, will be no violation of the spirit of isolation. To refuse, for selfish reasons, to assume the duty and the responsibility which a gracious Providence has thrust upon it would be to render the nation guilty of a great crime in the sight of high Heaven.

Although McKinley had succeeded in making minor inroads into the working-class and Catholic vote, his constituency still depended largely on business and Protestant groups. He had no choice but to take seriously the warning of the Presbyterian *Interior* that "the churches will stand solidly against abandoning the islands."[11]

Religious and missionary spokesmen were not only the first to insist upon annexing the Philippines, but, unlike most other advocates of this policy, they rarely felt a need to avoid the term "imperialism." The Reverend Wallace Radcliffe explained:

Imperialism is in the air; but it has new definitions and better inventions. It is republicanism "writ large." It is imperialism, not for domination but for civilization; not for absolutism but for self government. American imperialism is enthusiastic, optimistic and beneficial republicanism. Imperialism expresses itself by expansion. I believe in imperialism because I believe in foreign missions. Our Foreign Mission Board can teach Congress how to deal with remote dependencies . . . give the President points on imperial republicanism. The peal of the trumpet rings out over the Pacific. The Church must go where America goes.

Some religious journals went so far as to insist that Jesus had favored imperialism. "Has it ever occurred to you that Jesus was the most imperial of the imperialists?" asked the *Missionary Record*. On the other hand, anti-imperialism was "the invention of the devil to oppose foreign missions," readers of the *Foreign Missionary Journal* were warned.[12]

Some religious spokesmen felt compelled to stipulate that the annexation of the Philippines was not "territorial expansion," but rather "the expansion of civilization." The *Congregationalist* explained that "only in carrying out divine purpose can we advocate the adoption of a colonial purpose." Possibly to assuage a sense of guilt, missionary publications frequently mentioned "freedom" or "liberty" for the Filipinos. But it is clear that these terms meant emancipation from the Spanish or the separation of church and state with free, secular, public schools. The *Baptist Home Missionary Monthly* explained that such freedom meant "soul-liberty," as political independence for the Philippines could only be realized by long preparation under "military control."[13]

Like secular imperialists, missionaries bristled with an aggressive and highly romantic Anglo-Saxonism. Britain and America not only shared the same civilization, but also the same "race instincts." American expansion into the Pacific marked the beginning of the "Anglo-American Mission of the Holy Trinity." Indeed, to one missionary it marked the real beginning of the world's history, and "the English-speaking empires" would "go on expanding." Infuriated by anti-imperialist doubts, a contributor to the *Missionary Record* asked, "What kind of men are we?"

Are we less able than our English and Dutch ancestors to take part in the work of the world? Has the rich Anglo-Saxon blood re-enforced by a good

Celtic strain, grown thin in our veins during the past one hundred years? Are we a less virile and resourceful race than the elder branches of our family across the sea? And yet we are told that we have no capacity for the government of colonies and foreign dependencies![14]

Such blatant imperialist demands led to sharp attacks on the Protestant clerics, who "preach the gospel of peace" while they "look upon war, and its horrors, as of divine origin" and think "the last places touched by the Holy Ghost were Manila and Santiago." Senator Hoar accused them of "preaching the new commandment to do evil that good may come." A colleague demanded that Protestant leaders explain "how grand larceny and 'criminal aggression' could become high Christian civilization in the Philippines?" Catholic editors were understandably upset by all the "loose talk" by these "preachers on the rampage" about "Christianizing" a population that was largely Roman Catholic. Rather than export "Christianity" or "morality," it was more likely that Protestant America would bestow on the Filipinos divorce, "atheistic public schools," a "Godless Constitution," and "other blessings of a similar nature," the *Catholic Review* wryly observed. If any "religious reconstruction" was necessary in the Philippines, it should be carried out by "good American priests," Archbishop Ireland declared.[15]

The group most adamant in its opposition to the annexation of the Philippines was the German-American community, or at least the German-language press gives that impression. This opposition was due partially to the suspicion that all the talk of Anglo-American world domination was aimed at the "Fatherland," which was not without some foundation. Such hallowed members of the military elite as Admiral Dewey and General Lawton had both casually opined to reporters that America's next war would be with Germany. Early in 1898, a combined Anglo-American fleet did line up in battle formation to intimidate a smaller German squadron off Samoa. The confrontation was reported with some fanfare in the nation's press, whose editors invariably blamed it on the "arrogant boy emperor" in Berlin. One historian has discerned "an almost pathological suspicion of Germany . . . prevalent in American political and diplomatic circles" at that time.[16]

But many Germans had fled the militarism that dominated their native country and feared that an American empire would nurture similar conditions in their adopted land. Milwaukee's *Freidenker* declared that "the coming militarism is already here" and expressed gratitude that "the overwhelming majority of our citizens of German descent stand by common sense and high principles" on the issue of imperialism. Newark's *Freie Zeitung* warned that the Filipinos would resist being colonized again and would have to "be taught with powder and lead" that "the Declaration of Independence was only for Americans." If the government was truly interested in helping the oppressed, it should go to the aid of the "poor Hindus," this editor taunted. Once it was known that annexation was to be part of the "peace with honor," the *Volks-Zeitung* in New York City scoffed, "And why not? Rascals, thieves, and robbers have a code of their own."[17]

In the midst of this debate over the Philippines, a peace protocol was signed with Spain on August 12 calling for treaty negotiations in Paris. McKinley again obfuscated his intentions by sending a shrewdly balanced commission to France: two avowed imperialists, Maine's Republican Senator William Frye and the *New York Tribune*'s Whitelaw Reid; Delaware's Democratic Senator George Gray, who was adamantly opposed to expansion overseas; and two limited imperialists of the Mahan stripe, Senator Cushman Davis, Minnesota Republican, who chaired the powerful Foreign Relations Committee, and William Day, who resigned as secretary of state to chair the commission. Clearly, McKinley had no intention of coming away from Paris empty-handed. He instructed the commission to demand no more than Luzon, Guam, and Puerto Rico, possession of which would mean a limited empire of pinpoint colonies to support a global fleet and provide communication links. Puerto Rico was close enough that Gray might have compromised his position, although it did pose "racial" problems. Frye might have limited his appetite, but Reid was bent on "converting the Pacific Ocean into an American lake."[18]

Once in Paris, the commission was besieged with advice to demand the entire Philippine archipelago, particularly from American generals and European diplomats. General Wesley Merritt arrived directly from Manila to convince the commission that any single island would be militarily indefensible should unfriendly powers colonize other ones. He brought corroborative statements from other generals and surprisingly from Admiral Dewey, who had privately expressed a very different opinion. Merritt also brought a statement from the Belgian envoy in Manila, Edouard André, predicting civil war, anarchy, and European intervention should the Americans not retain control of all the islands. These spokesmen totally distorted for the commission the political conditions in the Philippines, and depicted Emilio Aguinaldo, the leader of the Filipino nationalists, as "a Chinese halfbreed adventurer" with no legitimate claim to govern the Philippines or as an opportunist who could easily be "managed." His native troops were even dangled before the commission by one general as potential American sepoys. Only the American consul in Manila, Oscar Williams, dissented in writing, and, since he was not present, Merritt was able to ridicule his position unopposed. The unanimous recommendation of the self-appointed advisors to the commission who had journeyed to Paris was that "it would certainly be cheaper and more humane to take the entire Philippines than to keep only part of it." Frye and Reid needed no convincing, and Davis quickly capitulated, leaving the majority in favor of this course. Day refused to budge from the president's original instructions, and Gray had been isolated from the beginning as a staunch anti-imperialist.[19]

The major obstacle to an imperialist policy was the nation's political traditions of anticolonialism, the Declaration of Independence, Monroe Doctrine, and isolationism. Gradually some Republican editors began to attack these traditions as outmoded, fit for the age of sail, not steam. "As a people, we are the most practical of races, and care more for conditions, than theories," the editor of the *Hawk-Eye* in Burlington, Iowa, explained in his endorsement of annexation. "Unexpectedly and through the unseen hand of divine destiny, we have the Philippine Islands. Surely the fetish of tradition" will not "stand in the way" of all the "compelling moral, military, religious, and commercial reasons for keeping them," he pleaded. In Chicago, the *Journal* warned against being fettered by the past:

> Unless the President shall take immediate steps to protect and hold the Philippines, generations to be will read the history of this time and curse the purblind folly that threw away a world out of Chinese reverence for mouldy traditions and dead men's opinions.[20]

Elections were coming up, and Lodge carefully reported to the president that state "Republican conventions are all declaring that where the flag goes up it must never come down." Senator Orville Platt concurred, informing McKinley that ninety percent of the voters in Connecticut favored keeping all territories won in the war and warning him that "if in the negotiations for peace, Spain is permitted to retain any portion of the Philippines it will be a failure on the part of this nation to discharge the greatest moral obligation which could be conceived." Platt went on to explain, "Those who believe in Providence see, or think they see, that God has placed upon this government the solemn duty of providing for the people of these islands a government based upon the principle of liberty no matter how many difficulties the problem may present."[21]

Apparently, the issue was touchy enough to convince Democratic leadership to ignore it during the midterm congressional campaigns that summer and autumn. The Democratic standard-bearer in 1896, William Jennings Bryan, flatly refused to comment on the issue until after the election. Although the *Democratic Campaign Book* for 1898 included nothing on the Philippines, it did reproduce two letters written by the party's founder, Thomas Jefferson, that called for the annexation of Cuba almost a century earlier, implying that the Republicans had no monopoly on overseas expansion. It also praised the Teller

Amendment, which forbade Cuban annexation, thereby attempting to be all things to all men. A survey of platforms in twenty-five states revealed a similar pattern of ambiguity and reticence. In twelve states the Democrats made no mention of the Philippines, in five states they opposed annexation, and in three favored it. The remaining five platforms mentioned the issue in such an equivocal manner that it is impossible to interpret their positions.[22]

Two youthful Republican candidates received near-hysterical responses to their bombastic demands to nail the flag to the mast wherever it was flying as a result of the war. In Indiana, Albert Beveridge, a handsome aspirant to the United States Senate with a golden voice, thrilled audiences in provincial hamlets by informing them that they were about to be in "the very center" of "the greatest empire known to man." Beveridge explained that "the rule of liberty" was only for people "capable of self government," and certainly not for the Filipinos. In New York, Teddy Roosevelt, fresh from the war in Cuba, delivered a similar message in his gubernatorial bid:

> The guns of our warships have awakened us to new duties. We are face to face with our destiny, and we must meet it with a high and resolute courage. For ours is the life of action, of strenuous performance of duty; let us live in the harness striving mightily; let us rather run the risk of wearing out than rusting out.[23]

Roosevelt was so sure of the popular appeal of keeping all of the Philippines that he pinned the anti-imperialist label on the Democrats and went on to equate that position with that of the copperheads during the Civil War. He demanded:

> Do you wish to keep or throw away the fruits of what we have won in war? If you wish to throw them away, then vote against President McKinley; vote in favor of his opponents, and give heart . . . to every Spaniard in Spain, to every man in Continental Europe who wishes us ill. Vote that way if you please. . . . But if you choose to vote for America, if you choose to vote for the flag for which we fought this summer . . . then you will vote to sustain the administration of President McKinley.[24]

Actually, the upstate Democratic boss and former senator, David Hill, had joined Roosevelt in calling for the annexation of the Philippines. "American valor has easily triumphed on both sea and land, and the American flag floats over newly acquired territory—never, as it is fondly hoped, to be lowered again," Hill declared. Roosevelt's main opposition in New York came from within his own party. Senator Carl Schurz denounced his fellow Republicans for sponsoring "a vulgar land grabbing" scheme "glossed over by high-sounding cant about destiny and duty and what not." Likewise, in Massachusetts, Republican Senator Hoar most strongly opposed his party's endorsement of imperialism. In Boston, a group of mugwump reformers placed a last-minute newspaper advertisement calling upon the voters to reject this "new and dangerous policy."[25]

Democratic caution on the Philippine issue was not simply a question of fear that the "war fever" had not yet subsided and was playing into the hands of the imperialists. The party itself was badly divided over the Philippine question. Crucial spokesmen, such as Adolph Ochs and William Randolph Hearst, respectively the publishers of the *New York Times* and a growing transcontinental journalistic empire, favored annexation, as did such party intellectuals as Walter Hines Page and Woodrow Wilson. Putting aside his initial misgivings over constitutional implications, Wilson came out in favor of annexation during the summer. On the other hand, labor leaders and the Catholic press and hierarchy for the most part were opposed to keeping the Philippines, while the party's leader refused to state his position.[26]

Bryan's concern and Roosevelt's optimism were fully justified by a landslide Republican victory in midterm elections, which ordinarily favor the party out of power. Of course, the Democrats tried hard to keep imperialism out of the campaign, but Roosevelt demagogically made it a key issue and scored an awesome victory. The *Springfield Republican* fatuously interpreted the fact that most Republicans in Massachusetts won less handsomely than did the Republican governor as an anti-imperialist victory. But only in South Boston could the defeat of a Republican be remotely connected to the issue. In fact, the president broke his silence on October 25 and declared officially that he favored keeping all the Philippine islands. Always cautious, McKinley would never have done so two weeks before election day if there had been the slightest hint that the decision would be unpopular.[27]

Early in October, McKinley had stumped for candidates in the Midwest and noted the thunderous applause evoked by the vaguest reference to retaining the Philippines. "Territory sometimes comes to us when we go to war in a holy cause, and whenever it does the banner of liberty will float over it and bring, I trust, blessings and benefits to all people," he told an ecstatic audience in Chariton, Iowa. Wild cheers followed comments on "America's moral obligations" overseas and on the necessity "to keep the flag flying" over Spain's former colonies. It must have been as clear to McKinley as it was to Bryan that expansion was immensely popular. Privately, McKinley confided to a friend, "You and I don't want the Philippines, but it is no use disguising the fact that an overwhelming majority of the people do." His close friend, Charles Dawes, opined that "whatever the result to our nation, the retention of the Philippines was inevitable from the first. No man, no party, could have prevented it." One of the president's biographers insists that this comment "reflected McKinley's own temper." Other historians, convinced that McKinley was an imperialist all along, have dismissed such comments as attempts to color the record and clear the president's conscience. But McKinley's cautious path to his decision that fall indicates his reluctance to retain the Philippines. English and French experiences in India and Algeria were enough to sober a prudent statesman considering the annexation of a large territory populated by a racially and culturally different people.[28]

Deemed even more hypocritical was McKinley's claim to have gone down on his knees "for light and guidance from the 'ruler of nations,'" to perceive "plainly written the high command" that it was America's duty "to educate the Filipinos, and uplift and Christianize them." But the president was a devout man living in an age of religious revivalism and renewed evangelical missionary efforts throughout much of the world, so his actions and perceptions were likely to have been sincere.[29]

After sounding out the people as well as God, McKinley wired the peace commission on October 28, 1898 that "cession of Luzon alone, leaving the rest of the islands subject to Spanish rule, or to be the subject of future contention, cannot be justified on political, commercial, or humanitarian grounds. The cession must be of the whole archipelago or none. The latter is wholly inadmissible, and the former must therefore be required." The majority had already reached that conclusion. Senator Gray may have hoped that McKinley would have prevented such a course. He wired back a protest that the change would lead to entangling alliances, militarism, and financial disaster. Day, too, seemed upset over the new plans, but he was not one to protest openly. The Spanish negotiators were furious over the "immodest demands of a conqueror." But they had little bargaining power, as Americans held Manila and the Philippine nationalists controlled Luzon and were successfully spreading their movement to other islands. Only a diplomatic device could assuage the wounded Spanish pride. When the commission offered twenty million dollars for "Spanish improvements" to the islands, the Spaniards capitulated and signed the treaty on December 10, 1898.

The news was, at first, hailed in the United States. Republican and imperialist editors had been insisting that the recent elections had "closed" the issue. The "people" had "spoken," and it was time to give the president's policy bipartisan support:

The administration is to be congratulated upon finally taking this vigorous stand, in which it is backed by the sentiment of the entire country. . . .

The desire for the retention of the Philippines is not confined to either party. It is broad as the continent and is entertained by men of every political faith. It would appear that President McKinley was a little slow to discover the breadth and strength of the popular demand that we should hold all that Dewey won.[30]

Such editorial self-satisfaction was highly premature. Once McKinley spelled out his intentions and the details of the pending treaty were made public, the debate got under way in earnest. Up to that point, the president's vague references to keeping the flag flying gave his critics little to swing at. Finally, there was something concrete to attack, however effectively the president had diluted the issue by wedding it to the final peace accord.

A few imperialist editors were dismayed over the purchase of territory already conquered: "Twenty million for what? For Dewey's victory?" But most of them used this point to launch self-congratulatory editorials on "America's generosity in victory." Anti-imperialist editors, particularly those who had held abolitionist sympathies, bitterly attacked the purchase of ten million natives at two dollars a head. For those whose anti-imperialism was motivated by racial fear, the purchase proved the inferiority of Filipinos in that they could be sold like cattle. These editors would have had no objection if the Filipinos were to remain chattels, but they feared that some muddleheaded Boston reformers, backed by the federal government and the Supreme Court, would repeat the mistakes of Reconstruction and bestow citizenship and constitutional rights on yet another "inferior race."[31]

Warily, the president embarked on another speaking tour in December to the South, whence came the most virulent congressional opposition to the Treaty of Paris. He bypassed the Southern representatives in Washington by appealing directly to the people, as he had done in the Midwest two months earlier. On this trip he made the startling statement that the Philippines was already in American hands and that "it is the duty of the army of occupation to announce and proclaim in the most public manner that we have come, not as invaders or conquerors, but as friends to protect the natives in their homes, in their business, and in their personal or religious liberty." McKinley's actions weeks before the vote on ratification was an extraordinary attempt to hand the Senate a fait accompli. He was apparently influenced by his military commander, General Elwell S. Otis, who strongly advised him that only the immediate and clearest statement of America's intention to remain in the Philippines would nip in the bud Aguinaldo's "political pretensions" and prevent imminent warfare with the native troops surrounding the American position in Manila.[32]

Naturally, McKinley's maneuver infuriated his critics, who interpreted it as "a complete usurpation of the Senate's power to ratify treaties." Missouri's Senator Vest opened the new session that December with a resolution that no power existed under the Constitution "to acquire territory to be held and governed permanently as colonies." A holiday recess provided a temporary respite before the debate resumed in the new year with a shower of resolutions limiting, if not precluding, a policy of imperialism. The Vest Resolution was too sweeping for senators opposed to annexing the Philippines but desirous of keeping bases there, as well as in Guam and Puerto Rico. Resolutions were made ranging from a very general one by Louisiana's Samuel McEnery that the nation's goal was to prepare Filipinos for self-government to a more specific stipulation by Georgia's Augustus Bacon that independence had to be granted as soon as the natives formed a stable, autonomous government. Hoar wanted to amend the treaty to recognize the future right of the Filipinos to be free and independent. Resolutions by Mississippi's William V. Sullivan, Kentucky's William Lindsay, and Nebraska's William V. Allen all stipulated that ratification of the peace treaty would neither constitute senatorial approval of a colonial policy nor preclude future independence for the Philippines. William E. Mason of Illinois was one of the few Republicans to question his party's direction, and his resolution would have outlawed "forced annexation." Allen further resolved that "any aggressive action" by the military in the Philippines would be "an act of war unwarranted on the part of the President and the exercise of Constitutional power vested exclusively in Congress."[33]

Vest's resolution was the subject of public debate in January, while serious discussion of the treaty took place in executive session. Daily leaks to the press, however, made mockery of any pretense to secrecy. Opposition to annexation ranged from the lofty idealism and humanitarian concerns of Senator Hoar to the flagrantly racist fears of his colleagues from the South and West. Filipinos were "a heterogeneous compound of inefficient humanity," thundered South Carolina's John McLaurin. He warned that such "a mongrel and semibarbarous population . . . inferior but akin to the Negro in moral and intellectual development and capacity for self-government" could spell doom for the Republic. South Carolina's junior senator, "Pitchfork Ben" Tillman, who liked to bill himself as "the senator from Africa," insisted that it was absurd to talk about teaching people self-government when they were racially unfit to govern themselves. Southern Negrophobes and Western Sinophobes in the guise of anti-imperialists thought the Filipinos should be left to fend for themselves or turned over to a friendly power.[34]

As in the earlier debate over Hawaii, the opposition, with few exceptions, lent to the imperialists an aura of moral self-righteousness that was hardly deserved, but fully exploited. "Providence" and "moral duty" were evoked often enough to more than balance the crassly commercial reasoning of a few Republicans. Of course, the imperialists acknowledged that America stood to gain rich profits from these "stepping-stones to China," but these profits would be but fringe benefits for having done one's duty and followed God's will. "Providence has given the United States the duty of extending Christian civilization, we propose to execute it," declared Minnesota's Knute Nelson. A former abolitionist, Nelson was more sensitive to the charge of wanting to exploit "racial inferiors." We are not there "to enslave or enthrall the Filipinos, but to uplift them," he protested.

The opposition worked hard to lift this cloak of hypocrisy and reveal underneath "the lust for power and greed for land veneered with the tawdriness of false humanity." Opponents to annexation also tried to bring some reality to the expectations of the imperialists. "God almighty help the party that seeks to give civilization and Christian liberty hypodermically with thirteen inch guns," Mason warned his fellow Republicans—a warning that was amply vindicated in the years to come. With chilling accuracy, Senator Swanson predicted it would take 50,000 soldiers, "as a very conservative estimate," and several years to subdue hidden guerrillas in disease-infested jungles. Continued frustration would lead to inhuman retaliation and a repetition of the Spanish atrocities. Endless warfare would require conscription and a huge standing army would drain the economy and vitiate the country morally and politically. It was not unreasonable to expect a martial hero to return from the Philippines and cross the political Rubicon, imperialists were warned. But historical analogies had little appeal. Where Spain had failed, America, of course, would succeed. Filipinos would quickly recognize that America was very different from European nations and had come to help and develop, not to conquer and exploit. If force was necessary, American soldiers would never resort to the tactics of Europeans in similar situations. In short, Swanson's valuable warning fell on deaf ears.[35]

The severity of the senatorial debate put the administration on notice that ratification would be no easy matter. McKinley did have certain strategical advantages. For one, he could avoid a premature vote by keeping the treaty bottled up in Davis's Foreign Relations committee until two-thirds of the Senate supported it. For another, a defeat would return it to the committee and bring it to a new vote in March, when a new Congress would be more favorably disposed to the treaty, thanks to Republican successes at the polls in November. Seven avowed opponents were lame-duck senators. But McKinley was under pressure from Otis to secure the treaty's ratification as soon as possible so that he could confront the nationalists with a legitimate claim to their islands. Without it, warfare was likely any day, Otis warned.[36]

The Administration began to buy key Democratic votes with promises of pork-barrel legislation, patronage, and federal judgeships. Arthur Pue Gorman, the minority leader from Maryland and a presidential aspirant, complained bitterly of the flagrant bribery taking place before his very eyes. "It is an outrage the way Hanna and others are working this treaty through the Senate. All the railroad influence, . . . all the commercial interests and every other interest that can be reached are bringing pressure on Senators in the most shameful way. Some of the things they are doing transcend the bounds of decency." Senator Richard Pettigrew, a South Dakota Silver Republican, protested "the open purchase of votes to ratify this treaty on the floor of the Senate." Years later, Tillman and McLaurin exchanged physical blows in the Senate when the former accused the latter of having sold his vote for ratification for federal patronage in their state.[37]

Imperialists received help unexpectedly from William Jennings Bryan, who broke his silence after the elections and, as expected, opposed annexing the Philippines on the grounds that they "were too far away and their people too different from ours to be annexed even if they desired it." Once articulated, his position was lampooned in the imperialist press, compared to his attack on the gold standard, and contrasted with McKinley's "Americanism" and "sound money." It was "after all not such a long step from the proposition that 46¢ worth of silver and 44¢ of wind are worth as much as a dollar's worth of gold to the other and newer proposition that a nation has no rights to the fruits of a victorious and honorable war," one editor observed.[38] In January, however, Bryan decided that ratification of the treaty would separate the need to end the war from the issue of imperialism. The future status of the Philippines could then be decided by a simple majority of the Senate by passing a resolution attached to the bill appropriating twenty million dollars for Spain or by passing the Bacon resolution.

Although his reasoning was sound enough, Bryan was vilified by anti-imperialists. Pettigrew attributed his "apostasy" to the need to create an issue for the 1900 presidential campaign. "He was seeking political capital and he was willing to take it where he found it, without paying too much attention to nice questions of principle." Actually, Bryan's error was in not trading his support for passage of the Bacon resolution *before* the vote for ratification, if such a trade was possible. Senator Jones of Arkansas had, in fact, warned Bryan that the Republicans would promise anything and then renege after ratification. Either Bryan was overconfident that the majority of the Senate was opposed to imperialism, or he was politically naive on this issue.[39]

By the end of January, both sides were ready for a showdown; both were worried that warfare in the islands could adversely affect its own position. Gorman was sure that a war would patriotically compel some wavering Democrats to vote for the treaty, while Lodge was just as certain that it could make annexation much too formidable a proposition for some of the bribed Democratic senators. Also, a Supreme Court decision on the sale of liquor in Alaska worried the opposition because it implied, at least, that tariffs against colonial competition might be constitutionally permissible. The realization that such tariffs were possible would certainly mitigate one crucial fear over annexation. Finally, Gorman had to realize that time was against his side. The president could resubmit the treaty in an extra session or in the next Congress when several foes, including Gorman, would not be in the Senate. For the opposition, it was a question of now or never, so Bacon called for a vote on February 6, after two more weeks of debate. In spite of the fact that the Republicans appeared to be still three votes shy of victory, Lodge agreed to Bacon's proposal, probably due to pressure from General Otis to secure the treaty's ratification as soon as possible.[40]

The leaders of the newly created New England Anti-Imperialist League angrily charged Gorman with selling out their cause by bringing the treaty up for a vote before they had had sufficient time to educate the public on the dangers of annexation. Apparently they had advised Gorman to delay the vote for ratification until a more enlightened electorate was able to pressure the Senate into rejecting the treaty. But men like Gorman and Bacon were, above all, practical politicians who had little faith that a handful of professional reformers in Boston, already famous for championing lost causes, could make a difference. Both voted against the treaty, though, as a lame-duck senator, Gorman did not have to had he had ulterior motives, as charged.

On the last legislative day before the vote, the Kansas Populist William Harris swung his vote in favor of the treaty, but the Republicans still needed two more. Four vociferous anti-imperialists, Henry Heitfeld, an Idaho Populist, McEnery and McLaurin, both Southern Democrats, and John Jones, a Silver Republican from Nevada, were being courted. Heitfeld publicly denounced a Republican bribe for his vote, but the other three senators succumbed. Most shocking was the affirmative vote of Jones, which has been attributed to the influence of Bryan rather than Republican bribery. His betrayal, along with that of fellow Populists Harris and Allen, embittered Pettigrew, who charged Bryan with having upset Democratic calculations by personally influencing eighteen votes. Senator Hoar pared this number down to seven, and more recent scholarship suggests that Bryan influenced only Jones and Allen. Even so, the smaller number does not lessen the importance of Bryan's "apostasy," as the vote was so close that a shift of two positive votes would have defeated the treaty. Surprisingly, Gorman, Bryan's possible rival for the Democratic nomination in 1900, did not exploit his defection. Instead, he attributed his party's defeat to Republican wheeling and dealing in the cloakrooms. "The result only shows the power of an administration in controlling votes in the Senate."[41]

Even more surprisingly, almost no one among the contemporary politicians or subsequent scholars attributed the Administration's success to the outbreak of warfare in the Philippines the day before the vote. President McKinley alone felt that the war assured ratification. Years later, Senator Patterson insisted that ratification would have been impossible without the war. "Senators who had stood against the treaty, incensed by what they were led to believe was a wanton, deliberate, and unprovoked assault upon the American Army by Aguinaldo's forces, changed their purposes and voted for ratification." Years later, Roosevelt attributed ratification "partly to the Senate, partly to Providence, and partly to the Filipinos." But neither Patterson nor Roosevelt named any specific senators who switched their votes at the last minute for patriotic reasons. All the late shifts are better explained by Republican bribery and Bryan's influence. Possibly the Republican Mason was affected by the war, but even if he had quietly been considered a doubtful vote, party loyalty could just as easily explain his support for the treaty. Lodge's insistence that he, Hanna, and other Republican leaders had carried the day seems accurate, if immodest. "We were down in the engine room and did not get the flowers, but we did make the ship move," Lodge contended.[42]

An even bigger Republican victory occurred two weeks later, after Bacon's endless clamoring for a decision on the pending resolutions. His own proposal received a tie vote, and Vice-President Garret Hobart decided against it. The imperialists again outmaneuvered the opposition by passing the innocuously worded McEnery resolution, which one historian characterized as "little more than a pious hope." Mason had warned Carnegie that his party had made a deal "for four votes" in return for "an absolute agreement to pass the McEnery resolution." Bacon vainly tried to put some teeth into this amendment through a pledge of ultimate independence for the Philippines, but it was defeated and the fate of the islands was simply left open.[43]

The voting on ratification and the subsequent resolutions was essentially partisan. Only two Republicans, Eugene Hale of Maine and George Hoar of Massachusetts, broke ranks and voted against the treaty. The real effect of the outbreak of war seems to have been that it momentarily stifled senatorial criticism of the Administration's Philippine policy, but not that it affected the voting. As Bacon declared when the war was only three weeks old, "the oft-repeated expression 'our country right or wrong' has a vital principle, and upon that principle, I stand." In the early days of stunning American victories in Luzon and Panay, the whole country seemed too drunk on the heady wine of national power to heed the witty, but astute, observation of Mr. Dooley, who explained, "We've got th' Philipeens, Hinnissey; we've got thim the way Casey got th' bulldog—be th' teeth."[44]

3

The Soldier as Diplomat

American relations with the Filipino nationalists were, from the beginning, left to professional military men, who were ill-suited to play diplomatic roles due to their training and temperaments. They egregiously mishandled diplomatic functions and, more seriously, failed to keep Washington accurately informed of the nature and complexity of the insurrection against Spain and on the degree of organization of and popular support for General Emilio Aguinaldo's revolutionary government. Significantly, the only two professional American diplomats involved, who remained on the periphery of the earliest relations with Aguinaldo, made very different assessments of his abilities and political goals. Because it was a wartime situation, however, America's military commander had sole authority to deal with the Filipinos.

The isolation of the Philippines, long imposed by Spanish policy, began to break down with the English invasion and occupation of Manila between 1762 and 1764. Trade with non-Spanish Europe, initiated by the English, continued after their departure, by bribery at first and then officially condoned. By the end of the eighteenth century, Philippine exports were permitted to be carried in foreign bottoms, and soon thereafter European and American firms established commercial houses in the islands. It was not long before foreigners dominated the export-import trade in the Philippines. The age of steam, opening of the Suez Canal, and laying of submarine cables greatly accelerated the process of foreign domination, which made westernized portions of Luzon, Panay, and Cebu increasingly dependent upon European markets. With traders from Europe came new ideas, particularly the liberalizing philosophies that were sweeping capitalist countries in the nineteenth century. In turn, the Filipinos who prospered from the expanding trade could afford to send their sons to European universities. The students brought back such ideas as natural philosophy, nationalism, secularism, and democracy. Madrid itself contributed to these impulses as it oscillated between liberal and conservative moods.

31

Economic development, along with other worldwide changes, rapidly re-structured society in the Philippines. Those who prospered from the changes—mostly hispanicized mestizos, and some *indios*—formed a new native elite, the *ilustrados*. Armed with increasing wealth and education, they challenged their Spanish "betters" and the carefully nurtured colonial myth that the natives were incompetent, uneducable "monkeys." Lower- and middle-class Filipinos began to break out of their provincial isolation, long enforced by Spanish policies, and to challenge the Chinese domination of domestic trade and certain types of labor. Anti-Chinese sentiment has a long history in the Philippines, but the virulent Sinophobia of the late nineteenth century probably reflected and enhanced a new and rising spirit of nationalism among the masses.

With the loss of Spain's colonies in the western hemisphere, the number of Spanish-born immigrants to the Philippines, *peninsulares*, increased dramatically. They competed with those Spaniards born in the Philippines, creoles, for jobs traditionally reserved for the Spanish. An attempt to give preference to peninsulares for such jobs forced some creoles to entertain more revolutionary perceptions of Filipino nationalism, which only frightened the conservative colons, particularly the friars, into resisting all change, even that emanating from Madrid. In short, the seeds for a colonial rebellion were being sown during the last few decades of the century.

In 1868, liberals came to power in Madrid and proposed so much reform that Queen Isabella fled to France. A new constitution guaranteed basic freedoms not only in Spain, but in the colonies as well. A new governor general, Carlos Maria de la Torre, enjoyed such a liberal reputation that he was ecstatically greeted in Manila by the ilustrados, well-versed in liberal thought. As is so often the case, sudden reform for peoples long oppressed can enhance revolutionary fervor. The outbreak of armed rebellion in Cuba, following these reforms, contributed to the fall of the liberals in Spain. With the return of the conservatives to power in 1870, the short-lived reforms were hastily rescinded, and de la Torre was recalled from Manila. These events helped fuel a workers' rebellion at the arsenal at Cavite in 1872. It was brutally suppressed by the Spanish, leaving behind a sullen resentment that would be exploited by a later revolutionary movement.

Filipino intellectuals reacted more cautiously to this turn of events and utilized their persuasion to press for the return of the liberal reforms. Organizing under the label of the "Propaganda Movement," they never advocated independence, however much the movement may have contributed to the spirit of nationalism and to the intellectual foundation of the coming revolution. The celebrated surgeon, poet, novelist, and artist, José Rizal, was the unofficial spokesman for this informal group. While studying in Spain, Rizal had traveled to England and Germany to observe political developments. His novel, *Noli*

Me Tangere, has been compared to *Uncle Tom's Cabin*, in that it had a similar galvanizing effect on Filipino nationalism to that which Harriet Beecher Stowe's work had on American abolitionism. Like Stowe's book, Rizal's novel had more political than literary significance.

In spite of the conservative nature of the Propaganda Movement, Spain overreacted to it, exiling Rizal in 1892 and executing him four years later. Thus Rizal was made a martyr for a revolution in which he was not interested; in fact, he was on his way to Cuba to serve as a surgeon for the Spanish Army at the time of his execution.[1]

A more important base for the Insurrection of 1896 than the Propaganda Movement was the *Katipunan*, a secret society founded by Andres Bonifacio, a laborer from Manila's Tondo District, on the very day of Rizal's banishment in 1892. Although he had had little formal education, Bonifacio had read the works of Rizal and other European-educated ilustrados, as well as books on the American and French revolutions. His appeal was largely to urban, lower-middle-, and working-classes. Because of the nature of his support, the Katipunan has been traditionally likened by later scholars, mostly university-trained ilustrados, to secular European revolutionary and nationalistic movements. Hence, it has been compared to the Levelers, Jacobins, communists, and even Freemasons. Reynaldo Ileto, however, has put the Katipunan in the context of Philippine history, in which previous, contemporary, and later revolutionary movements were almost all of a religious nature. Such fanatical and heretical religiopolitical cults were popularly, and collectively, labeled *colorums*. Ileto has discerned idioms and symbols similar to those of Christ's passion and other biblical themes in the initiation rites and other rituals of the Katipunan, placing it more squarely within this Filipino revolutionary tradition. At least, "the original *Katipunan* of Bonifacio conceived of revolution as an experience of *pasión*," Ileto argues convincingly.

After several years of secret existence, the Katipunan was betrayed in the confessional by a Spanish priest. In a wave of hysteria, induced partially by the history of heretical religiorevolutionary sects, the Spanish rounded up thousands of Katipuneros and suspects and incarcerated, tortured, and executed many of them. Rizal was one of the victims, although he, like most of his class, had rejected the Katipunan. Bonifacio was forced to raise his red flag prematurely at Balintawak, on Manila's outskirts, and make a formal declaration of independence. After initial skirmishes around Manila, the fighting spread to other parts of Luzon and to Panay and Negros. Spanish repression had created an uneasy alliance between Katipuneros, ilustrados—conservative rural ones, such as Pedro Paterno, and urban radical ones, such as Apolinario Mabini—and the provincial *gobernadorcillo* leadership, symbolized by Emilio Aguinaldo. This alliance was actually the first real expression of modern Filipino nationalism, one that, although partially and only temporarily, managed to transcend the very sharp vertical divisions of class and the formidable horizontal, ethnic ones. Passionate ideological positions, however, kept the insurgency divided.

The young latecomer to the Katipunan, Emilio Aguinaldo, who had joined only after Rizal's execution, quickly distinguished himself as a tactician and martial leader with one of the few Filipino victories at the Imus River in his own province of Cavite. He soon rose to a position of rivalry with Bonifacio, who lacked military skills. The ensuing struggle between them has been seen as a result of a struggle for power and of conflicting personalities and class interests, but Ileto has discerned an ideological division of religious and secular parameters as well. Aguinaldo, as a Chinese mestizo of relative wealth and provincial status as the town mayor of Kawit, had—much more than Bonifacio—what Ileto calls "a genteel regard for secular ilustrado ideas of nationalism." He thus attempted to secularize the Katipunan and came into conflict with Bonifacio's faction on this point. Bonifacio made the strategic error of shifting his base of operations to Cavite, Aguinaldo's bailiwick, and a showdown quickly followed. After the angry confrontation, marked by inflamed rhetoric, Bonifacio was charged with treason and sedition when he refused to be demoted. Following a farcical trial, he was executed. Aguinaldo's last-minute commutation to exile of the death sentence failed to reach the firing squad in time. As the undisputed leader of the insurrection, Aguinaldo then outmaneuvered Bonifacio's following by transforming the Katipunan into a revolutionary government.[2]

After nine months of fighting, the revolutionaries were badly mauled by the Spanish. Aguinaldo retreated to Biyák-na-bató, a mountain redoubt scarcely thirty miles from Manila, from which he directed guerrilla warfare, almost exclusively in Cavite, and wrote a constitution, modeled after the American constitution and that written by Cuban revolutionaries in 1895, for his recently declared republic. Realizing that an assault on Aguinaldo's headquarters would merely force him to relocate elsewhere in the mountains, the Spanish wisely decided to negotiate a peace. Aguinaldo had little choice, as his cause had been greatly weakened by the understandable desertion of Bonifacio's followers after their leader's execution and as he had little influence beyond Cavite. The death of the ilustrado General Mamerto Natividad of Pampanga, who would hear of no compromise with Spain, paved the way for negotiations. Even then, some revolutionaries refused to accept Aguinaldo's Pact of Biyák-na-bató with Madrid and continued ineffective resistance after their leader went into exile.

Many reforms were discussed with the Spanish negotiators, ranging from expulsion of the hated friars and dissolution of their monasteries and large landholdings to the restoration of the briefly bestowed liberties of 1868. Also discussed were tax reform, equality under the law between Spaniards and Filipinos, and representation in the Cortes. Amnesty was promised in return for the surrender of the rebels' arms to Spanish authorities. The insurgents naively accepted a verbal promise for unspecified reforms "deemed wise" by Her Majesty's Government. Spain agreed to settle the claims of Filipino noncombatants who had suffered damages at the hands of Spanish soldiers for a sum not to exceed a total of $900,000. In addition, Aguinaldo and forty followers would go into exile with half of the $800,000 promised to the insurgents. When a stipulated number of guns were surrendered, half of which had to be modern, Aguinaldo's group in exile would receive the second half of the money, a general amnesty would be proclaimed, and a final *Te Deum* would be sung in Manila's cathedral, signaling the end of the civil war.

Actually, both sides flagrantly violated the terms as well as the spirit of the settlement. Aguinaldo, hoarding the $400,000 he had taken from the Spanish in order to buy arms, organized a revolutionary junta in Hong Kong to plan the next round in the struggle for independence. In the islands, insurgents surrendered only their oldest arms and secreted the others in the mountains for future use. Spain, on the other hand, failed to make the second payment to Aguinaldo or to honor any civilian claims. None of the discussed reforms were forthcoming. Even the amnesty was violated almost immediately following its lavish celebration feast. Many Filipinos implicated in the revolution were arrested on trumped-up charges by the Spanish police and tortured to reveal the locations of hidden arms. By March 1898, unorganized and scattered gunfights had again erupted throughout Luzon. If the insurrection had ever ended, it began anew with little leadership. Bonifacio's former secretary, Emilio Jacinto—long considered the brains behind the Katipunan—began a new recruitment drive, and for the first time members of the better-educated classes began to join in significant numbers.

More than three months before the revolution revived, Aguinaldo began to make contact with American officials in the hope of gaining American support for the junta in exile and making a formal alliance should the United States go to war with Spain. To these ends he sent his "Foreign Secretary," Felipe Agoncillo, to see the American consul-general in Hong Kong, Rounceville Wildman, in November, 1897. When Dewey's squadron arrived in Hong Kong, Commander Edward P. Wood, on Dewey's instructions, invited Agoncillo aboard the U.S.S. *Petrel* for serious negotiations. Wood urged members of the junta to return to the Philippines as soon as possible in order to join and lead the incipient rebellion there. He assured them of American support in the event that the United States went to war with Spain, hinting that the latter was inevitable. Members of the junta were granted an audience with Dewey him-

self to give the plans the imprimatur of his office, although he made it clear that
he was not in a position to commit his nation officially.

These conferences were broken off suddenly when Aguinaldo and his en-
tourage were forced to flee to Singapore to escape a lawsuit by one member of
the junta who wanted to divide their treasury for personal use. Aguinaldo's English contact in Singapore, Howard H. Bray, quickly put him in touch with
E. Spencer Pratt, the American consul-general there, and the secret interviews continued. During these negotiations the United States declared war on
Spain, and Dewey cabled Pratt, "Tell Aguinaldo to come as soon as possible."
But Dewey was already at sea by the time the junta got to Hong Kong, and the
Filipino leaders had to wait there for three weeks for the U.S.S. *McCullogh* to
return for them. Meanwhile, Aguinaldo gave Wildman $115,000 with which to
purchase arms for him.

Again Aguinaldo was in the awkward position of not having a written commitment. Having learned a painful lesson from his earlier negotiations with the
Spanish, he agonized over the lack of formal accords. The fast pace of recent
events made impossible the making of binding agreements approved in Washington, he reasoned. The act of transporting him to the Philippines aboard an
American warship constituted a de facto alliance, or, at the very least, recognition of his political claims. America's traditional anticolonial policy and the
Teller amendment forbidding the colonization of Cuba further assuaged his
fears. Aguinaldo was more than willing to cede a port and naval bases to the
United States even before they were demanded. Indeed, he was ready to turn
foreign policy over to the United States in return for protection against other
major powers and for complete autonomy over internal affairs. Such details had
never been discussed, no less committed to paper, and Aguinaldo had only the
hope that history and geography militated against an American attempt to replace the Spanish in the Philippines.

Aguinaldo also counted on the continuous encouragement of Dewey,
Pratt, and Wildman to think in terms of a Philippine Republic. The State Department was, in fact, so alarmed over the remarks of diplomats Pratt and Wildman that it admonished them for acting without authorization. Wildman's
reprimand read, "If you wrote to Aguinaldo as reported . . . your action is disapproved, and you are forbidden to make pledges or discuss policy." Pratt was
told that his remarks caused "disquietude" in Washington and created "a doubt
as to whether some of your acts may have borne a significance and produced an
impression which this government would be compelled to regret."[3] Dewey was
too revered to be disciplined for his indiscretions, although anti-imperialist editors did publish his conversations with "Don Emilio"—or, at least, Aguinaldo's
recollection of them—which enraged imperialist editors. The Admiral was re-

peatedly forced to deny Aguinaldo's version of their early relationship. "I never treated him as an ally, except to assist me in my operations against the Spanish." As damning as this explanation was, imperialist editors ecstatically hailed it as the "final refutation" of Aguinaldo's claims. "Dewey of Manila Bay" had "ruthlessly destroyed one of the foundation stones of the anti-imperialist temple of falsehoods and delusions," crowed the *New York Times*. The *Hartford Courant* pointed out that "it is the word of a Malay adventurer—a Malay 'patriot' if you please—against the word of an American admiral and gentleman." The popular choice was obvious enough, and even the *Springfield Republican* hesitated to call the hero a liar and advised that it would be wiser "to leave it up to future historians" to decide, "when calm statement and the full record" would count more than "violent denunciation and concealment."[4]

General T. M. Anderson, the first American commander in the Philippines, understood better than any other military leader the full diplomatic implications of Dewey's and Wildman's assistance to Aguinaldo. "If an incipient rebellion was already in progress, what could be inferred from the fact that Aguinaldo and thirteen banished Tagals were brought down on a naval vessel and landed at Cavite?" Anderson asked in the *North American Review* after his return from the islands and retirement from the army. Unfortunately, Anderson's command was all too brief. Although he was patronizing and paternalistic in his treatment of Aguinaldo, he at least treated him as a partner, albeit a junior one. If any officer was capable of salvaging the good feeling that Aguinaldo had for the United States, it was Anderson.[5]

Once the United States Navy returned him to his homeland, Aguinaldo immediately demonstrated the amazing organizational and military abilities that had catapulted him to leadership during the first phase of the revolution. Within the first week of his return he had full command of the revolutionary forces and insisted on making public his gratitude to the United States for being there. The Filipino forces were allied to "the great North American nation, the cradle of liberty, and therefore the friend to our people," he told his troops. At every opportunity he sang lavish praises for the United States. "America has come to us manifesting a protection as decisive as it is undoubtedly disinterested toward our inhabitants, considering us as sufficiently civilized and capable of governing for ourselves our unfortunate country," he declared on May 24, 1898. Such statements may show that Aguinaldo still believed in America's good intentions, that he was trying to convince himself, or that he hoped to stir the conscience of America's military commanders.[6]

While bottling up the Spanish in Manila, directing the conquest of Luzon, establishing ties with other *insurrectos* on the various islands, and creating a revolutionary government, Aguinaldo also found time to write a Declaration of

Independence and even to design a flag for the new republic. On June 12, 1898, when the only American troops on Luzon were a handful of marines guarding naval stores at Cavite and a small army advance party making preparations for Anderson's arrival still two weeks away, Aguinaldo, along with other Filipino leaders, signed the Declaration of Independence with great fanfare. Ironically, Aguinaldo asked L. M. Johnson, Colonel of Artillery, United States Army, as the highest-ranking American officer on land at the time, to witness the document; not having been briefed to the contrary, the American colonel obliged. The declaration was also "witnessed by the Supreme Judge of the Universe" and was "under the protection of the Mighty and Humane North American Nation," Aguinaldo vowed as he unfurled the flag of the Philippine Republic. This was significantly not the red flag of the Katipunan, but a red, white and blue one symbolizing the special friendship and protection of the United States, as well as "courage, independence, and eternal resistance to invaders," Aguinaldo explained. Three stars on the flag symbolized the union of Luzon, the Visayan islands, and Mindanao; eight rays of the sun represented the areas placed under martial law by the Spanish during the earlier rebellion; and finally a white triangle in the middle, symbolizing the blood pact of the Katipunan, acknowledged the role played by that society in the revolution against Spain. Interestingly enough, Aguinaldo neglected to explain the symbolism of the white triangle that day in the presence of Colonel Johnson. The Filipino leaders were apparently learning the ideological imperatives of their American "allies" and wished to avoid seeming radical or secretive. Similarly, Aguinaldo altered the original title of "dictator" that he had assumed upon his return to "president," although this change may have been to placate his Filipino followers as much as to satisfy American critics. At any rate, few imperialist editors acknowledged the change in order to exploit the draconian implications of the earlier title.

As in all revolutionary movements, there were sharp divisions within the ranks, in which the ilustrados were the most unstable element. During Aguinaldo's exile, they had drifted back to the Spanish side. Upon his return, Aguinaldo worked hard to recruit them back and angered Katipuneros by appointing such elitist "collaborators" to key posts in his government. His key advisor who ran the cabinet was Apolinario Mabini, an ilustrado of lower-class origins with radical ideas of a "simultaneous external and internal revolution." His ideas terrified the elite, which wanted "an oligarchy of intelligence," not one of the Katipunan, the army, and "ignorance." With the shift of his government from Cavite to Malolos, Aguinaldo lost more power and was soon dominated by these conservatives, who seemed willing to accept almost any form of government that would continue to legitimize their dominant position in Philippine society. Some were convinced that an American protectorate would best maintain their status. Pardo de Tavara, Aguinaldo's director of diplomacy, for example, recommended that President McKinley be asked not to abandon the Philippines. Florentine Torres informed Aguinaldo that educated and propertied Filipinos were "convinced that . . . the only possible way of saving these islands from anarchy in the interior, from the ambitions of certain powers, or from some other colonial system similar to Spain . . . [is] the frank and loyal acceptance of the sovereignty of America."

Ilustrados dominated the constitutional convention and used their persuasive powers to shape that document and the legislative branch of government. Highly emotional issues—such as the role of friars, the separation of church and state or nationalization of the Church, the choice between a loose confederation with regional and tribal autonomy and a more centralized authority, or the powers and relationships of executive and legislature—merely cloaked the real struggle to limit the powers of the Katipunan, and lower classes in general, and to diffuse any radical thrusts. The ilustrados emerged victorious. As David Joel Steinberg explained it:

> The landowning *ilustrado* community, embodied by Pedro Paterno, Felipe Calderón, Benito Legarda, and Felipe Buencamino, established legislative hegemony over the executive coalition of Aguinaldo and Mabini. The radical goals disappeared as private property was guaranteed, and as the suffrage was limited to men of high character, social position, and honorable conduct. Eighty of the 136 delegates were trained professionals (43 were lawyers). The government as inaugurated on 21 January, 1899, was dominated by conservative *ilustrados*.[7]

Possibly because he, as a conservative Katipunero, was in the middle of the struggle, or more probably at the instigation of Mabini, Aguinaldo did win an amendment granting him the power to rule by decree "during the time the country may have to struggle for independence." This limited victory chased a few of the most conservative ilustrados to Manila, where they reenforced the narrow view of General Otis that Aguinaldo's government represented little more than ignorant and self-serving men who could never control the archipelago. Many ilustrados remained, however, to provide Aguinaldo with crucial civilian and military leadership until the cause seemed militarily hopeless.

In addition to class differences within his following, there were also rival revolutionary movements that plagued Aguinaldo, such as the *Guardia de Honor* in the Ilocos region of northwestern Luzon. Created in 1872 to uphold orthodox Catholicism, it was transformed over the next few decades, through clerical neglect, into a revolutionary, millenarian, and anarchistic sect opposed to all authority and preying on its nonbelieving neighbors for supplies. The Katipunan courted it unsuccessfully, possibly due to the more secular orientation of Aguinaldo's faction, or possibly to Ilocano-Tagalog rivalry. At any rate, the Guardia de Honor challenged the revolutionary government's authority in the fall of 1898, just when General Otis was escalating his diplomatic demands of Aguinaldo on another front.[8]

It was the responsibility of American military leaders in Manila to provide Washington with an accurate assessment of these political movements and to perceive in Aguinaldo's government the most viable segment of the population with which to work. Aguinaldo had not demanded independence of Spain in his peace proposal, and possibly he, and certainly the dominant ilustrado wing of his government, took this issue far less seriously than did the Katipuneros. A face-saving compromise may have been possible. In order to make such a bargain, however, Otis had to transcend the class biases being fed to him by former Spanish rulers and those friendly ilustrados in Manila who had either rejected or deserted Aguinaldo's cause. Above all, he had to refrain from assuming that the banditry of offshoot revolutionary sects was Aguinaldo's responsibility.

To a limited extent, Admiral Dewey and General Anderson did attempt to portray Aguinaldo in a realistic manner. At one point, the admiral informed Washington that he viewed "the insurgents as friends," who were "far superior in their intelligence and more capable of self government than the natives of Cuba." Anderson also cabled his early impressions of Aguinaldo: "When we first landed he seemed very suspicious and not at all friendly, but I have come to a better understanding with him and he is much more friendly and seems willing to cooperate." As more American soldiers streamed ashore, however, Aguinaldo understandably grew suspicious of America's real intentions. At one point he threatened to cut off Anderson's food supply until the general threatened to "pass over" Aguinaldo and "make requisition directly on the people." The Filipino leader backed down and permitted Filipinos to sell food to the Americans.[9]

In spite of this encounter, however, Anderson continued to challenge prevalent shibboleths in Washington regarding the capabilities of Aguinaldo and his followers. "I submit with all deference that we have heretofore underrated the natives," he pleaded with Washington. "They are not ignorant, savage tribes, but have a civilization of their own; and though insignificant in appearance are fierce fighters, and for a tropical people are industrious." Unfortunately these assessments, however patronizing, never got past the War Department, where they languished until congressional critics of the war in the Philippines forced the secretary of war to make them public. By then, however, Anderson was already retired and publishing articles on his early relationship with the "insurrectionists."[10]

One other general, Charles King, also disagreed with the official view of the situation. Unfortunately, he was a volunteer and had little means of influencing Washington. When he returned from the Philippines, the war was already six months old. As an established novelist before his service, however, King quickly took up his pen in place of his sword and expressed his views in the *Milwaukee Journal*:

The capability of the Filipinos for self government can not be doubted. Such men as Rellano, Aguinaldo, and many others whom I might name are highly educated; nine-tenths of the people read and write, all are skilled artisans in one way or another; they are industrious, frugal, temperate, and given a fair start, could look out for themselves infinitely better than our people imagine. In my opinion they rank far higher than the Cubans or the uneducated negroes to whom we have given the right of suffrage.[11]

A report by two lower-ranking naval personnel who made a trip through Luzon in the summer of 1898 should also have challenged any doubts about Aguinaldo's ability to command popular support. After interviewing many local officials, these two Americans reported that "universally . . . all declare they will accept nothing short of independence." The officials also desired and expected American protection, but were fearful of "any interference on the land and suspicious of American intentions," the report concluded. Dewey read the account and forwarded it to the Navy Department on December 1, 1898, with a strong endorsement that insisted it "contains the most complete and reliable information obtainable in regard to the present state of the Northern Luzon Island." But the document remained in the Navy Department until the two authors returned to the United States and published a popular account of their trip.[12]

Dewey and Anderson were also the only American commanders to maintain direct communication with Aguinaldo, a practice that was abruptly halted when Merritt assumed command. They constantly stipulated that their dealing with him did not mean they recognized "his assumption of civil authority." Aguinaldo naturally pressed them on this point. "He asked me at once whether the United States of the North either 'had recognized' or 'would recognize' his government—I am not sure as to the form of the question," but "in either form it was embarrassing," Anderson recounted years later. As if to assuage his conscience, Anderson explained in writing to the Filipino leader on July 23, 1898, that "your fine intellect must perceive that, happy as I am to see you fighting so bravely and successfully against a common enemy, I cannot without orders recognize your civil authority." On another occasion Aguinaldo asked Anderson more bluntly if the Philippine Islands were to become "dependencies" of the United States, to which the American commander responded that in 120 years his country had yet to establish any colonies. "I have studied attentively the Constitution of the United States and I find in it no authority for colonies, and I have no fear," Aguinaldo concurred.

In order to strengthen the impression that their meetings with the Filipino commander were not official and did not constitute recognition of his government and his claim to independence, Dewey and Anderson went to almost childish lengths to impart an air of informality. They contrived to forget their swords, to show up without tunics, or to leave them carefully unbuttoned. Anderson remained uncomfortable about such subterfuge and the role he had personally played in deceiving Aguinaldo. But the politically ambitious Dewey went on to betray further his "friend, Don Emilio," insisting to reporters and congressmen that the junta had been foisted on him by those foolish diplomats, Wildman and Pratt. "They seemed to be all very earnest boys," the Admiral recalled: Aguinaldo was childishly preoccupied with selecting an appropriate cane for himself, and his lieutenants had declined his invitation to join the admiral on his historic dash to Manila because they had not brought their toothbrushes! However, a cane was an important symbol for Spanish rulers in the islands, and unquestionably the junta members did not want to join Dewey in the absence of their leader and used what they considered to be the least offensive excuse. At any rate, their actions were no more childish than Dewey's visiting Aguinaldo without his sword or wearing an unbuttoned tunic, or refusing to attend Philippine Independence Day ceremonies on the excuse that it was "mail day."[13]

Years later, Dewey astounded members of a senate committee by insisting it never dawned on him that Aguinaldo "wanted independence." He felt Aguinaldo's declaration was so unimportant that he mailed it, rather than cabled it to the Navy Department "for information." When pressed for his opinion of Aguinaldo's goals, Dewey answered, "revenge, plunder and pillage." This remark provoked one flabbergasted senator to demand why the navy had transported a "looter" to the Philippines in 1898, whereupon the admiral blithely informed him, "you know the old saying that all things are fair in war." He might more accurately have said "politics."[14]

With the arrival of General Wesley Merritt on July 25, 1898, to assume overall command, the United States was represented by an imperious leader devoid of any diplomatic inclinations. His first edict was to forbid any communication with Aguinaldo's headquarters. As one of the Civil War's boy generals who had matured in the Indian wars, Merritt thought he was better equipped to deal with "savages" than was a naval leader. All that appears to have held Merritt in check were his orders to avoid at all costs "a rupture with insurgents. This is imperative."

Unable to communicate with Merritt, Aguinaldo turned to America's top civilian, Consul Oscar Williams, asking him, "Why do not the American generals operate in conjunction with the Filipino generals? Is it intended to carry out the annexation against the wish of the people?" Williams had learned from the reprimands of Wildman and Pratt not to commit himself to anything in writing. Moreover, as the supreme commander in time of war, Merritt had jurisdiction over Williams and included the consul's office in his directive "not to hold any direct communication with insurgent leaders." So Williams was unable to give Aguinaldo even the courtesy of a reply.[15]

Merritt's dilemma was that he wanted to defeat the Spanish in Manila without aid from Aguinaldo, whose army ringed the city and separated the Americans at Cavite from their objective. No doubt, Merritt would have preferred simply to drive the native army out of the way, but his orders precluded this solution. As Anderson later explained it, "This anomalous state of affairs, namely, having a line of quasi-hostile native troops between our forces and the Spanish position, was, of course, very objectionable, but it was more difficult to deal with owing to the peculiar condition of our relations." Merritt was forced to resort to diplomacy and reopen lines of communication. He turned to Dewey, the "liberator and benefactor of the Filipino peoples," as Aguinaldo had once hailed him, to use once more his persuasive powers on his "good friend Don Emilio." This time Aguinaldo risked a mutiny by his angry lieutenants by accommodating the Americans to make room for them on his front line surrounding Manila.

At the same time, Merritt and Dewey were negotiating with Manila's commander behind Aguinaldo's back. The Spanish knew it would be futile to fight and preferred to surrender to the Americans. All that was needed was a sham battle to save the commander's reputation—and rank—in Madrid. Ironically, the *opéra-bouffe* assault was planned for August 13, a few hours after a peace protocol had been signed. But Dewey had cut the cable to deprive the Spanish of its use, and there was no way of advising Manila immediately that the war was over. The few casualties on both sides in the phony attack were due to some "actors" bungling their "lines," or possibly to the fact that very few officers were let in on the charade. Even Anderson claimed to have been ignorant of the real nature of the "battle."[16]

The major problem for the Americans was to prevent the Filipinos from joining the attack on Manila. This objective was accomplished by threats and some exchange of fire between the two armies. Anderson sent a "most urgent" message to Aguinaldo, "Serious trouble threatening between our forces. Try and prevent it." Aguinaldo answered, "My troops are forced by yours by means of threats of violence to retire from positions taken." Anderson explained that "if you apparently have been forced to retire it is from military necessity and not the want of confidence." Always more diplomatic than his fellow generals, Anderson added, "While we may admit the justice of your insurrection, to prevent all possible complications it is thought judicious and necessary to have only one army in Manila at once." Aguinaldo had been bested and could only plead for joint occupation of the city. This time Merritt at least answered his plea: "The government of the United States, you may be assured, for which as its agent I can make no promises, will deal fairly with the Filipinos, but we must now insist for the good of all there shall be no joint occupation of Manila." Perhaps sensing that relations between Americans and Filipinos were at a breaking point and remembering his strongly worded orders to avoid a rupture, Merritt appeased Aguinaldo with the only diplomatic statement of his brief command, "For myself and the officers and men under my command, I can say that we have conceived a high respect for the abilities and qualities of the Filipinos, and if called upon by the Government to express an opinion, it will be to that effect."[17] Within six weeks Merritt journeyed to Paris to deliver a very different opinion to the U.S. Peace Commission.

Aguinaldo's only recourse was to occupy the Spanish outer defense network, reversing its direction so that the Filipinos had the Americans hemmed in on the land side of Manila. This maneuver incensed Merritt, who felt that such "impudence" could not go unpunished. As soon as the cable was repaired on August 17, Merritt used it to demand from Washington an "urgent" clarification of his orders:

> Since occupation of the town and suburbs the insurgents on outside are pressing for occupation of the city. Situation difficult. Inform me how far I shall proceed in forcing obedience in this matter and others that may arise. Is government willing to use all means to make natives submit to the authority of the United States?[18]

Within hours Merritt received confusing and contradictory instructions in the best McKinley style. "The President directs that there must be no joint occupation with insurgents. . . . Use whatever means in your judgement are necessary to this end." But lest that message unleash Merritt, the cable emphasized that he must "preserve the peace."[19]

Unable to attack the native army, Merritt tried another ploy. Since his orders were to occupy the city in its entirety, he decided to demand the withdrawal of the Philippine Army from two suburbs that were legally part of Manila. Again, Aguinaldo had to bargain for a meager concession to save face in front of his own officers. Merritt agreed to assure the Filipino president in writing that the two positions would be returned to him should the Philippines be

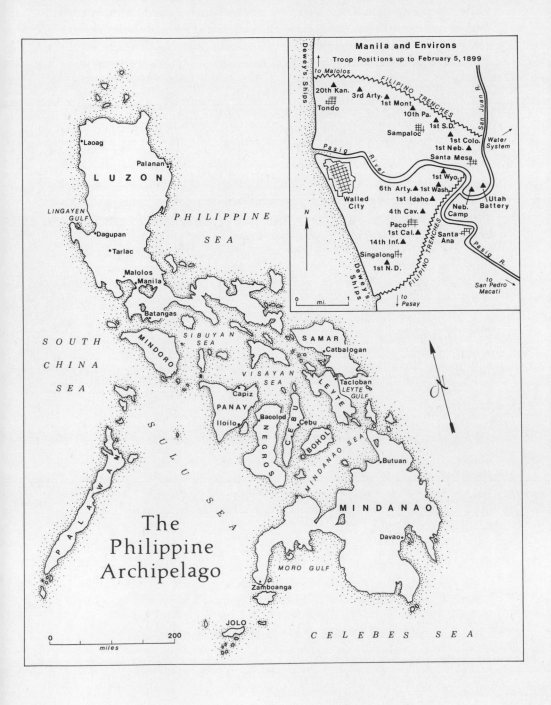

Manila and Environs

Troop Positions up to February 5, 1899

Dewey's Ships

to Malolos

FILIPINO TRENCHES

San Juan R.

20th Kan.
3rd Arty.
1st Mont
Tondo
10th Pa.
1st S.D.
Sampaloc
1st Colo.
1st Neb.
Water System
Santa Mesa
Pasig River
1st Wyo.
Walled City
6th Arty. 1st Wash
1st Idaho
Utah Battery
4th Cav.
Neb. Camp
Paco
1st Cal.
Santa Ana
14th Inf.
Pasig R
FILIPINO TRENCHES
Singalong
1st N.D.
to San Pedro Macati

N

0 mi. 1

Dewey's Ships

to Pasay

•Laoag

Palanan•

L U Z O N

PHILIPPINE

LINGAYEN GULF

•Dagupan

SEA

•Tarlac

Malolos•
Manila•

•Batangas

MINDORO

SIBUYAN SEA

SAMAR

•Catbalogan

S O U T H

SOUTH CHINA SEA

C H I N A

VISAYAN SEA

LEYTE

Tacloban•
LEYTE GULF

S E A

Capiz•

PANAY

Bacolod•

•Cebu

NEGROS

CEBU

BOHOL

Iloilo•

MINDANAO SEA

•Butuan

PALAWAN

S U L U   S E A

N

The
Philippine
Archipelago

M I N D A N A O

Davao•

MORO GULF

Zamboanga•

JOLO

C E L E B E S   S E A

0   200
miles

left to Spain in the pending peace treaty—not so remote a possibility in August. But Merritt departed too hastily for Paris to write the requested stipulation, and the Filipinos still occupied the disputed sectors when a new American commander arrived on August 22.[20]

Major General Elwell S. Otis, like Merritt a Civil War hero, was a fastidious, pompous, and fussy man who inspired few of his subordinates. In many ways he was a harbinger of today's desk general rather than an example of the swashbuckling, hard-riding cavalry type so adored by soldiers of the nineteenth century. He was unable to delegate the slightest authority and ensconced himself in the governor's mansion, working late into the night at the Sisyphean task of reducing stacks of paperwork. The papal delegate to the Philippines, Archbishop Chapelle, described Otis accurately as "of about the right mental caliber to command a one-company post in Arizona." It was to such a man that the United States entrusted the tasks of working out accommodations with Aguinaldo and his followers and of supplying Washington with accurate intelligence. But Otis rarely ventured from his headquarters and seemed uninterested in appeasing the wounded pride of the Filipinos. In the end he supplied the coup de grace to any remaining pretense of cooperation between the two nations.

Aguinaldo attempted to outflank the Americans in Manila in two ways. On the grounds that his government was not a signatory to the peace protocol, he continued to assault successfully Spanish military garrisons outside of Manila. And since American leaders in the Philippines had continually insisted they were powerless to make any commitments to him, he sent Felipe Agoncillo to Washington to represent the Philippine Republic and begin negotiations with the American government. As one historian described this attempt: "The McKinley administration at this time was in a delicate position. . . . No promise of independence could be made because American public opinion would not tolerate it. But the rebels could not be rebuffed entirely lest they turn against the Americans." McKinley handled the situation in his usual style. He received Agoncillo and spent an hour talking to him, but refused to give him any assurances about the future of the Philippines since that was still being negotiated in Paris. Agoncillo then went to France in an attempt to testify before the Peace Commission. There he was completely cold-shouldered, and he "returned to the Philippines with considerable bitterness toward the American government."[21]

Meanwhile, Aguinaldo faced the diplomatic aggression of Merritt's successor. Picking up where his predecessor had left off, Otis demanded immediate Filipino withdrawal from the two suburban positions specified by Merritt. But whereas Merritt had at least couched his demand in reasonably polite language, Otis issued a blunt edict and refused to honor Merritt's promised face-saving concession. Instead, the general delivered to Aguinaldo and "his so-called government" on September 8 one of the most arrogantly worded ultimatums in the annals of American diplomatic history. Paradoxically Otis had informed Washington on September 5 that "our relations [are] friendly but require delicate manipulation." There was nothing delicate about his first communiqué to the revolutionary government. Otis disavowed "any obligations" inherited from Merritt, refused to acknowledge that the Filipinos had aided the Americans in any way in the war against Spain, and warned that if the Filipinos did not withdraw from the disputed suburbs by September 15 he would be "obliged to resort to forcible action" and would hold Aguinaldo personally "responsible for any unfortunate consequences that may ensue." He went on to remind Aguinaldo of American military might, before assuring him that rather than "devastating" the Philippines, he would prefer to advise Washington that no more troops were necessary.

The language of this communiqué was so outrageous that Aguinaldo sent a commission of three officers to ask Otis to withdraw it in favor of a simple request to evacuate the positions in question, to which the Filipinos would comply. When Otis refused, they begged him to delete his threat of force from the original message. Again they were imperiously turned down. Finally Otis agreed to issue a second ultimatum in slightly more temperate language without withdrawing his first one. Aguinaldo could then pretend he had never received the American commander's first message, which a senator investigating the war was later to characterize as "tantamount to a declaration of war" and to which General Anderson attributed the beginning of an irrevocable split between the Filipinos and the Americans. If Otis did not understand what he was doing, it was not lost on his young aide, Lieutenant Frederick Sladen. In his diary, Sladen expressed both amazement and disgust that the Filipinos did not fight in the face of such humiliation.[22]

Instead, the Filipinos put up a good front, retired from the suburbs in question on September 15, and, accompanied by a military band, smartly rendered honors to the American troops sent in to relieve them and to Old Glory as it was raised to replace the flag of the Philippine Republic. Needless to say, Brigadier General R. P. Hughes, provost marshal of Manila, ignored the salute; he was not in the habit of returning honors to an "undisciplined mob," he later explained. Otis, however, responded to the Filipino retreat with a note of appreciation to Aguinaldo for "the friendly spirit" in "retiring his troops." But this "courtesy" was merely a gambit for the next aggressive move by the American commander. It seems that the city's "exact boundaries," about which Otis had confronted the Filipinos on September 8, were not so "exact" by October 14. A "careful search of the city's records and an actual survey" by Otis's engineers produced a new boundary, one that included Pandacan, which was "unfortunately" occupied by the Philippine army and, incidentally, on strategically high ground. He appended a map with the new boundary marked in blue to another aggressively worded ultimatum to the Philippine president:

> I am therefore compelled, by reason of my instructions which direct me to execute faithfully the articles of the Spanish capitulation, because of the interests of my government, and, as I sincerely believe, the welfare of your own forces, to ask that you withdraw all your troops beyond the lines marked in the accompanying blue print which are above described, and I must request such withdrawal on or before the 20th instant, else I shall be forced into some action looking to that end.[23]

Again Aguinaldo sent representatives to see Otis about the "mysterious blue line" on the map. Pandacan had never been considered part of Manila, the Filipino officers protested. This time Otis's demand had more serious military consequences for Aguinaldo's army: it meant giving up not only high ground that could be used to outflank a large portion of the native line of defense, but also some Spanish blockhouses that Aguinaldo needed to shelter his troops in the coming wet season. The Filipino officers attempted a compromise and pleaded with Otis at least to adjust his blue line to permit their continued use of the blockhouses. The latter had no military value except as barracks, certainly not in the face of American artillery. "All concessions refused" was Otis's arrogant reply, although he "generously" granted the Filipinos an extra five days to clear out of Pandacan.

Aguinaldo followed up this one-sided negotiation with a copy of a letter from General Merritt dated August 20 in which he specifically recognized that Pandacan was "outside" the boundaries of Manila. The Filipino leader expressed the hope that the American commander's "high sense of justice" would cause him to rescind his latest demand in the light of his predecessor's statement. Gruffly informing the envoy who carried the letter that "the subject had been discussed sufficiently and that insurgent troops must retire on the specified date or suffer the consequences," Otis refused to answer. Not until after Aguinaldo backed down once more and withdrew from Pandacan on October 25 did Otis acknowledge the existence of Merritt's letter, explaining that:

> I have referred to General Merritt's letter of August 20th, which you mention, and find that it is as you state. Unfortunately, I am bound by the terms of capitulation, which recite "the city and defenses of Manila and its suburbs." Pandacan is certainly far within the line of defenses and, from

information obtained from two weighty sources, I have been led to believe that it has, of late, been considered one of the city's suburbs, although we have been unable to find any Spanish decree which fixes its status with definiteness.[24]

This explanation was full of holes. Merritt had been just as bound by the terms of capitulation on August 20 when he agreed in writing that Pandacan was not part of Manila. Furthermore, Otis failed to specify who or what sources had led him to believe that Pandacan was part of the city; the absence of a Spanish decree on the subject hardly proved his case. But Otis's real *coup de maître* was his sudden shift in emphasis from the boundaries of Manila to its "line of defense." Years later, before a senate committee, Otis made it clear that Manila's line of defense could be anywhere he wanted it to be and that the concept of a defense perimeter authorized him to demand that the Philippine army retreat from Luzon if necessary. So, while the general's letter was more conciliatory in tone than his previous messages to Aguinaldo, it actually opened the way for a sharp escalation in demands.[25]

Otis had another motive for using more reasonable language in his acknowledgment of Merritt's letter. He wanted high ground outside of Manila for a convalescent camp for his growing list of sick soldiers. It is hard to believe that he had the temerity to include this request in his harsh ultimatum of October 14 ordering Aguinaldo out of Pandacan. The Filipino leader responded with understandable sarcasm. He conceded that he fully understood Otis's "humane sentiments" in trying to care for his sick soldiers, but he was forced to remind the American commander that the joint occupation of Manila had been denied by Merritt in order "to prevent friction" between the two armies. Would not the establishment of an American hospital behind Filipino lines be similar to the joint occupation of the city? And if he granted Otis this request, what would it lead to, Aguinaldo wondered bitterly. Would General Otis then begin to demand that the native forces retreat further and further away from the hospital in the interest of maintaining "the friendship that constitutes the welfare of both peoples?" he asked with feigned wonder. Ignoring the sarcasm, Otis repeated his request for a hospital on high ground. But this time Aguinaldo—or possibly his clever advisor, the lawyer Apolinario Mabini—saw in the request an opportunity to wring from Otis a formal recognition of the Philippine government and its claim to sovereignty over all territory outside of Manila. Aguinaldo told Otis that an agreement in writing would be necessary:

The only solution possible is to completely cede to you the use of this encampment, and this, as you will understand, requires some fixed basis of arrangement more concrete than can result from a verbal one made in a conference. It is not a lack of confidence which obliges me to proceed in this manner, it is necessity.[26]

But Otis was also a lawyer by training and knew better than to put in writing anything that could be construed as a formal recognition of "their Malalos arrangement." He promptly informed Aguinaldo that he would be able to care for the sick within the confines of Manila, and then pondered a new diplomatic offensive against the Filipino nationalists.

The next American demand was that Aguinaldo release all his Spanish prisoners. It is not that Otis was concerned over the plight of these prisoners, but that he hoped that compliance with his directive would demonstrate Aguinaldo's recognition of American control over the internal affairs of the Philippines. On this point Aguinaldo remained firm and refused to release the prisoners. Except for a pretentious and pedantic lecture from Otis on "the laws of warfare," Aguinaldo suffered no serious consequences as a result.[27]

Otis then embarked on another aggressive maneuver in the hope, apparently, that it would drive Aguinaldo over the brink. A Spanish garrison in Iloilo, the major city of Panay in the Visayan island group, was still holding out against Filipino attacks. The Spanish sent an offer to surrender to the Americans, and Otis was very eager simply to accept it and report it to Washington as a fait accompli. But Dewey vetoed his plans, and without his ships the army was going nowhere outside of Luzon. Lieutenant Sladen was sent to negotiate with the admiral, who had already vetoed earlier plans for expeditions to Cebu and Samar, where some Europeans had requested American protection when the Spanish garrisons left those islands. Sladen warned Dewey that the Germans had threatened to intervene if the Americans did not "take hold" of these islands. But German threats did not bother Dewey. More than once he had confronted the German flotilla on Manila Bay. Dewey simply was uninterested in acquiring anything more than Manila and possibly a base or two elsewhere. "We should leave everything but this place entirely alone unless ordered by Washington," he told Sladen. "Admiral, don't you think that it would look like a display of a white feather and wouldn't it have a bad effect on the insurgents around us here? Don't you think it would be better and less trouble to take these places now than to do so later on after the insurgents become more firmly located?" Sladen pleaded. Dewey's laconic reply was, "Let it appear so. We will disapprove [sic] that idea if we are ordered to take these islands."[28]

The admiral's refusal to budge without specific orders from Washington had nothing to do with respect for the justice of Aguinaldo's cause. On "his bay," Dewey could be just as aggressive as Otis. Sladen was aboard the *Olympia* when Dewey ordered two gunboats in Aguinaldo's "mosquito fleet" seized for daring to fly their colors. Their flags and guns were removed, and the two native skippers were hauled before the admiral, who "told them to 'git'" or he would "blow them to pieces." "And still we are at peace with them," Sladen recorded, wondering what it would take to get the "insolent natives to fight." On another occasion, a group of Filipino captains assembled aboard Dewey's flagship to protest his restrictions on their activities. Dewey informed them their flag was merely "a piece of bunting" of no more value than "a yacht pennant" that he would not allow to be flown from their "boats." One Filipino muttered an angry response, which was interpreted to Dewey as meaning "that he will get even with you." Whereupon the admiral had the man thrown from the *Olympia's* main deck into the bay. A flabbergasted Aguinaldo protested that his captains had gone to protest politely to the admiral but were not permitted to speak and were subjected to "aggressive phrases and other abuses." [29]

Otis was forced to request orders from Washington in order to secure Dewey's cooperation for an Iloilo expedition. His request of December 14 was not answered for ten days, and then the approval carried the stipulation that he was to proceed only if Iloilo could be taken peacefully. Nevertheless, when young Sladen deciphered the coded message, he was delighted that nothing was said about "coming back if pacific measures failed." Sladen interpreted this oversight as permission to fight if necessary, and wrote, "The fun begins now. Will the Aguinaldo party come off the perch or will they wait for us to take them off?" [30]

Otis lost no time in getting a task force under way led by General Marcus Miller, only to discover that the Spanish garrison had abandoned Iloilo and sailed for Manila, probably passing the American flotilla under cover of night. By the time that Miller's contingent arrived, Iloilo was already in the hands of insurgents who swore allegiance to Aguinaldo's government. *Presidente* Lopez of the "Federal Government of Visayas" sent an extraordinary message to General Miller, full of standard diplomatic flourishes and the traditional Filipino reverence for the obligation of a host to his guest, but also asking as politely as possible "the purpose of this unexpected visit." When Miller more bluntly informed Lopez of his intentions, the general was told that "foreign troops" could not be landed "without express orders from the central government of Luzon." The next day a group of Iloilo businessmen petitioned Miller not to land his troops, protesting that the Filipino troops were maintaining law and order and needed no help from the Americans. Miller, eager to fight but wanting specific permission from Otis to attack, advised Manila that "the longer they [the insurgents] remain in possession, collecting customs, and running post offices, the more they will be confirmed in the idea they can do it." [31]

Perhaps Otis should have sent clippings from the *New York Times* to convince the Filipinos that they were far too ignorant and savage to run a city like Iloilo. Instead, he sent a copy of President McKinley's recent "Benevolent Assimilation" proclamation, which he had just received. Miller passed it on to Lopez so that he could learn that the intention of the United States in the Philippines was to "assert its sovereignty, that its purpose is to give them good government and security in their personal rights." Otis neglected to tell Miller that he had politically bowdlerized the copy he had sent to Aguinaldo by removing the mention of American sovereignty over the Philippines "to stress our benevolent purpose" and not "offend Filipino sensibilities," the general later explained. He substituted "free people" for "supremacy of the United States," and deleted "to exercise future domination" in the president's proclamation, because:

> After fully considering the President's proclamation, and the temper of the Tagalos, with whom I was daily discussing political problems and the friendly intention of the U.S. Government toward them, I concluded that there were certain words and expressions therein such as "sovereignty," "right of cession" and those which directed immediate occupation and so forth, which though most admirably employed and tersely expressive of actual conditions, might be advantageously used by the Tagalog. The ignorant classes had been taught to believe that certain words such as "sovereignty," "protection," and so forth had peculiar meanings disastrous to their welfare and significant of future political domination, like that from which they had been recently freed.[32]

Such inferences were hardly unreasonable or as perverse as Otis seemed to think. If Aguinaldo was not fully aware of American intentions at this stage, Otis's deceit certainly drove the point home and added Machiavellian proportions to the scenario. Possibly Otis fell victim to his own propaganda and did not expect the Filipinos to be efficient enough to get the two versions of McKinley's message together. Even before Aguinaldo received the original and observed the "curious changes" in Otis's doctored copy, he was upset that the general had altered his title to "Military Governor *of* the Philippines" from "*in* the Philippines." Aguinaldo did not miss the significance of the alteration, which Otis made without authorization from Washington.[33]

Interestingly, the justification for the Iloilo expedition was "to prevent lawlessness" there. Yet McKinley had usurped senatorial power by proclaiming American sovereignty over the Philippines before ratification of the treaty, and Otis had arbitrarily altered his official title to reflect this premature assumption of annexation. The general's lawlessness went even further when he ignored his orders of January 1, 1899, to avoid a showdown at Iloilo: "Conflict would be most unfortunate, considering the present [treaty debate]." Only the day before Otis had cabled Washington, "Am waiting to hear results from Iloilo and am meditating action in the islands of Samar, Leyte, and Cebu, in all of which Luzon insurgents have been operating for several months." It was this cable that alarmed the administration and elicited strongly worded orders to preserve the peace. Yet Otis tried to get Dewey to provide ships to reinforce Miller and confided to his aide, "I still hold to my view that Iloilo must be taken." According to Miller, Otis gave him permission to attack the city on January 3. Elements of the Iowa regiment were landed only to be greeted by up to one hundred native soldiers ready to open fire. The colonel commanding the amphibious force protested landing his troops "under such conditions of hostility," but Miller signaled him that it was "better to strike the first blow here." The colonel thought otherwise and returned his men to the transport that had been their home since leaving San Francisco sixty-three days earlier. They remained aboard for another twenty days in stifling heat, at which point they became too sick to fight, and Miller was forced to order them back to Manila.[34]

On January 9, 1899, Miller decided to ask Lopez again for permission to land in order to "enforce the orders of the President of the United States." Lopez answered with a terse historical lesson:

> The supposed authority of the United States began with the Treaty of Paris, on the 10th of December, 1898. The authority of the Central Government of Malolos is founded in the sacred and natural bonds of blood, language, uses, customs, ideas, sacrifices.

Miller remained riding anchor off Iloilo until the war began on February 4. The insurgent troops then burned the city and fled before his troops could get ashore. Even then Miller was cheated of his glory by a contingent of U.S. Marines who dashed ashore and raised the flag over Iloilo before Miller entered the city, much to his chagrin and Otis's outrage.[35]

The result of the Iloilo fiasco was the birth of a myth, that the failure to attack the city immediately upon the arrival of American troops on December 28 caused the war between the Filipinos and Americans. The correspondent J. F. Bass, who had accompanied Miller, returned to Manila in disgust when the attack was delayed and labeled it an "exploded bluff" that would be interpreted as "weakness" by the Filipinos. Otis played on this theme and insisted that had he been allowed to take Iloilo there would have been no war. Instead, American "magnanimity" was translated into "softness" and "emboldened" the natives sufficiently to begin the war. This line of reasoning was, of course, a variation of the prevalent myth that "Asiatics" only understood force.

After the Iloilo affair, Aguinaldo took his case to other foreign powers. Out-

lining the American betrayal of his cause, he explained that he had acceded to
every outrageous American demand until his back was against the wall. Any
"violent and aggressive seizure of the Philippines would require an endless
struggle for the United States, a nation which has arrogated to itself the title
'champion of oppressed nations,'" the Philippine president declared. "I denounce these acts before the world, in order that the conscience of mankind
may pronounce its infallible verdict as to who are the true oppressors of nations
and the tormentors of mankind." Otis called this international appeal "a virtual
declaration of war" and "noticeable proof of Aguinaldo's premeditated intent"
to begin the war.[36]

One final act of American duplicity remained to be played, however, before the war was to begin. Aguinaldo was more realistic about the power differences between his forces and the Americans than were some of his hotheaded lieutenants, such as General Antonio Luna, who had had his fill of
humiliation at the hands of Otis. He was also aware that the American army
would be a much more formidable enemy than the Spanish forces, against
which he had had some success. In addition, he was greatly influenced by
the more conservative ilustrados, who dominated his government, and thus
avoided a showdown. To this end, he vainly pleaded with Otis for a conference
in which to discuss their differences. Suddenly, Otis agreed to a meeting in January, 1899. Manila's provost, General Hughes, Colonel James F. Smith, a highly
successful lawyer commanding the California regiment, and Colonel E. H.
Crowder, an aide to Otis, met five times between January 11 and January 29
with General Ambrosio Flores, Lieutenant Colonel Manuel Argüelles, and a
distinguished civilian lawyer, Florentino Torres. The Filipinos arrived with a
list of five basic grievances they wished to discuss:

1. Failure to include the Filipino army in the capitulation of Manila
2. American expansion of its territory around Manila beyond the city's
   recognized boundaries
3. Seizure of the Filipino steamer *Abbey* and several steam launches by
   the U.S. Navy
4. Prohibition to fly the Philippine flag on Manila Bay
5. The American attempt to take Iloilo.[37]

In contrast, the Americans had no agenda, and seemed unwilling to discuss the Filipino grievances. Several years later, Hughes mocked the native negotiators, telling a senate committee that they thought that independence was
"something to eat":

For instance, we asked them: "What are we to understand by your absolute independence? Do you mean that you wish the Americans to go

out . . . ?" "Oh no; for God's sake, no. No: we will make the laws and you will stay here and see that outsiders do not disturb us." And we never, from the day we began until the day we quit, could get the definition of what they really wanted. They did not know themselves.

When pressed by a senator as to what the general thought they might have wanted at these meetings, Hughes informed the committee that all any Filipino wanted was "to go to cock fights, gamble and whet up their bolos." Possibly some did want "absolute independence and somebody to take care of them," he conceded, then warned the senators to keep in mind that "we are simply fighting children." In fact, Torres was a European-trained jurist with an education and intellect far superior to General Hughes's. Moreover, he was a conservative, who continued to work for reconciliation after warfare broke out, and served the Americans as attorney general and finally as a justice on the Philippine Supreme Court. He was interested in independence in name only to satisfy such firebrands as Luna. Yet Otis dismissed his position at these meetings as "irresponsible." What was, in fact, truly irresponsible was that the United States trusted delicate negotiations to a soldier of such marginal understanding and limited ability as General Hughes.[38]

"Finally, the conferences became the object of insurgent suspicion and of amusement to those who did not wish beneficial results," Hughes explained. Of course, after five months of refusing to negotiate, the Americans had come to the talks with nothing to say or give, at a time when reenforcements were on the way from San Francisco. Hughes himself in a comment before the committee vindicated Filipino suspicions:

> We were sorry, at least I was, to have the conference stopped because I was trying to prolong them until General Lawton's ship could get there with four battalions which we needed very much. But we could not stretch it out any longer. The papers had begun to attack us and stated absolutely in words that we were doing nothing but trying to gain time, and a telegram had been received by them from Agoncillo in the United States to make the attack before reenforcements got there and it came.[39]

Agoncillo had kept his government informed of troop movements to the Philippines—a legitimate part of the intelligence role played by diplomats—but there is no evidence that he advised his countrymen to attack the American forces. At best, warfare broke out as a result of overwrought tempers on both sides and of the spontaneous combustion resulting from a minor incident, one of many during the American presence in the Philippines. At worst, Otis had deliberately planned to goad the Filipinos into attacking by skillfully maneuvering them to the point at which the slightest incident would touch off a war. Parallel to this brinkmanship, the American military commanders had made careful plans for the armed showdown they were so eager to have. Of course, given the political reality of American annexation, open warfare between the two armies was inevitable, but the specific moment of its beginning appears to have been an American decision.[40]

4

The Dividends of Brinkmanship

Exactly one week after the last meeting of the negotiating teams led by General Hughes and Torres, warfare erupted between the two armies. Its immediate origin remains as obscure today for the historian as it was eighty years ago for the politician, editor, and average American citizen, obfuscated by a mire of claims, counterclaims, and recriminations by both sides. Washington quickly mounted a propaganda offensive to prove that the Filipino army started the war by unsuccessfully assaulting the American lines on the evening of February 4, 1899.

Angry, jingoistic threats by Filipino officers were fully exploited by American apologists. Colonel Cailles once shouted at an American officer, "War! War is what we want." General Otis also produced an intercepted letter from Aguinaldo to a friend in Manila advising him to get his family out of the city, "although it is not yet the day of the week." This last phrase was "proof" that a "premeditated attack" on Manila was being planned. All that was needed to gain world support for Aguinaldo's cause was an incident to draw American fire and make it appear that the Yankees had started the war, Otis reasoned.[1]

To this end Filipino soldiers were exceedingly rude to their American counterparts, Otis reported, shoving them off sidewalks and taunting them with aggressive gestures, such as running their fingers across their own throats to signify they would soon kill these intruders from the United States. But under strict orders from Washington to avoid a rupture, he would not permit American soldiers to retaliate in kind. The soldiers were thus forced to grin and bear the indignities heaped upon them. One medical officer later recalled:

As an American acquainted with Oriental ways, I was so ashamed of myself the last month or two that I hated to leave the house. Our soldiers received and submitted to untold insults from insurgent troops, and bore

them patiently, all because of the most stringent orders from headquarters
to avoid trouble if possible, without actual sacrifice of dignity.

Then suddenly in January Aguinaldo refused to allow American parties "seeking health and recreation" through his lines. The Filipinos even turned back a
Royal Navy funeral party, Otis related in a tone of disbelief.[2]

A much better case can be made for indicting General Otis and the U.S.
Army for starting the war. It is easy enough to gather evidence that these soldiers, from privates to generals, were "just itching to get at the 'niggers.'" The
outraged innocence with which Otis complained of the decision not to allow
any more American recreation behind Filipino lines does not jibe with the evidence that, rather than "seeking health and recreation," many of the parties
were actually spying on native defense networks. Colonel Frederick Funston
readily admitted to such reconnaissance missions. Three American engineers
and the correspondent J. F. Bass were arrested for taking measurements and
photographs of Filipino military installations. In demanding their release, Otis
insisted they were making "surveys for the completion of the map of Manila."
Possibly Aguinaldo was just as concerned that another "mysterious blue line"
would appear on the general's map to expand the city's boundaries.[3]

Contrary to official accounts, American soldiers did not grin and bear "the
insult and abuse heaped" upon them, or respond "with constant submission as
the only means of avoiding a rupture." They addressed the Filipinos as "niggers" or "gugus." One, more sensitive, American complained that "almost
without exception soldiers and also many officers, refer to the natives in their
presence as 'niggers' and the natives are beginning to understand what the
word 'nigger' means." The English-language *Manila Times* pleaded for an end
to this practice, and Otis issued an official order forbidding the use of these
terms by military personnel.[4]

But American soldiers went well beyond calling the natives derogatory
names. As early as October, 1898, *Collier's* reported that Filipinos crossing the
American lines on their way to Manila "have been surly, and have *not* submitted to being searched with good grace." This reaction was understandable,
since it was common practice to knock down a native with the butt of a Springfield merely for "seeming disrespectful." One native charged that he was
robbed rather than searched. Several females complained that searches were
lecherously improper and humiliating. Sentries also shot at Filipinos on the
slightest pretext. "We have to kill one or two every night," Private William
Christner wrote to his father on January 17, 1899, when the war was still weeks
away. Christner may have exaggerated the case, but the official record indicates
that a Minnesota sentry killed a civilian for "looking suspicious." A Filipino captain was gunned down without warning for approaching an American position

while armed, even though his sidearm was safely secured in its holster. Another native soldier was killed by a sentry who claimed that, after saluting, the Filipino swung a bolo at him. On January 23, Otis reported that a woman and child were "accidentally shot." As Christner explained it, "We killed a few to learn them a lesson and you bet they learned it." During the six months preceding the war, only one American was killed and two wounded in a single incident behind Filipino lines. Aguinaldo explained to his outraged American counterpart that the three soldiers had shot each other in a drunken argument over cards. Otis apparently accepted this explanation and dropped the matter.[5]

Roughing up or even shooting natives by American sentries was not part of a plan to provoke an incident that could initiate the desired war. It was more likely an outgrowth of racist attitudes and of the belief that violence was the only way to deal with "Asiatics." Such activity was usually carried out by volunteers, who had a reputation for being undisciplined in their use of rifles. Less than a year later San Francisco got a taste of this lawlessness, when some Montana volunteers home from the war got drunk at the Presidio and used a schooner entering the bay for target practice. Angry city officials successfully demanded that all volunteers be disarmed before leaving the Philippines.[6]

A series of orders and maneuvers by Otis during the final three weeks of peace, however, indicate that he may have planned and provoked the war. On January 16, he persuaded Dewey to move warships close to the water flanks of Aguinaldo's semicircular line around Manila. Two days later, he ordered his troops into "fighting khaki." This order overjoyed one private, not just because he hated the "dress whites," but because it indicated that at last some action was in the offing. Otis then carried out a most provocative maneuver on January 21 by moving part of the Nebraska regiment out to the hitherto unoccupied Santa Mesa, a finger of high ground that extended behind and above the entrenchments newly dug by the Filipinos who had been forced to evacuate Pandacan months earlier. Aguinaldo protested "one and a thousand times" that under no stretch of the imagination could this territory be considered part of Manila. But Otis argued, with a dazzling verbal maneuver worthy of his legal training, that Aguinaldo's forced withdrawal from Pandacan, which Otis now agreed was not part of Manila, was an act of recognition of the American right to expand beyond the city's traditional boundaries. He reassured the Filipino commander that the mesa would be used "for sanitary reasons only," not military ones, whereupon he immediately transferred elements of the Utah Battery there and ordered them to train their artillery on the rear of the vulnerable Filipino positions. If pressed, Otis might have assuaged Aguinaldo's anxiety over this aggressive maneuver by telling him that these big guns had been moved to high ground to cut down on rust![7]

Otis continued to look for the appropriate sensitive spot to provoke his war. General Arthur MacArthur decided that one village occupied by Filipino soldiers was actually behind American lines and demanded their immediate withdrawal. To avoid a confrontation, Colonel San Miguel complied but only with the stipulation that the matter be arbitrated. Instead, MacArthur moved his own troops into the disputed village as the Filipinos withdrew. Aguinaldo vainly pointed out that his army had occupied the village for five months, that San Miguel had no authority to withdraw, and that he had done so with the understanding that the position was to be negotiated. Otis ignored this protest, as by then he had found the opening for which he had been looking. When the Nebraskans posted a sentry at a position on the mesa known as the "pipeline" on February 1, they were confronted by angry Filipino officers, who swore at them and posted their own sentry at the very same spot. Undisciplined American volunteers confronting outraged Filipino officers, driven to the brink by months of humiliating capitulations to unreasonable demands by Otis, was an ideal combination to set off the desired "incident."

Since Otis still had a few final preparations to make, he ordered the Nebraskans not to man the "pipeline post" on February 2 so as to avoid a premature rupture before he was fully ready. That day Otis discharged all native employees on American military installations and placed his troops on "full alert." He notified Dewey that the war could begin at any moment and ordered General Miller, anchored off Iloilo, to hang on "until something happened." He also sent an aide to Aguinaldo with an appeal to preserve the peace, a gesture that he later cited to demonstrate that he had exhausted every means to avoid a rupture. One would assume that the motive behind this appeal for peace was either to buy some time or to put Aguinaldo off guard, except that it was an arrogantly worded ultimatum. But then, Otis seemed incapable of using diplomatic language.[8]

Having cleared his decks for action, to use a naval metaphor, the general once again turned his attention to the very sensitive and disputed "pipeline post." Colonel John Stotsenburg, commanding the Nebraska volunteers, was on hand personally to post a sentry at this volatile spot on February 3. That sentry, Private Hermann Dittner, described in a letter home "the trouble with the nigs" on that occasion:

> It then became apparent that a fight was imminent. So on February 3 we posted our sentry at the same old place. The insurgents kicked but without avail. Our colonel was down there and an insurgent lieutenant called him a s-n--b-h. Of course this made Stotsenburg mad and he gave orders to arrest the lieutenant as soon as they could catch him.[9]

February 4 was the ideal day to begin the war, as the leading officers in the Philippine army were scheduled to attend a formal celebration in Malolos, followed by a lavish ball that would go on until the early hours of the next day. By his own admission, Otis raised the stakes, so to speak, by not only instructing Stotsenburg to man the disputed post, but to order his sentries to fire on any intruders. Two members of the eight-man detail assigned to guard the "pipeline" around the clock acknowledged in letters home that they fully understood the significance of these orders. Early in the evening, Privates Grayson and Miller were on duty when they were approached by four Filipino soldiers, now believed to have been drunk and unarmed. According to Grayson:

> I challenged with another "Halt." Then he immediately shouted "Halto" to me. Well I thought the best thing to do was to shoot him. He dropped. Then two Filipinos sprang out of the gateway about 15 feet from us. I called "Halt" and Miller fired and dropped one. I saw that another was left. Well I think I got my second Filipino that time. We retreated to where six other fellows were and I said "Line up fellows; the niggers are in here all through these yards."[10]

This was all the overeager volunteers needed. For the next six hours, they unleashed fusillade after fusillade at the Filipino positions, long after darkness prevented them from seeing what they were firing at. Otis claimed that the Filipinos sent up rockets to signal their attack and were repulsed with heavy losses by a gallant thin American line. As Secretary of War Elihu Root explained in the official version:

> On the night of February 4th, two days before the U.S. Senate approved the treaty, an army of Tagalogs, a tribe inhabiting the central part of Luzon, under the leadership of Aguinaldo, a Chinese half-breed, attacked, in vastly superior numbers, our little army in the possession of Manila, and after a desperate and bloody fight was repulsed in every direction.[11]

Root's version is very different from subsequently written regimental histories, which make no mention of Filipino assaults on the regiments' positions that evening. Years later, when pressed by Senator Patterson on whether there had been "any attempts to advance upon American troops that night or that morning," MacArthur, who commanded the sector that was allegedly under attack, answered, "I have no knowledge of that kind and I presume that it was not so. . . ." MacArthur further confessed that his troops did the first firing following the "pipeline" incident. "Our soldiers were under great provocation, and it was getting hard to restrain them," he explained. Three regular officers who had been on the scene made it clear that not only did the American volunteers fire first, but they also did most of the shooting, as relatively few shots were returned by the Filipinos.[12]

Sladen and Lieutenant William Connor, an aide to General Wheaton, had been friends at "the Point" and compared notes on the action that evening. Both officers had armed themselves and galloped off in search of some action upon hearing the widespread firing. Privileged as aides to generals, they covered the entire northern sector only to find green volunteers everywhere firing wildly into the dark. Hearing that the South Dakota regiment was under heavy attack, Connor dashed to its position, but found nothing, except "green Dakotans" shooting away for dear life at no discernible targets. Sladen returned to headquarters to complain of all the "wasted ammunition." Major William Kobbe, who commanded the only regular outfit in the northern sector, the Third Artillery, sent an aide to see if the Kansans needed assistance when he heard all the furious firing from their positions. The aide returned to report with dismay that there had been no attack on the Kansans. Kobbe entered into his diary that "it was another false alarm brought about by the excited confusion of the volunteers."[13]

If any advances were made during the night, they were by the South Dakota and Nebraska regiments to be in better positions for the charge planned for the next morning. "We hiked out and lay in a skirmish line in front of their posts and in the morning charged and chased the niggers across the San Juan River," Dittner wrote to his parents. Such testimony indicates the existence of a general plan to attack all along the line as soon as an incident was provoked. MacArthur testified several years later:

> Yes, we had a prearranged plan . . . I had instant contact . . . and within an instant after the firing at the outpost I received a message from Stotsenburg . . . "the pipe-line outpost has been fired on; I am moving out my entire regiment." His move was in accordance with a prearranged plan. . . . When I got Colonel Stotsenburg's report I simply wired all commanders to carry out prearranged plans.[14]

In his testimony MacArthur also revealed that the heavy guns that Otis had placed on the Santa Mesa began firing as soon as the shots were first heard from the "pipeline post."

> Patterson: Did you hear the firing when it commenced?
> MacArthur: I heard the guns from Colonel Stotsenburg's position; that is, the field artillery.
> Patterson: Did you open up with field artillery that night . . . the American side?
> MacArthur: Oh yes. . . . We had a section or a platoon of artillery in a very favorable position.[15]

The initial comments of key officers upon hearing the firing confirm the existence of a general plan to attack at the moment the long-desired incident to start the war had occurred. "The thing is on," Hughes shouted ecstatically. Sladen confessed to knowing immediately that the long-awaited war was on at last. "The ball has begun," Major Wilder Metcalf roared at Colonel Funston above the delicious noise of gunfire. Apparently Kobbe was one of the few commanders willing to consider the possibility that it was a false alarm.[16]

Otis was not about to repeat his mistake in the Iloilo fiasco by asking Washington for permission to launch an attack. He was not dependent on the more cautious Dewey this time, and, if the navy refused to cooperate, he could go it alone with his own artillery. Had he wished, he could have treated the battle as an isolated incident when the firing suddenly stopped around 2 A.M. and simply registered a complaint with Aguinaldo. Until then, there had been few casualties on either side. Two South Dakotans had been killed around 11 P.M., when their regiment moved forward to the slope of a hill in preparation for the morning charge. Years later, MacArthur implied that there had been many more American casualties, but, when challenged by Senator Patterson, he refused to say there had been any "officially." Otis had even been proffered the services of Florentino Torres as a mediator before he had launched his offensive, but, according to Hughes, he had "sternly replied that the fighting having begun must go on to the grim end." After the Philippine army was routed the next day, Otis did permit Torres to slip through the lines to get a Filipino offer. He returned with Aguinaldo's proposal for an immediate armistice and the creation of a neutral zone of any width deemed necessary by Otis, but the American commander refused to accept anything less than unconditional surrender from "a rag tag army" in full retreat, a position he maintained throughout his tenure in the Philippines.[17]

Clearly, Otis, like every other soldier in Manila, wanted the war he had been seeking for months. There is no evidence that he ever considered the effect that warfare might have on the pending vote to ratify the Treaty of Paris. The treaty was rarely if ever mentioned, and if February 4 had any special significance, it was because the ranking Filipino officers had gone to Malolos, and not because the U.S. Senate was going to decide on the fate of the Philippines in two days. Otis had no authorization to attack the Filipino lines on the morning of February 5. Even a secret agreement, or plan, with Washington would have been leaked to the press a few years later by the army's chief of staff, General Nelson Miles, along with other damaging evidence that he made public to serve his own political ambition. Remarks by Otis in 1902 make it clear that he considered it well within his prerogative to start the war without consulting Washington. "I recognized that the taking of Iloilo meant war throughout the country," he told a group of astonished senators when recounting his motives for sending General Miller on his ill-fated mission. When pressed on this, Otis declared:

I not only had the right, but it was my duty, to make them remove beyond the city and its defenses; and I had the right to drive them farther away from the city, a perfect right; and there is no nation, except for the United States, in the world which would have allowed those people to have hemmed in that city the way they did.[18]

An uneasy Senator Albert Beveridge quickly prompted the general at this point, asking if the Iloilo expedition had not actually been "in the interests of peace in every way at this time?" Otis dutifully agreed that it had been, but in the next breath suggested that shooting "savages" was a better means of preserving peace. Further evidence that Otis made crucial decisions entirely on his own was his response to Senator Rawlins's challenge as to why he had changed his title to "Military Governor of the Philippines" with no official authorization: "Because it occurred to me at the time to do it."[19]

If there was a conspiracy to start a war with the Filipinos, it appears to have begun and ended with Otis and his key officers, without any assistance, or even knowledge of such a plot, on the part of imperialist leaders in Washington. Given the repeated orders to Otis to avoid a rupture, these leaders would more than likely have disapproved of such a scheme.

Surprisingly, not until the war began to sour did Otis's role in starting it come under close editorial scrutiny. San Francisco's *Call*, which was to become one of the general's severest critics, initially accepted at face value the official version of the war's origins. "Aguinaldo Growing More Bold," and "Filipino Insurgents Threatening War" were daily headlines while Otis was arrogantly escalating his demands. Once the war began the *Call*'s editor agreed with most of his colleagues that "Aguinaldo forced the issue." Two other editors destined to be war critics initially concurred that "the Filipinos needed a good lesson" and that "coercion will be better than bribery."[20] Not until Otis's incompetency as a military leader became obvious was his role as a diplomat reviewed *post hoc* and sharply criticized in the press.

Two important exceptions were the *Springfield Republican* in Massachusetts and *City and State* in Philadelphia. But, while they criticized America's actions leading up to the war, they focused their editorial attacks on McKinley and his Administration and ignored Otis for the most part. In Boston, the *Evening Transcript*, which ended up in the imperialist camp, seemed more aware of the serious error of using military men as diplomats. "The Filipino leaders were from almost the first repelled and ignored. Hardly could men have set about in a better way to arouse resentment, suspicion, anger, and rebellion than the men in charge of the administration of American interests in Manila." But in the flush of patriotism that followed the outbreak of warfare, most editors overlooked the blunder.[21]

Republican and proimperialist editors never acknowledged the error. "The fact is, our government has been far too considerate of Aguinaldo's mercenaries," announced the editor of *Inter-Ocean* in Chicago. Aguinaldo was nothing but "a lying popinjay," and the "mischievous influence of this tricky little man must be broken," declared the *New York Times*. In upstate New York, the editor of the *Troy Times* explained to his readers that "the 'white man's burden' must be borne with the strength of red blood and not the weakness of a white liver." To these editors, the "real culprits" were those "partners in crime," Hoar, Hale, and that "repudiated political trickster, Gorman," who had encouraged the Filipinos to fight in the first place. "These men have sowed the wind for days and now the nation reaps the whirlwind," Republican editors charged. The *Call* refrained from making recriminations and counseled the president to make "the punishment of the 'half child' swift and sharp" and to then set about establishing a stable government leading to independence along the Cuban model.[22]

Ironically, it was Otis's own official report, made public in June, that called attention to his role in provoking the war. Otis was far too self-righteous to cover his tracks, and with great candor he documented each outrageous demand that pushed Aguinaldo and his army to the brink. The *Call* urged its readers to take a close look at this report, warning that "the facts of history are against us."[23]

Imperialist editors, however, read into the report whatever they wished to believe. The *New York Times* declared:

> The truth is now made clear by the official report. It is shown that the patience and forebearance of our men under insult and indignity were remarkable. General Otis was as considerate of Aguinaldo as one would be of a forward child. Our kindness and indulgence were thrown away, for it is now made plain that Aguinaldo was resolved to be content with nothing short of the recognition of his Malolos government.[24]

Nothing before or after the war began ever budged Otis from his self-deceptions. When his young aide attended a banquet for Aguinaldo in San Fernando in October, 1898, he reported back to Otis that the native leader was "a small insignificant looking man, very much like a Jap in appearance. He hasn't much to say but the influence he has over the natives and their devotion to him impressed me with his power over them. It really surprises me." Amazingly, Otis ignored Sladen's intelligence and continued to report to Washington that Aguinaldo was "a half Chinese adventurer" who demagogically incited the natives with "vile aspersions" and the "cry for liberty and independence (really license and despotism under their governing methods)." Otis still clung tenaciously to this myth in 1902, when he informed the Lodge committee that the

Filipinos "never intended to secure their independence; they proposed to set up a government under Aguinaldo possibly," but only "to loot and kill every white man" in the Philippines. Exasperation must have gotten the better of Senator Patterson, who vainly tried to disabuse the general of his obsessive delusion:

Patterson: When did you learn that the Filipinos wanted independence?
Otis: I do not believe that they ever wanted it.
Patterson: So you never learned it?
Otis: No. They were fighting to control the Philippines so they could loot them.[25]

For the rest of his life Otis defended another misconception—his original prediction that the Filipinos would not make more than a token, ephemeral effort to fight in order to save face. In all fairness, this miscalculation was widely shared by the military before the war began. "If we attack them we would give them the biggest surprise they ever had. The Spanish never gave any fight to speak of and they don't know what it is. They think that we will employ Spanish methods," Sladen predicted. But Sladen soon realized that he had underestimated the Filipinos' willingness to make enormous sacrifices to win independence. His boss never adjusted his opinion; Otis continually insisted that the natives had been decisively defeated after three months of warfare. Isolated bands of "outlaws" continued the struggle only because they received encouragement from "traitors" in the United States, the general charged. His young aide was too perceptive to take refuge in this rationalization.[26]

Some of Otis's defenders argued that it was the fault of the Spanish who remained in the islands that American predictions failed. Still smarting from their own defeat, the Spanish allegedly spread anti-American propaganda stressing the racism and anti-Catholicism of the invaders. Actually, a better case might have been made for the opposite effect. Sladen's diary indicated that Otis frequently dined with former Spanish officials and the hispanicized upper class, who may well have reenforced his misconceptions with their own ethnic and class prejudices. Unfortunately, they failed to convince Otis that the Tagalog "rabble" was capable of waging protracted guerrilla warfare.

Ultimately, McKinley must be held responsible for giving so much responsibility to a man of such limited ability and understanding. Upon Otis's return to Washington, the president effusively thanked him for "having handled a thousand and one cases for decision without reference to authorities in Washington, who were ignorant of . . . conditions in the islands incident to our occupation."[27] McKinley failed to understand that the government's ignorance of conditions in the Philippines was largely the result of the distorted intelligence that Washington received from General Otis.

5

The General as Warrior

Once the first light silhouetted the Filipino positions to the east of Dewey's gunners around 4 A.M. on February 5, the navy opened fire with devastating accuracy. Land-based artillery followed suit to soften up the enemy prior to the infantry charge scheduled for 8 A.M. Sladen rode behind the skirmish line and described how the Americans chafed at the bit waiting for the order to advance. Finally it came, and with a "Montana yell" and a "jayhawk cheer," the volunteers took off for the enemy positions, only to discover, to their chagrin, that the artillery had done its job too well. The Filipinos had not been prepared for heavy artillery salvos and had fled in panic, leaving behind only their dead and some wounded. The only Filipino stand was made in a cemetery on high ground, where some brave defenders kept the Montana regiment pinned down until Pennsylvania volunteers relieved their comrades. "With a good old Pennsylvania yell we charged up the hill" through "a hail of bullets," Private Christner reported to his parents, reassuring them that "I hardly think I was born to be killed by a nigger." The Fourth U.S. Cavalry pierced the enemy line so fast that it crossed the Pasig River well ahead of the retreating Filipinos, and in the only boats available. Once the Washington and Idaho regiments reached the river, the enemy was trapped at midstream in a murderous crossfire from both banks. "From then on the fun was fast and furious," as dead Filipinos piled up "thicker than buffalo chips," Sladen recorded. Several western lads informed their dads that "picking off niggers in the water" was "more fun than a turkey shoot."[1]

Most of the exuberantly charging and shouting volunteers, however, found little more than dead Filipinos in the trenches that they overran, so they just kept on going in pursuit of the fleeing enemy until they were far beyond their designated objectives. The rambunctious Colonel Funston led his Kansas outfit up the coast so swiftly that he came under fire from the U.S.S. *Charleston* and had to stop. Colonel James Smith dutifully and vainly attempted to halt the Californians when they captured the huge ammunition dump at Santa Ana assigned to them, but enthusiastic inertia carried them on for two more miles along the Pasig to San Pedro Macati. Finally exhaustion was able to do what Smith could not. Only the southern end of the American line advanced in orderly fashion. The Fourteenth Infantry was a more disciplined unit of regulars, for one thing, and a half-mile of swamp in front of the eager North Dakotans left them no choice but to allow the navy to bombard the retreating foe while they inched forward to their assigned objective.[2]

By the day's end, this wild scramble for glory left the American line "so greatly extended that any civilized foe could easily break it," Sladen, a West Point professional, observed with obvious disdain. The major problem caused by this undisciplined advance was that it left too many enemy stragglers behind the American lines. Reports of heavy sniping from the rear led to a scorched-earth tactic to deny concealment for snipers. Otis would later blame the excessive burning on the retreating Filipinos, but Sladen's diary makes clear that it was ordered by American commanders, if not Otis himself.[3]

The American command had to have been pleased with some of the results of the first day's offensive. The Nebraskans had captured the crucial San Juan Bridge, which enabled this regiment to take the water system for Manila before the enemy had a chance to dismantle the pumps completely. The Filipinos had sustained enormously heavy casualties and severe material losses. Their supplies had been stockpiled too close to their front lines and so were vulnerable to capture by the rapidly advancing Americans. Approximately 3,000 Filipino soldiers perished that first day, compared to sixty Americans.[4]

Even more important for domestic consumption was the production of a couple of instant heroes. A glowing eulogy for Lieutenant Mitchell of the Fourteenth Infantry was cabled to Washington that described how he had called out to his platoon after falling mortally wounded, "Forward men, advance; don't mind me." Lieutenant Charles Kilbourne of the engineers was recommended for the Congressional Medal of Honor for having climbed a telegraph pole to restore communications in the face of withering fire. Kilbourne probably shared the general contempt for Filipino marksmanship. One officer shouted from his rearing horse, "These fellows can't shoot! As long as they aim at us, we are all right." In truth, some Filipinos did remove the rear sights from their guns in order to concentrate on the front ones. Also, the limited supply of ammunition never permitted much in the way of target practice. Indeed, the differences in preparation and readiness of the two armies were so vast that one English observer noted skeptically:

If the Filipinos were the aggressors, it is very remarkable that the American troops should have been so well prepared for an unseen event as to be able to immediately and simultaneously attack, in full force, all the native outposts for miles around the capital.[5]

The easy success on the first day of warfare set a naively optimistic tone in the nation's press over the next few months. Teddy Roosevelt had once complained of the conflict with Spain that there was not "war enough to go around." It now appeared that warfare in the Philippines would be of even shorter duration. On the morning of February 6, a carnival atmosphere prevailed at the base of La Loma Hill, less than a mile behind the overrun enemy trenches, as Americans gathered to witness what was thought to be possibly the last battle of the war. Some Filipino survivors of a Pennsylvania charge had begun sniping from the hill the evening before. Civilians and soldiers vied for the best vantage points as the Pennsylvanians theatrically fixed bayonets and charged the hill a second time. The result should have given Otis a clue to what was in store for him. The enemy holdouts had evaporated during the night, probably burying their arms and slipping through the American lines to fight again. Disappointed, Otis reported that they had "skulked back to their homes disguised as civilians" and predicted that the shattered remnants of the Philippine army would soon do the same. Only Aguinaldo's demoralization kept him from surrendering unconditionally, Otis informed Washington on the second day of the war. The front page of the *Call* announced that

Aguinaldo Weeps for His Blunder
Sits Crying in His Quarters
Afraid to Surrender to the Americans.[6]

When Florentino Torres brought an offer of conditional surrender, however, Otis refused it. Instead, he planned a strategy to trap the enemy. General Lloyd Wheaton was to lead a thrust to the southeast, along the Pasig River and across the narrow isthmus that separated Manila Bay from Laguna de Bay (see map, p. 223). However, he soon faced the usual frustrations of pursuing an elusive enemy adept at setting up boobytraps and ambushes before vanishing and two American companies fell into a trap and suffered many casualties. Wheaton then ordered the first American reprisal against civilians—and the war was only one month old. Every town within a twelve-mile radius of the site of the ambush was burned to the ground. A soldier who participated in the "punitive expedition" described the "people's shrieks and torments" as one village after another was put to the torch. His letter home found its way to Boston's *Evening Transcript*, which published it with no editorial comment. Otis denied the incident, although Wheaton detailed it in his own report. A retraction was quickly extracted from the letter-writer since he was still in the army, but similar allegations became so common over the next few years that it was impossible to deny such conduct, or that it was either ordered or condoned by high-ranking officers. Ironically, Wheaton would have to preside over the court-martial of a general three years later for having employed the same tactics.[7]

Simultaneous with Wheaton's probe, MacArthur moved northward along the rail line, but he only succeeded in capturing abandoned trenches and villages. Moving swiftly beyond the objective assigned to him by the cautious Otis, MacArthur hoped to catch the enemy at Malolos. The general predicted "a premeditated battle" there after running into some sharp skirmishes as he approached Aguinaldo's capital. But these confrontations were merely staged as a delaying tactic to cover Aguinaldo's retreat to San Isidro, some thirty miles to the north. When the impulsive Funston made a solo charge into Malolos on horseback well ahead of his troops, he found it deserted, with nothing to fight but the fires set by the retreating enemy. MacArthur ignored both Aguinaldo and the cautious instructions of Otis and dashed five more miles to Calumpit, an important railroad junction with the Rio Grande de Pampanga. There, he was rewarded with a battle, only because General Antonio Luna was too proud to obey his orders to destroy the bridge and retreat. It was here that Funston won his first acclaim in the Philippines for a foolhardy maneuver that would have been suicidal against a more efficient foe. Nevertheless, the Kansans crossed the river and forced Luna to retreat before he could destroy the bridge so coveted by MacArthur for his "armored" and supply trains. The jayhawk commander was rewarded with a promotion and the Medal of Honor. Always vying with Funston for glory, Colonel Stotsenburg was not so lucky. He was killed leading a Nebraska charge on Quinqua before his regiment crossed the river. Otis translated MacArthur's advance into "brilliant" and "smashing final victories" for Washington, and, of course, the press.[8]

Meanwhile, a popular hero, Brigadier General Henry W. Lawton, arrived as Anderson's replacement, bringing two regular infantry regiments with him. In some ways, Lawton was America's Lord Kitchener. He had had a string of successes from the Civil War, in which he won the Congressional Medal of Honor, to the Indian Wars, in which he captured the legendary Geronimo, and finally in Cuba, where he led the attack on El Caney on the outskirts of Santiago. The contrast between this tall, dashing, and imaginative leader and the fussy, overly cautious Otis was not lost on the correspondents, who gave him good copy and even suggested that he should be running the show in the Philippines. Otis kept him cooling his heels in Manila for weeks before allowing him to lead a force of 1500 men, collected from fragments of various commands, on a lightning strike on Santa Cruz on the southeastern shore of Laguna de Bay, where, it was believed, the enemy had regrouped following Wheaton's campaign. This time, gunboats would land marines on one side while Lawton approached by land on the other. Relying on faulty charts inherited from the Spanish, however, the amphibious force got hung up in shallow water too far from shore to surprise the enemy, while Lawton got bogged down in swamps and dense jungle when a road on a Spanish map proved nonexistent. Nevertheless, Otis managed to squeeze out of this fiasco headlines proclaiming "The Filipinos Flee Before General Lawton." But Lawton knew better, and was rapidly learning the realities of warfare in the Philippines.[9]

By then the war had been of longer duration than the conflict with Spain had been, and Americans had probed only thirty miles out of Manila to the north and to the south. Insufficient troops were left to occupy permanently a minuscule portion of this area around the capital. Even if there was a sufficient number of men to occupy conquered territory, the cautious Otis always ordered his commanders to return after each successful advance, much to their chagrin. Otis desperately needed a real "brilliant victory" before the rainy season arrived. Wildly, he released details to the press of his imminent "master stroke of the war" to force the Filipinos into another "final battle," as though enemy intelligence were unable to pick this information up. Even the president seemed taken in by Otis's grandiose plans; he cabled his commander "to force the fighting; penetrate far into the interior and capture every warring Filipino." A second glance at that famous globe of his might have warned McKinley of exactly what that would have involved.[10]

On June 10, 1899, two columns commanded by Lawton and Wheaton moved southward from Manila for Cavite, a hotbed of rebel activity. They were accompanied by a naval force steaming down the coast. The first few days were not exactly auspicious as the soldiers faced intense heat, impassable swamps or jungles, and the inevitable attack at dusk by swarms of mosquitoes. The surviving letters of several officers involved spell out the awesome confusion wrought by the elements. In desperate attempts to escape the heat, men jettisoned equipment and clothing during the first day's march, which only rendered them more vulnerable to the mosquitoes when the sun went down. One outfit reported 500 stragglers of a force of 750 men. Not a single enemy soldier had been so much as sighted and Lawton's army was in disarray and its commander was signalling for reinforcements. None of this was reported to the press, however, and Otis would have censored the dispatch of any correspondent intrepid enough to describe it. Instead, the press was fed descriptions that produced headlines in the United States announcing that "Insurgents Flee as Lawton Advances."[11]

Finally, Lawton did make contact with the enemy. Headlines described this battle as "Success of the Moment Against Filipino Braves." General Otis informed reporters that four Americans were killed while 400 "Indians" perished. The *Call* also explained that "the insurgents again proved their facility as dodgers. Between three and four thousand warriors who seemed destined to be captured have disappeared. The majority got away under the cover of the night." Wheaton complained angrily that "the whole country is networked with trenches and tunnels and the enemy scurry from shelter to shelter."[12]

The Americans engaged "at least 5,000 Southern Tagals" in what Otis hailed as "the hottest battle of the war." Even the realistic Lawton conceded that it was "a real battle," his first in the Philippines. But the enemy was not trapped and rapidly retreated along the coast with the U.S.S. *Helena* in hot pursuit, leveling one coastal village after another. When naval intelligence reported to Lawton that the enemy had taken refuge in the town of Bacoor farther south, the general halted the pursuit while he worked out maneuvers to trap the Filipino soldiers there. The navy would land marines south of Bacoor while Lawton personally led the Fourth Cavalry on a dramatic gallop down the coast from the north. The Ninth and Fourteenth infantry regiments would move more slowly through the jungle to cut off the western avenues of escape. Once these three elements were in position, the navy would move in its warships from the east to spring the trap with shore bombardment. It was a good plan, but it required precise timing. It seemed that at long last a sizable enemy force was trapped and that the "insurrection" in Cavite would be terminated.[13]

Unfortunately, the naval commander sprung the trap prematurely. Apparently, he felt that the publicity-hungry Otis had been grabbing too many headlines for the army, and in the interest of generating a little glory for himself and his own branch of the service, he began to bombard Bacoor before Lawton's cavalry, the infantry, and even the marines were close enough to the town. The report in the *Call* must have sounded to its readers like a broken record:

> General Lawton rode five miles along the coast, without discovering the enemy, to Bacoor, and found the town full of white flags. But there were no soldiers. The women and children, who had fled the bombardment, were camping in the ruins of their homes. The shells had almost knocked the town to pieces. The big church was wrecked and many buildings were ruined. Even the trees and shrubbery were torn as by a hailstorm.[14]

The Filipino force managed to avoid the two infantry regiments in its retreat inland to Imus, which was out of range of the naval guns. The mayor of Imus was eager to avoid the fate of the coastal towns left in ruins and, informing Lawton that his people had always opposed Aguinaldo's government and needed American protection, asked him to take possession of the town. Lawton was shrewd enough to know that this request meant that the Filipino soldiers had concealed their weapons and blended in with the local peasantry. He reported back to Otis his negotiations with several mayors but warned his commander that the enemy had merely "turned 'amigo', while peacefully planting crops," and that they were capable of operating in Cavite again as soon as the Americans departed. Nevertheless, Otis ballyhooed Lawton's report as "a warm welcome" for American rule. "Inhabitants rejoiced at deliverance and welcome with enthusiastic demonstrations arrival of our troops," he cabled Washington. He also ordered Lawton's army back to Manila, but to reenforce his delusion that Cavite had been conquered, Otis allowed Lawton this time to leave behind token garrisons in Imus, Bacoor, Las Pinas, and Paranke, or what the navy had left standing in the last three towns.[15]

Otis had anticipated the style of later warfare appropriate to societies with more sophisticated mass media, in which impressions back home would be as crucial as the reality of the battlefield, and in which a good public relations officer is as important as a good field commander. Press releases full of exaggerated claims were as essential to Otis as any traditional military strategy. Every military probe was launched with great fanfare and the claim that it was to be "the last stroke of the war." Otis invariably called each probe a "complete success" in press releases to correspondents who were well aware that it had failed. Technological innovations were introduced to the press in similar fashion. MacArthur's command featured an "ingenious combination" of Hotchkiss cannon, Gatling guns, and borrowed naval batteries mounted on flat cars that would follow the rail system deep into the interior to get at enemy sanctuaries. A new explosive, "Thorite," would soon rock the Filipinos "to their senses," Otis bragged to reporters, who knew through more candid officers, such as Lawton, that using this explosive would be the equivalent of shooting a mosquito with a Krag and that "armored trains" lacked the maneuverability to be effective against an elusive, fast-moving enemy. At any rate, it was rumored that Aguinaldo had destroyed the rail system north of MacArthur's position. One new weapon that Otis did not publicize in such fashion, for reasons of delicacy, was a steam fire-fighting engine converted, or more accurately, inverted, to spray villages with petroleum to make them burn more rapidly. Since the enemy had become increasingly more dispersed, the reporters knew that the civilian population had to bear the brunt of the use of such indiscriminate weapons.[16]

By the time Lawton returned from Cavite, Otis was well into his first rainy season in the Philippines. Heavy clouds threatened his publicity campaign as well as his military one, as more editors suddenly realized that they had been hoodwinked by his inflated and fatuous press releases. "Conditions Are Most Serious in the Philippines. The Roseate View Not Born Out By A True Statement of the Facts," a huge, front-page headline in the *Call* announced. Other dramatic headlines declared: "Otis Has Seriously Blundered" and "Otis To Blame For the American Losses." This last headline referred to news that a battalion of the Fourth Infantry had fallen into a trap and had been badly mauled before being rescued. "That the news that the 'hardest battle of the war' should have been fought just when we were positively assured that the fighting in the Philippines was all over cannot overcome the average man like a summer cloud without his special wonder," warned one editor. Even imperialist editors had become concerned that the end was still "many months away" in spite of "encouraging reports from General Otis." The *Salt Lake City Tribune* cautioned, however, that a longer war should not dishearten America:

> The struggle must continue til the misguided creatures there shall have their eyes bathed in enough blood to cause their vision to be cleared, and to understand that not only is resistance useless, but that those whom they are now holding as enemies have no purpose toward them except to consecrate to liberty and to open for them a way to happiness.[17]

A long editorial in the *Call* summed up the disillusionment of many antiimperialists, who had patriotically held back their criticisms of the war for the first four months or so:

> The undeclared war in the Philippines has now been nearly twice as long as the war with Spain. The Filipinos, without effective artillery and lack of military form, have proved their touch and common feeling with all people who are fighting for the soil they were born on and for independence and self-government against an invading host.

> Our superior arms, aim, and formations, our great guns and support of warships that with one broadside can destroy a town and leave its men, women and children heaped in a mass of torn flesh to spume in the sun . . . our inadequate forces have destroyed the country by raiding . . . and their hosts have closed in behind advancing columns, as water closes after the hand that is drawn through it.

> Meanwhile General Otis has been dealing "crushing blows." He has ended the "rebellion" repeatedly. But the "crushing blows" do not crush. We have probably killed thousands. There is much mourning in American homes where the first born of many a house has died under the blistering tropical sun. . . . Our troops have pushed the unavailing butchery of war with uncomplaining endurance and dash. Yet the barefooted enemy, remembering his hut burned and his paddy field destroyed, lurks in the jungle and fights.[18]

However much the *Call* challenged the basic assumptions of the war and the competency of Otis as a general, the paper did not at this juncture call for a halt to the struggle. Instead, it counseled the Administration to remove Otis from command and to ship more troops. "War is hell. We have made it hell in the Philippines, let us get through with it as soon as possible." In this case the *Call*'s editor reacted the same way his disillusioned imperialist colleagues did. In Los Gatos, a small town in California's Santa Clara Valley that boasted more churches and fewer saloons than any place in the state, the *Mail* took time out from its daily tirades against booze, whores, and the ungodly in general to wonder what Otis and the Administration were doing in the Philippines:

> There is no use dilly-dallying with these uncircumcised, uncivilized, unthankful and treacherous cutthroats; the sooner soldiers are sent there in sufficient numbers to finish up the business, the better it will be for Christianity and human progress. Let sympathizers with the Filipino in this country hold their peace, and let the fight go on. . . . Let it not be said at the close of the nineteenth century that the hands on Liberty's clock were turned back! Let the fight go on.[19]

In the face of escalating criticism of his leadership, even in the imperialist press, Otis desperately tried to salvage his claim to victory. When some Filipino soldiers assassinated General Luna and his aide at Cabanatuan in June, Otis seized upon the execution as proof that the war was as good as over. The Filipinos were so demoralized that they were fighting among themselves, he crowed. Otis argued that Luna, not Aguinaldo, had been the real "evil influence" behind the "insurrection," and the one who had not allowed Aguinaldo and his "pseudo rebels" to surrender. The war had long been over, but its formal ending was now at hand, the American commander predicted. "Optimistic Dispatches From Otis Cause President to be Hopeful," the *Call* headlined this story, but its editor observed caustically that "the General does not even have enough sense to come in out of the rain."[20]

There was some truth to Otis's interpretation of Luna's murder. Luna had been adamantly opposed to any compromise on the issue of independence. He had had Manuel Argüelles charged with treason for merely suggesting privately that Filipinos accept autonomy under American sovereignty. He had also ordered Pedro Paterno, Felipe Buencamino, and the entire "peace cabinet" arrested for having voted to negotiate the terms of autonomy with the Americans. Paterno had negotiated the peace with Spain in 1897 and was therefore suspect among irreconcilables. But there was also a highly charged personal rivalry between Luna and Aguinaldo, one with striking parallels to the earlier confrontation with Bonifacio. This time, however, certain features were reversed. Luna had emerged as a superior military leader in the war with the Americans, and he had had more status as an ilustrado. He probably looked down on the less educated Aguinaldo as his social and intellectual inferior, as well as a less competent general. The fact that Luna was an Ilocano added another dimension to his conflict with Aguinaldo's Tagalog generals, particularly over the issue of discipline, which the Philippine army sadly lacked. In fact, two of Luna's assassins had been dismissed by him, only to be reinstated by Aguinaldo. Aguinaldo feigned innocent surprise over the news, promising an investigation, but circumstantial evidence points to Aguinaldo's culpability. Luna was clearly a threat to him and was on his way to confer with Aguinaldo when he was cut down by soldiers from Cavite loyal to Aguinaldo. Later, Mabini bitterly accused Aguinaldo of having ordered Luna's murder and attributed the defeat of the revolution to this despicable act.[21]

What Otis overlooked, however, was that he, and not Luna, had stymied every attempt to negotiate peace during the spring of 1899. He had young Sladen inform emissaries from both Aguinaldo and the "peace cabinet" that either they "lacked proper credentials" or that an audience with Otis might be construed as "recognition of their so called political organization." This explanation ignored the fact that he had already met with Torres on February 5, and later with General Gregorio del Pilar, who offered Otis peace on any terms that would permit the Filipinos to save face. When young del Pilar was arrogantly informed by Otis that "complete submission" was the only possible basis for peace, he was reported to have "turned red under his brown skin."[22]

Not until October, 1899, did Otis agree to another meeting, this time with General Jose Alejandrino, carrying a peace proposal from Aguinaldo. The proposal to negotiate was sweetened with the offer to release some American prisoners if the meeting with Otis took place. European-educated and extremely urbane, Alejandrino was so conservative that even the Spanish considered him "level headed." But he fared no better than earlier emissaries. Otis curtly informed him that he had no authority to negotiate an armistice, which could only be done in Washington. He then informed the flabbergasted Filipino general that he could not even recognize any released Americans as legitimate prisoners of war. They were "merely stragglers from within our lines captured by robbers," he told Alejandrino. Otis reported to Washington, falsely, that "the insurgents never intended to give prisoners up unless they could force money payments and recognition in exchange."[23]

Aguinaldo attempted to bypass the imperious Otis by sending Argüelles to see Jacob Gould Schurman as soon as he arrived to chair the Philippine Commission. But Schurman was in a difficult position in that Otis, who had been appointed a member of the commission by the president, refused to meet with this civilian body and made it clear that he would tolerate no interference on its part in military affairs. Schurman's only choice was to advise gently that "unconditional surrender" was Aguinaldo's only option. When Argüelles protested that that option was "too humiliating," Schurman argued that there was "no humiliation in General Otis treating our brother Filipinos as General Grant treated our brother Americans at Appomattox." At any rate, only Otis had the authority to negotiate a settlement, Schurman apologized, unaware that Otis had already denied having such authority.[24]

Aguinaldo also tried once again to deal directly with Washington by sending Antonio Regidor from his post in London to sue for peace. But when Otis got wind of this maneuver, he frantically cabled warnings that any armistice was "unsafe to grant" and would upset "military plans" to destroy Aguinaldo's army. The peace proposal carried by Regidor was "merely a trick" to "gain time" now that Otis had "trapped the insurgents." Officially, Regidor was a nonperson representing a government that simply did not exist. Thus he was completely ostracized, as earlier Filipino emissaries to Washington had been. Senator Hoar denounced such arrogant, imperious, and inhuman responses to every Filipino attempt to negotiate a peaceful settlement:

> Was it ever heard before that a civilized, humane, and Christian nation made war upon a people and refused to tell them what they wanted of them? You say you want them to submit. To submit to what? To mere military force? But for what purpose or for what end is that military force to be exerted? You decline to tell them. Not only do you decline to say what you want of them, except bare and abject surrender, but you will not even let them tell you what they ask of you![25]

Otis received a good deal of support in the imperialist press for his intransigence. Even the most trivial face-saving compromise was perceived as bribery by some jingoistic editors. The natives "had to be whipped into respectful submission," advised the *Omaha Bee*, insisting that "the Filipinos will love us later, for the fullness of the lesson we taught them." Even the *Call* agreed at this stage that there could be no peace until Aguinaldo understood that "unconditional is a word with no modifiers." On May 29, the *Call*'s front page announced, "No More Dallying With Belligerent Filipinos." Only in October, 1899, did the *Call*'s editor suddenly discover that the Filipinos had been "willing to accept a protectorate under the United States" for at least five months and that only Otis's demand for "a humiliating unconditional surrender" kept going "the cold-blooded butchery of a people who are crying for quarter." Imperialist editors ignored this crucial fact and continued to evoke the harsher

"British model for dealing with alien races" or the belief that Asians only understood force.[26]

A few anti-imperialist editors astutely cautioned the Administration that a bloodbath would prove counterproductive to the work of missionaries and teachers, who would have to face the bitter residue of hatred caused by the destruction and slaughter. The war was not very old when the *Criterion* in New York raised this very point:

> Whether we like it or not, we must go on slaughtering the natives in English fashion, and taking what muddy glory lies in the wholesale killing until they have learned to respect our arms. The more difficult task of getting them to respect our intentions will follow.

But no one, critic or imperialist, considered at this point that the war could continue for years. It took a second dry season under Otis's leadership for this painful reality to sink in.[27]

From a military perspective, the worst consequence of the American commander's unrealistic assessment was that he left himself woefully short of troops in June, 1899. Up to half his force of almost 30,000 soldiers were state volunteers slated to be repatriated and discharged during that summer. They had been recruited to fight the war with Spain, which had officially ended on April 11, 1899, with the formal exchange of ratified treaties. Technically, these volunteers had to be discharged within six months of that date. Yet throughout the spring, Otis had blithely refused offers of more troops from the secretary of war and had insisted that the war was all but over and that he had sufficient troops for the mopping-up operation. Several subordinates attempted to disabuse Otis of this dangerous notion, but to no avail. Lawton attempted to bypass Otis by telling correspondents that 100,000 soldiers were needed to pacify the Philippines, a remarkably accurate estimate and the exact number requested by MacArthur upon relieving Otis of his command in May of 1900. Lawton's action enraged Otis, who forced his subordinate to deny he had ever made such a statement to the press. Even the enemy tried to influence Otis with the reality of his dilemma. General Alejandrino warned Otis that he needed "ten times as many soldiers" and "years not months" to conquer the Filipinos. "We perceive what an American requires in this climate. On the other hand a Filipino exists on a handful of rice and a pair of linen trousers. . . . We could keep your army occupied for years." This advice turned out to be as painfully accurate as Lawton's prediction. But if Otis refused to listen to his own generals, he was hardly going to take advice from the enemy.[28]

To add to the woes of Otis and the Administration, some state governments pressured Washington to return their volunteer regiments immediately after the war ended. The outspoken Populist governor of South Dakota warned McKinley that keeping the volunteers any longer would be as "unconstitutional as the war itself." Moreover, his state would never recognize

> the present attempt of the government to enforce title with bayonets to a nation of brown men purchased from a disgraced and vanquished despot and [must] regard the further sacrifice of our soldiers, in a conflict waged against liberty and in the interest of exploiting capitalism as totally incompatible with the spirit of our institutions.[29]

The president could dismiss Governor Lee's statement as being politically motivated, but he could not so easily ignore General Reeves's cable to Governor Lind of Minnesota demanding the recall of his state regiment at once or the same demands made in scores of letters from parents and at public meetings in Oregon, Washington, Tennessee, and Nebraska. In the end, however, the governors of these states followed Sacramento's more restrained policy asking that the Californians be returned as soon as they were properly relieved by regulars. On this basis, the War Department advised Otis that the volunteers could not be kept for more than six months and that by law this retention had to be voluntary. Otis assured Washington that these soldiers were eager to remain and that six months was more than he needed to wind down the war. The president foolishly accepted this estimate and turned down offers from states to raise new volunteer regiments to serve in the Philippines.[30]

When it became obvious that more time and troops would be needed, the president hastily authorized recruitment for new national volunteer regiments. This move was the first sign that Washington was growing wary of Otis's judgment. Because Otis had been so certain that the state volunteers wanted to remain in the islands, he was instructed to flesh out the new regiments by recruiting these veterans. Possibly nowhere else was Otis's power to deceive himself more evident than in his assurance to Washington that these regiments could easily be raised in the Philippines. Getting soldiers already in the field six months to reenlist would be a signal feat in any war, hence enlistments are usually frozen for the duration. But the refusal to recognize that a "war" was being fought in the Philippines precluded that option. On top of this, it was hardly an ordinary war, but a "dirty" colonial one being fought in unbearable climate and led by a general totally lacking in charisma.

From private to general, Otis was held in near universal contempt by those serving under him. Commanders of the Nebraska and Colorado regiments, respectively Colonel Stotsenburg and General Irving Hale, not only made their disrespect for Otis obvious, but even engaged in shouting matches with him in front of their men. On one such occasion, Otis threatened Hale with "official action" and was in turn threatened with the charge of "cowardice" by Hale, much to the delight of their audience of Colorado soldiers. The Astor Battery informed the press that its members refused to reenlist because of the "blundering despotism and incompetence of Otis." In all likelihood, few of these volunteers would have remained under any leadership, but Otis certainly contributed to their disillusionment.[31]

Otis was authorized to offer a five-hundred-dollar bonus for enlisting in the national volunteer outfits. One correspondent estimated that only seven percent of the volunteers considered enlisting, although Otis reported that a surprising 1,229 men had signed up, a figure slightly better than ten percent. Nevertheless this number fell far short of Otis's rosy expectations and represented at best the skeletons, not flesh, of the three new regiments that Otis was expected to raise from the state volunteers. But Washington was not informed of this shortfall until June 3, when the first state volunteer regiment was already on its way back to San Francisco. If the president was not aware that his commander had left him in a terrible bind, it was not lost on the press. "The Failure of Otis To Grasp the Situation. Despite His Protests It Is Apparent That He Needs More Men," bellowed one front page. "Otis Has Seriously Blundered. Many More Troops Needed At Once," charged another. Momentarily, at least, the entire blame for the mess in the Philippines shifted in the public eye from Aguinaldo and the anti-imperialist critics to the American commander. The *New York Herald*'s editor polled his colleagues across the country that June and reported an overwhelming loss of confidence in the general. Virtually every editor polled demanded that Otis's recommendations at least be overridden, if he were not to be relieved of his command altogether.[32]

Almost in panic, the Administration set out to raise ten new volunteer regiments in addition to filling out the three being formed in the islands. The secretary of war began pushing more cavalry and artillery on Otis over the general's protests and instructed him to be "fully ready for the fall campaign." Otis refused two regular "colored" regiments because he worried that "racial loyalties" would conflict with national ones, but they were sent in June anyway. General Hughes was ecstatic over using "darky troops" in the Philippines, as he agreed with the surgeon general's prediction that they would be less susceptible to the tropical diseases that had already incapacitated one-quarter of the white force. Hughes also thought that the racial affinity American Negroes might have with the natives would better equip them to play an important diplomatic, as well as a military, role. These two regiments were soon followed by two black volunteer infantries, with black officers, and the legendary black Ninth Cavalry.[33]

Secretary of War Alger was replaced that summer by a young, energetic,

and highly successful lawyer, Elihu Root. Alger's replacement had been expected, as he had been made the scapegoat for all the logistical problems in the
war with Spain. Furthermore, he had naively attached himself to the Republican renegade governor of his home state of Michigan in a vain attempt to secure
a seat in the U.S. Senate. But Root was a political unknown whose appointment
surprised everyone, including one of his clients, Theodore Roosevelt. Even
Root protested that he knew nothing of war or the army, but he was one of the
president's shrewder choices. The Philippines was still under the jurisdiction of
the War Department, and McKinley wanted a good legal mind to influence the
Supreme Court on forthcoming constitutional questions. Root carried out
sweeping reforms to an archaic system that had changed little since the Civil
War. (In all fairness, Alger had started such changes, but with far less energy
and success.) Curtly informing Otis that he would "rather err on the safe side in
sending too many troops than too few," the new secretary foisted more soldiers
on the general. Root also overrode Otis on the issue of recruitment of native
soldiers.[34]

Captain Matthew Batson had carried the offer of service from the village of
Macabebe in Pampanga to Otis. The Macabebes had strong warrior traditions
and had loyally served Spain in her suppression of the earlier insurrection; they
had asked Madrid to relocate their village in the Carolines should the Filipinos
win independence. But Otis was "afraid that they would, if armed, turn traitors," complained Batson, who took the idea to Lawton, who in turn peddled it
to his very influential friends in Washington. Otis protested to Alger that it was
"not advisable to call into service in Luzon native organizations of any character
at present." Without even consulting Otis, Root ordered the formation of Philippine Scouts to be placed in active service as soon as possible. This order was a
particularly bitter pill for Otis to swallow as he had to surmise that the immensely popular and well-connected Lawton was behind Root's edict. Possibly
out of spite, he turned the recruited Macabebes over to Lawton, who had Batson promoted and placed in command of them.[35]

The decision to recruit native troops was immensely popular in imperialist
circles, as it triggered the fantasy that colonialism would produce American
"sepoys." Some American editors and statesmen were sensitive to English criticism or advice on this score. English editors liked to counsel their "provincial
cousins" in America on the proper manner of managing colonies in the European fashion, since Americans were so new to the game. Hence, a ranking English officer writing in the *London Daily Chronicle* chided the Americans in
April, 1899, for bearing the heaviest burden of the fighting with no plans to
raise local troops and set one tribe against the other in the fashion of the English in India and elsewhere:

Americans do not seem to understand the game, which is to use one set of natives against the other. This would not be a difficult matter in the Philippines; the suspicion of some tribes against the dominating Tagals could easily be aroused.[36]

Since American imperialists tended to be unabashed Anglophiles, they were eager to win English approval and validate themselves as "efficient" colonizers. Of course, America needed no advice on the divide-and-conquer tactic; it had long been used against the Indians. However, expectations to "Filipinize" the war proved to be unrealistic. No more than 5,000 Macabebes were recruited, and while they proved to be fierce and effective fighters, they represented a single group and only five or six percent of the forces serving under the American flag. Actually the Americans were more successful in enlisting the Hispanicized, better-educated Filipinos to serve in nonmilitary capacities, once they had wearied of the endless warfare.[37]

As if Otis did not have enough troubles with the press that summer, the correspondents in Manila rebelled against his heavy-handed censorship, a revolt that appears to have been encouraged by Lawton. Even before the war, Otis had subjected every press dispatch sent from Manila to censorship. "Troublemakers" were banished or denied access to his press briefings. The latter discrimination bothered journalists less and less as they realized that his briefings were too divorced from reality to be of much value. But they relied on the cable terminal that Otis controlled. Only at a heavy cost of time could they bypass the censor by mailing dispatches to Hong Kong to be cabled from there. Local newspapers were not dependent upon the cable, but any stories critical of Otis's interpretation of the facts prompted Otis to close down the papers that ran them for giving the United States "a black eye." Two English reporters who dared ask embarrassing questions were quickly deported, and even President McKinley's personal representative was declared persona non grata by the imperious commander for criticizing his leadership in the Philippines.[38]

Before making his final decision to annex the Philippines, McKinley had sent E. W. Harden in the fall of 1898 to assess the commercial and industrial potentials of the islands. Harden made a preliminary report in November, recommending that he return to the Philippines for a more extensive study after the first of the year. When Otis got wind of Harden's plan to return, he wired the War Department, "Harden not acceptable here in any capacity. See his abusive article published in the San Francisco *Chronicle*, November 11th." In that article, Harden said nothing critical of imperialism or in favor of independence for the Philippines. But General Otis, he wrote, was "too weak a man for the important office he fills and exhibits his incompetency by struggling with little matters of detail to the detriment of matters of graver importance." This view was shared by almost everyone on the scene, and the president should have heeded it rather than comply with Otis's objection.[39]

During the months leading up to the war, there were some complaints of the general's treatment of the Fourth Estate and his bald attempts to manipulate the news emanating from the Philippines. Otis denied this charge, insisting that correspondents could cable any "established facts." There were "trouble makers," such as Robert M. Collins of Associated Press, who tried to wire "numerous baseless rumors [which] circulate here tending to excite the outside world." What Collins had wanted to report was that Aguinaldo was not an isolated "looter," but a popular and effective leader who had defeated the Spanish throughout the islands with no help from the Americans. With the exception of Collins, "all correspondents here satisfied with present censors," Otis informed the War Department.[40]

Once warfare broke out, censorship seemed more legitimate as a means of denying the enemy military intelligence. The correspondents dutifully submitted to the whims of the censor until they became suspicious that censorship was being used to cover army mistakes and to support Otis's fictitious reports on the war. In March, one correspondent bootlegged a story to his editor via the Hong Kong cable that challenged the report that Americans had been enthusiastically welcomed on Negros. In fact, bitter fighting continued on that island. It was this report that opened the eyes of many editors, who demanded to be told the function of the general's censorship. Was it to deny Aguinaldo the knowledge that fighting was still going on in Negros? Surely he knew this, one editor mused. More correspondents followed suit, sacrificing up to a week's delay to file more accurate stories. All other generals disagreed that no more troops were needed or that the war was anywhere near over. The state volunteers were not eager to reenlist in the new regiments. Otis angrily demanded that Washington outlaw the use of the Hong Kong terminal by correspondents in the Philippines as it was the source of all the "detrimental reports alarming the country." The ensuing exchange with the War Department makes it clear that censorship was, from the beginning, entirely Otis's doing. Alger finally suggested that Otis relax the practice and replace the censor, Captain Thomson, with "a more moderate man." The suggestion, which ignored the fact that the general set the criteria for censorship, was followed by the secretary's customary assurances that Otis was running the show and that the Administration did not want "to interfere."[41]

The general's protest against the use of the Hong Kong cable was badly timed, as it coincided with a growing disillusionment with the war in even the imperialist and Republican press. Some of McKinley's strongest editorial supporters understood that Otis could not have passed off all "his fiction" without censorship. "The people want the truth," was a common plea in the press. Censorship merely engendered doubts, fears, and suspicion. Anti-imperialist editors used the revelation that censorship was being used to conceal the truth as yet another example of the "high handed militarism they had predicted would have to accompany imperialistic policies.[42]

As though encouraged by this editorial support back home, the correspondents followed a suggestion by Lawton that they band together to protest the military governor's autocratic and arbitrary management of the news. Even a few of Otis's "favorites" joined in and signed a collective statement charging the American commander with deliberately misrepresenting the real situation in the Philippines. His "ultra-optimistic view is shared by no one in the islands. Even his leading generals disagree with him," this round robin charged. By pleading that "the truth would alarm the people at home, Otis compelled us to participate in this misrepresentation by excising or altering uncontroverted statements of fact."[43]

Knowing that Otis would pigeonhole the statement and punish those who had signed it, each correspondent involved mailed a copy to Hong Kong for transmission to his editor. It caused something of a sensation as front pages headlined the story by inverting some of the general's pet phrases ("Situation Not 'Well in Hand'"). It was too much for the *New York Sun*, which refused to print the protest even though its own correspondent, O. K. Davis, had signed it. But the *New York Times* published the entire statement and editorially called for the general's head. Otis should be removed altogether, or his authority restricted to civil matters and the military command turned over to Lawton, it counseled. The general's worst sin, as far as Whitelaw Reid's *Tribune* was concerned, was the credence that censorship had lent to the charges of anti-imperialists—as though there were really nothing to cover up. *Public Opinion*'s survey of newspapers revealed heavy criticism of Otis's use of censorship to conceal his own failures. A few editorial defenders lashed out at the "incredible folly" of the rebellious correspondents, and the "vanity, effrontery, and impertinence of the statement."[44]

Collins followed up the collective statement with a personal account to his editor spelling out the egregious abuses that had motivated the revolt. He pointed out that he and some of his colleagues had covered Cuba during Weyler's command, and all agreed that the censorship imposed by Otis was "much more stringent." At first the reporters were patriotically compelled to go along with Otis. "Every fight became a glorious American victory, even though every one in the army knew it to have been substantially a failure, and we were drilled into writing, quite mechanically, wholly ridiculous estimates of the number of Filipinos killed." Feeling that it was "hopeless" talking to Otis, the correspondents took their case to "leading army officers," who suggested that they "tell the truth" and accused them of "cowardice." In response to this challenge, they decided to confront the censor with a totally realistic story of the Philippine situation. "Of course, we all know that we are in a terrible mess out here, but we don't want the people to get excited about it. If you fellows will only keep quiet now we will pull through in time without any fuss at home," the censor told them when he refused to cable the story. The correspondents persisted and were ushered in to see Otis one at a time. "When I went in to see him, he repeated the same old story about the insurrection going to pieces, and hinted so portentously about having wonderful things up his sleeve that I almost believed him," Collins recalled. Finally the general told each reporter that if he held the story for ten days, he would be "grateful" to Otis, as events about to unfold would so contradict the criticism that it would embarrass him.[45]

The reporters decided to capitulate to Otis's demand one last time and gave him not ten days but a whole month to carry off his promised miracle, after which they drew up their round robin. The dumbfounded censor gasped, "This is just the sort of matter the censor is intended to suppress," as he rushed in to show Otis the collective statement. Otis tried to interview Davis, one of his "favorites," but this time the reporters refused to see him individually. Instead, they formed a committee composed of Collins, Davis, Bass, and McCutcheon of the *Chicago Record*. All save Collins represented staunchly imperialist organs and had been considered "friendlies" by Otis. The general accused them "with some anger" of "espionage" and threatened to make formal charges against them:

> Gentlemen, you have served an extraordinary paper upon me; you accuse me of falsehood. This constitutes a conspiracy against the government. I will have you tried by court-martial and let you choose the judges.[46]

Collins pointed out that court-martial had been threatened before and that he did not believe that Otis could get a ranking officer in the Philippines to vote for a conviction on such silly charges. The committee demanded that the general reply to the specific charges raised in the protest. Otis explained that he did not permit them to report the number of sick because it would be misleading, as the hospitals were "full of perfectly well men who were shirking their duty and should be turned out." As for the story that the marines had actually taken Iloilo a full three hours before Miller could get his forces ashore, Otis had blocked it because "the Navy was so anxious for glory that it disobeyed the instructions by landing before the proper time, etc., although the correspondents could not have been permitted to send that explanation had they known it and were forced to send in a false account," Collins wrote. This was not the first time that Otis had used his control over the news to gain advantage over his adversaries:

> The only time Otis has given us any freedom was during his row with Schurman over the peace negotiations, when (by insinuations and those attempted diplomatic methods which public men seem to think that newspaper men do not see through) he was encouraging us to "roast" Schurman and take his side.[47]

After this disastrous interview, Otis again tried to isolate Davis from the others in order to work on him alone, but Davis would only meet the general with the committee. Otis again predicted that "final victory" was around the corner and promised "greater liberality" in censoring the dispatches if the correspondents would only refrain from mailing their protest. The round robin went out that very day, Collins reported disdainfully.[48]

McKinley responded to the protest in characteristic fashion declaring that the charges offered "nothing tangible except that the general's conclusions were unwarranted" and instructing the secretary of war to pressure Otis into relaxing the censorship. Root's instructions to Otis were ambiguous:

> In view of the public misconception here, created by the allegations of Manila correspondents . . . the Secretary of War inclines to advise most liberal treatment, even to the point of practically meeting your expressed willingness of July 20 that the censorship be entirely removed, only continue the requirement that all matters be submitted in advance, that you may deal, as you deem best, with any liable to affect military operations. . . . Do it without announcing that you are going to do it.[49]

Otis responded in predictable fashion. After denying that there was any censorship, he appointed a new censor and escalated the practice. Terminating censorship for Otis was a bit like ending the war. That is, he periodically announced that for all practical purposes the censorship that never existed had been abolished. The *Boston Herald* was in the awkward position of having congratulated Otis twice within the space of two months for having ended the censorship of news. The situation was so bizarre that the editor of the *Call* began to doubt the general's sanity.[50]

In reality, Otis was so incensed over the action of the correspondents that he became increasingly arbitrary following the unfavorable publicity connected with their statement. The word "ambush" was scrubbed from dispatches, and correspondents could not mention defective ammunition after one reporter wrote that up to half of the howitzer shells had failed to explode on impact. McCutcheon lost his cable privileges permanently when he filed a story that, because there were not enough troops to occupy them, towns frequently changed hands. This practice imposed enormous hardships on the civilian population. McCutcheon was so peeved that he went back to the Hong Kong cable to announce that the "abolished censorship" was very much alive and getting worse. Impervious to the public reaction, Otis turned his sights on some uncooperative local publications. He shut down the Spanish-language *La Democracia* and indicted the American editor of *Freedom* for "treason and sedition." E. F. O'Brien, a former state volunteer who had elected to be mustered out in Manila, had started a newspaper for the growing American colony in that city. As a Catholic, O'Brien was offended by General Funston's well-known antipapist bigotry and decided to publish a letter from Charles Fox, a former civilian teamster for the Kansas regiment, describing how his colonel had helped loot and desecrate a church by conducting a mock mass in stolen ecclesiastical garb to amuse his men from the Bible Belt. Funston responded to the charges in his usual ad hominem style, ignoring the specific accusations and insisting that Fox was simply "a worthless camp follower" who never really worked for the army. Otis charged O'Brien with libel and sedition without even investigating the validity of Fox's accusations.[51]

The Republican *Call* warned the president that the responsibility for this cavalier treatment of the press in the Philippines rested on his shoulders and would hamper his bid for reelection a short year away. "The Republican party must bear the burden of distrust of the people, and the situation is not helped by the continuing repetition that 'there is nothing to conceal' while nothing is disclosed. The people are not children."[52]

During the summer and fall of 1899, Otis came under sharp attack from still another quarter—the state volunteers back in San Francisco. Reporters invaded the Presidio, where these veterans awaited discharge and transportation home. They made good copy, and the headlines alone tell their story: "No Friend For Otis Among the Volunteers"; "Soldiers Call Otis A 'Foolish Old Woman'"; and "The True Situation in the Philippines Is Said to be Much Worse Than Official Reports Indicate." Almost in unison, these veterans insisted that the war could never be won under Otis and that "the silly old Grandmother" should be replaced by Lawton, who could "smash the 'gugus.'" After that the United States should get out of the Philippines. "Few of them have a good word to say of the islands, or their future, and not one of them will ever return there of his own volition," one reporter concluded. "Damn Otis and damn the Filipino" seemed to be the overriding sentiment.[53]

Among these veterans were three generals, who succeeded in getting even broader coverage for their criticisms of Otis. General Hale called a press conference to denounce the incompetency of the military governor. General Charles King, already an established writer and novelist before going off to war, lost no time contributing an article to the *Call's Sunday Magazine* criticizing not only Otis's military leadership, but also his diplomatic role in provoking the war in the first place. "There is no reason in the world why these people should not have the self-government which they so passionately desire, so far as their ability to carry it on goes," King wrote. This is rare sentiment for a volunteer, although he undermined it elsewhere in the article with a more typical assessment of the Filipino, whom he described as "half child, half devil . . . a most accomplished sneak thief . . . utterly without conscience and as full of treachery as our Arizona Apache." General Reeves also faulted Otis for treating the Filipino leaders "as half civilized savages" on some occasions, while on others he "ignored them completely." Reeves was so eager to make his views public that he held a press conference on the dock, while his Minnesota regiment was still disembarking. The *Call* reported it under a banner front-page headline, declaring:

> There Was No Necessity For War in the Philippines
> General Reeves Says Otis Was Inconsiderate
> Natives Were Ignored and Made Enemies Instead.

But, like King, Reeves went on to criticize Otis for not adopting the tactics used against the Indians in the West. In essence, Reeves thought that Otis was too tough on the Filipinos during peace and too lenient with them in war.[54]

There was yet another source of criticism of Otis and the military. From almost the beginning of the war, soldiers wrote home describing, and usually bragging about, atrocities committed against Filipinos, soldiers and civilians alike. Increasingly, such personal letters, or portions of them, reached a national audience as anti-imperialist editors across the nation reproduced them. Thus, on May 8, 1899, the citizens of Kingston, New York, shared a letter from a homegrown lad in the Philippines to his parents that found its way into the local paper. The very next day San Franciscans were reading his description of "the nigger fighting business":

> The town of Titatia [*sic*] was surrendered to us a few days ago, and two companies occupy the same. Last night one of our boys was found shot and his stomach cut open. Immediately orders were received from General Wheaton to burn the town and kill every native in sight; which was done to a finish. About 1,000 men, women and children were reported killed. I am probably growing hard-hearted, for I am in my glory when I can sight my gun on some dark skin and pull the trigger.[55]

About the same time a letter from Corporal Sam Gillis of the First California Volunteers to his parents appeared in the Salinas paper before traveling eastward:

> We make everyone get into his house by seven p.m., and we only tell a man once. If he refuses we shoot him. We killed over 300 natives the first night. They tried to set the town on fire. If they fire a shot from a house we burn the house down and every house near it, and shoot the natives, so they are pretty quiet in town now.[56]

Once these accounts were widely reproduced, the War Department was forced to demand that General Otis investigate their verity. His idea of an investigation, however, was to forward the press clipping to the writer's commanding officer, who would then convince the soldier to write a retraction. But one soldier, Private Charles Brenner of the Kansas regiment, resisted such pressure. He insisted that Colonel Funston had ordered that all prisoners be shot and that Major Metcalf and Captain Bishop enforced these orders. Otis was obliged to order the sector commander, General MacArthur, to look into the charge. Brenner confronted MacArthur's aide with a corroborating witness, Private Putnam, who confessed to shooting two prisoners after Bishop or Metcalf had ordered, "Kill them! Damn it, kill them!" MacArthur sent his aide's report on to Otis with no comment, and, incredibly, the governor general ordered Brenner court-martialed "for writing and conniving at the publication of an article which . . . contains wilful [sic] falsehoods concerning himself and a false charge against Captain Bishop." The judge advocate in Manila wisely convinced Otis that such a trial could open a Pandora's box, as "facts would develop implicating many others." Otis sent the case to Washington with an endorsement that indicts him before the court of history for having tolerated atrocities under his command:

> After mature deliberation, I doubt the wisdom of a court-martial in this case, as it would give the insurgent authorities a knowledge of what was taking place and they would assert positively that our troops had practised inhumanities, whether the charge should be proven or not, as they would use it as an excuse to defend their own barbarities; and it is not thought that this charge is very grievous under the circumstances then existing, as it was very early in the war, and the patience of our men was under great strain.[57]

The press was just getting warmed up on the subject of American atrocities at this stage. Initially, anti-imperialist editors approached the subject with utmost caution, as though it were tantamount to treason to suggest directly that

American soldiers were committing such barbarous acts. The best that the *Call* could say straight out was that "the real current history is being published in papers all over Iowa, Kansas, Nebraska, and Minnesota." The *New York Times* busily collected all the retractions elicited by the army from "these spinners of tall tales," gleefully announcing that "another yarn has failed to stand the test of time." The *Republican* in Springfield declared that "the *Times* is suffering morally from a case of blind staggers." Two journals of opinion attempted to gauge the editorial reaction to the letters describing American atrocities. The *Literary Digest* concluded that most editors assumed that where there was "so much smoke there had to be a fire." The more pro-Administration *Public Opinion* insisted that editors overwhelmingly believed that the subject had been grossly exaggerated for political purposes. "For every letter describing looting or killing prisoners, ten could be printed which mention nothing of the sort." The latter argument reminded the *Republican*'s editor of the old "joke that the thief proved his innocence against two witnesses who saw him steal by producing twenty who didn't see him."[58]

6

The General's Last Campaign

As 1899 entered its last quarter and another dry season approached, Otis seemed far more concerned with repairing his battered public image than with confronting military problems. He worked desperately to win new friends among the correspondents and bestowed favors on anyone giving him good copy. He managed to recruit E. C. Ross of *Frank Leslie's Weekly* and Theodore W. Noyes of Washington, D.C.'s *Evening Star* to help launch his new propaganda offensive. Ross wrote paeans to the general's military leadership and insisted that all the criticism of Otis had "originated in the United States and not Manila for political reasons." Noyes pointed out that every company in the army had its "champion liar" and that all the "purported" American atrocities could not have occurred without having been seen by war correspondents. Of course, Collins had explained that "everyone" knew of "the perfect orgy of looting and wanton destruction of property and the most outrageous blackmailing of the natives and Chinamen in Manila and various incidents like the shooting down of several Filipinos for attempting to run from a cock fight," but "by common consent" these particulars were never reported by correspondents. In any case, Noyes contradicted himself by declaring that "the charges that have been made, not only by volunteers, but also by the correspondents 'that our troops have shot down and killed in cold blood the poor and innocent Filipino' are a pack of lies." Abandoning any semblance to objective journalism, Noyes angrily asserted:

> The truth is that these scoundrels [Filipinos] have been treated too well and far too leniently by the American authorities. In fact Otis and his officers seem to have been afraid of the criticisms that might have developed into charges of cruelty on the part of the missionary and other organizations, who have the "welfare" of the poor nigger at heart.[1]

Otis also got aid in his public relations counterattack from Father William McKinnon, the former chaplain of the California regiment, who remained behind to be appointed bishop of Manila. Agoncillo had journeyed to Rome to protest his appointment and informed the pope that McKinnon had sanctioned the looting and desecration of Catholic churches by Protestant bigots in the U.S. Army. (The *Call* reported that "Agoncillo Lies Like a Tagallo.") The newly invested bishop defended Funston and insisted there had been no looting, or even disrespect, of churches by American soldiers. The "insurgents," along with "the pagan Chinamen," had done all the looting and desecrating, McKinnon declared, thereby evoking his own ethnic and Californian prejudices. One volunteer had brought back a photograph of a Kansan captain leaning against an altar he was using as a telegraph base with his hat on and smoking a cigarette. When it appeared in newspapers, Cardinal Gibbons, a strong supporter of the president's Philippine policy, registered a protest. Even the *New York Times* expressed outrage over the officer's lack of respect for an altar. McKinnon claimed to have investigated this and similar incidents and found no evidence of "sacrilege" or "bigotry." The bishop explained that churches, monasteries, and convents were often the only "substantial buildings" available and that they had enormous military value that could not be denied to the American army.[2]

The new propaganda offensive was not confined to Otis's efforts. In an effort to restore public confidence in the army, the Administration wheeled the affable and popular General Anderson out of retirement to serve as a spokesman for the army. Anderson denied that a single atrocity had ever been committed by an American soldier in the Philippines. General Shafter, commanding the Department of California, denounced the "rantings" of the returned volunteers, whom he characterized as "sulkers" and "riff-raff." Hearst's *Examiner* endorsed Shafter's opinion and expressed concern over the safety of the city's streets with "these idlers" and "despotic characters" who had remained in San Francisco to malign their country rather than return to their homes. "We have gained more glory as a nation in the space of one short year than we had any reason to expect at the beginning of hostilities," Shafter told reporters. He even agreed with Otis that the war was over, "no matter what ten millions of niggers think about it." Finally, the Administration exploited the country's biggest hero, Admiral Dewey, who landed at San Francisco that fall and received almost hysterical receptions in one city after another as he made his way eastward. Between ovations, he managed to brand all "the loose talk" about the origins and the conduct of the war as "a pack of lies." But always more realistic than Otis, he refused to comment on the war's end.[3]

Back in Manila, Otis escalated his own propaganda campaign on Filipino atrocities in order to fight fire with fire. "Insurgents" tortured American prisoners in "fiendish fashion," some of whom were buried alive or, worse, up to their necks in anthills to be slowly devoured. Others were castrated, had the removed parts stuffed into their mouths, and were then left to suffocate or bleed to death. It was even charged that some prisoners were deliberately infected with leprosy before being released to spread the disease among their comrades. Spanish priests were horribly mutilated before their congregations, and natives who refused to support Aguinaldo were slaughtered by the thousands, according to these accounts. Such press releases won headlines announcing the "Murder and Rapine" by the "Fiendish Filipinos." Otis was also able to capitalize on the fertile imagination of General "Fighting Joe" Wheeler, who spun daily yarns for the press about "Aguinaldo's Dusky Demons," who had "No Respect for the Usages of Civilization." Wheeler went so far as to insist that it was the Filipinos who had mutilated their own dead, murdered women and children, and burned down villages solely to discredit American soldiers.[4]

In his tirades against alleged enemy atrocities, Otis invariably made use of a captured fragment of a Filipino order signed by Aguinaldo's secretary of state, Teodoro Sandiko, ordering Manila to be put to the torch and every American man, woman, and child slaughtered in their sleep. Ignoring the fact that the order was almost a year old, Otis continued to use it as evidence. One correspondent noted wryly that the mere mention of American atrocities sent Otis scurrying to his desk for this "infamous order" of February 15, 1899.[5]

During the closing months of 1899, Aguinaldo attempted to counter Otis's propaganda by suggesting that neutral parties—foreign journalists or representatives of the International Red Cross—inspect his military operations. Otis would have none of it, but Aguinaldo managed to smuggle four reporters—two English, one Canadian, and a Japanese—through American lines. The correspondents returned to Manila to report that American captives were "treated more like guests than prisoners," were "fed the best that the country affords, and [that] everything is done to gain their favor." These efforts were reported in the *Call* under the headline, "Aguinaldo Playing a Very Deep Game. Trying To Make Good Treatment of American Prisoners a Card By Which To Gain Outside Sympathy." The story also revealed that American prisoners were offered commissions in the Philippine army and that three had accepted. "This is not believed," the *Call* advised. Naturally, the four reporters were banished from the Philippines as soon as their bootlegged stories were printed.[6]

Aguinaldo also released some American prisoners so they could tell their own stories. In a *Boston Globe* article entitled "With the Goo Goo's," Paul Spillane described his fair treatment as a prisoner. Aguinaldo had even invited American captives to the christening of his baby and had given each a present of four dollars, Spillane recounted. Naval Lieutenant J. C. Gilmore, whose release was forced by American cavalry pursuing Aguinaldo into the mountains, insisted that he had received "considerate treatment" and that he was no more starved than were his captors. Gilmore also warned that the enemy would fight until "the last Tagalog." Otis responded to these two articles by ordering that the "capture" of the two authors be "investigated," thereby impugning their loyalty.[7]

When F. A. Blake of the International Red Cross arrived at Aguinaldo's request, Otis kept him confined to Manila, where the general's staff bombarded him with Filipino violations of the laws of civilized warfare. On one occasion, however, Blake managed to slip away from his escort and venture into the field. He never made it past American lines, but even within them he witnessed burned-out villages and "horribly mutilated Filipino bodies, with stomachs slit open and occasionally decapitated." Blake saved his impressions until his return to San Francisco, where he told a reporter that "American soldiers are determined to kill every Filipino in sight." Otis seems to have fared as poorly in the propaganda battle as he had in actual combat. One headline declared, "General Otis Made Ill By Melancholia. Suffers From Insomnia. The Result of Worry Over Criticism of His Campaign." But if he was stung by criticism, he certainly was not enlightened by it. Otis decided to publish his own newspaper for army personnel, but the soldiers assigned to it protested that they had not come to the Philippines to run a printing press, but if they had to, they wanted the pay of typesetters and not of soldiers.[8]

In the fall of 1899 MacArthur, who had remained loyal to Otis, conceded to reporter H. Irving Hancock that:

> When I first started in against these rebels, I believed that Aguinaldo's troops represented only a faction. I did not like to believe that the whole population of Luzon—the native population that is—was opposed to us and our offers of aid and good government. But after having come this far, after having occupied several towns and cities in succession, and having been brought much into contact with both insurrectos and amigos, I have been reluctantly compelled to believe that the Filipino masses are loyal to Aguinaldo and the government which he heads.[9]

By the end of the year, Otis's only other supporter in the military hierarchy, General Shafter in California, had joined Otis's critics in advising the military governor that the war was not over and that the only way that it could be won was by "more stringent" methods. Shafter explained to reporters in San Francisco that it might be necessary to kill half the native population in order to bring "perfect justice" to the surviving half. An outspoken veteran of Wounded Knee, Colonel Jacob Smith, informed report rs in the Philippines that, because the natives were "worse than fighting Indians," he had already adopted the appropriate tactics that he had learned fighting "savages" in the American West, without waiting for orders to do so from General Otis. This interview provoked a headline announcing that "Colonel Smith of 12th Orders All Insurgents Shot At Hand," and the *New York Times* enthusiastically endorsed Smith's lawlessness as "long overdue." Jake Smith considered discretion in talking to reporters as much a waste of time as were trials, and two years later he won infamy in the world's press as an American version of Spain's General Weyler.[10]

Some correspondents in the Philippines were as bloodthirsty as any soldier. They, too, attacked Otis for "leniency" and "soft measures," although they attributed these faults to the general's fear of the civilians on the Philippine Commission, "who have the 'welfare' of the poor nigger at heart." One correspondent charged:

> To make some show, in view of the commission, Otis has established petty courts of justice (or rather a travesty) over which Filipino shyster lawyers preside. Fancy a court in the South presided over by a Negro judge and a white man as prisoner! What justice would he obtain? And this is the state of affairs here.[11]

Such correspondents served as mouthpieces for the generals who felt that the war could not be won unless distinctions betweeen Filipino civilians and soldiers were erased. Phelps Whitemarsh, a former missionary turned correspondent, wrote a blistering attack on Otis and the commission for putting leashes on the old Indian fighters. Of course, Senator Hoar was also responsible, not only for giving "immense help and confidence" to "our enemies," but also for intimidating the Administration. Contrary to "this misguided nanny and his associates," there were no "amigos" in the Philippines. "Everywhere one finds the same old hatred toward Americans, the same hope and belief in ultimate independence. With the exception of a mere handful, too insignificant, every Filipino is an *insurrecto* and wishes to drive the Americans from the islands." Unless "more stringent measures" are adopted, the war's end "will be a question of years, not months," Whitemarsh warned.[12]

As the rains showed signs of abating in October, Otis shifted his attention to the military campaign in the coming dry season. Despite his own resistance, a larger and better-equipped army had been forced on him. Richard Little of the *Chicago Tribune* painted a grim picture of the predicament facing the American command. The army occupied no more than 117 square miles of a total of 116,000 square miles, he claimed, or about one-tenth of one percent of the archipelago. It was virtually impossible for an American to venture out of

Manila with any degree of safety, Little warned. In effect, Otis was starting from scratch in the eyes of this correspondent.[13]

Actually, Little had exaggerated the picture, as bad as it was. During the rainy months, MacArthur had moved northward up the rail line and the Rio Grande to occupy most of eastern Pampanga, forcing Aguinaldo to move to Tarlac. Once the rains began to abate, a brilliant pincers movement planned by Lawton was executed. MacArthur pushed up the central plain toward Tarlac, Bayonbong, and Dagupan, although he was denied the use of the railroad beyond Angeles. Sealing off each pass into the mountains, Lawton moved up the eastern edge of the plain, while Wheaton made an amphibious landing from the Gulf of Lingayen to join up with Lawton at Dagupan north of the Filipinos retreating from MacArthur's offensive. It was an excellent plan, only frustrated by Otis's caution (see map, p. 223).

Otis had refused to allow Lawton to establish advanced supply bases earlier, when swollen rivers would have supported supply boats. As a result, Lawton's encircling movement got bogged down as boats were grounded, and he could not move much faster than his carabao-drawn carts and Chinese bearers. In desperation, he launched his chief of cavalry, General Samuel Young, and a "flying column" with very limited supplies, restricted to what each man could carry, to close the trap at Dagupan. Otis would never have approved of such a risky venture.

Meanwhile, Wheaton landed at San Fabian and, under verbal orders from Otis not to venture too far from the coast, took his time making contact with Young's forces. A feeble probe by Wheaton narrowly missed Aguinaldo at Rosario, and still he was reluctant to allocate his fresh troops to Young's exhausted expedition when it, without supplies or even shoes for many of its men and horses, started out in pursuit of the Filipino forces. Macabebe scouts provided Young with accurate intelligence, and had it not been for the betrayal of a Tagalog guide, Aguinaldo would have been trapped at Pozorrubio. As it was, Young captured Aguinaldo's hastily buried treasury, his printing press, his young son, and secretary of foreign affairs, Filipe Buencamino. Finally Young persuaded Wheaton to release Major Peyton March and a battalion to follow Aguinaldo fleeing into the mountains. March picked up the Filipino leader's mother and twenty-five American and many Spanish prisoners released to hasten the flight. At Tirad Pass, he faced General Gregorio del Pilar, the boy idol of the Filipino struggle, who fell while fighting a delaying action to cover his leader's retreat into the Cordillera. His body was stripped of clothing and possessions by souvenir hunters as March's battalion moved past him, and only days later did the Americans give him the hero's burial that he richly deserved.[14]

Lawton and Young were an excellent team in that they were both compe-

tent and daring and did not compete with each other for publicity. The eminent
success of these two generals had to have galled Otis inwardly. Given Lawton's
coverage in the press, Otis had to have felt threatened by and jealous of him,
and he hated Young. The latter had the temerity to pen a highly critical evalua-
tion of Otis for the War Department, which, foolishly, passed it on to the governor general. Otis vowed to destroy his career, but Young towered over Otis
both physically and professionally, just as Lawton did. Four years later, President Roosevelt would pass over Otis in favor of Young for the army's chief-of-
staff.

Otis's feelings, or his genuine cautiousness, may have motivated his orders
to Lawton to return to Manila and to leave Wheaton in command of the northern sector, even though Lawton had requested permission to cross the mountains into the Cagayan Valley before Aguinaldo got settled. But like MacArthur,
Lawton knew that he could defy Otis with impunity as long as he was successful, so he sent Captain Joseph Batchelor and 300 men anyway on a mini version
of his plan. Batchelor did not find Aguinaldo, but he met with astonishing success when Colonel Danilo Tirona surrendered to him with 1,100 men, 800
rifles, and other equipment. Aguinaldo had established a new, secret headquarters at Palanan in the mountain jungle of Isabella Province on Luzon's northeastern coast, but it was clear that his army in the north was, like Tirona,
thoroughly demoralized and ready to give up the struggle. It was the most impressive American victory in the war, rendered even more so by the fact that
the dry season had just begun. Otis faced an awesome credibility gap at home,
however, one that was not helped by his recycling of such shopworn and ridiculed phrases as "crushing blow" and "last movement of the war" to describe
Lawton's victory. The fact that Aguinaldo had not been captured further undermined the governor general's claim that his organization had been smashed for
good.[15]

Imperialist editors, of course, accepted Otis's claims at face value and began to discuss the imminent termination of the war with renewed confidence.
In their eyes, Lawton and Young were seasoned Indian fighters who knew how
to deal with savages and who would "pursue the rebel Filipinos just as they
relentlessly pursued the Modocs and Apaches in the triumph of civilization."
After all, Lawton had captured Geronimo, and "the puffed-up crack brained
egoists of Aguinaldo's had to realize that they were no match for him." The editor of the New York Times even chided the president for not recruiting a native
police force to replace the U.S. Army, now that the end of the war was so near.
"We shall hear very little of 'imperialism' as an issue from now on," another
editor fatuously predicted.[16]

In the midst of all this euphoria, Lawton was killed in a minor skirmish

outside Manila. While waiting for Otis to approve his plans for a major campaign in southern Luzon, he led a "scout-in-force," hardly appropriate for a
man of his rank, during an unseasonably late downpour on December 18. The
next morning, he confronted (ironically) General Lucerio Geronimo and 250
Filipino riflemen. His bright yellow slicker and white British pith helmet made
him an inviting target, particularly as he paraded upright behind his men, who
were firing from prone and kneeling positions. The "Pride of Indiana" was hit
when he returned to the front line after carrying his wounded young aide to the
rear.

But Lawton's death did not deflate the growing optimism of the imperialists. It took months for them to realize that Lawton's signal victory had merely
ended one phase of the war. Guerrilla warfare began in earnest with the year
1900. Having lost control over the central organization of the struggle, Aguinaldo delegated full authority to local commanders, which lessened the bitter
internecine and ethnic jealousies and rivalries in many areas. Major cities and
towns were abandoned in favor of the bush from which to launch guerrilla attacks. Local officials were instructed to appear to cooperate with the Americans
while serving as intelligence sources for local bands. At the same time the U.S.
Army began to expand its occupation of major cities, and even small hamlets.
General John C. Bates, who had succeeded Lawton, met only token resistance
as he carried out his predecessor's plans to occupy southern Luzon. The Visayan island group was occupied beyond Panay, where General Hughes had
beaten all formal opposition. The newly promoted Brigadier General William
Kobbe led detachments to Mindanao and Jolo in the Sulu group. Few editors
noticed that the army was being spread very thin in isolated garrisons, which
increased its vulnerability to guerrilla warfare. Station commanders did not
have to wonder for long what had happened to the armed Filipinos who had
disappeared upon their arrival. Telegraph lines were cut as fast as they could be
strung and repaired. Supply wagons were subject to well-planned hit-and-run
attacks. As soon as pursuing parties became the least bit careless, they fell into
ingenious ambushes. Soon, American editors became dismayed at the "renewal
of the war" everywhere, even in areas thought to have been completely
pacified.

As American frustration escalated, so did the stories of less than civilized
reprisals on both sides. One "treacherous official," under the pretense of leading Lieutenant Kohler to a cache of insurgent arms, led his force into the arms
of bolomen, who butchered the Americans. A soldier's letter bragged that Lieutenant Colonel House beat to death the several officials involved in the betrayal
of Kohler and his men. General Funston announced that to avenge Kohler he
had summarily executed twenty-four prisoners. Later, amidst rumors that he

and House were slated for courts-martial, Funston insisted that the twenty-four prisoners had been killed while "attempting to escape." Upon reporting this, the *Press-Knickerbocker*'s editor observed bitterly, "Meanwhile, the work of Mr. McKinley's 'benevolent assimilation' goes along."[17]

As the first anniversary of the war passed and another rainy season approached, the euphoric mood produced by Lawton's victory five months earlier soured into one of despair and bitter doubts that the war would ever end. But 1900 was an election year, and Republicans became alarmed that McKinley would have to go to the polls a scant six months away with the war still dragging on. "The dullest man must be impressed by the record. Another rainy season is at hand and the islands are less pacified than a year ago," warned the anti-imperialist, but loyally Republican *Call*. Even imperialist editors conceded that the entire archipelago was "a huge hornet's nest" and that "we merely hold a few towns, and that by main force." It was imperative to the Republicans among them that "the President appreciate the danger signals" that the war would be "a fearful stumbling block" in November. Generals Young and Bell defied Otis and informed the press that they were still desperately short of troops in Luzon and could not hold the towns taken. It was obvious to the staunchest imperialist that the country had been taken in a second time by Otis's lively imagination and self-serving fictional accounts. There was a bipartisan demand for the governor general's head, but the *Call*'s editor warned his colleagues that the war's end was still years away under any commander.[18]

For months rumors that Otis was about to be replaced, if not sacked in disgrace, necessitated the constant reaffirmation of the president's confidence in his commander. But clearly, some changes, if only cosmetic ones, were called for before the election campaign got under way. Finally, in April, it was announced that Otis, at his own request, would soon be relieved by Mac-Arthur. After twenty-one months in command, and "with the end of the war," the general had "earned a rest," the president explained. The press had an editorial field day with this announcement. "The opinion of the country is, that he ought to have taken it [the 'rest'] before he went to the Philippines," declared the *Kansas City Times*. The *Washington Post* suggested that "Otis might well have been 'permitted' to come home twelve months ago." Other editors expressed relief that the change in command would at least end "all the fairy tales" spun by this "grandmotherly martinet" masquerading as a general. "MacArthur may not do better, but the country will be glad that 'Otis is over,' if the war isn't," observed the *New York World*.[19]

Although he consistently got bad press, Otis rarely disappointed reporters. Immediately following the change of command ceremony in Manila on May 2, a reporter needled Otis by asking him if he thought that the war was over. "I have held that opinion for some time that the thing is entirely over. I cannot see where it is possible for the guerrillas to effect any reorganization, concentrate any force or accomplish anything serious," Otis exclaimed. The flabbergasted editor of the *Call* explained to his readers that on May 1, the very day before Otis made this insane declaration to the press, elements of the Forty-Third Volunteer Infantry had lost nineteen men on Luzon while fighting their way out of a trap that their captain described as extremely well-planned and well-executed. On May 3 regulars in the Twenty-Sixth Infantry had to battle their way out of yet another clever ambush on Panay. They abandoned their dead and severely wounded as they escaped with heavy casualties. "The Filipinos are not conquered. Their spirit is not broken. Their capacity for resistance has not begun to be exhausted," the *Call* declared as Otis embarked on his long sea voyage back to San Francisco.[20]

With the election only five months away, it was absolutely essential that the Republicans convince the public that Otis had won the war. To this end, a series of elaborate receptions were planned, and McKinley set the tone by sending a cable to Otis on the eve of his departure from Manila congratulating him on his "victory over the forces of barbarism in the Philippines." A monumental effort was to be mounted to convert this fiction into a reality for the electorate. Gala celebrations nationwide would outstrip the honors rendered to Dewey on his triumphal return. In New York, the *World* described the honors that awaited Otis as his transport approached the California coast:

> Otis to Return Like a Conquering Hero
> McKinley Plans a Roman Triumph For His Homecoming
> Highest of All Honors
> No General of Late War Has Received Any Such Distinctions.[21]

General Otis played the role to the hilt, pompously strutting down the gangplank on June 3 to the tune of "See the Conquering Hero Comes." After exchanging salutes and inspecting the troops with General Shafter, who had assembled an honor guard for him, Otis strode over to the waiting press corps to announce to them, "not for the first time be it observed—that the war in the Philippines was ended," the *New York World* reported. No longer able to confine the sarcasm to its editorial page, the *World* pointed out that while the general was at sea fierce fighting had erupted in the Philippines and his successor had already sent off an urgent request to Washington for additional troops:

> This only shows how indiscreet it is for a commander who has only just come ashore to talk for publication before he has time to consult the newspaper and learn what has been going on since he went abroad. General

Otis will have discovered by this time that he had scarcely left Manila before his successor General MacArthur felt obliged to cable Washington for "more troops". . . . "The war is ended," no doubt as far as General Otis is concerned—but General MacArthur is eagerly waiting for those "more troops."[22]

Otis ignored the journalistic jibes as he made his way slowly across the nation as guest of honor and "conquering hero" at increasingly elaborate ceremonies. It was as if the country wanted desperately to share the general's self-deception as he repeatedly declared in one city after another that "the war in the Philippines was over" and that "it had been over for some time." The only references in his speeches to different viewpoints were sporadic attacks on the "slanderers," reporters and editors, who fed on lies to criticize his command and to write "about depredations committed by men of our army." When Otis reached Washington, all doubts were washed away in a sea of toasts to his "victory" and in the thunderous applause a jointly convened Congress gave him in its standing ovation. The president thanked him again and congratulated him on his splendid military achievement in the Philippines. As one headline put it, "Otis Is Glorified By Uncle Sam."[23]

The culmination of the general's triumphant homecoming was reached in his hometown of Rochester, New York. The entire city was decked out in flags and red, white, and blue bunting. A parade several miles long honored the native son who had gone off to the Civil War and returned almost forty years later the "hero of the Philippines." Between the blizzards of confetti and the endless flattering toasts, Otis found time to write an article for *Frank Leslie's Weekly*, whose correspondent in the Philippines, E. C. Ross, was one of the general's "favorites." He simply put into writing what he had been telling the admiring crowds for weeks. Apologizing disarmingly for not being able to tell his readers when the war would be over, he explained, "That is impossible for the war is already over. The insurrection ended some months ago, and all we have to do now is to protect the Filipinos against themselves and to give protection to those natives who are begging for it . . . against the wild and savage bands who are too lazy to work." He assured his readers there was no need to worry about Aguinaldo, who was "merely the figurehead" for "armed robbers" and who could be "safely left skulking about the mountains." But above all, Otis concluded, "there will be no more fighting of any moment."[24]

This article produced more editorial hoots and catcalls. Under such headings as "The Incorrigible Otis," "Otis in Wonderland," and "Otis Through A Looking Glass," anti-imperialist and Democratic editors expressed their suspicion that the general had lost his senses altogether. With his unfailing touch for the worst possible timing, Otis's article reached the public along with news that an American battalion had fallen into a Filipino trap and suffered heavy losses. Reports of ambushes on the island of Mindanao accelerated at the same time, with ever-increasing American casualty lists. To some editors, these events indicated that the war in the Philippines was just beginning. The editor of the *Call* advised his colleagues that Otis actually believed what he was saying and was to be pitied. He urged each to turn his editorial gun on the myth-makers who knew they were lying. The reception given Otis was transparently a political act, he declared, aimed at fooling the voters into believing that the war was over.[25]

Teddy Roosevelt, at the New York Republican State Convention, beat everyone to the punch by declaring in April of 1900 that "the insurrection in the Philippine Islands has been overcome." The Republican National Convention followed suit two months later, making this fiction the official truth by declaring that "the American people have conducted and in victory concluded a war for liberty and human rights." This was one of the rare occasions that the "insurrection" was acknowledged as a "war" by Republicans. Possibly because it was over—by fiat, at least—it was safe to give it this label. The editor of the *Philadelphia Record* complained of the misrepresentations being handed out to the American people as they prepared to go to the polls to pass judgment on the man primarily responsible for the mess:

> Evidently a herculean effort is being put forth to make the facts square with the frequent announcement that "the war is over." The situation is dreadfully embarrassing for an executive reelection. Our sovereignty does not extend beyond our guns.[26]

One last detail to be handled in June, 1900, was that of an appropriate reward for its returned "conquering hero." Otis must at least be kicked upstairs lest anyone suspect he had been removed from command for incompetency. There was speculation that he would be made the secretary of war in McKinley's next cabinet if Root became the president's running mate. When Roosevelt instead was given the nod for the vice-presidency, rumors circulated that he would become the next chief-of-staff when General Miles was forced to retire. Miles enhanced the belief that he would quickly be eased out of his position by committing an unforgivable offense. Because he was so eager to assume command of the army in the Philippines in order to gain more recent martial glory as the means of obtaining the presidency, Miles publicly disagreed with the official decree that the war was over, or that its end was even "in sight."[27]

Otis was given the Department of Great Lakes and took command of its headquarters in Chicago, there presumably to await a more appropriate award.

But a year later, Roosevelt was in the White House, and it was obvious that Otis had reached the end of his military line. He quietly retired and exchanged his sword for a pen to write a few more articles, alternately defending his "victory" and attacking the anti-imperialists for encouraging the Filipinos to continue the struggle after he had decisively defeated them.

7

The American Opposition Organizes

In spite of the long history of opposition to American expansion, both continental and overseas, no formal anti-imperialist organization existed in 1898 when the news of Dewey's victory electrified the nation. A small group of Bostonians, most of whom had opposed the war with Spain in the first place, fully understood immediately the temptations involved. They feared that tradition alone would not deter American leaders from keeping far-flung Spanish colonies in the Pacific. They feared even more the militarism that imperialism would spawn. Senator Carl Schurz of New York, himself a refugee from German militarism, joined a prominent Boston lawyer and reformer, Moorfield Storey, in a vain attempt to sober a jubilant population with warnings that the success at Manila Bay might lead to a formal American empire. Such foreboding was lost, however, in the wave of self-congratulatory hysteria sweeping the nation.

One month later, another Boston reformer, Gamaliel Bradford, placed in the *Evening Transcript* a notice announcing a mass meeting at Faneuil Hall to protest the "insane and wicked ambition which is driving the nation to ruin."[1] The hour was late, however, as on the very day of the meeting Congress passed a joint resolution calling for the annexation of the Hawaiian Islands. If Bradford was disappointed over the response to his clarion call, he kept it to himself. Between 200 and 400 people showed up, half of them women; virtually all were familiar faces associated with other "good causes." The same rituals used to initiate previous crusades were reenacted at the meeting on June 15: the opening diatribe against this new evil, long and erudite, to convince an audience already opposed to imperialism; the retelling of Rome's fate to illustrate what happens to a republic when it embarks on the path to empire; the unanimous passing of familiar-sounding resolutions; and the formation of committees, new or recycled, to combat imperialism. As habitual political losers (except on the issue of abolitionism), these reformers usually concocted conspiracies to explain their

104

many failures at the polls. Hence it was only "a few ambitious men in Washington" who were "leading the nation on this new and dangerous course," not only against cherished traditions, but also against the specific wishes of its people, Storey informed the gathering. This political cabal was not simply in pursuit of power and martial glory, he explained, but it was also attempting to divert the nation's attention away from serious domestic problems, such as "a disordered currency, unjust system of taxes, the debasing influence of money at elections, [and] the uses of offices as spoils." The ease with which each resolution passed helped to resurrect the illusion that once again theirs was a popular cause. Protected by a cloak of self-righteousness, these professional reformers refused to face the reality that their causes, however just, were rarely the concern of very many of their compatriots.[2]

Shortly after the meeting at Faneuil Hall, Storey's Reform Club, at his urging, appointed a committee to oppose imperialism. In November, it arranged a series of meetings of reformers to discuss the formation of an organization to fight overseas expansion. These meetings were held in the Boston office of the businessman and perennial reformer, Edward Atkinson. Charles Francis Adams, descendant of two presidents and brother of Henry Adams, described these meetings as "pretty dreary and discouraging." But he had always been more realistic than the other reformers, and he worried about the public image of this group as "a parcel of cranks." He was certain that his colleagues would dilute the main concern in a potpourri of lost causes. Nevertheless, Adams permitted his name to be used as a vice-president of the newly formed New England Anti-Imperialist League.[3]

George Boutwell, ex-governor of Massachusetts and a former member of Grant's cabinet, was named president of the League, while Erving Winslow and Francis Osborne served as secretary and treasurer, respectively. David Haskins, Albert Parsons, James Monroe, William Endicott, and James Meyers made up the executive committee, which was chaired by Winslow Warren. Forty-five vice-presidents held honorary, rather than functional, positions and, also, created the illusion of a broader base of support since they were carefully selected to include labor leaders and southern politicos whose outlooks were very different from those of the League's patrician leaders. Almost all of the latter were liberal Republicans or mugwumps who had broken once with the party over the corruption of the Grant regime, and again in 1884 to support Grover Cleveland over James G. Blaine. The exception was Boutwell, who had remained loyal throughout the years. Parsons considered himself "a true independent," while Endicott, Warren, and Haskins were Democrats.[4]

Within months of its founding, the League claimed 25,000 members, a number that swelled to "more than 70,000" within a year. If accepted at face value, this figure probably represents its peak membership. The League's consistent failure both at the polls and to collect anywhere near the anticipated "ten million signatures" on a petition protesting the president's decision to keep all of the Philippines belie their claims. The preposterous target for the petition represented eighty percent of the total vote cast in 1896, and that the group expected to reach it betrays their sublime self-confidence and utter lack of realism. In December, Senator Hoar presented the petition to McKinley with a mere 2,000 signatures, to which another 3,000 were added ten days later—a minuscule fraction of the announced goal. It is small wonder that the numerical claims and projections of the League's leadership were often considered suspect. More practical anti-imperialists, such as Hoar and Adams, ended up having little to do with this organization.[5]

To enhance the impression that anti-imperialist sentiment was sweeping the country, the organization was soon converted into the nation-wide Anti-Imperialist League, with offices in Portland, Oregon, Los Angeles, Minneapolis, Chicago, Cincinnati, Philadelphia, Washington, D.C., New York, and, of course, Boston. Boutwell opened an office in the nation's capital for its symbolic value, but, significantly, he continued to operate out of the "Hub." The League reverted to its original title in 1904, when it became obvious that it was not a national movement. By no means, however, should the League's efforts be considered a total failure. The League sponsored mass meetings in various cities and promulgated countless pamphlets and broadsides to educate the public on the situation in the Philippines. Every publication bore the instruction to pass it along "to some person who would give it careful consideration." The League estimated that each piece of literature reached up to one hundred readers. When combined with the claim that several hundred pieces had been distributed, the number of persons exposed to the circulars comes to possibly thirty million, or forty percent of the population and practically every adult American. This claim also appears to be inflated. Besides, the League's literature tended to be intellectual, even pedantic, and put forth historical, constitutional, economic, and moral arguments that could not have had much mass appeal.

Had the League asked two of its vice-presidents, Senator "Pitchfork Ben" Tillman and Samuel Gompers, to inveigh against imperialism in the manner of their earthy philippics against Negroes and Chinese, its arguments would have had greater mass appeal. But these tactics would have offended the fine sensibilities of its patrician leadership, which was outraged enough by the Ohio Silver Democrat John Lentz calling President McKinley a murderer, and by ex-governor of Illinois John Altgelt leading cheers for Aguinaldo in the middle of a speech—both at League-sponsored rallies. Significantly, such speeches were not reproduced in League publications as were other, more refined and politically correct, discourses.[6]

The leaders of the League were concerned not only over the propriety of radical statements and actions, but also over lending credence to the demagogic charges of their critics, who had characterized them as little more than "unhung traitors." The *Inter-Ocean* asked, "Why should Chicago tolerate a conference of anti-imperialist traitors any more than it should tolerate a convention of acknowledged incendiaries or anarchists?" The *New York Times* suggested that the League go one step beyond simply playing host to a Lentz or Altgeld and "send rifles, Maxim guns and ammunition to the Filipinos," so that it would, at least, "be more openly and frankly treasonable." In Philadelphia, the *Press* posed the historical analogy, "What would have happened during the Civil War if a public meeting had been held . . . to cheer Jeff Davis and denounce Lincoln as a murderer?" The commander of the New York chapter of the Grand Army of the Republic had no doubts about the answer to that question and demanded that all League members be stripped of their citizenship and "denied the protection of the flag they dishonor."[7]

In reality, the leaders of the League were extraordinarily cautious and conservative. The executive committee did not approve of even the milder antics of Edward Atkinson, who wrote to the War Department for a list of soldiers serving in the Philippines so that he might send to them his privately published essays, bearing such titles as "The Cost of the National Crime," "The Hell of War and Its Penalties," and "Criminal Aggression: By Whom Committed?" Failing to receive a reply, Atkinson announced to the press that he was sending copies to Generals Otis, Lawton, and Miller, Admiral Dewey, the correspondent J. F. Bass, and to Schurman and Dean Worcester on the Philippine Commission, "in order to test the right of citizens of the United States to the free use of the mail." Postmaster General Charles Emory Smith foolishly took the bait and ordered that the pamphlets be seized in San Francisco. The attorney general hinted that he would have Atkinson indicted for treason and sedition. Crucified in the press as a "latter-day copperhead," Atkinson actually enjoyed his new role as a national cynosure. He effusively and sarcastically thanked the Administration for calling national attention to his essays and increasing the demand for them in every state in the union.[8]

Henceforth, anti-imperialists were denounced as "agitators of the Atkinson-Altgeld stripe" or "supporters of the three A's"—Aguinaldo being the third A. Boston's *Times-Herald* concluded that "whatever may be thought of the judgement and motives of the Boston school of national slanderers, there can be no doubt as to the treasonable nature of their acts." Arguing that Atkinson's stunt was "proof enough" that the League was "responsible for much unnecessary loss of life in the Philippines," the *Times* in Minneapolis concluded that "almost any other government would have a few Atkinsons in jail by now."[9]

Many anti-imperialist editors were uncomfortable with Atkinson's ploy and called upon the League "to squelch him" before he further damaged their cause. "There is a huge difference between criticizing the policy of the government and tampering with the soldiers who are fighting its battles," worried the *Omaha Bee*, which was moving into the imperialist camp and may have finally been pushed there by Atkinson. "Whether the practices of Edward Atkinson and his anti-expansionist associates are seditious or merely meddlesome, they are utterly distasteful to the vast majority of Americans," cautioned the usually neutral *New York Herald*. Atkinson also had journalistic defenders, who argued that the Philippines could not be considered a legitimate war zone since the war was "unauthorized by Congress" and even insisted that it was McKinley who was lawless. Another editor considered it an "insulting reflection on the patriotism and manhood of the volunteers to say that they could be influenced to mutiny by having literature placed in their hands." The soundest advice was in the *Boston Journal*, which warned the government that Atkinson would consider a jail sentence "the crowning glory of his life."[10]

The League straddled the issue by disapproving of sending propaganda to soldiers in combat while denouncing the government's "mailed fist" response and making it an issue of freedom of speech. Atkinson was so stung by its disapproval that he offered to resign as a League vice-president, but Winslow would not hear of it. Nevertheless, Atkinson did not abandon the tactic, frantically trying to recapture the limelight with a new batch of "seditious essays for the Philippines." He teased Smith that "the demand is not universal, and I write to ask if it is practical for you to issue an order forbidding its circulation in the mails that go to 'our new possessions.'" The postmaster general had recovered his poise, however, and refrained from rescuing "this Boston crank" from oblivion.[11]

General Shattuck, an Ohio congressman and retired soldier, was not so wise. He returned the essays with instructions "to take my name off your list. I am no traitor to my country." Atkinson parlayed this request into an acrimonious eight-letter exchange that buried Shattuck in words. When the press ignored the incident, Atkinson privately published the letters in "A Special Edition for Circulation in the First District of Ohio and Other Districts Now Misrepresented." A covering letter promised to take Shattuck's name not only off Atkinson's mailing list, but also off "the list of Congressional candidates for 1900." Shattuck replied that "not a precinct in the First Ohio District would elect you or one of your kind as a delegate to a convention to nominate a director for the county poorhouse." A voluminous letter from Boston in response ended the debate, as Shattuck learned that it was wiser to give Atkinson the last word.[12]

Irreverent speeches at League-sponsored rallies evoked embarrassing boos, hisses, and cries of treason. Chicago's Professor J. Lawrence Laughlin was even threatened with violence when he called Old Glory "an emblem of tyranny and butchery." Ex-congressman Charles Towne angered students at the University of Michigan when he predicted the fall of the United States "within a single year . . . from the moral leadership of mankind into the common brigandage of the robber nations of the world." The *Times*, choosing to take literally sarcastic suggestions for altering the Statue of Liberty since the "colonial war" made it "an awkward object" so visible in the harbor, accused one speaker in New York City of inciting his audience to vandalism. The speaker had suggested extinguishing the torch, lowering the lady's arm, bowing her head, changing the inscription to read "Liberty Conquering the World," or simply shipping the statue back to France. Such rhetorical excess was not wise in an era of intense nationalism, which the League's leaders fully understood.[13]

Frequently a spectator, rather than the authorized speaker, would demand from the audience "three cheers for Aguinaldo," but the League got the blame nevertheless. The *Call* reported uneasily that far too often the cheers "were given with surprising vigor." Another anti-imperialist editor worried that such conduct would discourage loyal Americans who opposed the war from participating in such rallies. "Cooper Union has been the scene of all sorts of demonstrations by all sorts of people in the interest of all sorts of things, but probably never before was a Cooper Union crowd asked to cheer a leader of a people with whom this country is at war."[14]

The League was also held responsible for other radical acts totally beyond the pale of its sponsored activities, acts that could never have been given the imprimatur of that organization. Some war protesters, usually passing out League literature without having been authorized to do so, stationed themselves outside recruiting stations to discourage volunteers. For the most part they were ignored or denounced as traitors or copperheads. In all probability, only the fact that the protesters were mostly women and older men saved them from being thrashed. One frustrated group attempted to restrain physically some young men about to enter a recruiting station. "Meadville, Pennsylvania, seems to be afflicted by the presence of Aguinaldinos even more reckless in act and statement than those of Boston," the *New York Times* declared of this incident. Another group in Boston embarrassed their cause by collecting refuse in an American flag during an anti-war demonstration.[15]

Montague Leverson, an elderly resident of Fort Hamilton, tried to communicate with Aguinaldo, to advise him to kidnap and put on trial for "piracy" some American officials and name McKinley and Otis as codefendants. "Piracy would be shown by conducting a war in violation of the usages of civilized warfare, and the proof would consist in the fact of the consent to killing defenseless prisoners and non-combatants, men, women, and children, in cold blood and in robbery by officers and soldiers of non-combatants," he advised. Carefully identifying himself as a member of the Anti-Imperialist League, Leverson declared, "If I were not an old man of more than 69 years, I would willingly aid you in your just defense." Ignoring, of course, that membership was open to anyone and that Leverson held no policy-making position in the League, which had never authorized him to advise Aguinaldo, imperialist editors cited Leverson's letter as proof that the League was seditious.[16]

The League was also held accountable for actions by nonmembers, even those who held that organization in utter contempt for its cautious attack on the war. In Los Angeles, for example, Morris J. Swift, an avowed socialist who perceived the war in the Philippines as part of a worldwide capitalist conspiracy, formed his own organization, The Filipino Liberation Society. Probably no more than a handful of members sent off antiwar petitions to American soldiers in the Philippines. The League was blamed in spite of its disavowal of even the remotest connection with Swift, of whom the leaders probably had never heard before this incident. Nevertheless, the obscure Leversons and Swifts set off the imperialist press on a crusade to jail every member of the League—if not to string them up to the nearest lamp post. Cooler heads advised, however, that "the blathering of such perverse lunatics," "aunties," or "little Americans" was harmless. To bring them to trial would render their "mad ravings" more significant than they actually were. "Of course, the scribblings of these professional anti-everythings" should "be kept out of the hands of the young, for anything more immoral and unpatriotic has yet to be developed, since the days of the copperheads," counseled *Harper's Weekly.*[17]

Unfortunately, some of the scorn heaped on anti-imperialists was richly deserved. They seemed hopelessly out of touch with political reality at times. No individual symbolized this remoteness more effectively than the League's president, George Boutwell. At age 81, he was a relic of the Grant regime, and as Grant's secretary of the treasury, he had been responsible for some of the worst scandals of that Administration. Oblivious to Grant's public image, Boutwell tried to persuade the ex-president to run again in 1880. If Boutwell's name was remembered at all in 1899, it must have conjured up unpleasant and musty associations.[18]

Another ancient hack recruited as a vice-president of the League was McKinley's former secretary of state and long-time senator from Ohio, John Sherman. While his enlistment may have seemed like a great coup at the time, it underscores some of the major weaknesses of the anti-imperialist movement. Sherman was obviously senile and had been a constant source of embarrassment for the Administration during his brief stint as the nation's top diplomat. He had publicly denounced the Spanish as "barbarous robbers" and called on Congress to declare war. His contributions at cabinet meetings became so rambling and confused that the president had to bypass him and deal directly with his assistants. When McKinley could not keep Sherman away from the press, he nudged him into a retirement long overdue. The *Nation* described the episode as "one of the most discreditable in our political history." In his confused state, Sherman interpreted McKinley's action as a betrayal, and so this leading jingoist before the war, who once demanded that Hawaii be made a county of the state of California, suddenly became an anti-imperialist. But even in his younger, more rational days, Sherman was described by one reporter as "the most active wobbler in public life."[19]

While the League seemed indiscriminate, and even opportunistic, in recruiting Sherman, Tillman, Gompers, and others as officers, it failed to attract other prominent, more genuine and effective anti-imperialists, who preferred to function outside its fold. Of these, the most conspicuous was Senator Hoar. Although he shared some of the priggishness and intellectual arrogance of the professional reformers behind the League, Hoar was too practical to operate outside of his party. He certainly was not going to forsake the Republicans to join a group of perennial losers. In fact, Hoar and the League leaders had a mutual contempt for each other, one that was enhanced by their initial, futile efforts to cooperate in opposing imperialism. Hoar had suggested a more narrow focus for the opposition and warned that the annexation of Hawaii was already a fait accompli and that personal attacks on McKinley would be inappropriate and counterproductive. But the aging reformers who directed the League could not heed such practical suggestions. They insisted on including the obviously popular annexation of Hawaii, and the even more popular war with Spain, which only served to divide the anti-imperialists. In the end, it would appear that the League leaders and Hoar hated each other more than they hated the imperialists. Actually, Hoar was a far more effective opponent of imperialism and continued to struggle for Philippine independence long after men like Atkinson had lost interest. Imperialist editors, in fact, acknowledged Hoar's effectiveness by casting him as pariah for having betrayed not only his country, but his party as well. In political cartoons, Hoar was depicted as Judas, or sometimes as Brutus, in a Roman toga, stealing away from a fallen American soldier and carrying a bloody knife labeled "speech."[20]

Another crucial political leader missed by the League was the powerful Speaker of the House, Thomas Brackett Reed, whose influence in that chamber was so great he was called "the Czar." His enormous size and caustic wit enhanced his power. Once when President Harrison went on a jingoistic rampage, Reed suggested that he take on the Chileans himself since he was "just about their size." He told Teddy Roosevelt, "Theodore, if there is one thing for which I admire you, it is your original discovery of the ten commandments." He bestowed upon President McKinley the perfect accolade: "The Emperor of Expediency." Reed also had exceptional political courage, as evidenced by his having held up, against great pressure, the appropriations to prepare the country for war with Spain and the bill annexing Hawaii. Of the annexation of the Philippines he complained, "We have about 10,000,000 Malays at $2.00 a head, and nobody knows what it will cost to pick them." When this barb proved to be an all too accurate premonition, Reed pushed the point again in a later debate over appropriations to run the Philippine war:

> I have to hunt all over your figures even to find out how much each yellow man costs us in the bush. As I make it out he costs us $30 per Malay and he is still in the bush. Why didn't you purchase him of Spain F.O.B. with definite freight rates and insurance paid?[21]

Reed's humor would have produced doubts about his sincerity in the moralistic and deadly serious atmosphere of the League's headquarters. A splinter group of anti-imperialists planning a third party did approach Reed as a possible candidate in 1900, just as he retired from Congress. But Reed was much too shrewd to seek the presidency on a single issue, particularly one as unpopular as anti-imperialism. At any rate, Reed's pragmatism had to clash with the moral absolutism of these reformers. The lack of a sense of compromise doomed the cause of anti-imperialism from the beginning, although given the nationalistic mood and the inertial effects of the war with Spain, it is unlikely that any changes could have salvaged the cause at this time.

Perhaps a bigger mistake was the failure of the League even to attempt to court McKinley. By perceiving the world in black and white, the League's leaders were unable to distinguish between a McKinley and a Roosevelt. Even after the president's decision to keep the Philippines, there were occasions when disillusionment over the war was particularly severe and direct persuasion for a compromise might have been tried. During the summer of 1899, many doubts about the wisdom of annexing the Philippines were expressed by some of McKinley's advisors and imperialist politicians. Upon his retirement as chief of the Bureau of Statistics, Worthington C. Ford warned that it would be impossible to realize any of the "rosy prophecies that have been made freely as to [the islands'] commercial value." No less an imperialist than Senator Frye blamed General Merritt for having misled the peace commission in Paris as to the Filipino desire for independence and capacity to resist American rule. John Barret, a former diplomat and an advisor to the Administration on Asian affairs, conceded that summer that annexation of the islands had been a mistake and recommended offering the Filipinos independence under American protection, provided that the military bases could be retained.[22]

An increasing number of imperialist editors began to express very similar doubts, although few ever recommended American withdrawal. "The Philippines are pretty costly real estate," conceded the *New York Times*, "but the abandonment would entail consequences that only the hardiest experts in government finance would have the fortitude to figure out." Senator Carter assured the swelling ranks of doubters that "the Republican Party will return the Philippines as a matter of profit. This is a practical age. We are going to deal with the question on the basis of dollars and cents. Neither religion nor sentiment will have much influence in determining the verdict. The great question is 'will it pay?'" The *Call* let out some editorial hoots over the "crass and ignoble motives" beginning to show under all "the palaver" about "benevolent assimilation" now that things were not going so well in the war. The *Boston Traveller* wondered editorially who would reap the profits, if any, "the salesman, clerk, laborer, muni employee," who not only "shoulder the costs," but are further victimized by "the increased cost of living produced by inflation?"[23]

If McKinley would have modified his Philippine policy at any time, it would have to have been done with sufficient distance from his bid for reelection to avoid the wrath of the electorate. The summer of 1900 was both too close to the pending presidential election to be politically expedient and too far from the beginning of the war to escape the charge that American lives had been needlessly sacrificed. By the end of the third summer, McKinley had been assassinated and the opponents of the war were faced with a more genuine imperialist in the White House. It is most doubtful that the course of this history could have been altered at any time during those three years, but less rigid critics might have at least kept Senator Hoar company in his almost solitary and futile efforts to counter the influences that military leaders, the "young Turks," such as Lodge, Roosevelt, and Beveridge, and possibly even historical inertia, exerted on President McKinley.[24]

Much has been made of the high caliber of the opponents of imperialism in the League, whose list of officers reads like a combination of the *Social Register* and *Who's Who in America*. One historian has calculated that seventy-three percent of the League's leaders were college graduates, and that half of these went on to earn graduate or professional degrees, at a time when less than one percent of the population held college degrees. Most of these officers were products of Harvard, Yale, and Princeton, which places them in a very small elite. The names Adams, Storey, Bradford, Winslow, Higginson, Wentworth, Warren, and Endicott are among the oldest and most prominent in New England's history. Two college presidents became officers of the League, Henry Wade Rogers of Northwestern and David Starr Jordan of Stanford. Some of the nation's foremost scholars did likewise, such as Columbia's Felix Adler, Yale's William Graham Sumner, Chicago's Herman von Holst and Edwin Burritt Smith, and Cornell's I. J. McGinty. Samuel Bowles and Herbert Welsh, publishers of the *Springfield Republican* and Philadelphia's *City and State*, respectively, became vice-presidents, as did prominent members of the Protestant clergy, such as Leonard Woolsey Bacon, Charles H. Parkhurst, Theodore Cuyler, and New York's Episcopal Bishop Henry Codman Potter. Senator Carl Schurz, one of the nation's more erudite politicians in an age that produced little brilliance in government, also lent his name to the League. Indeed, if one goes beyond the confines of the League to include others who expressed their opposition to expansion and the war of conquest, it is possible to add many more distinguished names, including four university presidents, another dozen leading scholars, and, of course, Senator Hoar. Some, such as Hoar, Chicago's Professor J. Lawrence Laughlin, and Harvard philosopher William James, were more active critics and were constantly writing or speaking out against the course of events in the Philippines. Others made their opposition known less stridently, or even privately in some cases, as was true of Presidents Charles W. Eliot of Harvard, E. Benjamin Andrews of Brown, Daniel Coit Gilman of Johns Hopkins, and James Burrill Angell of Michigan; and of Professors Charles Eliot Norton and John Fiske of Harvard, John Burgess and Frederick W. Starr of Columbia, G. Stanley Hall of Clark, George P. Fisher of Yale, David Ames Welles of M.I.T., J. Scott Clark of Northwestern, Arthur Latham Perry of Williams, and the historian Goldwyn Smith. However one wants to define its membership, the anti-imperialist movement adds up to a very impressive group of distinguished Americans. Its leading historian, E. Berkeley Tompkins, concluded, "It is doubtful any other organization could boast a more outstanding leadership. If the nation could be said to possess an elite, these gentlemen would surely qualify."[25]

One problem of drawing conclusions from this assessment is that it is equally applicable to the leading proponents of imperialism. Henry Cabot Lodge, Theodore Roosevelt, or Albert Beveridge could match degrees, pedigrees or erudition with any anti-imperialist in or out of the Anti-Imperialist League. Leading men of the cloth, famous publishers, university presidents and scholars also justified and supported the conquest of the Philippines. This was true of Presidents Benjamin Ide Wheeler of California, Charles Kendall Adams of Wisconsin, David Jayne Hill, who left Rochester to become under-

secretary of state, and Jacob Gould Schurman, who left Cornell to head the first
Philippine Commission; and such prominent scholars as John Bach McMaster,
Albert Bushnell Hart, James Ford Rhodes, James Morton Callahan, Franklin
Henry Giddings, James Harvey Robinson, John Spencer Bassett, Nathaniel
Southgate Shaler, James Bradley Thayer, David Prescott Barrows, E. A. Ross,
Charles A. Cooley, Henry Pratt Judson, Abbott Lawrence Lowell, Paul Reinsch,
William McDougall, Dean Worcester, Theodore Woolsey, Jr., E. Spencer Bal-
dwin, and Woodrow Wilson. As was true of the anti-imperialists, some more actively supported their cause than did others. Worcester served on the Philippine Commission, and Barrows organized and ran the school system in the
islands. Some, such as Wilson, Woolsey, and Schurman initially opposed, or
were uneasy with, the acquisition of colonies, but ended up supporting the
Philippine venture. When it became impossible to deny that American atrocities were being committed, Schurman returned to the opposition in 1902.

Actually, few academicians left any record of their sentiments on the issue
of imperialism. Very limited evidence would suggest a rather even division
among those professors who did record their opinions on the issue, however
much the contemporary press distorted their activities. Turn-of-the-century
editors greatly exaggerated the criticism to be found in universities. The "professor" was a favorite target of the *New York Sun* for behaving as though he
were "a creature of special illumination and inspiration," whereas he was actually "a narrow minded prig, habitually regarding himself as superior to the 'un-
sheep-skinned man.'" Indeed, this "professor" was "little more than a mere
pedagogue and his intellectual equipment and acquired knowledge are not
such to make his 'thought' trustworthy or valuable or to prevent its being falla-
cious, immature and unsound," the editor assured his readers. Probably due to
this bias, he launched a series of attacks on the tenure system which "protected
these cranky and shallow reasoners," concluding that "no professor holds his
chair by divine right." Ironically, it was an advocate of imperialism in the academic community, E. A. Ross, who would prove this proposition, although his
firing in one of the nation's first tests of tenure rights had nothing to do with the
issue of expansion. (Professor Ross had the temerity to impugn the reputation
of his university's benefactor while Mrs. Leland Stanford was still alive and able
to exert pressure on Stanford's anti-imperialist president to get rid of him.) In
fact, the resignation of Henry Wade Rogers at Northwestern may have had
more to do with the issue, as his opposition to the Methodist McKinley's war
may have offended the Republican trustees at this Methodist school.[26]

The *Sun* was not alone in attacking professors for being the leading con-
tributors to the cause of anti-imperialism. New York's *Journal of Commerce* reminded its readers that professors were, more often than not, "Socialists," and

even "Populists," so that it should not be "surprising" that they would also be "sympathizers with a public enemy." The *Times* in New York gleefully endorsed this observation and expressed outrage over a petition urging Philippine independence from Harvard's faculty to President McKinley in May of 1899. Yet, by the editor's own account, the petition bore only seventeen signatures, at a time when Harvard's faculty numbered 134 teachers of professorial grade, 277 teachers and research fellows, and fifty-five officers. As though he were aware that his initial outrage may have been out of proportion, the editor added that "many friends of that institution will think that it would have been better if the number had been smaller." Likewise, imperialist editors in Chicago railed against the subversive influence of their new, but already prestigious, university, whereas very few of its professors were active in the antiwar protest. A Chicago petition to the president in 1900, similar to the one from Harvard a year earlier, attracted thirty-six signatures from a total of 130 who held professorial rank that year and many others in lower categories. Often, anti-imperialist editors would distort the number of dissenters in order to claim near unanimous support in the universities for their position. One exception to this view was the *Call*, whose editor angrily denounced the apologies for imperialism emanating from leading universities. "It is difficult to keep one's patience in reading such utterances from a professor," he declared. The political cartoons in the imperialist press depicted professors indoctrinating students to be ashamed of their country, or deliberately falsifying the facts to serve their own political ends. Anti-imperialist cartoons showed them as the latest victims of the nation's first colonial war, being gagged by President McKinley personally while seated next to an already gagged correspondent from Manila. Actually, the University of Chicago's ruling "Congregation" publicly reaffirmed its commitment to freedom of speech for its faculty in response to editorial demands that the war critics on campus be fired or silenced.[27]

If students had been indoctrinated at all, it appears more likely that it was to support expansion, if the wildly enthusiastic receptions that Roosevelt received on college campuses, including the University of Chicago, in 1900 is any gauge. Addressing a gathering of Harvard alumni and students, Professor Charles Eliot Norton was rudely hissed at when he criticized the government's handling of the Philippines. For every Professor James at Harvard, there was a Professor Giddings at Columbia who countered academic criticism of the war with intellectual justification of American conquest. It is impossible to guess even which position represented the faculty majority. If one looks closely at the university presidents and scholars already cited, however, it is possible to discern an important generational difference. Of the twenty-three mentioned as opponents of imperialism, only five were born after 1850, whereas eight were born before 1840, and five of the latter, before 1830. In contrast, the twenty-four cited as apologists for expansion were, on the whole, much younger. All but five of them were born after 1850, only two before 1840, and none before 1830. Six of them were born after 1860, and two of these after 1870. In 1900, the average age of these campus critics of the war was slightly under 58, while that of the imperialists cited was between 43 and 44. This difference reflects perfectly the gap in the average ages between nonacademic advocates and critics of expansion. Boutwell was well into his eighties at the turn of the century, Bradford was 69, and Schurz, 71. The average age of the officers of the League in 1900 was well over 60. In contrast, Roosevelt turned 42 that year, Beveridge, 38, and, at 50, Lodge was the old man of the group. Basically, most of the war's critics had reached manhood before, or during, the Civil War, when most imperialists were still infants. Any casual sample turns up an average 15-year difference between the two groups, not quite a generation, but sufficiently great for Roosevelt to be able to characterize anti-imperialists as "men of a bygone age having to deal with facts of the present."

Oddly enough, this age differential does not hold up when one examines the positions taken by intellectuals—novelists, poets, playwrights, and humorists—working outside of campus confines. But then, this group as a whole appears to have been overwhelmingly opposed to expansion and the war in the Philippines. Such writers as Thomas Bailey Aldrich, George W. Cable, Henry Blake Fuller, Edgar Lee Masters, Hamlin Garland, Edwin Arlington Robinson, Bliss Perry, William Vaughn Moody, John Jay Chapman, Lincoln Steffens, Finley Peter Dunne, and George Ade made clear their opposition to imperialism and the war. Only one of them was over forty. William Dean Howells, Charles Dudley Warner, Ambrose Bierce, and Joaquin Miller, pushing, or over, 60, were the old men of this group, except for Warner, who was 71 in 1900. Mark Twain, at 65, was the most famous—or, at least, his caustically critical essay, "To the Person Sitting in Darkness," has better survived in our historical imagination. But Twain got into the act very late in 1900, when the atrocities, both in China and in the Philippines, seemed to have gotten to him before any moral concerns over imperialism in general. Then, too, missionaries looting in China and the antics of General Funston were perfect targets for his brand of humor. Some intellectuals also provided support for the imperialist persuasion, such as Brooks Adams, Julian Hawthorne, Gertrude Atherton, Richard Hovey, William Bliss Carman, Walter Hines Page, and Julia Ward Howe. Surprisingly, many of the imperialists were women and, even more unexpectedly, Miss Howe was both 81 in 1900 and a social reformer, a combination that typically was found in anti-imperialists.[28]

The imperialists were no less successful than their critics in attracting

prominent men of the cloth to support their cause. Once McKinley made it
clear that he did not intend to interfere with the established Catholic church in
the islands, *ex cathedra* approval from Rome lined up the Catholic hierarchy
behind him. Perhaps his biggest coup was the weaning away of Bishop Potter
from the ranks of anti-imperialism. This League vice-president returned from
an army-sponsored tour of the islands a convert to imperialism in 1900. Potter
explained in *Century Magazine* that the leaders of the "rebellion" were "unscrupulous and ambitious men." Espousing the "white man's burden," Potter
declared:

> Time alone can demonstrate how far we may be able to persuade a fickle,
> restless, impulsive, unreasoning people, embittered by many wrongs at
> the hands of those we have expelled, or ought to expel [friars, probably], to
> trust us, to learn from us, and under our tutelage to grow into the status of
> competent citizens in a self-governing state.[29]

Needless to say, this article infuriated his former friends, who carried on a
running debate with him. "I think it ill-advised and unfortunate that we originally held the Philippines. But I think also that to abandon them *now* would be
to abandon them to internal warfare of rival leaders and rival tribes. At present
they are no more fit to lead themselves, or organize a government, than a parcel of children," the prelate wrote in defense of his change of heart. When it
was suggested that his army-sponsored tour may have been rigged, Potter
angrily answered, "It does not follow that because you think otherwise persons who differ from you are frauds and time servers. They have seen the
Philippines."[30]

During the Boxer crisis, Potter carried his apostasy further by praising
McKinley's contribution of American troops to the European invasion of China.
"She has been guilty of the gravest crimes against international rights and com-
munities. Let her be punished as she deserves," the bishop wrote of China
in *Century Magazine.* Not until 1901, when reports of western excesses in punishing China and of increased American atrocities in the Philippines became
impossible to deny, did Potter revert to his original opposition to imperialism. Meanwhile, throughout his political vagaries, he remained listed on the
League's masthead as a vice-president.[31]

Not only did the imperialists and their critics draw from the same social
strata for the most part, but more surprisingly, there was even some ideological
overlapping. Of course, the terms "imperialism" and "anti-imperialism" are se-
mantically and historically confusing. There were enormous intragroup differences between McKinley, Taft, and Roosevelt on one hand, and between
Atkinson, Storey, and Tillman on the other. Some anti-imperialists not only had

uneven personal histories on the issue of overseas expansion, but a number advocated the more subtle forms of imperialism that were to evolve in the twentieth century. Thus, Carnegie had cabled McKinley during the war with Spain
to keep Puerto Rico—and possibly Cuba, the Teller amendment forbidding the
latter notwithstanding. He also advised the president to swap the Philippines
for the British West Indies, nearer to home. But essentially, he argued that formal empires were obsolete because economic penetration could achieve control over foreign lands without the cost of conquest and administration. Atkinson argued along the same lines and, on the pages of his *Anti-Imperialist*, of all
places, that the English economic controls over Egypt could be the basic model
for the United States, rather than her military conquest of India. "Lord Cromer
administers the affairs of Egypt under a khedive," he wrote with obvious admiration for the resultant reduction in overhead costs. Schurz, Jordan, and William Graham Sumner advanced similar alternatives to the military conquest of
"backward" people. What he called "the peaceful conquest of Mexico" was, in
Jordan's eyes, "a perfectly legitimate form of expansion." He recommended
that the "Mexican experience" be expanded on a global scale. "We could fill all
of the tropical countries with consular agents, men trained to stand for good
order and to work for American interests, for less than it costs to subdue a single tropical island," Jordan enthused. To classify this "peaceful penetration," he
coined the term "permeation." Professor Sumner endorsed a similar idea and
argued that it would be at long last a cure for the "earth hunger" that had
caused so much war.[32]

One historian of the anti-imperialist movement, Robert Beisner, concluded that only "in their advocacy of free trade and opposition to direct control
over foreign territories" can these critics of the annexation of the Philippines
accurately be labeled "anti-imperialists":

> They favored subtle forms of American domination and looked on the
> world as a society in which some nations were more equal than others, in
> which American commercial agents were granted special privileges, Amer-
> ican government officials were treated with special deference, and the
> American navy was allowed special access to harbors and coaling stations.[33]

Indeed, some Marxist historians have suggested that the anti-imperialist
movement was a clever cover for the more sophisticated indirect control and
exploitation of the nonwestern world that evolved over the next five decades.
But this interpretation, with its conspiratorial overtones, smacks of reading history backwards. Other historians have done likewise in their attempts to read
into anti-imperialism some of the humanistic concerns and liberal policies associated with opposition to neocolonialism later in the twentieth century. Pro-

fessor Christopher Lasch warns us that this anti-imperialist movement "did not foreshadow the liberalism of the Good Neighbor. It was in fact no more liberal than that of the expansionists."[34]

Both sides tended to be contemptuous of the common man, to whom they attributed responsibility for such social ills as corruption in politics and yellow journalism. As patricians, both groups were uncomfortable with the "new immigration" that was emptying the "sewers" of eastern and southern Europe after 1870 and flooding America's industrial cities with culturally disparate, and allegedly inferior, types. The men on either side of the issue of imperialism perceived themselves as the heirs to the Jeffersonian tradition, particularly its emphasis on a "natural" aristocracy, individualism, and laissez-faire economics. Indeed, the economist Laughlin's opposition to imperialism appears to have had as much to do with the ideas of Adam Smith as it did with those of John Locke. Neither the imperialist nor his critic was happy with such collectivistic responses to industrialization as trusts, unions, and urban, largely ethnoreligious, political machines. The leading advocates of imperialism were very often the young Progressives, such as Roosevelt and Beveridge, who saw overseas expansion as essentially an extension of domestic reforms, and they brought to it the same crusading zeal with which they fought slums, trusts, unions, child labor abuse, poor health and safety standards, and urban political corruption. As Professor William Leuchtenberg explained it, "The Progressives, contrary to orthodox accounts, did not oppose imperialism, but with few exceptions, ardently supported the imperialist surge, or at the very least, proved agreeably acquiescent."[35]

The elitist bias of anti-imperialists is easily discerned in the diatribes against mass democracy and the leveling effects of egalitarianism written by E. L. Godkin, Charles Eliot Norton, William James, and Charles Francis Adams. "Ignorance" elected the likes of a McKinley, who in turn catered to "savage instincts" and the "fighting mob hysteria" of "common men." The "vulgar" daily tabloids enjoyed a similar symbiotic relationship with the uneducated and the unwashed, a combination that had launched the war with Spain and set the country on the road to empire, as far as C. F. Adams was concerned. Unlike some anti-imperialists, Adams did not fool himself that his cause was a popular one. He proposed at one point a scheme for weighting votes to give disproportionate electoral power to the "better elements," whom he considered intellectually and biologically superior. Without such a reform, the nation was in danger of sinking into "a European and especially a Celtic proletariat of the Atlantic coast, an African proletariat on the shores of the gulf, and a Chinese proletariat on the Pacific," Adams warned.[36]

Perhaps nowhere else is this elitism more evident than in the cavalier attitudes expressed by some anti-imperialists toward poverty and working conditions. Bread and circuses contributed as heavily to the destruction of the Roman republic as did imperialism, they insisted. It was "natural" to have poverty and inequality, and no matter what schemes were devised to alleviate them, "the intelligent and thoughtful of the race shall inherit the earth," Godkin argued. "Natural laws" as revealed by Adam Smith should not be tampered with, and Edward Atkinson vigorously opposed the Interstate Commerce Act of 1887 and all attempts to abolish child labor, raise wages, and reduce working hours. Atkinson personally designed a cooking device he called "Aladdin's Stove," which "the fourteen-hour wives of eight-hour husbands" should use to prepare "more appetizing food from the shinbone of beef and the scrag of mutton," instead of demanding higher wages. He had the audacity to justify the use of scabs at a Knights of Labor meeting. Immensely egotistical, highly opinionated, and invariably armed with reams of statistics that rarely proved his point, Atkinson was never shy about pontificating to any audience and remained impervious to the hoots and catcalls of "shinbone" from workers. But even Atkinson never went as far as Godkin, who once advised the government to deal with the strikers at Homestead in "the old fashioned way," that is to shoot them down. When Carnegie protested that shooting Filipinos would destroy the Republic, Secretary of State John Hay was able to observe, "He does not seem to reflect that the government is in a somewhat robust condition even after shooting down several American workers in his interest at Homestead." It is small wonder that the anti-imperialists failed to win the support of workers, beyond the token gestures of a few labor leaders in lending their names as vice-presidents of the League.[37]

Another shared characteristic of the two groups was a highly romantic Anglo-Saxonism. The Boston Brahmins and the Southern anti-imperialists were unabashed Anglophiles, who repeatedly made it clear that their attacks on imperialism should in no way be construed as criticism of "our mother country." Senator Augustus Bacon emphasized:

> I am proud of the English race: I am proud of the grand civilization given to the world by England. I am proud of her history; I am proud of her achievements; and if the time came that the great powers leagued themselves together to destroy her, I would be willing to go to her side . . . in her defense.[38]

Likewise Atkinson stipulated that he admired the British imperial system, however much he did not want the United States to emulate it. English expansion had brought free trade, human rights, and other Anglo-Saxon ideals where none had existed before. Indeed, Atkinson's hysterical letter to Cleveland over the Venezuela boundary dispute in 1895 was more related to the target of the president's jingoism than to any pacifistic concerns. Atkinson suggested that, instead of attacking England's aggressive moves against Venezuela, Cleveland propose "a British protectorate" for "the whole of South America":

> What a boon it would be to the world if systems corresponding to English law, English administration, and the English regard for personal rights, could be extended over the continent of South America.[39]

Carnegie, too, defended British imperialism as beneficial to the world and even wanted to reunite the "two leading Anglo-Saxon nations," a process he called "race imperialism." A flag of his design, combining Old Glory and the Union Jack, flew from the Scottish castle of this "star spangled Scotch man," as he was labeled in the press. Another anti-imperialist, Cleveland's secretary of state, Richard Olney, justified his devotion to England as "a patriotism of race," which was, he averred, as important as "patriotism of country," and added that "the Anglo American is as little likely to be indifferent to one as to the other."[40]

This romantic Anglo-Saxonism rested firmly on the belief in racial inequality as an established fact of life. Because American imperialism coincided with racist extremism at the end of the nineteenth century, some historians have linked the two together in a causal relationship. As evidence, one historian noted that McKinley had never spoken out against lynching or the mushrooming Jim Crow laws in the South. But there are obvious flaws in this interpretation. For one thing, more ardent imperialists than McKinley, such as Roosevelt and Lodge, did protest racist developments. Lodge was the author of the 1890 "Force Bill," designed to end the growing disenfranchisement of blacks. When Roosevelt denounced lynching and Jim Crow, he was attacked as "a narrow minded bigot," a "modern Judas," and "a prostitutor who smites the South." What kind of a white man would defend "negroes who outrage our womanhood"? asked one Southern editor. "Burning and hanging negro rapists is a terrible crime in the eyes of this would-be Caesar. This is the low estimate President Roosevelt places on the virtue of our women." Roosevelt also outraged the "lily white" faction of his party in the South by making Negro appointments there, and Lodge lectured Southerners that they had to "learn and broaden."[41]

In direct contrast, anti-imperialist Thomas Wentworth Higginson, a former abolitionist who once supported John Brown, counseled a hands-off federal policy for the South as a result of disillusionment over the frustrations of the Reconstruction experiment. This policy would have meant abandoning the Negro to the mercy of white extremists. Carnegie even defended lynching, explaining to a Scottish audience that "'Judge Lynch' is rarely, if ever, accused of punishing the innocent—undue haste or excessive 'efficiency' is his fault. The number who suffer, not from injustice, but undue haste, is not very great."[42]

If racism was related to America's imperialistic venture in the Philippines, the two were connected in an unexpected way. The imperialists were paternal racists while their opponents, at least in the South and West, were almost invariably race haters. The young progressives who supported imperialism were politically tied to moderates in the South, not to the extremists, who were usually anti-imperialist. The moderates were, in the words of one historian, "white Washingtonians," who believed that with patience and careful tutoring the Negro could become the equal of the white man. They were clearly indebted to Booker T. Washington for their ideas, and John Spencer Bassett was almost fired from Trinity College (later Duke University) for declaring that this black leader was "the greatest man save General Lee, born in the South in a hundred years." It was no accident that Bassett's good friend and confidant, Teddy Roosevelt, invited Washington to the White House in 1901. The invitation angered William Jennings Bryan, the defeated anti-imperialist Democratic candidate, who protested, "When Mr. Roosevelt sits down with a negro he declares that the negro is a social equal of the white man."[43]

Once these moderates, or "accommodationists," were hounded from the South, they established close and influential relations with Northern progressives, who invariably were imperialists. Walter Hines Page and Nathaniel Southgate Shaler became personal advisors to President Roosevelt on racial policies in the South. A major outlet for their views was Lyman Abbott's proimperialist *Outlook*. These Southern advisors not only supported imperialism, but argued that the experience gained in the South best equipped Americans to assume a "new missionary and pedagogical spirit" that will "uplift the child races everywhere." The South would continue to serve as an ideal training and testing ground for "this characteristic problem of the world." To them, domestic blacks were but a small part of the "white man's burden."[44]

These ideas were lent academic respectability by the relatively new field of sociology expounded in the works of Professors Ross, Cooley, and Giddings. The latter argued that although the nonwhite races lacked "intelligence and inventive genius," they were "capable of imitation and improvement." By virtue of their experience in dealing with "racially inferior types," it was the responsibility of Anglo-Saxons to ensure "orderly development" for such "unfortunates," Giddings reasoned. The British Empire had already extended "English sacredness of life" and the "requirement of social order" to "less able races," a system based on what he called "ethical homogeneity," due to the propagation of English morality. To explain the lack of traditional democratic institutions in this "democratic empire," Giddings coined the marvelous contradiction "consent without consent" to epitomize his conclusion that "if in later years, they [the colonized] see and admit that the disputed relation was for the highest interest, it may be reasonably held that authority has been imposed with the consent of the governed."[45]

While the progressive and imperialist view of nonwhite races at home and abroad was rife with paternalism, the racist fears of the anti-imperialists were closer to traditional racism. This is clear enough in the Southern opposition to imperialism. "We understand what it is to have two races side by side that cannot mix or mingle, without deterioration and injury to both and the ultimate destruction of the civilization of the higher," "Pitchfork Ben" Tillman, senator and vice-president of the League, explained his opposition to imperialism. His colleague from Virginia, Senator Daniels, hypnotically inveighed against the "mess of Asiatic pottage" that would be created by expansion—"a witch's cauldron" of "black spirits and white, red, gray spirits . . . spotted peoples with Zebra signs on them." Writing about "the White Man's Problem," Mrs. Jefferson Davis made clear that she was opposed to keeping the Philippines "because three quarters of the population is made up of negroes" and, worse, "hybrids," and "everyone knows the trouble mulattoes cause in the South." Western anti-imperialists portrayed Malays as Mongolians and simply recycled earlier pleas not to "open the doors" to the "yellow hordes." Senator Rawlins's frequent tirades against imperialism were invariably studded with references to an "Asiatic pottage."[46]

Much more surprising is that well-educated anti-imperialists in the Northeast were not above expressing such racial fears. E. L. Godkin warned earlier in the *Nation* that the annexation of Hawaii would admit "alien, inferior, and mongrel races to our nationality." Senator Schurz warned that immigrants would come from the Philippines and that it was not possible to assimilate "Spanish-Americans, with all the mixture of Indian and Negro blood, and Malays and other unspeakable Asiatics by the tens of millions!" C. F. Adams contended that "protection against race mingling" had long been an American policy. He justified the "harsh treatment" of Indians, blacks, Chinese, and Mexicans because it had "saved the Anglo Saxons from being a nation of half breeds" and argued that imperialism would reverse that historic policy. William Larrabee, former governor of Iowa, and a League officer, countered the paternalistic arguments of the imperialists by insisting that the Filipinos were the "worst and most unmanageable savages" who could not possibly be taught "the first principle of American citizenship in a thousand years." It is in this spirit that the quip of one anti-imperialist hero and League vice-president, Grover Cleveland, must be understood: "Cuba ought to be submerged for a while before it will make an American state or territory of which we will be particularly proud."[47]

Possibly more shocking is that similar racist anxieties can be discovered in the anti-imperialist objections of academicians. Stanford's President Jordan declared that "the degenerate and alien races within our borders today constitute a menace to peace and welfare," without adding more from possessions overseas. Harvard's Professor Norton echoed this sentiment and insisted that "mixing races of varying ability within an institutional framework must lead to the irreparable impairment of that institution." Even the erudite Storey and Hoar on rare occasions inserted the phrase "aliens in blood" into their attacks on imperialism. When Senator Knute Nelson of Minnesota quickly pointed out to Hoar that he had voted for the annexation of Hawaii, where "ninety-five per cent of [its] people are of inferior race," the senator from Massachusetts explained that within fifty years those islands would have "a Northern, largely New England population."[48]

Indeed, the most effective anti-imperialist tactic was to exploit such racial fears by threatening to insist that full citizenship be extended to Filipinos unless this foolish venture in imperialism was abandoned. "Are you ready to grant citizenship to those whom your laws exclude from coming into this country?" taunted Henry Johnson, Indiana congressman and vice-president of the League. The Honorable Champ Clark warned that very soon "Almond-eyed, brown-skinned United States Senators" would destroy the very Constitution that had granted them the rights of citizenship. His ringing peroration drew heavy applause from his fellow anti-imperialists in the House, "No matter whether they are fit to govern themselves or not, they are not fit to govern us!"[49]

Whitelaw Reid recognized that "the chief aversion to the vast accessions of territory . . . springs from the fear that they must be admitted into the union as states." McKinley's rationalization that imperialism was merely continental expansion overseas did little to assuage such fears. Imperialist spokesmen were increasingly flushed out of their earlier, more humanitarian position to argue, as did Undersecretary of State David Jayne Hill, that it was never intended to bestow American citizenship on "half civilized peoples" who were "so adverse to social order." To bolster this position, imperialists were able to line up a number of prominent law professors, such as Theodore Woolsey of Yale, E. W. Cutting of Cornell, Abbott Lawrence Lowell, and Christopher Columbus Langdell, both of Harvard, to outline just how ridiculous would be such a proposition. Woolsey informed the august American Academy of Political and Social Sciences that Filipinos "are incapable of gratitude, profligate, undependable, improvident, cruel, impertinent, superstitious, and treacherous . . . all are liars even in the confessional." Granting such people constitutional rights would be "a *reductio ad absurdum*," and military rule was the only possibility, he concluded. How could anyone expect Filipinos to have the intellect, instinct, and morality "developed in the Anglo Saxon fiber through all the centuries since Runnymede," protested Reid in the face of this subtle anti-imperialist blackmail. "We have full power and are absolutely free to do with these islands as we please," Senator Lodge reassured America.[50]

Actually, the McEnery resolution, passed after the ratification of the

Treaty of Paris in 1899, precluded making Filipinos citizens or their islands "an integral part of the United States." There was, however, a nagging fear that the Supreme Court might rule this provision unconstitutional in the near or distant future. Already an anti-imperialist challenge was in the lower courts. There was also the possibility that "wooly-headed reformers from the 'Hub'" would start another crusade to bestow constitutional privileges upon Filipinos as they had once done for African slaves. How seriously such inferred threats were taken is impossible to calculate, but as a people culturally committed to rationalism, Americans seem to have been uncomfortable, at least, with logical inconsistencies. As a result, some imperialists actually felt compelled to attack the very sacred document on which their nation was founded. "It is time to begin teaching the American people the absurdity of that clause in the Declaration of Independence which derives all the just powers of government from the consent of the governed," Whitelaw Reid declared. But very few expansionists went quite so far as the Reverend Henderson, who, in his zeal to defend the conquest of the Philippines, branded from his pulpit the Declaration of Independence "the most damnable lie as the devil ever invented." Since Senator Beveridge was more dependent on public support, he explained more cautiously that the Declaration of Independence applied only to "self governing races" before exploding in outrage, "How dare any man prostitute this expression of the very elect of self governing people to a race of Malay children of barbarism?"[51]

Such admissions delighted senators from the South, particularly when made by young progressives who had been so critical of racially motivated political restrictions in their states. The staunchly anti-imperialist Senator McLaurin of South Carolina taunted:

> It is passing strange that Senators who favored universal suffrage and the full enfranchisement of the negro should now advocate imperialism. If they are sincere . . . they should propose an amendment to the Constitution which will put the inferior races in this country and the inhabitants of the Philippines upon an equality as to their civil and political rights, and thus forever settle the vexed race and suffrage questions.

The junior senator from South Carolina, Ben Tillman, even wrung an apology for the "dead past" from Senator Nelson, a former abolitionist turned imperialist, on which he refused to elaborate to avoid making "the South's burden that much heavier."[52]

Anti-imperialist spokesmen in the North attempted to exploit this inconsistency in the imperialist position in order to pin the racist label on them and win black support for their cause. Archibald Grimke of the famous abolitionist family declared:

Scratch the back of Republican leaders like Hanna, Lodge, Roosevelt, and McKinley, and you will find race prejudice underneath, an invincible belief on their part in the divine right of the Anglo Saxon to govern the Republic and subjugate the darker races.

William Lloyd Garrison rather foolishly declared that black Americans would refuse to fight in this racist war. In fact, two "colored" regiments already had distinguished themselves in the Philippines by the time he made this statement.[53]

Although considerable anti-imperialist sentiment had been expressed in the Negro press, the League was not successful in enlisting organized support from this quarter. One black minister in the Boston area, the Reverend William H. Scott, did address anti-imperialist rallies as a self-appointed black spokesman, and was later made the only Negro vice-president of the League. Professor Kelly Miller of Howard, Clifford Plummer, a Boston lawyer and secretary of the National Colored Protective League, and other black leaders contributed strong anti-imperialist statements to the cause. Negroes were just as divided on this issue as were whites, and other black leaders, particularly ministers, endorsed the conquest of the Philippines. The scholar W. S. Scarborough was enthusiastic over projected opportunities for his fellow blacks in these islands.[54]

A group of Boston blacks held a meeting at Faneuil Hall in 1900 to condemn imperialism and endorse Bryan's candidacy. Erving Winslow urged Plummer to create a "Colored Auxiliary" to the League, in keeping with the "separate but equal" doctrine of the day, although it pales in comparison with the acts of some imperialists, such as President Roosevelt's appointment of black Republicans to federal offices in the South a year later. At any rate, the auxiliary never materialized. The National Negro Anti-Expansion, Anti-Imperialist, Anti-Trust and Anti-Lynching League was formed in 1899 at Cairo, Illinois, but it disappeared after the election of 1900.[55]

It seemed that most blacks were not yet ready to abandon the party of Lincoln. They would have been uncomfortable with the leaders of the League, many of whom had advocated letting the South work out its racial problems on its own. On the other hand, young progressive Republicans still wanted to use federal leverage to affect the outcome. Of course, at that time most blacks still lived in the South, where the imperialists were more likely to be moderates on the race question and where anti-imperialists were often extremists. There were exceptions, naturally. George W. Cable was both an anti-imperialist and a racial moderate. Thomas Dixon, whose protagonist in *The Clansman* is portrayed as a dedicated knight in the racist organization, was an imperialist. One of the South's leading imperialists, Senator John Tyler Morgan of Alabama, substituted the Philippines for Africa as an ideal destination for American blacks, but his reasoning was closer to moderate thinking. He accepted black capacity for progress with careful tutelage, but he feared that the educational and vocational successes of Negroes would escalate the hostility and demands for a caste system on the part of less successful whites. Therefore, Morgan saw emigration as the only hope for American blacks. In contrast, the anti-imperialist publisher of the *Louisville Courier-Journal*, General A. G. Greenwood, wanted to kill two birds with one stone by shipping the blacks to the Philippines before granting those islands independence. In essence, many anti-imperialists resembled "little Englanders"—to whom Roosevelt compared them—who opposed British imperialism more out of fear that it would inundate their island with alien races than out of any humanistic concern for the colonized.[56]

SAVED FROM THE CRUEL SPANIARD.

—*The Chronicle, Chicago.*

THE WHITE MAN'S BURDEN. — *The Journal, Detroit.*

General Emilio Aguinaldo
(National Archives 111–SC–98358)

General Arthur MacArthur
(National Archives 165–PF–2)

General Adna Chaffee
(U.S. Army Military History Institute)

General Henry W. Lawton
(U.S. Army Military History
   Institute)

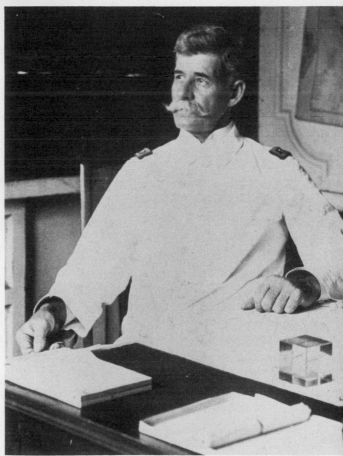

Filipino victims of American bombardment on the first day of the war
(National Archives 111–RB–1037)

Filipino prisoners at the Rio Grande in Pampanga
(U.S. Army Military History Institute)

Filipino officers posing before the war
(Reproduced from the Collections of the Library of Congress)

Macabebe scouts in formation, Pampanga
(U.S. Army Military History Institute)

The Filipino leaders; Aguinaldo at center
(Reproduced from the Collections of the Library of Congress)

General Elwell S. Otis and his aides on the porch of Malacanan Palace: *front*, General
R. P. Hughes, Otis, Colonel T. H. Barry; *back*, Captain C. H. Murray, Lieutenant
Louis P. Sanders, Lieutenant Frederick Sladen (U.S. Army Military History Institute)

Aguinaldo saluting as he boards the U.S.S. *Vicksburg*
(National Archives 111–SC–85795)

General Frederick Funston aboard the
Vicksburg with his prize
(National Archives 111–SC–83545)

DID HE DO IT?

—*The St. Paul Dispatch.*

FEBRUARY 12.—"LEST WE FORGET."

—*The New York World.*

BRYAN'S ROAD TO THE WHITE HOUSE.

—*The Chicago Inter Ocean.*

TRADE FOLLOWS THE FLAG.

—*The New York World.*

From the editorial page of the *New York Evening Journal*, May 5, 1902
(Courtesy of the Newspaper Collection, The New York Public Library,
Astor, Lenox and Tilden Foundations)

8

Armageddon, 1900

Both sides of the Philippine question girded themselves for a final showdown in the election year of 1900. Each was certain that the people would overwhelmingly endorse its position. Anti-imperialists rationalized their earlier political defeats: They had not been organized in 1898 and had fared no better a year later because the truth about the Philippines had not yet transcended Otis's censorship and the Administration's propaganda. But the election of 1900 would be a different story. It was obvious to all that the war was going badly. Its cost was staggering, and there were too many stories of American atrocities to deny all of them. Even imperialist politicians and editors were losing heart, the war critics convinced themselves. But on the other hand, Governor Roosevelt exuded confidence and was eager to meet his opponents in the political arena, particularly if the Democrats were going to add to their advocacy of the coinage of silver the issue of anti-imperialism.

Congress adjourned near the end of 1899 in a sour mood, after Senator Pettigrew's last-minute protest that once again the Administration had deliberately withheld evidence of the real conditions in the islands, this time in a report made by Assistant Secretary of State Micklejohn. Believing that his tour of the islands was supposed to have been a genuine fact-finding mission, Micklejohn had submitted a report that challenged official views of the war and berated Otis's leadership. Root had quickly pigeonholed the report, but someone in the War Department had leaked it to the press. In a fury, Pettigrew rose dramatically in the Senate, brandishing a newspaper with a headline that announced "Startling Disclosures," and demanded to know why he, a senator, had to learn of Micklejohn's report in this manner. His resolution requiring the Administration to release to the Senate every scrap of information it held on the Philippines was tabled until after the holiday recess.[1]

As soon as Congress reconvened in January, apologists for the Administra-

129

tion took the offensive by impugning Pettigrew's patriotism and warning that such a resolution would jeopardize American soldiers. Senator Walcott angrily pointed his finger at Pettigrew's empty seat and declared that it might as well be occupied by Aguinaldo "to represent the people of South Dakota who sent their sons to the Philippines." Once again, as had happened so often in the debate over the islands, each side shifted its definition of the conflict. Anti-imperialists railed against "peacetime" restrictions on information, implying at least what imperialists had long contended—that there was no "war" in the Philippines, merely an "insurrection." Imperialists, on the other hand, now evoked the historical excuse of withholding information "in time of war." Angry over the defeat of Pettigrew's resolution, the *Call* conveniently overlooked its own inconsistencies on this score and complained of the Administration's semantic opportunism:

> Though not said officially, it is in the air that nothing can ever be whispered about the Philippines, because there we are at war! . . . As Congress has no control over that war which it never declared, its technical prolongation may be indefinite and no fact concerning it, including the cost, will ever reach the people.[2]

The Administration discovered a new weapon in this election year—the freshman senator from Indiana, Albert Jeremiah Beveridge, who took a prominent part in the verbal fray that continued right down to the wire in November. This "golden orator" was unintimidated by seniority, and at the slightest hint that all was not well in the Philippines, he was on his feet to invoke God, patriotism, and "national destiny" and to chastise those who "shirk" their duty and "foul the nation's honor." The Hoosier senator was forever being "forced to say" that the "so-called anti-imperialists" had "started the war" and were now "the chief factor in prolonging it." When Hoar merely suggested that the time had come to negotiate with Aguinaldo, Beveridge demanded:

> What shall history say of us? Shall it say that we renounced that holy trust, left the savage to his base condition, the wilderness to the reign of waste; deserted duty, abandoned glory, forgot our sordid profit even, because we feared our strength and read the charter of our powers with the doubter's eye and the quibbler's mind? Shall it say that called by events to captain and command the proudest, ablest, purest race of history's noblest work, we declined that great commission?[3]

It was virtually impossible to respond to such bombast, particularly when it elicited thunderous applause from galleries packed with spectators who wanted to see and hear this young marvel, who was handsome enough to be a

matinee idol. The *Call* expressed wonder over the ease with which Beveridge
thrilled an audience with banal and repetitive nonsense about "God's preparation of the English speaking and Teutonic people for 1,000 years," not for "vain
and idle contemplation and self admiration," but for the "mission of our race,
trustee under God, of the civilization of the world." Beveridge neither recoiled
from the word "imperialism" nor felt any need to invent euphemisms. "If this
be imperialism, the final end will be the empire of the Son of Man." If his Democratic colleagues refused to heed God's will, those in the galleries would not,
he warned. Pointing to his audience, Beveridge swore that

> we will move forward to our work, not howling out regrets, like slaves
> whipped to their burdens, but with gratitude for a task worthy of our
> strength and thanksgiving to Almighty God that he has marked us as his
> chosen people, henceforth to lead in the regeneration of the world.[4]

What the *Call*'s editor failed to appreciate was that this combination of patriotic and religious appeals struck deep into the heart of a populace in a highly
nationalistic mood and in the midst of an evangelical revival. But Beveridge
also enjoyed a practical advantage in these debates. He had toured the Philippines to see the war at close quarters, something that his critics had not done,
or perhaps been able to do. The shrewd Hoosier milked his special experience
for all it was worth by studding his speeches with personal observations of
America's brave boys in blue in the thick of battle against an unseen and treacherous foe. When critics raised the objection that the islands would never return
a profit, Beveridge dramatically produced from his pocket a golden nugget he
had brought back to symbolize their untapped wealth. Differences of opinion
were settled by the "insider's" curt comment, "I was there." In the American
cultural context there could be little doubt that direct experience was the best
source of reality. A Boston editor pressed this advantage when he observed of
the freshman senator's presumptuous duel with the venerable Senator Hoar,
"Beveridge has travelled to and seen the Philippines whereas Hoar has studied
the Filipinos through books, documents, and reports. One man has seen, the
other has heard." Of course, Secretary Micklejohn had also seen first hand, but
after the initial furor over the suppression of his report, its contents were
quickly forgotten.[5]

McKinley used the testimony of another eyewitness to bolster his position
on the Philippines as the election approached. It had been rumored that Jacob
Gould Schurman of the Philippine Commission would break with the official
view in a dissenting report, particularly after some comments by him shortly
after his return from the islands. In a magazine article Schurman had praised
the sincerity and honesty of Aguinaldo's quest for self-government, and was

critical of the drunken and lawless conduct of American troops. On two other occasions he had mentioned publicly ultimate independence for the islands. Such rumors of Schurman's pending heresy proved unrealistic, however, and the chairman concurred with the commission's total whitewash of the mess in the Philippines. Indeed, once it was determined that Schurman would not dissent, the Administration rushed into print a preliminary report by the Philippine Commission two months before the final one was ready.[6]

General Otis was the only member of the commission who refused to sign the report, either the preliminary or the final version. He had been hostile to Schurman's group since its arrival and viewed the commission as an infringement on his authority. The breach widened when the civilians on the commission recommended local self-government for areas already declared "pacified." They also recommended civilian control for Manila, which Otis interpreted as a slap in the face, even though the proposal allowed that he would retain veto power over the city government. Otis could not even get along with Dean Worcester and Charles Denby, both of whom consistently stipulated that they would tolerate no civilian interference with military operations. Both were avid imperialists, and Denby had been a career army officer before becoming a diplomat. Denby's proposal to allow a few municipal governments to function on a limited and trial basis was viewed by Otis as a betrayal. Denby complained to Secretary of State Hay that "a civil board" to run Manila would relieve Otis of all the hours "taken up by him in the determination of matters which scarcely deserve his personal attention." He warned Hay that the current situation "pleases nobody." But Denby's concerns were omitted from the commission's report, understandably so in an election year.[7]

Imperialist editors were delighted with the findings and recommendations of the commission, which they hailed as the definitive account of the conflict. "If this report is not to be believed, then we may as well abandon scholarship, renounce reason and grant that judgement is 'fled to brutish beasts,'" crowed the New York Tribune. The Times in that city hailed it as "proof of our unselfish intent: It must carry conviction to every reasonable mind." The editor of the Evening Transcript in Boston, who, like Schurman himself, had been hesitant initially to endorse imperialism, confessed to "a great relief" that the report had at last "put an end to the swarm of rumors which have confused public judgement of the Philippine question."[8]

Anti-imperialist editors dismissed both reports as "campaign documents" having more to do with McKinley's reelection than the situation in the Philippines. The Springfield Republican countered by publishing Aguinaldo's "authentic version" of the war. Pettigrew had once tried to read this article on the floor of the Senate but was shouted down with cries of "treason." Another interpretation by Apolinario Mabini was published in the *North American Review*. The *San Francisco Call* and *New York Herald* printed a letter from Mabini to "friendly editors." The charges raised in these accounts were hardly new, but once again Dewey was forced to deny that he had ever betrayed an alliance with Aguinaldo. "The statement of Emilio as recently published in the Springfield *Republican* as far as it relates to me is a tissue of falsehoods," the hero of Manila Bay declared to the press, a denial that Lodge read into the *Congressional Record*. Imperialist editors thanked the admiral for having "set the record straight," as though this were the first time that Dewey had carried out this ritual. The *New York Times* followed Dewey's denial with its own repeated announcement that "Admiral Dewey has ruthlessly destroyed one of the foundation stones of the anti-imperialist temple of falsehoods and delusions," along with a familiar warning: "Any politician or editor who so much as peeps about a 'broken alliance' or 'broken promise' will be saying in effect that the Admiral of the Navy is a liar. That will be inadvisable. To put the matter mildly, it will displease the American people. Who knows more about the matter—George Dewey or the 'anti-imperialist' spouters and ink splashers?"[9]

Dean Worcester took to the stump to defend the commission's report against anti-imperialist charges that the commissioners had "prostituted themselves" to produce "campaign literature" for McKinley's reelection. As a former scholar at the University of Michigan, Worcester thought it fair to concede that the war critics "may be sincere in their convictions, but by freely giving voice to them they are encouraging the ambitious Tagalo leader to prolong a hopeless struggle . . . costing us millions of dollars, and what is far worse, good American blood." He insisted that if such encouragement ended so would the war, and American "benevolence" could get under way in earnest. The *Call* expressed amazement that even a scholar could "so totally miss the point—'til we give them self government, there can be no good will." Why is "Professor Worcester so certain that that 'benevolence' will follow conquest," when "similar British takeovers elsewhere have failed to produce beneficial results?" this editor demanded.[10]

McKinley shrewdly seized upon one recommendation in the report—to appoint a second commission with the power to implement limited local self-government, independent of the military. For this task, the president appointed a highly distinguished group: Professor Worcester was retained, this time joined by Professor Bernard Moses, a political economist at the University of California and author of a book on Spain's former colonies in South America; Judge Henry Clay Ide, former chief justice of the United States court in Samoa; and Luke Wright, lawyer, former general and vice-governor of Tennessee, and a Democratic expansionist. McKinley's biggest coup was getting the brilliant young jurist, William Howard Taft, to serve as chairman. Like his predecessor, Schurman, Taft was a Republican suspected of harboring anti-imperialist sympathies. The president gained further advantage by announcing that the new commission would immediately assume legislative powers for the islands and begin preparations for a complete transfer to civilian rule as soon as feasible.[11]

Anti-imperialist editors were left sputtering over this development and for the most part could only praise the quality of the appointees and the power and intent of the commission. Indeed, some imperialist editors worried that the president was moving much too fast in order to placate his critics in an election year and was possibly jeopardizing military operations in the process. If Filipinos were going to be given the right to vote in local elections, cautioned the *New York Sun*, there should be educational and property qualifications.[12]

The Second Philippine Commission was still en route when MacArthur relieved Otis as military governor, and it was thought that one potential obstacle to Taft's success had been removed. The new commander enhanced this belief by immediately cabling Taft at Hong Kong, his first port of call, that "cordial greetings and warm welcome await the commission." If this message had disarmed Taft, he should have been alerted by the petty slights he received upon his arrival at Manila. Instead of personally meeting the ship, MacArthur sent a junior officer to escort the commission to his headquarters, although the general did pay a visit to the ship the next day. It would not take Taft long to realize that he was expected to court America's first "proconsul," rather than cooperate with a mere general.[13]

MacArthur's announcement in June of a general amnesty helped to allay some of Taft's suspicions. The amnesty pledged "complete immunity for the past and liberty for the future," along with a bounty of thirty pesos for each surrendered rifle. This excellent ploy in the midst of McKinley's campaign for reelection permitted the Republicans to grossly exaggerate the Filipino response to the "generous offer." By the end of the summer, they even claimed "a final victory by amnesty." Taft added to the euphoria with glowing reports full of such phrases as "the Philippines for the Filipinos," although he shared Roosevelt's paternalistic racism and assured President McKinley that "our little brown brothers" would need "fifty or one hundred years" of close supervision "to develop anything resembling Anglo-Saxon political principles and skills." Nevertheless, such sentiment won Taft few friends among the military, which greeted his assertions that "Filipinos are moved by similar considerations to those which move other men" with utter scorn. It was clear to the generals that McKinley's choice to head the second commission knew even less about "Oriental character" than did Schurman.[14]

The first real rift between Taft and MacArthur was over a "catch-22" provision in the amnesty offer. Filipinos who had violated the "rules of civilized warfare" were not eligible for amnesty and could be tried and punished for their crimes after having laid down their arms and signed a loyalty oath in good faith. As one Boston editor explained approvingly, "insurgents who murdered or tortured prisoners or inflicted outrages on friendly natives need not apply." But MacArthur used the provision to keep surrendered native leaders in line. Thus Pedro Paterno was arrested merely for privately expressing that he favored independence under American protection. Taft protested that the amnesty had carefully stipulated "liberty for the future" and to his wife expressed the opinion that such arrests had effectively wrecked the amnesty. Worse, the censorship and harassment of local editors continued under MacArthur's command, which Taft deemed "revolting," "unnecessary," and "unAmerican." By the end of the summer, Taft complained directly to Secretary Root and warned him that MacArthur had never taken the amnesty seriously and that he "regards all the people as opposed to the American forces and looks at his task as one of conquering eight millions of recalcitrant, treacherous and sullen people." This ever-widening breach between Taft and MacArthur was carefully kept under wraps until after the election.[15]

Several external developments across the globe played into the president's hands that election year. In February, he was able to claim success for his open door policy for China when Britain, France, Germany, Russia, and Japan agreed to maintain equal commercial rights in all Chinese territories. William Rockhill, who played a crucial role in the formation of this policy, attributed its success to the American presence nearby in the Philippines.[16] This conclusion was enhanced four months later when Chinese Boxers attacked western missions and embassies, and the United States was able to send troops from the Philippines to join the Allied Expeditionary Force. Editors and missionaries demanding "rapid and utter annihilation of the Chinese government" for its collusion with the Boxers thanked the Lord for a base nearby from which to deliver "timely justice." The imperialists also reasoned that the presence of American troops, alone, had prevented the great powers from carving up China during this crisis. One editor advocated a joint Anglo-American administration of China, but his imperialist colleagues warned that the problems inherent in such a scheme would be greater than those faced by England in India. A watchdog role from the Philippines was the cheapest and most effective means of keeping the Germans and Russians at bay and guaranteeing an open, independent China. It was a persuasive line that added immensely to the value of the islands just when anti-imperialists and some candidates were arguing to the contrary during the campaign. John Barrett crowed in *Harper's Weekly* that "any doubts over the strategic and political value of the Philippines were washed away in the Boxer Crisis."[17]

The reality of the situation was that few troops could be spared from the

Philippines, and MacArthur was unhappy about having to send any at a time when he was urgently requesting reinforcements himself. As it was, the American troops did not remain in China long and were quickly returned to combat in the Philippines. The war critics tended to remain respectfully silent as long as the fate of the besieged Americans in Peking remained in doubt. After their rescue, criticism for McKinley's "latest caper" was more noticeable in the anti-imperialist press, which denounced the decision to commit troops as "yet another declaration of war by the executive without the authority of Congress." Such illegal interventions "are the very worst phase of imperialism," and more could be expected if McKinley were not rejected at the polls in November, warned one editor.[18]

Another foreign development that affected the election of 1900 was the Boer War. Oddly enough, McKinley and the imperialists seem to have benefited from the war in South Africa in that it divided the opposition. The Anglophiles in the Anti-Imperialist League were uncomfortable in criticizing their beloved England, which embittered the German-Americans with strong sympathies for the Boers and for anti-imperialism. While it is impossible to say how solidly Negroes and the Irish supported anti-imperialism—whatever the League claimed—they lined up on opposite sides of this issue. The Irish compared South Africa to Ireland and became much more concerned over the "rape of the Boers" than they ever were over the plight of the Filipinos. Blacks focused on the issue of slavery, which was still practiced by the Boers, and were certain that the England that had pioneered in the abolition of slavery would end that practice in South Africa.[19]

The war in South Africa had no such divisive effect on the imperialists, who soundly cheered England for extending her "civilizing Anglo Saxon hand" to the Boer Republic. Long after the election, the revelation of British atrocities against the Boers did make imperialists uncomfortable, particularly when they invited comparison with similar American tactics in the Philippines. Some Democratic imperialists, such as San Francisco's Mayor James D. Phelan, seemed unconcerned over the inconsistency of denouncing England for using techniques in South Africa that had been perfected in Ireland while praising the war in the Philippines as "the most sacred in history." But then the likes of Phelan would not have voted for McKinley on any account.[20]

Quite possibly, McKinley's biggest boost for reelection was the Democratic nomination, for a second time, of William Jennings Bryan. His anti-Eastern, antiurban, and fundamentalist, evangelical Protestant biases put a strain on the Democratic coalition. His followers' stress on moralistic issues, such as strict Sabbath laws and prohibition, might attract midwestern Republicans, particularly the Scandinavians, but it could also repel Germans and Catholics who might have voted against "McKinley's war." In essence, Bryan's candidacy represented what one historian has dubbed an "imperialistic pietism," an attempt to apply age-old moral codes to the complexities of a twentieth-century industrialized, urbanized, and pluralistic America. Worse, Bryan's brand of class conflict would have less appeal this time around in the more prosperous year of 1900.

One of Bryan's first campaign declarations was that "imperialism" was the "paramount issue," made, possibly, to attract the German and Catholic vote or to deter the formation of a third party on this issue. At any rate, Bryan's anti-imperialism was never very convincing, and as the campaign unfolded, the issue was increasingly ignored. "Of all men in this country, Bryan is the least entitled to a hearing against imperialism." His party was even "less deserving, with Hearst in its vanguard, the same Hearst who once demanded that the flag be nailed to the Philippines, not hoisted, but nailed!" And as for "the Irish Catholics who run that party, [their] version of anti-imperialism [is that] if we must expand, we should take Canada," ridiculed the *Call*.[21]

This "bogus anti-imperialism of Colonel Bryan" was also evident in the Democratic platform, which ignored the war but did pledge a stable government for the Philippines and eventual independence under American protection in some vague future. It failed to mention Hawaii, Guam, and Puerto Rico and was not that much different from the Republican pledge "to put down the insurrection" and "to grant the Filipinos the largest measure of self-government consistent with their welfare and our duties." This position was strengthened in September with the publication of the president's instructions to Taft, which granted to the Filipinos the Bill of Rights, except trial by jury and the right to bear arms, and replaced military rule for civil control in those areas already pacified. Actually, most Democratic speakers, including Bryan, tried to avoid the issue, but Teddy Roosevelt kept it alive, if only to lump war critics, silverites, and Populists together as "irresponsible," "anarchistic," and "treasonable."[22]

Some anti-imperialists either refused to forgive Bryan for his "apostasy" in the treaty fight or were skeptical of his dedication to their cause. They attempted to form a third party but were unable to get much support, or even to convince anyone prominent to run on the ticket. Gompers had long refused to endorse political candidates for president, and Carnegie withdrew an earlier offer to finance a third-party ticket. Pettigrew charged him with capitulating to John Pierpont Morgan's threat to leave him out of a pending steel merger if he backed a third party, but it is hard to believe that Morgan would have been so concerned over an effort that could only have hurt Bryan, not McKinley. Gold Democrats, and less "pietistic" ones, were wooed, but they scorned such a naive effort in favor of McKinley. The list of solicited candidates, alone, symbolizes the bankruptcy of the idea: eighty-year-old General William Birney, son of the Liberty Party's candidate in 1840; retired Senator John B. Henderson, one of the "Recusant Seven" who had refused to vote for the impeachment of President Andrew Johnson several decades earlier; and Lew Wallace, retired general and author of the novel *Ben-Hur*, who was a youngster by comparison at seventy-three. Ex-President Cleveland and former Speaker of the House Thomas Reed also declined to run. Senator Donelson Caffery of Louisiana finally accepted the nomination only to reverse himself on second thought. A "Liberty Congress" held in Indianapolis by anti-imperialists that August killed all hopes for a third party by endorsing Bryan. This action so offended some anti-imperialists that they collectively announced they would not vote in the coming election. But then, scarcely three hundred had attended the "Liberty Congress," and it should have been apparent that they were politically irrelevant, however justifiable and righteous their cause.[23]

While such labor leaders as Henry Demerest Lloyd and George McNeil did stump for Bryan, the more powerful Gompers maintained his policy of not endorsing any candidate. Most local labor councils followed suit and refused to comment on the war, imperialism, or even on the election. In Cleveland, the American Federation of Labor refused to allow Bryan to address its members, while in Chicago, labor leaders agreed to hear Bryan only if Roosevelt appeared to present the other side. Labor leaders in Indianapolis and San Francisco defied tradition by endorsing the Republican candidate.[24]

The Roman Catholic hierarchy further splintered the Democratic coalition by endorsing McKinley's Philippine policy. With the election only weeks away, Archbishop Ireland declared upon his return from the Vatican:

> As a plain matter of fact the only safety which the Catholic Church has at the present time in the Philippines for the possession of her properties and for the lives of our priests is the protection of the American flag and all this is fully recognized in Rome.

Bishop Keene corroborated this position and brought from Rome the pope's *ex cathedra* blessings for the American conquest of the Philippines. "His Holiness is determined that the priests in the islands shall support the American government in all things. On this subject the Pope is very firm." Cardinal Gibbons added his voice to the chorus. "I believe it wise and proper to retain the Philippines. I think the government we enjoy in the United States is the best government for us in the Philippines." Archbishop Chappelle concurred. "The Philippines should be ours on moral, legal, commercial, sociological, and religious grounds." He even denounced anti-imperialists as being "devoid of the conception of national 'honor,'" and insisted that "to retire under fire is unAmerican."[25]

Ordinarily one would expect an uproar in the Protestant press over such flagrant electioneering by the Catholic hierarchy, but on this issue there appears to have been a tacit agreement that transcended the historical enmity between the two groups. Indeed, the strongest reaction was in the Catholic *Monitor*. "It still remains to be said that there are many millions of American citizens whose sentiments do not concur with those of His Holiness in that matter."[26]

McKinley's success in winning the pope's endorsement of his Philippine policy was partially the result of his retreat on the friar question. Initially, the Americans were no more willing to compromise on this issue than were the insurgents and seemed intent on confiscating the vast landholdings of the friars. But an understanding with Rome was McKinley's only practical option. The Aglipayan Church of native priests was inextricably woven into the insurrection, and converting the natives to Protestantism was unrealistic, at least in the short run—all the prattle about "Christianizing" the Filipinos notwithstanding. Rapprochement began with the Vatican's appointment of Father McKinnon as bishop of Manila, while McKinley made Archbishop Chappelle an unofficial advisor on the Philippines, or, as the press dubbed him, "the President's agent to rehabilitate the friars." Funston was incapable of compromise and continued to make such idiotic statements as "If Congress would drive out the friars and confiscate every piece of Church property, the bottom would drop out of the insurrection in one week." In spite of Bishop McKinnon's protest to the press that Funston was "not of the class of bigots that hate the name Catholic and all that it means," that description fit him well. General Otis, too, threatened the evolving alliance by turning over 160,000 acres of friar land to a British syndicate and reporting it to Washington on February 19, 1900, as a fait accompli. One of the priority tasks given to the Taft Commission was to work out a compromise on the friar question that would be acceptable to Rome.[27]

It is impressive that McKinley's overtures to the papacy did not fragment his Protestant support in this era of intense anti-Catholic feeling. A few religious editors continued to rant on about the "priest-ridden, defrauded, revolting adherents of a formal religion" in the Philippines who needed to be "saved" from the friars by "the plain, simple gospel message," but they refrained from attacking McKinley's new tack. The Reverend Lyman Abbott even turned over space in *Outlook* to Bishop Ireland for a defense of the friars, an act that would have been unthinkable a year earlier. McKinley continued to enjoy the status of an evangelical hero in the Protestant establishment. He was wildly cheered at a missionary conference in New York just before the election, as he and clerical speakers exchanged effusive kudos. As far away as England, the London Missionary Society hailed McKinley as the answer to the prayers of all evangelists around the world. Dean Ferrar penned a well-timed theological justification of the war, one that was denounced by anti-imperialist editors as "profoundly un-Christian." The *Springfield Republican* lamented bitterly that "the religious press is as a unit for McKinley," and a Jewish publication complained that Christ, Mammon, and the dogs of war were running "shoulder to shoulder with imperialism in the name of religion and civilization."[28]

The League leaders attempted to counter the impression of clerical unanimity behind the war, if not necessarily in favor of McKinley's reelection, with their own list of prominent clerical dissenters. If not long, it was impressive in terms of quality, but significantly, there was not a single Catholic priest among them. Since the influential *Catholic World* had featured attacks on the "preachers on the rampage" advocating the need to bring the benefits of Protestantism to the Philippines, the League did attempt to enlist the support of Bryan Clinche, a leading writer, and Father A. P. Doyle, the editor. Both declined abruptly, and Doyle informed the League that "I consider that while my country is at war and American soldiers are being shot down in the Philippines, to institute any such league as you propose is constructive [*sic*] treason."[29]

Bryan's candidacy not only threatened to sway the loyalty of the labor-Catholic-immigrant-urban constituency of the Democratic Party, but it also divided the small band of anti-imperialists. Atkinson had already lost interest in anti-imperialism and all but gave his blessings to McKinley. The *Call*, along with C. F. Adams, Carnegie, and Hoar, supported the incumbent, albeit reluctantly. Grover Cleveland's reaction was not atypical. "Bryanism and McKinleyism! What a choice for a patriotic American." His former secretary of agriculture advised the ex-president of how he intended to solve the dilemma. "It is a choice between evils, and I am going to shut my eyes, hold my nose, vote, go home and disinfect myself." Even the League's support for Bryan was not enthusiastic. He was "the least objectionable of the two candidates to whom our choice is limited." His anti-imperialist supporters became bitter when Bryan simply ignored the Philippine issue after July. Schurz complained that Bryan had "strangely ignored" what was to him the main issue and instead "indulged in all sorts of loose talk which sounded far more dangerous than it was, bringing various other things, especially the money question into the foreground."[30]

If Bryan had difficulty getting Cleveland's support, McKinley fared little better with the only living ex-president in his party, whose silence led to Democratic jibes about Benjamin Harrison's "masterly inactivity" for the Republicans. When party leaders did finally coax a statement from him, it was enigmatic enough to produce a headline announcing "Harrison's Statement. Brilliant Flashes of Silence." As Mr. Dooley explained it to a friend:

No wan is going to vote th' way he believes. Says me friend Binjamin Harrison: "Th' condict iv th' administhration has been short iv hellish. Th' idee

that this gover'mint shud sind out throops to murdher an' pillage an' elope
with th' sthrugglin' races iv th' boochoos Ph'lipeens, makes me blood bile
almost to th' dew pint. I indorse ivrything Willum J. Bryan says on th' subject an' though it goes hard f'r me to say it, lifelong Raypublican that I am,
I exhort ivry follower iv mine to put inmities aside, f'rget his prejudices an'
cast his vote f'r William McKinley."[31]

When Democratic campaigners did raise the issue of imperialism, they
sometimes chose words that became double-edged swords. Bryan asked one
audience if it wanted its country to be "a bully and braggart" in the international arena. Governor William Amos Poynter of Nebraska complained of the
militarism spawned by imperialism that would lead to swollen federal budgets
to support more "idlers" and "hirelings" in an ever-expanding army. Such
words were tailor-made for Roosevelt's demagogic talents. Did the people of
Nebraska want men with such low opinions of their country and of its fallen
heroes to occupy the White House or Lincoln's governor's mansion? he demanded while campaigning in the cornhusker state. "I fought next to these
'hirelings,'" he reminded listeners:

> I saw them . . . shed their blood for the honor of the flag . . . and the re-
> ward is that these men should be sneered at as "hirelings" and "idlers."
> Colonel Stotsenburg, General Lawton no longer walk about in idleness,
> nor does Liscum nor Reilly who died at Tientsin. They have found rest
> where their comrades from 1861 to 1865 who gave their lives have found
> their rest. Woe to the country that has lost its capacity to appreciate the
> sacrifice of the gallant souls who do and dare and die for its honor and
> glory.[32]

With enormous showmanship, Roosevelt asked audiences across the country to stamp their feet if they disapproved of the Democratic slander against
Lawton, Stotsenburg, and the heroic dead "when the mould is fresh on the
graves of 'hirelings,'" who had made "the ultimate sacrifice for their country."
Reporters invariably likened the response to a stampeding herd of buffaloes.
Conveniently forgetting that it was Poynter, not Bryan, who had allegedly
made the remark, in Cheyenne Roosevelt introduced veterans of the Wyoming
regiment as "Bryan's idlers." All these "gallant lads" ask is that the comrades
left behind in Philippine soil "at least be spared the slights and sneers of our
own people," Teddy pleaded. In Detroit, he invited veterans and "boys in
blue" to share the stage with him. When the tumultuous applause for those
assembled died down, Roosevelt dramatically pointed at them, and bellowed,
"Behold your tyrants!"[33]

As if the hapless Democrats needed to give the opposition another oppor-

tunity to impugn their patriotism, a group of naive anti-imperialists supporting
Bryan made public their own direct negotiations with Aguinaldo, who allegedly
had agreed to end the guerrilla warfare if Bryan were elected. Aside from the
implied blackmail, corresponding with the enemy in time of war could only be
regarded as treasonable. Democratic leaders understood this and tried desperately to keep the matter secret. Already, they had been embarrassed by a
League announcement that Aguinaldo supported the Democratic Party of
America. Party leaders assured the people that this endorsement was un-
wanted, unsolicited, "ill timed and ill advised." Now they had to deny that any
party official had corresponded with the enemy. Hearst suggested that his party
had brought this calamity on itself by allowing to go unchecked "the appearance
of an alliance with a group of traitors":

> Is there not material here for some pretty solemn reflections? What do
> Democrats think of the sort of management that has enabled the enemies
> of their country to greet their party as an ally . . . ? The Democratic Party
> is as patriotic a party as ever existed. Its only trouble is indiscreet leader-
> ship. Aguinaldo's proclamation is a cold shower bath that ought to bring
> the inebriated leaders to their senses.[34]

The *Republican Campaign Book* for 1900 had already noted that Bryan was
toasted at *insurrecto* banquets. The publication of Aguinaldo's offer in the middle of the campaign was conclusive proof of the treasonable nature of Bryan
Democrats. "The distinguished sign of Democracy today is not a flag, but a
flagstaff, from which Bryan, the friend of Aguinaldo and the enemy of American
sovereignty in the territory won from Spain, has hauled the national banner
down." Political cartoons often placed Aguinaldo on Bryan's right, cheering
Bryan on with bloody hands or standing on the bodies of slain American soldiers to make himself as tall as his Nebraskan ally. Bryan's shadow cabinet always included the "three traitorous A's," Aguinaldo, Atkinson, and Altgeld,
along with the ghosts of Benedict Arnold and Charles Vallandigham and, of
course, assorted Tammany types, incendiaries, and wild-eyed Populists to plan
"the country's destruction." But the real nadir in this scurrilous campaign was
reached by a New York magazine, *Judge*, one issue of which featured a sinister-
looking Aguinaldo standing on the body of an American soldier. The caption
asked, "What is behind Aguinaldo?" By raising a flap superimposed on the
cover on which Aguinaldo was depicted, the reader exposed Bryan's picture.[35]

The naiveté of the anti-imperialists supporting Bryan succeeded in destroying the single advantage enjoyed by Democrats that summer. Guerrilla
warfare had greatly intensified in many areas by August, possibly to undermine
Republican claims for the success of the amnesty program. Operating in small

bands, Filipino soldiers were able to wreak havoc on American communication and supply lines and on occasion to inflict serious losses on a careless patrol. Headlines announced with horror that Captain Shields and fifty-one men had fallen into a trap and were badly mauled before the enemy disappeared as a relief column approached. It was a familiar story, but in the wake of the alleged "victory by amnesty" it caused an editorial uproar. "This disaster to American arms is considered the worst since the outbreak of the war," the *Call* lamented. Even the cocky General Funston conceded that he had underestimated the difficulties in "exterminating the enemy" because of the fact that "when pursued too closely they hide their rifles and scatter to their homes, and no longer wear uniforms or any distinctive insignia but use the dress of noncombatants of the country."[36]

Such setbacks undermined official claims that the war was winding down and that its end was in sight. The revelation that some Bryan supporters had communicated with Aguinaldo merely lent credence to Republican charges that the new enemy offensive was the result of "false hopes" given them by Bryan's candidacy and a form of blackmail to force the electorate to vote for Bryan. That "Aguinaldo's bandits will stop killing our soldiers very soon after he becomes convinced that he will receive no aid in the effort from the party of which Mr. Bryan is chief" was a typical assertion in the Republican press. Intoxicated on this theme, the Republicans recklessly pledged that the fighting in the Philippines would die of its own accord within sixty days of McKinley's re-election. Secretary Root, at least, had to have known that this guarantee was a deliberate deception, for he was sitting on MacArthur's more realistic assessment, which he did not release until after the election.[37]

The Democrats bungled another highly charged campaign issue, that of "law and order." Roosevelt and others insisted that Bryan stood for disorder; that domestically he supported "labor violence," Irish "hooliganism," and a "frightful, panic inducing monetary system," while abroad he advocated abandonment of the Philippines, which would lead to an international scramble for the islands and set off global warfare. Holding up a newspaper that was already a year old, Roosevelt would launch his pet topic by flashing a banner headline reading, "Rowdyism Reigns at Democratic Convention." The fact that the headline referred to a much earlier attempt by followers of Eugene Debs to disrupt a Democratic convention did not bother Roosevelt. Invariably, members of the audience chose this moment to disrupt Roosevelt's speech by hurling debris at him and shouting vulgar epithets or chanting, "Teddy, Teddy, who shot a Spaniard in the back?" Roosevelt would then apologize to the audience that he had with him "neither cane nor umbrella" with which "to teach these 'Bryanites' a lesson." But, inevitably, there were some less patrician Republican heavies on hand, always identified as "veterans," to eject the "rascals" with their hands. The hecklers were never removed, however, before their performances were sufficiently noted to produce appropriate headlines on "The Foul Mouthed Hirelings of Hearst" and "The Desperate Democrats Sowing Seeds of Anarchy, License, and Mob Rule."[38]

These interruptions occurred with such perfect timing that it is difficult to avoid the suspicion that they may have been staged. In Elizabethtown, Kentucky, debris and shouts filled the air in the middle of Teddy's diatribe against the "enemies of order" who supported Bryan and opposed the "ordered liberty" of McKinley. As the "veterans" began to throw out "the rowdies and anarchists," Roosevelt was able to shout after them, "I call your attention to the attitudes of Bryan's friends on the subject of law and order." Sometimes this charade varied, and the vice-presidential candidate verbally took on the hecklers. "Teddy's Repartee Causes Confusion to Bold Bryanites. Shouts for the Nebraskan Promptly Met With Query, 'Why Don't You Hurrah For Altgeld or Aguinaldo?'" one headline reported.[39]

From the very beginning of the campaign, Roosevelt's energy and enthusiasm were overwhelming. He arrived at the Republican convention in his Rough Rider campaign hat and took the place by storm. From then until election day he never stopped, crisscrossing the nation and making speeches at a frenetic pace, while McKinley hibernated on his front porch in Ohio. The incumbent remained above the fray, solemnly announcing, "This is an age of patriotism, my friends," as he unveiled a veterans' memorial or exchanged banalities with groups of missionaries. It was as though Roosevelt, rather than McKinley, were the presidential candidate.[40]

Reporters described wildly ecstatic crowds heaping adoration on Roosevelt during his campaign marathon. In Chicago, "crowds had been waiting around the hotel entrance for hours to catch a glimpse of the governor, and when he finally made his appearance he was greeted enthusiastically. He was repeatedly cheered during his ride to the university, and was greeted with a storm of cheers and college yells when he appeared before the students." Back in his home state during the final week before the election, Roosevelt was given receptions in Elmira and Rochester that approached mass hysteria. "Never Has A Political Candidate Received Such Honors," conceded a headline in the *Call*, whose editor was no fan of what he called "Rooseveltism." Long before his nomination, this editor worried that such a "boorish adolescent" would be placed on the ticket with McKinley. When Roosevelt told the National Convention of Mothers that they must raise their sons "to fight" and "to die" for their country, the *Call*'s editor labeled him "an American Boulanger." Throughout the campaign he insisted that "the frenzied utterances of Governor Roosevelt," who had "all the youthful enthusiasm of a freshman at a college rush, or the unthinking muscular zeal of an amateur at football," did not represent the Grand Old Party. But the *Call* had to acknowledge that he was an awesome campaigner in headlines such as "Roosevelt Completes One of the Most Remarkable Campaigns Ever Made. In 8 Weeks Visits 24 States Makes 673 Speeches." Even the Democratic press admitted that he was met everywhere by "a sensational greeting," given by "wildly cheering crowds," however much it railed editorially against Roosevelt's whirlwind of demagoguery.[41]

Roosevelt was not the only Republican pinning the label of treason on the opposition. Beveridge, Root, Lodge, Platt, and a host of imperialists pitched in to convince the electorate that Bryan represented Aguinaldo. "I will not say that the men who are encouraging the Filipino soldiers here are traitors to their country," Root declared with feigned magnanimity, "but I will say, and I think with justice, that the men who are shooting from ambush there are allies in the same cause, and both are enemies to the interest and credit of our country." Bryanism was the main cause of "our dead soldiers, the vacant chair, flag draped, in the homes of the Republic," Indiana's "golden boy" declared. Beveridge went on to ask his audience:

What said Lawton—Lawton, Indiana's pride? "If I am shot down by a Filipino bullet it might as well come from one of my own men . . . because the continuance of the fighting is chiefly due to reports that are sent out from America." Who will wear this on his forehead, the everlasting brand which Lawton's words burn?

But Beveridge cautioned that he was "appealing to no passions" as his party stood for "law and order," and the matter had to be settled by ballots, not fists or bullets. He was "merely stating the truth. . . . I state the facts. The defeat of the opposition to the government here is the defeat of the opposition to the govenment there."[42]

Senator Platt stooped so low as to attack Bryan's military record and asked one audience to compare it with Roosevelt's. Bryan "deserted his regiment to run for office," whereas Roosevelt left his office "to rush into battle." This sentiment was echoed in the *New York Sun*, whose editor continually asserted that the country needed "selfless" leaders like Teddy, who "left office to be in the thick of the fight and not the other way around." Implicit, of course, was that Bryan's motivation was cowardice.[43]

From the Philippines, General Funston tried to get into the act by writing a letter to Charles F. Scott, who was running for the congressional seat once held by the general's father. He told Scott that he held captured Filipino documents "that would make fine Republican campaign matter." One consisted of "instructions transmitted by Aguinaldo to his subordinates to keep up the fight hoping that it may bring about the defeat of McKinley." Funston's interference infuriated the Republican editor of the *Call*, who predicted that more electioneering from generals in the field would go hand in hand with imperialism. He cited the fact that so few Americans were outraged by Funston's action as evidence that the feared militarism had already arrived. Actually, Funston's offer was late. The Administration had already released a captured letter from Aguinaldo praying to "God that he may grant the triumph of the Democratic Party in the United States" and praising such "illustrious North Americans" as Bryan and Atkinson.[44]

Not all Republican oratory was demagogic. Along with humanitarian appeals and evangelical arguments, there was an attempt to create a tradition of expansionism built on actions of past Democratic leaders. Jefferson and Jackson had seen no contradictions in controlling the Louisiana and Florida territories, inhabited by people "as yet incapable of self government as China" and who were also "bitterly opposed to the transfer of sovereignty," Roosevelt lectured to an audience at Pocatello, Idaho. Yet no one then demanded "referendums for self determination" or accused Jefferson of "imperialism" or "militarism." Why not? "Because our ancestors were of finer mettle," he explained. "Imperialism you hear talked of. What does it mean?" he asked rhetorically:

> It means nothing. There is not an imperialist in the country that I have yet met. Expansion? Yes; playing the part of a great nation. . . . Expansion has been the law of our national growth. Our fathers worked, we rest; our fathers toiled, endured, dared, and we stay at home to avoid trouble; our fathers conquered the West, but we are a feeble folk and we cannot hold the Philippines.[45]

Roosevelt dismissed the accusation of militarism as "the most shadowy ghost that ever was raised to frighten political children." Anyone who loves his country is a "militarist" to Bryan and his supporters, who ask Americans "to dishonor their flag" to prove they are not militarists, he charged. "Slander" of this sort is to be expected from "the political heirs of the copperheads," who once accused "the patient and kindly Lincoln" of militarism and of imperial ambitions. *Harper's Weekly* joined Roosevelt in arguing that such terms as "imperialism" and "militarism" were "the empty wind of rhetoric" and "bogies constructed to frighten the timid" by "a party which stands for everything which is essentially subversive of good government, as a cloak under which its leaders may creep into power and put their pernicious doctrines into an operation."[46]

Other Republicans felt no obligation to provide any justification for the

war other than *realpolitik*. Lodge set the tone for this argument at the June
convention:

> We make no hypocritical pretense of being interested in the Philippines
> solely on account of others. While we regard the welfare of these people as
> a sacred trust, we regard the welfare of the American people first. We see
> our duty to ourselves as well as to others. We believe in trade expansion.[47]

In his endorsement speech for Roosevelt's candidacy, Chauncey Depew emphasized the importance of power and commercial gain to justify the conquest
of the Philippines and the invasion of China. Dewey's guns did not just speak at
Manila, but "echoed through the palace at Peking and brought to the Oriental
mind a new and potent force among western nations . . . striving to enter the
limitless markets of the east. These people respect nothing but power," Depew
declared. The *Sun* in New York had always felt more comfortable with this
straightforward argument, based on self-interest alone, and attributed the hesi-
tancy with which it was used to the "snobbery" of "college doctrinaires" whose
"sole occupation is minding other folks' business and issuing commands to the
country." They were the ones who invented "the anti-imperialist prattle about
'commercialism.'" There was nothing wrong with the profit motive, advised
the *Sun*, and gain should be the only reason for American expansion into the
Pacific.[48]

This trend toward economic justification of the Philippine situation was
forced on Republican campaigners by the Democrats, whose best argument
was that the islands could never return a profit large enough to cover the cost of
conquest. The war had cost "thus far $186,678,000, a war tax, and 2,394 Ameri-
can lives. All this is more than the Philippines are worth," announced the *Saint
Louis Republic*. "Feeble attempts are being made to show that our trade with
the islands is improving, but it would seem that as a cold-blooded business
proposition, we are engaged in a very bad speculation," observed the *New York
Herald* in the middle of the campaign. Political cartoonists depicted Uncle Sam
throwing money bags into the Pacific Ocean or shoveling gold coins endlessly
down "the Philippine rat hole." Indeed, the *Chattanooga Times* expressed
utter astonishment at the end of that summer over the "unanimity of the country in support of the government's policy to permanently retain all we got out of
the war with Spain," in view of the fact that the war in the Philippines was such
"a bad business proposition."[49]

At least this last editor had no illusions over the outcome of the pending
election. Possibly others anticipated a bitter defeat when, on election eve, they
began to protest the distortion of Bryan's position on the Philippines, as well as
all the "garbling, misrepresentation, perversion, and apology which have ema-

nated from the administration's defenders, beginning even with the President himself during the Presidential campaign." The Democratic Party advocated neither "surrender" nor "immediate withdrawal," nor "anarchy," the editor of the *Springfield Republican* pointed out. The alternative was not American rule in the Philippines, at any rate, but "the hideous spectacle" of continuous warfare, he protested. Contending that only one in twenty Filipinos surrendering under MacArthur's amnesty program that summer carried a rifle with him, the *Nation* charged the Administration with hiding from the voters the possibility of continuous warfare. In order to give the impression that the war was winding down, the Administration also made misleading claims of reductions in the number of American troops on the islands. As one lieutenant explained in a letter to his wife, "It looks good on paper, but there really has been no reduction of the force here. These 'battalions' [being sent home] are made up of men . . . about to be discharged." By November it was clear to many Democratic editors that they had been outmaneuvered by Republican deceit and distortion. Mark Sullivan recorded in his chronicle of the times how the "rancor grew with debate." "Dissension at home became more disagreeable than fighting the Filipinos. The spirit of America became sour."[50]

"Once the people spoke" that November, as Bryan had repeatedly warned that they would, the message was vastly different from what he had had in mind. It was the greatest Republican victory since 1872. McKinley not only kept all the states that he had won four years earlier, but also added Washington, South Dakota, Kansas, Wyoming, and even Bryan's Nebraska. One cannot isolate the issue of imperialism from the others, and, unquestionably, it was far less important than the monetary, trust, and labor issues. The people voted for McKinley's "full dinner pail," rather than for his Philippine policy.

Nevertheless, the fate of those few candidates who did tackle the issue rather vigorously indicates that anti-imperialism had little popular appeal. Governor Poynter failed to win reelection in Nebraska, and Pettigrew lost his support in South Dakota for another term in the Senate. On the other hand, Roosevelt and Beveridge, whose spread-eagle nationalism featured overseas expansion, were joyously received wherever they spoke. As though taking cues from the style of General Otis, however, the anti-imperialists rationalized their egregious defeat by stressing that McKinley's plurality was off slightly from 1896. In its second annual report, the Anti-Imperialist League stated that "we dare not and cannot recognize that the question of anti-imperialism was settled by that election." The *Call* informed its readers that only Bryanism was defeated and that any "good and able Democrat of higher character" could "have beaten McKinley on the anti-imperialist issue." Boutwell interpreted the election as an indication that the "masses" were somehow "losing faith" in the president and his Philippine policy! The *New York Sun* ridiculed such fatuous statements and counseled its readers:

> The rabid anti-imperialists are not to learn anything. Their monomania must be permitted to wear itself out. Their impotence to affect public opinion was shown by the election. Their impotence any longer to help the enemies of the United States in the Philippines is also evident. They will not cease to be noisy, but practically, they have become a negative quantity.[51]

Unfortunately there was at least a germ of truth in this.

Teddy Roosevelt, on the other hand, saw in McKinley's smashing victory a resounding endorsement of "ordered liberty" at home and expansion overseas. Although he had oversimplified the results, Roosevelt understood that anti-imperialism was an Achilles' heel for the Democrats, even more so than the silver issue, and advised that it be kept "to the fore in the Congressional campaigns, for if it is made the main issue we can certainly beat the Democrats out of their boots."[52] The Republicans had won an easy political victory in 1900, but winning the war would not be so easy. It certainly was not about to end within sixty days as pledged during the campaign.

9

The War under MacArthur, 1900–1901:
Déjà Vu

One of the new commander's virtues was that he was a realist who, unlike his predecessor, refused to delude himself about the course of the war in the Philippines. His first report in September, 1900, after four months in command, warned Washington that the war was not winding down and that the end was not even in sight. On the contrary, MacArthur believed that the guerrilla stage of the war was just beginning and that the Filipinos were refining their techniques with experience. Aguinaldo's strategy, moreover, had to rest on popular support, MacArthur cautioned:

> The success of this unique system of war depends upon almost complete unity of action of the entire population. That such unity is a fact is too obvious to admit of discussion; how it is brought about and maintained is not so plain. Intimidation has undoubtedly accomplished much to this end, but fear as the only motive is hardly sufficient to account for the united and apparently spontaneous action of several millions of people. One traitor in each town would eventually destroy such a complex organization. It is more probable that the adhesive principle comes from ethnological homogeneity, which induces men to respond for a time to the appeals of consanguinous leadership even when such action is opposed to their interests and convictions of expediency.[1]

MacArthur's report was just what was needed to rescue the anti-imperialists from postelection gloom. Why did all this "truth-telling become available only after the election?" demanded Sam Bowles of the *Springfield Republican*. It was just such "cruel and stupid ignoring of facts" in the past that "plunged us into the horrible mire in which we have now been floundering," opined the *Baltimore News*. By refusing to recognize the national feeling and aspirations of the Filipinos, our policy was bound to fail whatever our intentions, the *New*

150

York World concluded from the general's report. "Is it not plain now that the whole policy of pacification by force of arms is as unpracticable as it is un-American?" a chorus of anti-imperialist editors asked after reading the report. If MacArthur's assessment did not "sober the people," the latest "bill of over $100,000,000 a year to be presented indefinitely" for "McKinley's gems and glories of the tropic seas" would, advised the *Evening Post* in New York. Almost to a man, anti-imperialist editors insisted that the report would have changed the results of the election had it been released before the people went to the polls.[2]

The anti-imperialists should have been sobered by the reaction of their opponents. Almost no expression of surprise or any real acknowledgment of fundamental errors in the official interpretation of the Philippine situation was to be found in the imperialist press following MacArthur's report. Quite to the contrary, the editor of the *New York Sun* went so far as to hail the report as "one of the most illuminating documents on the subject that have as yet emanated from the Philippines." He went on to cite it as irrefutable proof of the soundness of the president's policy. "Now that the November election in the United States has dispelled one hope of the conspirators, it may be assumed that even the irreconcilables will give up their piratical warfare," the *Inter-Ocean* declared. It was as though these editors had not bothered to read the report at all. It is next to impossible to conceive of the editor of the *Philadelphia Press* concluding his discussion of the general's report with the recommendation that "a native police force with white officers" would be more effective against "scattered bands of guerrillas"—when MacArthur himself had reached very different conclusions. The *Evening Telegraph* argued that:

> No candid reader can peruse the report without arriving at the conclusion, already reached by all impartial observers, that the native tribes of the Philippine Islands are totally unprepared for self government, and that chaos and anarchy would be the inevitable result of abandonment by the United States. Under the circumstances, the people and Government of the country have no choice of alternatives; they must go forward without hesitation and without flinching, in the assumption of the onerous duties and responsibilities laid upon them by the fortune of war.[3]

Paradoxically, it was the editor of the *Army and Navy Journal* who seemed most affected by MacArthur's report. He reluctantly reached the opinion that the Philippine problem was "not altogether a military one" and cautioned his readers that "there is something required beside the rifle." The editor of the *Boston Herald* vainly expressed the hope that the report would at least compel Teddy Roosevelt to temper his language on the subject of the Filipinos:

The next Vice President has been in the habit of denouncing them in gross as "savages" and the example has been widely imitated. More than once in the course of a speech, he has compared them to the Apaches, a tribe formerly noted for their excessive barbarity of disposition and cruelty in war. General MacArthur gives no support to such representations of their nature.[4]

Meanwhile, the war continued with one discouraging report after another emanating from the Philippines. New Year's Eve revelers awoke to a new headache in 1901; the first editions of the year carried reports of "unprecedented activity everywhere around 477 American posts. Scouting parties and small expeditions strike day and night." January 5, the sixtieth day since McKinley's reelection, was greeted with irreverent hoots in the anti-imperialist press. Sam Bowles gloated as much as he dared in the face of American setbacks and reminded the victorious Republicans that they had scheduled the war to end by that day:

Never was a prediction more completely and ignominiously falsified by events as this one. . . . Bryan was licked and the traitorous anti-imperialists were sternly rebuked and the election did "confirm Presidential policy." But what has followed? By the admission of a leading administration senator [Republican William J. Sewell of New Jersey] military conditions in the Philippines have occupied themselves these sixty days in getting worse and worse. It seems to us that conditions which show no more respect than that for the honorable Philippine Commission and our *sacrosanct President* are too ungentlemanly to be noticed in polite society.[5]

Not even imperialist editors let the day go by entirely unnoticed. The *New York Times* conceded that the war was not going as expected:

The American people are plainly tired of the Philippine War. The administration must be aware that the case of its enemies is not weakened nor the confidence of its friends augmented by the daily reading about all this cost and killing. To kill rebellion by inches and trust to patience and slow time to bring back peace and contentment is not a humane or wise policy. It cannot be the lack of money. Is it the lack of troops, supplies, transportation, ammunition, artillery? Is it the lack of a competent commander? The public simply does not know where the trouble lies. It does know that there is trouble somewhere. Where is it? How long is this Philippine War going to last?[6]

Another staunchly imperialist editor admitted to being greatly confused by the conflict:

The United States at the present moment is not, technically, engaged in any war. But it is engaged in the warlike enterprise of putting down what is technically an insurrection—a large and baffling one. It seems strange to Americans that the Filipinos—or so many of them—are bitterly opposed to our sovereignty. They must know it is likely to be a great improvement over former conditions. . . . Nevertheless they fight on. The situation is a depressing one from every point of view. Good men are perplexed. Questions of right and wrong, of consistency with American ideals and principles, of stifling the "passion for independence," of national responsibility, of prudence—all are hard to decide.[7]

Each anti-imperialist editor kept his own tally of what he perceived to be defections from the cause of imperialism. It was impossible to resist the temptation to twit a Republican colleague or two with reminders of their earlier predictions and anticipations of glory and wealth that would inevitably follow McKinley's decision to keep the Philippines. The editor of New York's *Evening Post* gloated over the conversions:

It ill becomes a preacher to ask converts why they have been so long in coming to a knowledge of the truth, and so we shall not put any unpleasant queries to the New York *Times*, Boston *Herald* and Indianapolis *Journal* and other newspapers which are now making the belated discovery that everything Philippine is not for the best in the best possible of worlds. All that we care to note is that they are at last under conviction of sin, and crying out, "what must we do to be saved?" Is it not time to confess the whole policy a hideous blunder?[8]

But a careful reading of editorials in the imperialist press questions whether there had been many genuine conversions to the anti-imperialist cause. What these editors wanted was a greater military effort to speed up the end of the war, not a reconsideration of the policy that sent American troops to the Philippines in the first place. The *New York Times* angrily advised that whatever was necessary to conquer the Filipinos quickly must be carried out immediately. There was "neither economy, humanity, nor statesmanship in dallying with the present situation," advised the *Portland* (Oregon) *Journal*, warning that the war must be ended swiftly "at whatever cost." The *Oregonian* in the same city concurred, "The Philippine situation is not good from our standpoint, and it is not satisfactory to us; but it is as good as the Spanish had it for 300 years. We shall not be content with it, however. We shall make it better by the double method of force—*arms* and *persuasion*." By this time imperialist editors were aware of the hard line taken by Generals Young, Wheaton, Funston, and the outspoken Colonel Jacob Smith, and they urged McKinley and MacArthur to follow their counsel.[9]

Some of the president's strongest apologists, while fewer in number but more significant in terms of reputation, began to advise the opposite course in the first few months of 1901. The Englishman John Foreman, who had been so often cited by imperialists as the leading authority on the Philippines and who had personally advised the peace commission in Paris to keep all the Philippine islands, now decided that the conduct of American troops there made the continuation of such a policy impossible without heavy costs well beyond the value of the archipelago. The highly respected journalist George Kennan reached the same conclusion a few weeks later. Like Foreman, Kennan was by no means converted to the cause of anti-imperialism. He simply realized that the "deep-seated and implacable resentment" of American rule made the proposition uneconomical. He warned that:

> We have offered them many verbal assurances of benevolent intentions; but at the same time, we have killed their unresisting wounded; we hold 1,500 to 2,000 of them in prison . . . and we are resorting directly or indirectly to the Spanish inquisitional methods . . . that the present generation of Filipinos will forget these things is hardly to be expected.[10]

In theory, crucial defections of this sort from the cause of imperialism should have aroused greater opposition to the war, but the people seemed instead to be growing as weary of anti-imperialist demonstrations as they were of the conflict itself. A call went out for "mass protests" on February 4 to mark the second anniversary of the war, but the turnout was anything but massive. With few exceptions, the anti-imperialist press acknowledged this dubious rite of passage with bitter stoicism. More radical anti-imperialists then called for massive disruptions of the president's inauguration in March, an activity that could not have won the approval of the conservative Anti-Imperialist League. The *New York Evening Post* encouraged the scheme, if only to let McKinley know that no one had been "hoodwinked" by the phony Republican campaign pledge that the war would end within sixty days following his reelection. "We are aware, of course, that the role of patriotic Americans is to stand mute before the wisdom and goodness of their government in all that relates to policy in the Philippines," the editorial concluded, tongue in cheek. Some imperialist editors gleefully responded to the suggested "disorder" with ridicule. "Will the foes of the despot McKinley allow him to ride unrebuked along Pennsylvania Avenue? Will there be no protest of outraged freeborn men against him and other murderers of the heroic rebels in the Philippines?" taunted the *New York Sun*. The *Sun*'s editor proposed a ludicrous scenario for the event, in which a counterparade would be led by the vanquished Bryan, ringing a liberty bell amidst thirteen shackled Filipinos "hired for the occasion in the Bowery" and followed by "professors of the University of Chicago in a six-ass drag." But McKinley marched up Pennsylvania Avenue without incident.[11]

A better index of war-weariness than poor protest turnouts might have been the low enlistment rate for a third wave of volunteers as the second one approached its eighteenth month of service. The rate was low enough to foster rumors of pending conscription. Forgetting that he had long contended that there was a war and not an insurrection in the Philippines, the Reverend Adolph A. Berle, a pacifist and anti-imperialist, actively spread the alarm of a peacetime draft that would destroy American democracy. General Leonard Wood lent credence to such rumors when he told the Economic Club of New York, "Of course we want a volunteer service, just as we want volunteer morality . . . but none but the fool expects to get it." The alternative to a draft, he warned, would be "the murder of our sons and the dishonor of our women," a proposition that ignored the fact that most of the army was in the Philippines, rather than guarding our shores.[12]

By 1901, senatorial debate over the size of the regular army had become an annual affair, and the debate inevitably spilled over to the conduct of the war in the Philippines. Senator Teller used the occasion to present the Senate with a petition signed by two thousand of Manila's most prominent citizens, who had taken no part in the struggle and were presumed to favor American rule. The petition demanded the same degree of autonomy enjoyed by Canada within the British Empire, praised Aguinaldo as a worthy leader, and carried a warning that "for every insurgent killed another thousand will spring up." Invoking the names of Washington, Jefferson, Lincoln, and God, in that order, the petition appealed to the conscience of Americans, "as a people who once struggled for independence" themselves, to reconsider their position in the Philippines. Filipinos were struggling "against greater odds and greater wrongs than those which inspired the Republic," it averred. Senator Hawley was on his feet immediately following Teller's reading of the statement, shouting "flat treason": "It is an attack upon the United States, its authority, and its troops, and a passionate appeal to Filipinos to continue to kill our men. If Jefferson Davis had brought forth a similar appeal after the Battle of Gettysburg . . . it would have been a mild crime in comparison."[13]

But Sentor Hoar angered his fellow Republicans even more during the debate when he raised the question of American atrocities in the Philippines, a topic "more inadmissible," in the eyes of his colleagues and imperialist editors, than that of greater autonomy for the Filipinos. "Mr. Hoar should be grateful to Massachusetts for his re-election and ashamed of himself for coddling rebellion," the editor of the *New York Sun* observed icily. In a rare concession to the fact that "things are not going well" in the Philippines, the *Sun*'s imperialist editor argued that at such a time criticism of the army could not be tolerated—even though he had been intolerant of any criticism when General Otis was allegedly winning the war two years earlier. It was the duty of every patriotic American to stand by his country in this moment of trial, he insisted, denouncing the country's detractors, such as Hoar:

> Instead, some Senators have chosen to besmirch American honor. To represent American soldiers as murderers, ravishers, drunkards and licentious reprobates has been the habit of the curious citizens who shudder at imperialism and the facts. To bring reproach upon the annexation of the Philippines, it has been deemed necessary to foul the honor and character of the American army. The most extravagant and nauseating assertions have been made; and some worthy folks have been bamboozled by the dealers in lies, wholesale and retail, into believing that Americans in the Philippines had suffered sea change [turning] into brutes.[14]

The *Evening Post* responded to the *Sun*'s editorial by complaining that "the chief fact about the Philippines appears to be that if you lay any disagreeable truth before the administration you are a liar and a traitor." But while imperialist editors reacted defensively to the charges raised in the debate, President McKinley, according to one reporter in Washington, was deeply disturbed by Hoar's comments, as well as by other damaging concessions made by Republican leaders in the Senate:

> The frank acknowledgements made in the Senate by leading Republicans, in the debate over the army organization bill, that the military situation in the Philippines is extremely bad, are causing a good deal of comment as to the future purposes of the administration. President McKinley has several times lost heart to some extent, if the reports of certain private conversations are to be believed, in the effort to enforce American sovereignty with the bayonet.[15]

The same reporter advised that the president was waiting for a pending Supreme Court decision on whether the United States Constitution had to follow the flag. If the Court ruled affirmatively—and the rights of American citizenship had to be conferred upon the Filipinos and tariff barriers could not be raised against goods from the islands—then McKinley would greatly alter his policy and even consider backing out of the archipelago gracefully, this reporter predicted. After interviewing aides in the White House, he reported that the president was profoundly influenced by the example of France, which had taken seventeen years to subdue Algeria, and wanted to avoid a similar fate for the United States in the Philippines.[16]

The Supreme Court partially buoyed the foundering president when it ruled that spring not only that the possession of colonies was constitutional, but also that not all the guarantees in the Constitution need apply to such possessions. The legal reasoning behind the decisions of the "Insular Cases" was so tortured that four of the five concurring justices could not agree on a single rationale to justify each one of them. Secretary Root, an extremely capable corporate lawyer, was at a loss to explain the exact meaning of the rulings. "Ye-es as near as I can make out the Constitution follows the flag—but doesn't quite catch up with it." In his own inimitable style, Mr. Dooley had a better explanation:

"Some say it laves the flag up in th' air an' some say that's where it laves th' Constitution. Annyhow, something's in th' air. But there's wan thing I'm sure about."

"What's that?" asked Mr. Hennessy.

"That is," said Mr. Dooley, "no matter whither th' Constitution follows th' flag or not, th' Supreme Court follows th' illiction returns."[17]

The Administration struggled during 1901 to counter the deteriorating image of the Philippine situation. A new political organization, the Partido Federal, had been formed late in 1900 by former insurgent leaders and moderately conservative members of the propertied class, who had grown weary of the struggle and hoped to work out a compromise. They bombarded Washington with petitions asking for "American protection" against "Aguinaldo's outlaws" and suggested that a civil government replace the military one and that self-governing experiments on local levels be allowed. Such demands followed the recommendations of the Schurman Report, as well as Republican campaign promises. When this party sent the names of thousands of Filipinos who had joined, clamoring for "peace under American sovereignty," McKinley was able to announce a turning point in American-Filipino relations.[18]

If the Administration exaggerated the significance and size of the constituency of the Partido Federal, the opposition press was even more deceitful in misrepresenting it. The *Evening Post* attempted to deflate the president's "latest propaganda balloon" by reporting, quite inaccurately, that only four members of the seven-man "Directory" of this "pro-American party" were "natives" and that these four were employed by the Philippine Commission. Anti-imperialist editors picked up this false charge and attempted to establish its validity through repetition—a trick they may have learned from their imperialist counterparts. Thus, the *Evening Post* went on to express outrage over this charade that was of its own making:

For cool effrontery the attempt of a cooked-up "Directory of the Federal Party" in Manila to impose on the American public has been rarely equaled. It has struck the imperialist newspapers dumb. . . . They even think the Philippine Commission takes them for ninnies to send such humbug "petitions."[19]

Another curious organization that raised anti-imperialist suspicions was the Philippine Information Society, also formed at the end of 1900, which turned out position papers in 1901. It appears to have been the brainchild of moderate anti-imperialists such as Fiske Warren and C. F. Adams and imperialists such as Harvard's historian Albert Bushnell Hart, whose purpose was allegedly to avoid propaganda from both sides in order to uncover the truth. The *New York Sun* was satisfied that "Aguinaldo's friends are not connected with it," and well might this imperialist organ have been content, as the society's first report was a complete whitewash of the army and its role in provoking the war. Aguinaldo was depicted as little more than a terrorist who started the conflict to gain native support. Once this assessment was published, several prominent Americans protested the use of their names as supporters of the society. The report and later ones corroborating the official view were fully exploited by the imperialist press. "If any doubt has existed in the minds of unprejudiced observers and students of affairs in our Far Eastern archipelago, regarding the blame for the outbreak of hostilities," let them read the report of the Philippine Information Society, crowed the *Evening Transcript* in Boston.[20]

It is possible to infer from the contents of these reports that this group was fronting for the Administration. Schurz had warned Warren to stay "entirely clear of administration influences which are very insidious" and then protested the "misleading presentation of facts" in the Society's reports. Months before its formation, the *New York Times* cited "special information" that the Administration was attempting to form a private organization to counter the propaganda of the Anti-Imperialist League. James LeRoy, who had served as an aide to the Philippine Commission, was suspicious of some of the documents supplied to the Society but saw no direct link to the government. It is unlikely that Warren or Adams—or the highly respected scholar Hart—would have gone along with subterfuge. At any rate, it was easy to exaggerate the efficacy of such propaganda. Like the League, it is doubtful that the Philippine Information Society influenced many conversions.[21]

The Army Bill was passed in February with appropriations that raised editorial eyebrows and produced such headlines as "Our Staggering Military Budget For Militarism, $400,000,000 a Year." The *World* in New York demanded to know why "the more 'pacified' the Filipinos become, the more soldiers are necessary to keep them so." As soon as the money was appropriated, the reports from the Philippines became increasingly favorable. Several editors asked whether the bad news had been allowed to filter through in order to pass the biggest peacetime military budget in the nation's history. The *World* observed that:

> A truly heroic optimism now pervades the Philippine dispatches. Everything has suddenly become the best possible in the best possible of archipelagos. . . . The best of it is that the inhabitants are now giving us "truthful information" about affairs. We know it is truthful because it is the kind we want to hear.[22]

The Administration was even able to cajole a more optimistic report from MacArthur. His second report was so vastly different from his first that the editor of the *Evening Post* paused to wonder if, in view of the general's reputation for realistic assessments, conditions had actually improved:

> Everyone must hope that General MacArthur's sanguine dispatch really foretokens the speedy ending of hostilities in the Philippines. He has not so long a line of unfulfilled predictions to his credit as General Otis and has, in general, shown less disposition . . . to take the thing he would have as the thing that is.[23]

Early in 1900, the powerful Republican senator from Wisconsin, John C. Spooner, had proposed a bill authorizing the president to create a government for the Philippines once the Filipinos were subdued. Anti-imperialists opposed such a step because it suggested permanent American retention of the islands following the insurrection. Rather than risk a Democratic filibuster, the Republican leadership never brought Spooner's bill to the floor. But Taft was eager to begin the economic development of the Philippines, and he argued that building permits for railroads, mining concessions, and bank charters could not be granted until a government was formed. "It is this which we need now to assist us in the development of this country and make these people understand what it is to have American civilization about them," Taft wrote to Spooner. In 1901, Lodge shrewdly attached Spooner's bill to the army appropriation bill as an amendment. To placate the opposition, however, he made some crucial changes at Root's urging. Although the bill would authorize the president to institute civil government in the Philippines, it stipulated that this was a temporary step pending final action by Congress. Changes also put severe limits on the disposition of public lands and the granting of franchises that would be subject to amendment or even repeal by Congress. Indeed, leases and concessions were only to be made when "great public mischief" would result from postponing them. In any case, all such franchises would be terminated one year after the establishment of a permanent civil government.[24]

Spooner had never been a very enthusiastic imperialist and preferred to label himself a "commercial expansionist." As such, he consistently supported naval expansion and the acquisition of coaling stations and bases overseas, along with the plans to construct an isthmian canal. But he just as consistently opposed the annexation of larger territories "inhabited by people alien to us" and voted against the annexation of Hawaii on these grounds. He was most reluctant, for the same reasons, to vote for the treaty of Paris and did so largely out of party loyalty. He called the annexation of the Philippines "one of the bitterest fruits of the war."[25] But once the islands were in American hands, he was not above exploiting them commercially. More ardent expansionists, like Roosevelt and Root, actually feared unchecked economic exploitation by American corporations.

The severity of the attack on the Spooner amendment by some anti-imperialists is difficult to understand, since it accelerated the transfer from military to civilian control and provided a legislative check on the president's power over the islands, while limiting rather severely the degree of commercial exploitation. One historian writes that "Root's changes struck a responsive chord in Congress. Anti-imperialists and most Democrats approved them in principle."[26] But this appears not to have been the case in the anti-imperialist press, in which editors, parroting Senator Hoar's attack on the Spooner provision, insisted that it would "confer absolute monarchical powers over twelve millions of human beings." Hoar called it "pure, simple, undiluted, unchecked despotism." Possibly the Spooner amendment, coming on the heels of the Supreme Court's decisions on the "Insular Cases," destroyed the last, illusionary hope of the anti-imperialists that the United States would withdraw from the Philippines "with honor" after suppressing the "insurrection."[27]

Meanwhile the war in the islands went on in earnest. MacArthur's leadership differed from that of his predecessor in some respects. Unlike Otis, MacArthur did make sincere—or what he felt were sincere—attempts to negotiate with the Filipino patriots. He had been privately critical of Otis on this score, particularly once he recognized Aguinaldo's popular appeal.

Although MacArthur's amnesty program was ridiculed by anti-imperialist editors as a "grandstand play" aimed at the presidential election in the United States, he intended it as a genuine step toward reconciliation and negotiation. He lost no time in initiating discussions with Filipino leaders who were released from jail under the program. MacArthur's problem was that he was far too imperious to permit anything resembling a free and open exchange of viewpoints. He refused flatly "even to discuss" an eight-point program of Pedro

Paterno's that included civil government, constitutional rights, and the acknowledgment of military ranks in the Philippine army. In fact, the American military commander had the audacity to lecture the highly-educated Apolinario Mabini during one such discussion and subsequently recounted his own sophomoric platitudes:

> Mabini was expatiating to me on the desire of himself for independence. He said independence was absolutely essential to good government. "No," said I, "Mabini you have a confusion of ideas, I think. Tell me what government on earth you think is the worst." Well, he mentioned a number. . . . Said I, "Mabini, they are all independent nations. A nation to be entirely bad has to be absolutely independent, and," said I, "your desire is for personal liberty such as is enjoyed under the American Constitution. The independence of a nation does not insure good government." Said he, "that is very true; that precise idea had never entered my head." "Reflect on it," said I. . . . Said he, "that is a new idea, and I will think it out." What he accomplished in thinking it out I do not know because I never had another conversation on the point with him.[28]

Mabini's reaction was never recorded, but one can assume he must have been either too polite or too flabbergasted to pursue the matter.

Because MacArthur chose to believe that he was negotiating genuinely with the Filipinos, he would become enraged over what he felt were betrayals of his good faith. On one occasion he granted permission to Pedro Paterno to host a huge banquet and fiesta to express Filipino gratitude for the amnesty, with careful stipulations that politics be avoided in the celebrations. Instead, Paterno decorated the banquet hall with pictures of Aguinaldo draped with the flag of the Philippine Republic over cleverly worded double entendres and thinly veiled pleas for autonomy. As soon as MacArthur got wind of the decor, he and the members of the Philippine Commission refused to attend the banquet as honored guests unless the decorations were removed under supervision of the U.S. provost marshal of Manila and Paterno's planned speech politically bowdlerized. When the atmosphere was rendered properly antiseptic, Taft and Luke Wright of the commission arrived two hours late, and MacArthur failed to show up at all. Taft wrote to Root that the affair was a "fiasco."[29]

By the end of the summer, MacArthur's ninety-day limit on his amnesty offer expired. The results were disappointing after the initial flurry of surrenders had tapered off, and even then it was suspected that many of the natives surrendering were merely opportunists collecting bounty for obsolete weapons. Once MacArthur felt that it was time to change tack, the new commander began to listen seriously to the advice that Otis had so long rejected: that harsher methods be employed, similar to those used against the Indians in the American West. Actually, the leading advocate of such tactics, General Samuel Young, preferred to call them "European methods" developed specifically for "rebellious Asiatics." The French had published theories about colonial warfare based on their experiences in Indochina and Algeria, which Young had recommended as required reading at West Point.[30]

Young returned to the United States that fall and began to accustom American audiences to the idea that harsher measures had to be adopted if the insurrection were not to go on forever. As keynote speaker at a Grand Army of the Republic celebration honoring Ulysses S. Grant's birthdate, Young portrayed the war as a racial, rather than a political, struggle:

> The keynote of the insurrection among the Filipinos past, present and future is not tyranny, for we are not tyrants. It is race. This then, gentlemen, is the whole thing in a nutshell. If you ask me the quickest and easiest way to bring peace and good order to the Filipino, I can only say that, like a chameleon, we must put him on such a background that he can change his color.

Young insisted that "the Filipino is happiest when most unhappy. He is born that way. He revels in wrongs and can't get along without them." According to a reporter on the spot, this nonsense received a standing ovation from a distinguished audience that included several congressmen, governors, and a bevy of senior army officers. In other speeches in 1901, Young praised Kitchener and hailed British techniques in South Africa as the model for America. "The Anglo Saxon has been gaining wide experience simultaneously fighting enemies full of wile and cunning," Young declared, insisting that future wars of conquest would be that much easier.[31]

Young was hardly alone in advocating harsher treatment of the Filipinos. It appeared that the entire American army, from private to general, demanded severe retaliation for the constant sniping, small ambushes, and clever booby traps that claimed the lives of their comrades one or two at a time. The correspondent for the *Evening Post* warned that an angry mood was pressuring MacArthur to wage "unrestricted warfare":

> A spirit of bitterness has crept into the rank and file of the army in the Philippines because of the policy which permits the American soldiers to be murdered in the most dastardly manner and the murderers remain at large. . . . Official reports to the contrary, officers and men who know the situation and natives are all agreed that the Filipino hates us as he never hated the Spaniard; that every Filipino is an insurrecto; and that the pres-

ent guerrilla warfare will continue for years unless some strong policy be inaugurated. Fear is the only force that the Tagal savage recognizes, and he is not much afraid of the American as he was of the Spaniard. In plain language the Filipino thinks the American a fool because he does not use his power or retaliate.[32]

MacArthur himself tried to prepare the American public for the possibility of unconventional methods. He decreed that henceforth captured Filipino guerrillas would no longer be treated as soldiers but as "criminals" and "murderers," for

men who participate in hostilities without being part of a regular organized force, and without sharing continuously in its operations, but who do so with intermittent returns to their homes and vocations, divest themselves of the character of soldiers and if captured are not entitled to privileges of prisoners of war.[33]

General Otis had threatened such action but had refrained from carrying it out. Anti-imperialist editors protested vigorously that such a step would remove any difference between American and Spanish rule in the Philippines. Executing prisoners on the pretense that they were murderers would serve no earthly purpose, warned the *Call*, as "there is no instance in history proving that such aspirations [nationalism] can be eradicated by any cruelty or slaughter that stops short of extermination." It reminded MacArthur that Spain had taken the same first step in Cuba on the path to tyranny. "It is worthwhile to remember that she [Spain] began with moderation and finally was compelled to do wholesale murder." But MacArthur went ahead with his plans and had several Filipino prisoners of war executed for the "murder" of American prisoners. Such "inhuman conduct" had removed these Filipino prisoners "from the pale of law," he declared.[34]

Other directives made it clear that MacArthur had capitulated to the hardliners. Headlines announced, "MacArthur tells Filipinos 'Be Good or Be Shot'" and "Forbearance Has Ceased To Be a Virtue in the Philippines." The frontpage headline in the *Boston Herald* declared of the new strategy:

Will Show No Mercy
Real Warfare Ahead For Filipino Rebels
Kitchener Plan Adopted
The Administration Weary of Protracted Hostilities.[35]

The reference to Kitchener made eminently clear MacArthur's intent, as the British general's tactics in South Africa had already earned him comparison to

"Butcher Weyler" in Cuba. Like Otis, Kitchener would consider only unconditional surrender, an attitude that served to stiffen Boer resistance. Kitchener then constructed concentration camps and executed prisoners and hostages. He defended these measures by accusing the Boers of savagery and of disregarding the laws of civilized warfare. Several English journalists smugly suggested that Kitchener would soon teach the Americans how to quell colonial rebellion. One young English journalist by the name of Winston Spencer Churchill lectured New Yorkers on the subject after his tour in South Africa. A graduate of Sandhurst and imbued with high professional standards, the young Churchill assured his American audience that he personally deplored such tactics but accepted that they were absolutely necessary in South Africa and in the Philippines simply because the Boers, like the Filipinos, did "not know when they are whipped." [36]

South Africa and the Philippines were not the only sites of brutal slaughter at the time. Reports from around the globe tended to mitigate MacArthur's plans for harsher methods. Newspapers were full of incredible tales of atrocities in the Belgian Congo, and it appeared that the Mexican government was bent on exterminating the troublesome Yaqui Indians. British and French naval commanders were constantly shelling coastal villages in Africa as though for target practice. In the Pacific an American squadron under Admiral Kautz teamed up with the Royal Navy to shell villages in Samoa, and the skipper of H.M.S. Porpoise told a reporter that shore bombardment relieved the boredom of tedious patrols in the middle of nowhere. "We are out here in this beastly, Godforsaken country and we had to have some fun to keep alive," he explained. American Consul Osborne did not appreciate the recreational firing, however, when a shell from the U.S.S. Philadelphia narrowly missed his house and killed an American Marine sentry. Osborne protested to Washington that Kautz was firing on villages "in which there were only inoffensive old men, women and children." [37]

Although MacArthur in his own mind was sure that the new and harsher tactics were justified, he nevertheless tightened the censorship that he had inherited from Otis and forbade correspondents to spell out any new methods being used. Those who refused to comply were repatriated to the United States; native editors were exiled to Guam. Ironically, the revelation of this censorship, supposedly ended by Otis, did not involve a war critic at all, but a veteran of the Minnesota volunteers, George T. Rice, who had remained in Manila to edit the Daily Bulletin, a maritime journal that focused on the port of Manila. Like most veterans, Rice was critical of Otis for not having pursued the war more vigorously. He was equally critical of civilian controls over the military and attacked the Philippine Commission for being too soft on the natives.

In short, Rice's views on the war and on imperialism in general were not too different from those of Fred Funston. But Rice ran afoul of MacArthur when he exposed corruption along the waterfront. He accused Lieutenant Commander William Braunereuther, the captain of the port of Manila, of charging excessive piloting and mooring fees and pocketing the surplus. Rather than ascertain the validity of the published charges, however, MacArthur immediately banished Rice from the Philippines as "a dangerous incendiary and a menace to the military situation."[38]

Such front-page headlines as "Muzzling the Press," "Militarism in Operation," and "MacArthur and George III" heralded the Rice affair in the anti-imperialist press. Once again editorials complained that "the knowledge of facts about the Philippines has been limited at all times by the most insolent censorship. . . . Now they deport reporters for doing their job." Just how long, "God, how long," would the American people continue to tolerate "the arrogant demands of these military martinets?" asked one exasperated editor in Chicago.[39]

In the wake of the sensationalized revelation of MacArthur's cavalier treatment of Rice, Clemencia Lopez arrived in the United States to secure the services of the famed jurist and future Supreme Court Justice, Louis Brandeis, to aid her brother's fight against deportation to Guam. Miss Lopez told reporters that her brother, General Sixto Lopez, and many others who had surrendered in good faith, had been arbitrarily deported by MacArthur. The general simply ignored the terms of his own amnesty agreement when it suited him and allied himself with Filipinos "of evil life and conduct who have no sense of honor," she complained. Reminding his colleagues that arbitrary deportation of this sort had been a key grievance of the American colonists against George III, Senator Hoar took up Miss Lopez's cause on the senate floor.[40]

Unsurprisingly, imperialist newspapers such as the *New York Sun*, insisting that those banished and deported were "war traitors," defended MacArthur's actions. In some way, Rice had given "comfort and aid to the enemy," the *Sun* declared; moreover, criticism of MacArthur was "ignorant, much of it malicious, and all of it ill-advised." It was obvious to most people that "a wartime commander has police power of the highest order," observed the *Sun's* editor, conveniently forgetting that he himself on other occasions had insisted the activity in the Philippines was merely an "insurrection." Indeed, at the very moment the *Sun* was justifying censorship and deportation as wartime measures, the War Department, in order to avoid combat pay, reasserted its position that there was no "war" in the islands. McKinley's spokesman, Senator Hanna, also declared that "there is no war in the Philippines." In the very same speech Hanna stated "there are no trusts," as though *ex cathedra* denials eliminated the existence of such evils. The *Sun's* editor ignored these official pronouncements, however, in order to deny the historical analogy between Mac-Arthur and George III:

> Some persons have pretended to find a parallel between MacArthur and George III, the latter of whom was charged in the Declaration of Independence with "transporting colonists beyond the seas to be tried for pretended offences," but there is no parallel actually because . . . [it was done] in times of peace.[41]

Actually the analogy may have been unfair to the English monarch, who had been far less arrogant, arbitrary, and imperious than MacArthur in many ways.

MacArthur's most serious obstacle to carrying out his plans was not the press, however, but William Howard Taft, who had become uncomfortable over the legality of the general's action and used the increased powers of the Philippine Commission to challenge the military leadership. In order to bypass the obstinate Taft, MacArthur went to Commissioner Wright, a lawyer and former general himself, and induced him to write the Treason Laws used to deport people and to put prisoners of war on trial for "murder." In these laws, Wright defined treason as joining any secret political organization or even as "the advocacy of independence or separation of the islands from the United States by forcible or peaceful means"; taking up arms against American authority was a "criminal act," and any death resulting from such an act was "murder." As one of the nation's outstanding constitutional lawyers, Taft conceded that the legality of these laws was highly questionable, except as emergency wartime measures, although he later warned a senate committee that such laws would have to be retained after peace was restored and "well into the foreseeable future."[42]

Taft's differences with MacArthur were personal as well as legal. When Taft broached the subject of the constitutionality of the Treason Laws, as well as some of the military commander's arbitrary acts, MacArthur lectured Taft on constitutional law! The civilian governor was astounded, not only by MacArthur's unorthodox interpretation of the Constitution, but by the general's presumption that with no formal training whatsoever he was the more expert in Taft's professional field. MacArthur advised the astonished Taft that the president's instructions to the Second Philippine Commission constituted "an unconstitutional interference with his prerogative as military commander in these islands." Taft quickly relayed MacArthur's thoughts to Secretary Root, another professional lawyer with a national reputation, and added in a tone of utter disbelief:

> The Constitution has not often been used to maintain undiminished the absolute legislative, executive, and judicial power of a subordinate military commander as against the express orders of his commander-in-chief.[43]

It would appear that MacArthur actually perceived his role as that of America's first "proconsul," with absolute power in the Philippines. A bit of a peacock to begin with, he deliberately played the part of an emperor in the belief that it would impress the "Oriental mentality," and to Taft's chagrin, he got away with his presumptions. The feistier Teddy Roosevelt might have been able to cut him down to size, but MacArthur left the Philippines almost three months before McKinley was assassinated.

It is not that Taft considered the Filipinos capable of governing themselves. He later informed the Lodge committee investigating conditions in the islands that "unquestionably chaos would follow self government" and that "even the educated Filipinos are below par." They were "glib," able "to run off phrases," but rarely could they "understand concepts." This inability was the basic problem in discussing politics with them, Taft informed the committee. The Filipinos became "intoxicated" on words, particularly by the "oratorical use" of terms such as "independencia," without understanding their meanings. But Taft angered the military by discussing politics with them at all and by characterizing the Filipino as "our little brown brother" who needed to be uplifted through kindness and gentle understanding. The soldiers retorted in song that "he may be a brother of William H. Taft, but he ain't no friend of mine."[44] Once MacArthur began formulating and announcing plans for reprisals and for the treatment of civilians as the enemy (until proven otherwise), the rift between the military and Taft grew wider. When MacArthur failed to end the war with such measures, Taft became a convenient scapegoat.

MacArthur's one break in the spring of 1901 was the capture of Aguinaldo. When Otis departed from the islands, he claimed that Aguinaldo was "probably dead" and that he was "merely a figurehead" at any rate, "too unimportant to worry about." His capture changed that story, of course, and provided MacArthur with the illusion he had won the war. According to the imperialist press, the capture broke the back of the rebellion, particularly when Aguinaldo swore allegiance to the United States and urged his followers to surrender.

Aguinaldo's capture was brilliantly masterminded by General Funston when a message requesting more troops from the Filipino leader to his brother, Baldomero, was intercepted by the Americans. The courier revealed his leader's location—possibly with the help of the "water cure"—and his coded message was finally deciphered. Funston then recruited eighty-one carefully screened Tagalog-speaking Macabebe scouts to pose as the requested reinforcements, equipped with captured Filipino weapons, and in some cases, uniforms. He added several renegade "insurgents" and a former Spanish secret service agent to serve as leaders, while he and four other American officers went along in the guise of prisoners captured en route to Palanan. The navy dropped this contingent off at Casiguran Bay on Luzon's northeastern coast (see map, p. 223). From there they followed jungle trails for more than fifty miles to Palanan. To allay suspicions in villages along the way, as well as in Aguinaldo's headquarters, Funston sent messages ahead bearing the forged signature of General Lacuna. The only hitch occurred when Aguinaldo sent back a message ordering that the American prisoners be left under guard several miles from Palanan and informing them that he was sending out his own detachment to take them over. Instead, the Americans plus some of the Macabebes hid in the bush and circumvented the enemy soldiers, who had been misinformed that the "prisoners" had been left behind on the coast as directed.

The disguised Macabebes entered Palanan in the middle of a birthday celebration for Aguinaldo. They were saluted by his honor guard and personally congratulated by the Philippine president for their capture of American soldiers along the way. Appearing to return the salute, the Macabebes opened fire, while Funston's group rushed the village in such a way as to give the impression that many more enemy soldiers were involved. The defenders fled in panic, leaving behind their leader. Funston dashed to the coast and a prearranged rendezvous with the U.S.S. *Vicksburg* before it was discovered how few men he actually had.[45]

Washington directed MacArthur to impose total secrecy on the mission, and under no conditions to make public any propositions or comments by the prisoner, "particularly any references to earlier claims or promises by American officers," without obtaining prior clearance from the War Department. But Funston's publicity-hungry staff had already leaked the details to the press before the mission was even completed. On the day that the navy picked him up, March 25, 1901, the *Boston Herald* ran a front-page story on "Funston's Plan to Capture Aguinaldo by Ruse." The *Call* ran that story a day earlier. Most editors, however, ignored it until Washington officially acknowledged the capture several days later. No doubt the many public plans of Otis's to trap Aguinaldo had made them cautious. Much earlier, a Japanese editor had warned accurately enough that:

> It will amount to this, that when Aguinaldo is taken—if he ever is—and when the Philippine army is smashed, people will not believe it. Most people will wink the other eye and say the Americans must be getting badly cornered again.[46]

Once the reality of the feat sank in, Funston became the hero of the hour, basking in a glory that almost rivaled the nation's reaction to Dewey's victory at Manila three years earlier, at least in the imperialist press. Any doubts and ugly rumors about Funston's past military conduct were momentarily erased. Roosevelt wired his personal congratulations for this "crowning exploit of a career filled with cool courage" and "iron endurance." As a reward, McKinley pressured the War Department to grant Funston a regular commission as a brigadier general, the youngest in the army at the time. Funston even won over some of his soldier critics in the field. "What do you think of Funston's capture of Aggie? Out of sight, wasn't it? I used to think he was a trifle too spectacular and inclined to talk too much, but wherever he is things move," Sergeant Daley confessed to his brother back home. The cocky little Kansan was far less successful in winning over other critics in the states. Adjutant General Henry Corbin, calling Funston "a boss scout—that's all," publicly protested his reward. Corbin had plenty of company in the War Department, where one reporter recorded that the general reaction to the news was "anybody but Funston."[47]

It was a rare instance when senior army officers agreed with anti-imperialist editors on any subject, but they agreed that anyone but Funston should have carried off this spectacular capture. Sam Bowles gloomily predicted in the *Springfield Republican* the "militaristic nightmare" of a Roosevelt-Funston ticket in 1904. Worried about this possibility, the *Call*'s editor labored to debunk the general's legendary heroics, making some errors of his own. That heroic swim across the Rio Grande de Pampanga under fire was proved to be one of Funston's own inventions, he declared. And he called those "Death Valley explorations" being bandied about "a laugh, and now 'Munchausened' in the press—a summer geological-botanical survey sponsored by the University of Kansas!"[48]

A more serious criticism of Funston's exploit focused on the legality of the means used to capture Aguinaldo. The opposition characterized the successful scheme as the "basest treachery," "unbecoming a civilized military power or a United States soldier and a violation of the accepted laws of war." The *Call* and the *Republican*, on opposite coasts, perceived Funston's ruse as nothing more than a part of the lawless warfare being carried out under MacArthur's command. The Administration felt pressed enough on this charge to enlist the aid of Yale's expert on international law, Theodore Woolsey. This professor had gone through as dramatic a transformation on the subject of imperialism as Bishop Potter had done, albeit in the opposite direction. After initially opposing expansion, he became one of the leading academic defenders of the war to subjugate the Filipinos. Thus Woolsey's justification of Funston's tactics came as no surprise, although he went beyond purely legal reasoning to offer a curious end-justifies-the-means argument that further clouded the legality of Funston's actions.[49]

Writing in *Outlook*, Woolsey argued that Funston's plan was "well within the traditional 'ruses of war'" that are "as old as warfare itself." As long as the general "did not break faith," the forged documents and letters were acceptable, the professor decreed. The use of enemy uniforms, however, was not so easily explained, so Woolsey had to resort to the reasoning that since the United States was not at war "with a civilized power," and "since the Aguinaldo party was not a signatory of the Hague Convention . . . there was no obligation on the part of the United States Army to refrain from using the enemy's uniforms for the enemy's deception." On the other hand, one must infer, the Filipinos were obligated to follow the rules of the Hague Convention since they were fighting a civilized power and signatory of that agreement. As if this reasoning were not devious enough, Woolsey further declared that "it was not a question of either law or ethics, but of common sense." Thus he asked his readers to "contrast the good likely to flow from the hastening of the end of the insurrection by means of it, with the offense of the use of enemy uniforms—a stratagem illegal in war only with a lawful belligerent—and you have the measure of the justice of the criticism."[50]

Having captured Aguinaldo, the government faced the problem of what to do with him. After all the propaganda depicting Filipino atrocities against American prisoners, it would be difficult to avoid some sort of punishment, and yet any harsh treatment of him could backfire. The Administration was eager not to make Aguinaldo a martyr and repeat Spain's error in its handling of the Filipino patriot, Jose Rizal, in 1896. Some imperialist editors clamored for Aguinaldo's head. "It is impossible to forget even now that he directed the burning of Manila and the assassination of all Americans, without distinction of sex," the *Philadelphia Press* reminded its readers and added that "any power but England and the United States would execute him in a few hours." How could it be overlooked that Aguinaldo was a "vain, deceitful, cruel, tyrannical adventurer, who has betrayed all who trusted him, and who sought to aggrandize himself by means of systematic murder and arson," demanded the *New York Tribune*. Admiral Dewey completed the betrayal of his "good friend, Don Emilio," by recommending to reporters that he be shot, a good way to silence those tenaciously nagging charges that the admiral had betrayed an earlier alliance with the insurrectionists. Root knew better, however, and cabled MacArthur to prefer charges "only if it should appear that he had violated laws of war." Listing specific charges presented a major obstacle to bringing Aguinaldo to trial. As a *New York World* editorial asked sarcastically, "Of course he should be punished for his crime, but what was his crime? Was it his refusal to acknowledge Spain's right to sell him for $2.50 on the hoof?"[51]

Aguinaldo settled the question abruptly by swearing allegiance to the United States and appealing to his followers to surrender and follow suit. His image was dramatically reversed in the American press. Suddenly, anti-imperialist editors were borrowing Roosevelt's epithets to label Aguinaldo "a Filipino Benedict Arnold." The shocked editor of the *Philadelphia Record* observed with disgust that "few professional traders in patriotism have more successfully marketed their wares." The *Baltimore American* quickly shelved the encomiums it once showered on Aguinaldo and denounced his plea for surrender as "the bombastic, puerile, fawning, insincere statement of an opportunist in bad plight."[52]

Imperialist editors were, of course, delighted with this sudden turn of events and twitted the war critics over the confusion in their ranks caused by Aguinaldo's action, which left them "with nothing to abuse the administration about." This "Patrick Henry, Nathan Hale and George Washington of the Philippines" had, in the end, "nothing about him that suggests Hoar's ideal hero," teased one editor. Imperialist editors overlooked their own short memories and abruptly began to eulogize the man they had vilified for years. The *New York Times*, long in the habit of calling Aguinaldo everything from a "lying popinjay" to a thief and a looter, now described him as a "warm, friendly, intelligent, trustworthy, and reasonable person—a man of honor with the best interests of his countrymen at heart."[53]

Over the next few months, an impressive array of Filipino leaders answered Aguinaldo's appeal, which had removed the stigma of treason from the act of surrender. Generals Alejandrino, Tinio, Mescardo, Lucon, and Cailles turned in their swords and the armed men in their commands. Sandiko, Father Aglipay, and Aguinaldo's brother Baldomero and cousin Pedro soon joined Emilio in Manila. It appeared, at long last, that the bottom had dropped out of Filipino armed resistance to American rule by the summer of 1901. The mood in the United States became self-congratulatory, and even conciliatory on the part of imperialists, who advised burying the past in order to build for the future. "In good truth, a whole host of Filipino insurgents richly deserve drastic punishment," one editor observed. "They had a right, of course, to make war upon us . . . [but] no right to wage it according to the rule of uncivilized peoples." But punishing them now that the war was over would be counterproductive, he decided. "We should remember that, after all, the Filipinos are much like children, requiring to be petted and pampered, else they become stubborn and rebellious." It was even time "to forgive and forget" the "more despicable and traitorous acts" of the anti-imperialists at home, he advised, with presumptuous magnanimity. One editor argued that the war, in the end, was a valuable learning experience for America.

> Now that the war is over . . . the experience that the Philippine problem has given us is among the most helpful chapters in our whole national history. We showed again the character of American manhood . . . that when men of English stock set out to do a new task, hysterical critics cannot deter them. The race has found its development by doing things.[54]

Amidst this unctuous self-congratulation, two crucial realities were being ignored. First, and foremost, the war was not over. Two important pockets of resistance to American rule still existed: in Batangas, led by General Malvar,

and in Samar under General Lukban. Smaller bands fought sporadically elsewhere in the archipelago and, much more serious, the Moros were becoming
increasingly restive on Mindanao and Jolo. Secondly, little was being said about
the escalation of unrestricted warfare being waged to hasten the end of the conflict. Only the atrocities committed by enemy "diehards" were mentioned. It
was charged that, on assuming overall command after Aguinaldo's capture,
General Cailles ordered the execution of eight American prisoners. But Cailles
had long enjoyed a good reputation with American field commanders. A Colonel Cheatham once praised him for returning American dead with all their personal property. At any rate, when Cailles surrendered a few months later, no
charges were made against him, indicating that this widely reported execution
of prisoners probably had been invented for purposes of propaganda.[55]

Once Cailles had surrendered, even the more realistic MacArthur was certain the war was over. Of course, he was about to be relieved after thirteen
months in command and close to three years of service in the Philippines, so he
had a special interest in claiming victory. His final month in command was
flawed, however, by the exposure of commissary frauds. Rumors of the misuse
of commissary funds had been chronic during the war. One veteran had charged
that "high class wines were being purchased as hospital supplies," and another
outlined how commissary personnel received kickbacks from civilian suppliers.
Even Otis had once conceded "that men in high positions in Manila are getting
rich too quickly." He had vowed "stern punishment for offenders," but nothing
ever came of it, and Otis ended up reporting that there was no basis to the
charges of kickbacks. One reporter charged Otis with selling favors and claimed
to have seen personally a letter from Otis to John D. Rockefeller offering oil
concessions for a percentage of the profits. Lieutenant Colonel J. W. Pope, the
chief quartermaster under Otis, confessed that his former boss had granted
special favors to businessmen, but the matter was dropped until headlines revived it in May of 1901. MacArthur scoffed at the "exaggerated charges" in the
press and responded to worried inquiries from the War Department with the
assurance there was little to them:

> Commissary frauds being investigated; not sufficient gravity to cause con-
> cern: apparently irregularities due sales savings. Press reports inexact,
> misleading as all have been since removal censorship.[56]

MacArthur faced damning evidence uncovered by an enterprising reporter: The lavish house of Colonel Woodruff had been expensively furnished
by contractors, and the captain and seven sergeants who ran the commissary
had huge personal accounts in a Manila bank. Once this was reported, Mac-
Arthur was forced to indict the eight men, two of whom, Captain Reed and

Sergeant Meston, were convicted. In spite of their convictions, however, the inspector general sent from Washington to investigate commissary corruption returned to San Francisco to announce incongruously that "the frauds that are supposed to have occurred in Manila are not known officially in Washington and no official reports were made of them. I think it was a great stir over nothing." The *Call* reminded its readers that "officially there is no war, no censorship, and now no corruption in the Philippines."[57]

Following Aguinaldo's capture, the Administration speeded up the "benevolent" programs that had been for so long ridiculed as "soft" by some military leaders. The army was ordered to supervise the scrubbing of towns and their inhabitants. Since the natives did not share the antiseptic obsession of their conquerors, delousing was invariably carried out at gunpoint, as were other sanitary measures. "They certainly are an irritating people," Lyon declared after describing the resistance he encountered while spreading "benevolence." Work gangs were impressed by American soldiers, who were then shocked that these people wanted to be paid for cleaning up their own dirt. The Filipino worked little under any circumstances, Funston explained, because:

> A Filipino is chronically tired. He is born tired; he stays tired and he dies tired. If you hire him he will labor a few days, and then he goes out of the work business for about a week, while he attends a fiesta or two. It doesn't matter how much you pay him; a Filipino will work as hard for 50¢ a week as he will for 50¢ a day.

Because of this reputed laziness, many officers impressed Chinese workers whenever available, but also refused to pay them. "Rounded up all the Chinamen I could find and set them to work cleaning up the town which was very dirty. They wanted pay which I would not give them and I had great difficulty keeping them together," Major Kobbe recorded in his diary.[58]

No American basked more proudly in the warm glow of "victory" and the smug self-righteousness of paternalistic benevolence than did President McKinley. He embarked on a tour of the nation "to heal the sharp divisions" created by the conflict. Starting in New England, he visited the nation's sacred monuments at Lexington and Concord with his anti-imperialist critic, Senator Hoar, at his side. At Harvard University, he called upon Americans to forget their past differences over the Philippines and unite in peace to carry out the task assigned to them by Providence: to bring the benefits of American civilization to the Filipinos. Not all anti-imperialists were as conciliatory as George Hoar, however. The editor of the *Boston Globe* suggested that the erudite senator might lecture his companion at Lexington on the "true relationship of the 'embattled farmers' who fired the shot 'heard round the world' to the cause of imperialism." At Harvard, war critics on the board of overseers bitterly opposed Hoar's attempt to have an honorary degree conferred upon the president at the next commencement. In the end, they supported Hoar's motion twenty to three, but President McKinley diplomatically declined with the excuse that he would not be able to return in a month to receive it.[59]

The president's tour ended in San Francisco with a visit to the Presidio to thank personally soldiers who had just returned from the Philippines (although one editor maliciously claimed that the assembled troops were in reality on their way to the islands to continue the war that had not yet ended). McKinley told the soldiers that there was "no imperialism but that of the sovereign power of the American people" who knew the "arts of peace" better than "those of war." Climbing a nearby sand dune, McKinley gazed at the Pacific in the manner of the conquistador Balboa and claimed that vast ocean for "American freedom." A front-page headline in the *Call* caught the bathos of the moment, "President Journeys Within Sound of Breaking Waves of the Pacific, and Looking Out Over Its Broad Expanse, Declares For Extension of Our Liberty to Philippines."[60]

MacArthur carried out his final act as governor-general of the Philippines on July 4, 1901, by transferring his authority over civilian affairs to William H. Taft and his military responsibility to Major General Adna Chaffee. MacArthur warned that "the very gratifying conditions herein briefly recapitulated have not been brought about by Providence," but by military might, which was still needed. He was, however, optimistic that eventually the natives would be "warmly attached to the United States by a sense of self interest and gratitude." But "in the meantime," he warned, "the moulding force in the islands must be a well-organized army and navy." The Administration agreed with him and explained that the new government under Taft would be "military in name but conducted by civilians."[61]

In sharp contrast to the elaborate festivities honoring Otis a year earlier, MacArthur's return was greeted with surprisingly little pomp and ceremony. Possibly the Administration felt less need to create the impression that MacArthur was "a conquering hero," since the claim to victory seemed so much more legitimate. It may also have been thought that an austere reception would be the best means of forgetting the follies associated with Otis's return. The Administration may possibly have wanted to keep MacArthur away from reporters as much as possible because of his tendency to make pessimistic assessments. For whatever reasons, the honors rendered to MacArthur that August were decisively low key.

Maintaining the optimistic view that he had adopted six months earlier, however, MacArthur informed reporters that the surrender of General Cailles, along with 650 men and 500 rifles, made it impossible to doubt that the war was at last over. "The more they see us the better they like us," he claimed. "And Aguinaldo is a better man than we gave him credit for." Still, MacArthur betrayed a note of reservation by declaring that "excessive humanitarianism" by civilians might upset "the self regeneration by process of natural but rapid evolution." MacArthur explained the "danger" in his matchless style:

> If the stages of primary tuition, under the guidance and control of constructive statesmanship, are conserved by such freedom of action as is essential to spontaneous growth, there can scarcely be a doubt as to the ultimate result. Such procedure would, of course, contemplate sustained effort through a considerable period, and in that light would be somewhat in opposition to the spirit of the age, which demands quick and visible results. In this instance, however, the receptive mass consists of many millions of people, from which enormous friction may arise as a consequence of the efforts to carry into successful operation unwise or exceptionally unacceptable laws. One of the great dangers, therefore, is the tendency to excessive experimental legislation, much of which must inevitably operate to smother initiative, rather than to inspire confidence and hope.[62]

★ ★ ★ ★ ★ ★ ★ 10 ★ ★ ★ ★ ★ ★ ★

The Soldier and the War

From the beginning of the Philippine conflict, anti-imperialists fully expected a mutiny of some sort by American soldiers, who were allegedly being forced to fight a dirty colonial war in direct contradiction to their own political principles. When this rebellion failed to happen, war critics imagined an acute discomfort, even a tacit sympathy, in the rank and file for the enemy cause and for anti-imperialism. Low reenlistment rates, excessive drinking, insanity, and desertion to the enemy were indices of low morale, war critics contended, and the price the country had to pay for asking its soldiers to deny another people by force of arms the sacred American right of self-determination.

A surprising number of private comments by soldiers, in the form of letters, diaries, marching songs, and some unpublished literary efforts, has been preserved. Although these writings are not a representative sample in any technical sense, there is sufficient evidence to test the anti-imperialist thesis. Even before warfare began, there was an abundance of complaints about life in the army and in the Philippines. The food was considered barely edible, and the heat was rendered even less bearable by the required wearing of dress whites. There were difficulties in establishing relationships with Filipinas, and constant insults from Filipino soldiers had to be endured. But above all, the soldiers complained about the lack of any combat. They had enlisted to fight, had missed the action in Cuba, and were standing garrison duty in Manila. If Uncle Sam had no intention of taking on the "insolent" Filipinos, then they wanted to be relieved by regulars and returned home in time for spring planting. Contrary to the expectations of anti-imperialists at home, the most common assertion of the volunteers in the months preceding the war was that they were "just itching to get at the niggers."[1]

After the fighting had erupted, these soldiers wrote jubilant letters home describing their easy victories. The war was but six days old when Hugh Clapp wrote back to Nebraska, "Well I guess the niggers are whipped at last." The initial battles offered much glory and little risk, and all the complaints evaporated as the mood became one of exhilaration. Noting the obvious boost in morale, Lieutenant William Connor wrote that "the American soldier is a mighty poor 'peace soldier,' but more than a mighty good 'war soldier.'"[2]

It was not long before the Americans realized that they had won battles but not the war. Soon there were no conventional battles to be fought as the battered Philippine Army resorted to hit-and-run tactics. By April a distinctive note of despair had crept into Clapp's letters. "You have niggers you can't see shoot at you until you get close enough to shoot at them and then Mr. Nigger tears off to another good place and shoots again." Between volleys, Americans frequently had to march on the double, often dragging cumbersome field pieces over muddy terrain when the more sensible mules refused to budge. The effort would have been worth it to men like Clapp had it resulted in a good firefight, but, prepared for traditional, pitched battles, they were too slow to catch up with the lightly equipped Filipinos. At any rate, the enemy could always conceal his weapons and blend in with the local peasantry if escape were cut off—a ploy deemed "cowardly" by the overeager volunteers. Despite these tactics, the men dreamed of a final battle that would win the war, which kept them going to the limits of their endurance. When a sniper's bullet broke Clapp's leg in April, it also shattered this dream for him. He would end his tour in a Manila hospital. He had not covered himself sufficiently with glory, he felt, but above all he had wanted to take home the claim of victory.[3]

The traditional complaints about food, climate, officers, and army life in general were revived by the frustrations of guerrilla warfare. But such complaints are endemic to all wars, and were heard no doubt by Leonidas at Thermopylae. On the whole, these soldiers expressed a spirit that by today's standards would be considered embarrassingly gung ho. While the realities of warfare dulled their romantic illusions about combat, the Americans' ardent, effusive patriotism never diminished. Indeed, the most common complaint of the volunteers concerned the alleged restrictions that the cautious General Otis had placed on their mode of warfare. This allegation was also a convenient rationalization for their failure to reach victory. If Otis had only "unleashed" them, the war would have been won. Precious few expressed any concern over the principles of the Declaration of Independence.

In June, the first state volunteer regiment sailed for San Francisco, followed by others during the course of the summer. Anti-imperialist editors were eager to gather from these veterans signs of resentment over having fought a colonial war of conquest. A reporter from the *Pittsburgh Post* was at hand to greet the Tenth Pennsylvania Volunteers at the Presidio and ambitiously interviewed 600 men. His editor was able to glean from his notes sufficient evidence that these veterans overwhelmingly agreed with their late commander, Colonel Alexander Hawkins, that "any attempt to hold these islands as a colony is a menace to American institutions and not worth the cost of conquest." Editors, however, were incredibly selective in choosing the parts of the soldiers' commentaries they would publish in order to support a particular bias. Thus, the anti-imperialist *Call* abstracted from a Wyoming volunteer's letter only his sharp criticism of General Otis and his doubts about the potential value of the islands after the war. On the other hand, the *New York Sun* reproduced from this very same letter by Sergeant Charles Burrett his bitter tirade against the war's critics back home:

> Every soldier in the Eighth Army Corps understands that the responsibility of the blood of our boys rests on the heads of Hoar, Gorman & Co. . . . I don't like to call these fanatics by the ugly name of traitor but when I think of the four brave boys of my company, whose lives have been lost by this disloyalty in the U.S., it is hard indeed, to be charitable toward these men for their mistakes if they are mistakes. The soldiers in this army call them crimes.[4]

Unwittingly, Edward Atkinson undermined the anti-imperialist effect of the *Post*'s survey by publishing a less severely edited version for the League. This rendition indicated far less support for testimony like that of one officer who insisted that the Pennsylvania "regiment sympathizes with the native fighting for a liberty as dear to him as an American's is to him." While sixty-two percent of the officers and ninety-three percent of the men were highly critical of the war, they were nearly unanimous in opposing American withdrawal unless the Filipinos were "whipped first" or "made to knuckle." Even the few self-professed "anti-expansionists" were careful to make this stipulation. "I have always been opposed to this expansion idea. While I, in common with nearly all the regiment, believe that the Filipino must be whipped now, I also believe that the United States will do well to get rid of the islands as soon as possible with honor," Lieutenant George Gordon averred. Corporal John Findley agreed with him. "The country should get out as soon as it can with honor," but "only after we've beaten [the Filipinos] into submission." Sergeant James Stickel testified that "most of the men think the natives must be whipped before there is talk of withdrawal." Corporal Moses Smith added, "Now I don't believe there is a soldier or American but believes the Filipinos must be whipped thoroughly. After that we can give them independence under an American protectorate." Only Private John Kenney's opinion that "if the United States can drop the hot chestnut without burning its fingers, it should" implied that withdrawal short of victory should be considered. Kenney seemed to understand that he was in a minuscule minority, however, and rationalized that "if blood had not been shed, . . . if their comrades hadn't been killed, the men of the volunteers would have been ready to withdraw and let the Filipinos try their hand at governing themselves. Now they believe the job must be finished."[5]

But few of Kenney's comrades thought that the Filipinos were capable of governing themselves. Most were certain they were not fit to be American citizens. Almost to a man they agreed with Private Samuel Hays that "we have negroes enough in the country without hunting more trouble." Possibly Private Edward McKnight came closest to expressing the consensus of his regiment when he angrily informed the reporter, "You can put me down as despising a Filipino and opposed to any annexation of them or their islands." If these statements were expressions of anti-imperialist sentiment, it was of the sort expressed by Senator "Pitchfork Ben" Tillman or Samuel Gompers. A popular marching song summed it up:

> Damn, damn, damn the Filipinos!
>   Cut-throat Khakiac ladrones!
> Underneath the starry flag
>   Civilize them with a Krag
> And return us to our beloved home.[6]

Even the criticism of the conduct of the war uncovered by the *Post*'s reporter can be misleading, as it was directed almost exclusively at General Otis and his alleged "semi-conciliatory policy." A more aggressive leader was urgently needed "to soundly thrash the natives," the volunteers insisted almost in unison. Private Loman Tucker explained that:

> This thing of letting "amigos," really insurgent soldiers pretending friendliness, through our lines has resulted in the deaths of many Americans. As long as Otis is allowed to carry on his grandmotherish system, I can see no end to the war.

But Tucker was being coy. Calls to end the "half-hearted tactics" of "coddling 'amigos'" were in reality thinly disguised demands to drop all civilized restraints and to wage war against the entire native population. In short, these veterans believed that "Injun warfare" was necessary against such "savages." One Kansas veteran stated this sentiment quite directly to a reporter polling his regiment as it awaited discharge. "The country won't be pacified until the niggers are killed off like the Indians." Howard McFarlane agreed it was necessary "to blow every nigger into a nigger heaven." Adapting an old frontier adage, another veteran explained that "the only good Filipino is a dead one. Take no prisoners; lead is cheaper than rice."[7]

After the Filipino, the veterans most despised General Otis for his cautious tactics. To demonstrate their contempt for their former leader, some soldiers even sang for one reporter a favorite ditty that mocked the commanding general in the mode of *H.M.S. Pinafore*:

> Am I a man
> or am I a mouse?
> Am I a governor general or a hobo?
> This I would like to know
> Who is boss of this show—
> Is it me or Emilio Aguinaldo?[8]

The *Kansas City Times* also polled its state volunteers upon their return, and the *Call* attempted to cover each volunteer regiment as it was billeted briefly at the Presidio nearby. Although no subsequent survey was nearly as ambitious as that conducted by the *Post*, each produced remarkably similar results. The *Call's* editor was certainly justified in exclaiming, "Ask the volunteers who stood the first brunt of the fighting in the Philippines if they want the Filipinos as fellow citizens, and their practically unanimous decision is against it." There was almost a total absence of sympathy among veterans for the plight of the Filipinos or for the political justification of their struggle.[9]

Given the egalitarian nature of American society, it is understandable that these soldiers were scornful of officers, but some were singled out for criticism far more than others. Surprisingly, such heroes as Fred Funston and J. Franklin Bell were favorite targets of ridicule. They were accused of staging histrionics designed more to impress a correspondent at hand than the enemy. Bell earned the derision of his men when he leaped out of a rowboat to reconnoiter enemy defenses. "The newspapers featured this, ignoring the fact that from the level of the water his view wasn't nearly as good as it would have been with a good glass on one of the ships or even in the rowboat," Lieutenant Lyon explained to his wife. On other occasions, "Bell would pick out some small and inoffensive village, ride into it waving his sword and calling on the town to surrender, which it immediately did," Lyon wrote, insisting that such "heroics" took place only in the presence of reporters. Captain Batson also noted the war's "phony heroes" in a letter to his wife and complained that "brevets and medals are being liberally thrown around" for acts "of little military merit." But no officer was as much an actor or so skilled a self-publicist as "Fighting Fred" Funston. A junior officer listed the complaints about Funston after the Kansas regiment had been disbanded:

Since the regiment was mustered out numerous officers and men of the regiment have stated that this man Funston was a humbug, who never crossed a river under fire in the Philippine Islands . . . that he was a fraud who advertised himself as the performer of exploits that were accomplished by other men; that he used his official position to secure the publication in the newspapers of a series of fabulous accounts of his own imaginary deeds and to decry the actual achievement of better men who did not happen to be his partisans; that he maintained and supported an advertising bureau to build up himself and tear down other men; that he commanded, condoned, and rewarded rapine and murder simply because they sprung from his own partisans and associates.[10]

An enlisted man's newspaper, the *Soldier's Banner*, stated that "publicity is not always the best test of heroism."[11] Nevertheless, it paid off in rapid promotions. Bell, who had spent most of his career struggling to achieve his majority before the Philippine War, moved from that rank to brigadier general in little over a year.

General Lawton was less obsessed with publicity but was not above including in his operations a favorite correspondent, usually John Bass or O. K. Davis, who gave him good copy in the United States. The action would begin, typically, aboard a bombarding gunboat with an elegant lunch for the general, Bass or Davis, and Mrs. Lawton. Then Lawton and the correspondent would go ashore to join the troops on the firing line, where Lawton would parade among his troops fully exposed to enemy fire. His tall frame, elongated by a white British pith helmet, made an inviting target as he paced back and forth immediately behind his forward firing line. Such bravado, however, seemed designed much less to win favorable press coverage for him than to fulfill Lawton's perception of the proper role of a gallant, English gentleman officer in combat. Moreover, Lawton was scrupulously accurate in describing a battle, never attempting to inflate it or himself and always quick to praise the courage of others. Both reporters and troops adored Lawton and were ready to follow him anywhere.[12]

The soldiers in the Philippines were even more cynical about the press coverage of the war in general. Clippings mailed to them from home were frequently the cause of both amusement and contempt. "I do hope the idiotic newspapers haven't had you worried to death about the heavy engagements at Calocoon [*sic*]," Lyon warned his wife. "'Battles' out here are greatly exaggerated. This rebel is like a flea you can't see." Above all, he advised her to ignore the preposterous claims of General Otis that were played up in the press. "Every paper brings us the information that the 'backbone of the revolution is broken,'

that 'Aguinaldo is suing for peace,' etc., etc., whereas we are no nearer a conclusion of hostilities than we were three months ago," Batson told his wife. A
ridiculous proclamation by Otis that there were no rebels left in the Philippines, only "bandits," provoked a private guffaw from Lyon, who cautioned his
wife that "there will be lots of 'outlaws' in Luzon for years to come," and "a
strong force must be kept here—that means me."[13]

If a soldier arrived in the islands without a degree of racial hatred for the
Filipinos, he was not very long in acquiring it. Private Walter Cutter, Lieutenant Samuel Powell Lyon, and Captain Matthew A. Batson best illustrate the
process. Not only were these three soldiers prolific writers, but their more humanistic views of the Filipinos made them exceptions among their comrades.
They were not long in the Philippines before they were hounded by their comrades, who branded them "nigger lovers." But in each case, sympathy for the
Filipinos and their cause expressed early in their tours gave way to increasing
contempt for the natives the longer they remained in the islands. Very early in
the war, Captain Batson complained to his wife about the conduct of American
soldiers, particularly the volunteers:

> The conduct of the regulars is not so bad, but I am sorry to say that it has
> not been as good as it should be. However their bad conduct has generally
> been stopped at killing some chickens and taking what they wanted to eat,
> and they have not gone so far as to desecrate churches and burial places in
> search of loot.
>
> The volunteer outposts will see some natives—hear a shot and they turn
> loose and fire on everything they see—man, woman and child. They then
> report that they have been attacked by the insurgents and have driven
> them off with great loss to the insurgents.
>
> I now believe that if we had well disciplined regular troops we could soon
> pacify the natives here, but the conduct of the volunteers has been such
> that it could only irritate the inhabitants.[14]

A few weeks later, Batson expressed horror over the senseless destruction of an
innocent village as part of a reprisal ordered by General Lloyd Wheaton after
two companies under his command had been caught in an ambush:

> One of the prettiest little towns we have passed through is Apolit. A beau-
> tiful river—the Rio Grande de Pampanga—passes alongside it. A nice
> drive runs along the river for miles and on this drive were picturesque
> houses set off by the tropical plants and trees. I may add that most of the
> people living in Apolit desire peace and are friendly to Los Americanos.

> When we came along this road, the natives that had remained stood along the side of the road, took off their hats, touched their foreheads with their hands. "Buenos Dias, Senors" (means good morning) or "Aldo ming despu" (Pampangan). The 17th Infantry came into this place the other night and literally destroyed it—looted, ransacked, burned it—and we propose to civilize, Christianize, these people. . . . We come as a Christian people to relieve them from the Spanish yoke and bear ourselves like barbarians. Well I have said enough.[15]

Batson's early letters also praised the natives as "exceedingly interesting people." He even suggested that "when you hear of our people sending missionaries here, tell them they had better put their missionaries to work in New York." He expressed sympathy for Aguinaldo's political claims and was favorably impressed by the Filipino treatment of American prisoners, even those who had been captured while looting, whom Batson would have treated as common thieves.[16]

Yet, as commander of the newly formed Philippine Scouts six months later, Major Batson had greatly changed his tune:

> The time has come when it is necessary to conduct this warfare with the utmost rigour. "With fire and sword" as it were. But the numerous, self styled, humane societies and poisonous press make it difficult to follow this policy if reported to the world, so what I write to you regarding these matters is not to fall into the hands of newspaper men.

Batson certainly had no qualms about sending his Filipino troops, recruited largely from the Macabebes, archenemies of the Tagalogs, out on reprisal missions similar to the one that had once so upset him:

> I am king of the Maccabebes and they are terrors. Word reaches a place that the Maccabebes are coming and every Tagalo hunts his hole. At present we are destroying this district, everything before us. I have three columns out, and their course is easily traced by the smoke from burning houses. Of course, no official report will be made of everything.

When a close friend was killed in an ambush, Batson ordered the nearest town annihilated, explaining that "it helped revenge Boutelle."[17]

Quite possibly Batson was unduly influenced by the hatred felt by Macabebes for the Tagalogs. But Lyon went through a similar metamorphosis, and he commanded black troops, who were allegedly more sympathetic to the natives. Early in his tour Lieutenant Lyon expressed wonder that such ignorant and bigoted boors as some of his fellow officers could ever have won commissions in the army. He also obtained a copy of the English translation of Aguinaldo's history of the rebellion, which he shared with his wife, along with his doubts about the wisdom and legitimacy of the war that he was being asked to fight:

> Between you and me Molly, I think we (the U.S.) are making a big mistake in taking the Philippines. I believe it would be a mistake to annex them if they wanted, and I think the mistake becomes a national crime when we force them by superior strength in numbers, enormous financial advantages and mental supremacy, to become subjects of our republic. . . . There is no saying where the new policy of "expansion" (which really means "conquest") will end—what internal dissensions and what external entanglements may result. It is all very well to say as the exponents of expansion all do, that "it is our duty to elevate the people of the Philippines," etc., but the first duty of a nation is to our people. While the trade of these islands may be, and probably will be, a commercial benefit, to restrain them can only be a source of national weakness.
>
> I don't know perhaps that I should have inflicted all this on you, and of course I have never said such things to anyone else—I am an officer of the United States and the politics of the government is no affair of mine but I cannot help thinking. I don't know that you ever told me how you stand on this expansion business. I should like to know. I would like to make a speech in the House or Senate on my side of the question (that is after the war is over, before then no one ought to attack).
>
> I am disappointed in the United States, but it is still my country. I am sure the American people will see the right thing to do sooner or later. I only hope they see it in time.[18]

Lyon did have one experience in which he felt his trust had been violated by a native. His "muchacho," whom the lieutenant treated as a son, attempted to assassinate him as he slept. The boy claimed that he was cleaning the officer's gun when it discharged accidentally. Lyon was in the Philippines less than a year when he began to dismiss all the natives as "treacherous gugus." He confessed to torturing prisoners for information. "I fear that I will have to give the insurgent officer a touch of high life by means of a little water properly applied. The problem of the 'water cure' is in knowing how to apply it," he explained to his wife.[19]

Cutter's transformation is more difficult to explain in that he appears not to have experienced combat in the islands. His literary talent relegated him to a desk, to edit the *Soldier's Banner*. But only months after his arrival, he jettisoned his initial sympathies for the natives and their national aspirations. He explained this change of heart in his diary:

> I am forced to conclude that my first estimation of them was not justified. They are not to be trusted in public positions, no matter how much we might like them in private life. The agitation for independence is fomented by the educated class, who want to cut the melon of public graft; while the poor and uneducated classes are led to support their specious claims under pretext of patriotism.[20]

The final step in Cutter's conversion is evidenced by his insistence that counterterrorism had to be directed at the entire native population, because "knowing the Malay character" was to understand that any "humane" distinction between "insurrectos" and civilians would be "worthless." He compiled a lexicon for green replacements and newly arrived regiments that carried a similar message. "Amigo" was "a 'friend,' sarcastically applied to natives who wear white clothes and conceal guns and bolos beneath them for the benefit of Americans." Such commands as "siggie, siggie" and "vamose" kept "amigos" at a safe distance, particularly when accompanied by the thrust of a bayonet. But, Cutter advised, "nothing is better than a well placed shot while the 'gugu' is still 200 yards away to keep from being bushwacked by him." A young lad in a skit written by Cutter ignored such advice while standing guard for the first time. He offers a cigarette to a "brown brother," whom he had befriended, and even lays down his rifle in order to give him a light. The play ends with the anguished cries of the corporal of the guard kneeling over the slashed body of the young sentry: "Amigo be damned! I hate the very sight of their black hides."[21]

Possibly Batson, Lyon, and Cutter simply capitulated to enormous peer pressure to accept the military's conventional wisdom about the natives and their political aspirations. It is also possible that the paternalism implicit in their earlier attitudes had to sour sooner or later. But it is clear that their earlier assessments of Filipinos were not influenced by antiwar propaganda. Only ten days after expressing anti-imperialist sympathies, Lyon wrote:

> The Filipinos just now are keeping things stirred up as much as they can, in the hopes that the "anti-expansionists" will win out. It would surprise you what a close watch these people keep on American politics—every disloyal sentiment uttered by a man of any prominence in the United States is repeatedly broadcast through the islands and greatly magnified. While Congress is on the fence [debating over the Philippine Bill] there ought to be some way of muzzling these traitors. If Congress comes out decidedly for holding the Philippines—the insurgents will perhaps accept the hopelessness of further struggling.[22]

In his unpublished war novel, Cutter caricatured the anti-imperialists. His hero, Hank Harkins, rips down a poster informing soldiers that they "are engaged in the task of enslaving a helpless race, whose only crime is a love of liberty. They are brothers and this work must stop." Searching for the "descendant of copperheads," who was responsible for this "despicable treason," the hero spots "a professional looking man in linen duster, broad brimmed hat and sporting a beard," surrounded by angry soldiers. Spotting the shiny, new stripes on the sleeve of Corporal Harkins, this fussy, bookish, and pedantic "agitator" appeals for protection against the "uncouth language and menacing gestures" of his audience. Feigning anger, Hank lectures the men on the necessity of showing respect for their "superiors," then directs them "to escort this well meaning gentleman" to the railroad station and "see that he gets *a good start* for the next town!" Delighted, the soldiers lead their naive victim toward a deserted back street, while Hank laments that his recent promotion precludes his "joining in the fun." Cutter also made it clear in his diary that he was contemptuous of the war critics, "who in the security of their homes, have set themselves up as judges."[23]

Comments on anti-imperialism by other soldiers were invariably scornful. "I wish Bryan and his friends would come over here and talk to the soldiers. I think that they would last just as long as a snowball in h———. I would like nothing better than to string them up," Private Hambleton wrote. It was not lost on him that Senator Albert Beveridge toured the islands, whereas no one in the opposition came to find out what was happening firsthand. According to Hambleton, the bombastic Beveridge was wildly cheered by soldiers in the combat zones. Responding to Beveridge's speech in the Senate upon his return, Hambleton told his father, "I have read it carefully and I think from what I have seen and heard since I have been here that he is right."[24]

War critics were also vilified in song. In one ditty, a soldier from Dixie confesses that all the "argufyin'" was "confusin'":

McKinley is our President
　　An' as far as I can see
The old flag's jist as sacred
　　As it wuz in '63
An' his soldiers in the Philyppines
　　—True an' loyal men—
Deserve the same encouragement
　　That Lincoln's boys did then.

So if Davis, Lee an' Johnson
　　An' we who wore the grey

Were traitors to our country then
   Will someone kindly say
What Bryan, Hoar and Atkinson
   An' others of such fame
Expect to find in history
   Writ opposite their names?[25]

Any mention of the election of 1900 in the soldiers' letters and diaries indicated overwhelming support for the Republican ticket of McKinley and Roosevelt. Presumably most southern and western soldiers should have favored Bryan, but, according to Sergeant Beverly Daley, even the "howling Democrats" favored McKinley. "Of course, there are some boys who think Bryan is the whole cheese, but they don't say too much," Hambleton explained. Batson testified that McKinley's reelection was "a great satisfaction to most of the men, as Bryan's election would have been disastrous to us here." Such sentiment helps to explain the wildly enthusiastic receptions McKinley and particularly Roosevelt received from soldiers and veterans. The *Call* acknowledged the raucous cheering for these two "imperialists," but its editor insisted, somewhat bitterly, that it "only seems to be a unanimous endorsement of imperialism" by the men who fought in the Philippines.[26]

The most shocking characteristic of the American soldier in the Philippines was his penchant for lawlessness. Military spokesmen tried to pass off widespread looting and senseless destruction of property as "souvenir hunting." Since officers, sometimes ranking ones, were involved, maintaining discipline in the ranks was out of the question. Colonel Funston was accused of helping to loot a Catholic church and of personally desecrating its sacred precincts by leading a mock mass in ecclesiastic garb. Indeed, Funston may have set the tone for his regiment before it ever arrived in the Philippines. While leading his men down Market Street in a parade on July 4, 1898, Funston, by his own admission, charged and narrowly missed decapitating with his sword a San Franciscan who had thrown a firecracker under his horse.[27]

A few soldiers did complain about the conduct of their comrades. D. M. Mickle of the Tennessee outfit wrote, "You have no idea what a mania for destruction the average man has when the fear of the law is removed. I have seen them . . . knock chandeliers and plate glass mirrors to pieces just because they couldn't carry them. It is such a pity." Another soldier observed of his regiment, "Talk of the natives plundering towns: I don't think they are in it with the Fiftieth [Fifty-First] Iowa." But many others bragged of their plunder. E. D. Furnam of the Washington State Regiment wrote that "some of the boys made good hauls of jewelry and clothing. Nearly every man has at least two suits of clothing, and our quarters are furnished in style." Captain Albert Otis boasted that he "had enough plunder for a family of six. The house I had at Santa Ana had five pianos. I couldn't take them, so I put a big grand piano out of a second-story window. You can guess its finish." The citizens of San Francisco got a taste of this lawlessness when some drunken Wyoming volunteers at the Presidio used a schooner entering the bay for target practice. Thereafter, the returning volunteers were forced to leave their rifles in the Philippines.[28]

This lawless spirit made it that much easier to commit atrocities against the Filipinos, who had already been dehumanized by racial hatred. In addition, widespread stories of native mutilation of American captives helped raise the soldier's blood lust. "They cut their ----- off and put them in their mouths. That is the kind of people they have here," Hambleton reported to his brother. "No more prisoners. They take none, and they torture our men, so we will kill wounded and all of them," a Washington volunteer testified. For every soldier who protested that "we came here to help, not to slaughter, these natives," or who complained that he had "seen enough to almost make me ashamed to call myself an American," there were dozens who saw nothing wrong with shooting prisoners, enemy wounded, and native women and children. Some even professed to enjoy it, although most seemed to accept the slaughter stoically, as a necessary but onerous task. Anthony Michea of the Third Artillery wrote, "We bombarded a place called Malabon, and then we went in and killed every native we met, men, women, and children. It was a dreadful sight, the killing of the poor creatures. The natives captured some of the Americans and literally hacked them to pieces, so we got orders to spare no one." On the other hand, A. A. Barnes of the same regiment, describing the destruction of Titatia and the slaughter of one thousand men, women, and children, added, "I am probably growing hard-hearted, for I am in my glory when I can sight my gun on some dark-skin and pull the trigger. . . . Tell all my inquiring friends that I am doing everything I can for Old Glory and for America I love so well." Another soldier described the killing frenzy that developed in his Washington regiment:

> Soon we had orders to advance, and we . . . started across the creek in mud and water up to our waists. However, we did not mind it a bit, our fighting blood was up, and we all wanted to kill "niggers." This shooting human beings is a "hot game," and beats rabbit hunting all to pieces. We charged them and such a slaughter you never saw. We killed them like rabbits; hundreds, yes thousands of them. Every one was crazy.[29]

Clearly these soldiers had been ordered to take no prisoners and to kill the wounded, and again ranking officers set the example. Funston not only ordered his regiment to take no prisoners, but he bragged to reporters that he had personally strung up thirty-five civilians suspected of being insurrectos. Major Edwin Glenn did not even deny the charge that he made forty-seven prisoners kneel and "repent of their sins" before ordering them bayoneted and clubbed to death. Private Fred Hinchman recorded with some scorn seeing "a platoon of the Washingtons, with about fifty prisoners, who had been taken before they learned how not to take them." But it would be an error to believe that most, or even many, American soldiers only reluctantly obeyed unlawful orders. One soldier declared, almost joyously, that "when we find one that is not dead, we have our bayonets." Sergeant Leman reasoned that because a Filipino "is so treacherous," even "when badly wounded," he has to be killed. It was considered an uproarious joke when "some Tennessee boys" were ordered to escort "thirty niggers" to a hospital in the rear and "got there with about a hundred chickens and no prisoners." A private in the Utah Battery, reporting on "the progress of this 'goo goo' hunt" to the "home folks," explained that

> the old boys will say that no cruelty is too severe for these brainless monkeys, who can appreciate no sense of honor, kindness or justice. . . . With an enemy like this to fight, it is not surprising that the boys should soon adopt "no quarter" as a motto, and fill the blacks full of lead before finding out whether they are friends or enemies.[30]

The most damning evidence that the enemy wounded were being murdered came from the official reports of both Otis and MacArthur that claimed fifteen Filipinos killed for every one wounded. In the American Civil War five soldiers had been wounded for every one killed, which is close to the historical norm. Otis attempted to explain this anomaly by citing both the superior marksmanship of the Americans, largely rural Westerners and Southerners who had hunted all their lives, and the tendency of the Filipinos to drag off their wounded with them. MacArthur, under cross-examination by a senate committee, added a racial twist by asserting that men of Anglo-Saxon stock do not succumb as easily to wounds as do men of the "inferior races."[31]

War critics insisted that a high price in troop morale had to be paid for forcing Americans to fight in this manner, which was at such variance with their principles. Anti-imperialist editors contended that this low morale was the reason that Otis was able to persuade only ten percent of the state volunteers to reenlist in the new national units, in spite of the offer of a five-hundred-dollar bonus for doing so. They also charged that Otis had ignored a unanimous vote by the Pennsylvania volunteers not to remain in the islands following the formal exchange of treaties that officially ended the war with Spain in April, when the Philippine war was but two months old. According to Private William Christner, however, the men of that regiment had refused to vote on this sensitive issue: "We did not want to vote either way, nor do we intend to. We are ready to come home when they are ready to relieve us," a contention more consistent with the fervent patriotism expressed by the volunteers. Besides, these soldiers were enormously confident early in the war that it would be all over in a matter of months, if not weeks. Thus Christner vowed that "we will be returned as soon as we maul the Philippinos and if they let us go at them it won't take long to do it." As late as April 9, he wrote, "I am willing to stay as long as Uncle Sam needs me in the Philippines." Christner's mind was changed not by a distaste for fighting a war of subjugation, but the belief that the war would continue as long as Otis was in command. There had to have been, however, a realization that the Filipino ability to resist American power had been underestimated all around and not just by Otis. At any rate, another rainy season was at hand in June, and few volunteers were eager to remain. Since all of the nation's other wars have been waged with armies that were either conscripted or volunteered for the duration, with the exception of those in Korea and Vietnam, it is difficult to make historical comparisons. One can only wonder how many veterans of six months of combat in any war would elect to remain in the field for another two years. Few of the glamorized fliers in the more popular World War II volunteered to stay on after their fiftieth mission. Indeed, given the contempt for Otis, the climate, sickness, and boredom of remote barrios, along with the persistent belief that the volunteers had been deliberately kept in the field until the last minute to save the regulars languishing in Manila, it is difficult to believe that ten percent actually did reenlist in the new volunteer regiments.[32]

As for the other ninety percent, few wanted to depart before being "properly relieved." It was one thing to leave the despised Otis in the lurch, but quite another to do the same to Uncle Sam or to the comrades left behind. They felt simply that they had done their duty and that it was a question of another lad replacing them to carry on. In song, they apologized:

> I came and did my best, sir,
> And, General, taint no harm,
> I'm intending when I ask, sir,
> Can I go back to "Marm"?

> And so, General, as my duty's done,
> Don't think I mean any harm,
> When I tells yer I've a duty
> ter perform for Dad and "Marm."

They also made it clear that it would be their last war:

Ah, all may sing the glory great of being a volunteer
But when again the country calls, we'll all be deaf, I fear
We'll climb up on the street car roof the suckers for to see
And as they pass we too will yell: "Just give them hell for me."

Such sentiments pertain to any war and are not peculiarly a product of the conflict in the Philippines; they are produced by the disillusionment that occurs
when expected glamor fails to materialize and the dreary restrictions of army
life become a reality. Over and over again the soldiers warned younger brothers
to ignore the appeal for more volunteers. Even A. A. Barnes, who professed to
enjoy shooting Filipinos, advised his brother that "should a call for volunteers
be made for this place, do not be so patriotic as to come here." No doubt, such
advice fell on deaf ears, however. Most of the volunteers joined to escape the
boredom and isolation of life on the farm, as well as for patriotic reasons, and
the discovery that garrison duty in a remote part of the Philippines was no improvement was seldom learned vicariously.[33]

Drunkenness was a serious problem among American soldiers in the Philippines, although Christner makes it clear that it existed long before the outbreak of warfare. Excessive drinking was not confined to Manila's red-light district, but also occurred in the field under combat conditions, although one
scholar has recently argued that intoxication just before battle may be as old as
warfare itself. Nevertheless, a young shavetail fresh out of West Point and the
son of a general, Guy Henry, Jr., was profoundly shocked to discover sentries
hopelessly drunk on duty. He invented what he called "Henry's Keeley Cure,"
which was to sneak up on the befuddled culprit and fire several rounds over his
head before stationing him in the most forward and exposed post. "Most of the
men were fairly well cured after about three weeks there and did not need a
second tour," he testified. But the best description of the problem in the Philippines was a fictional one in the *Soldier's Banner*. It described the fruitless
chase of an unseen enemy by an exhausted and mud-splattered American company. The captain decided to bunk his men one night in a friendly barrio for a
hot meal and a much-needed rest. The men bargained for chickens, which native women dressed and cooked. As soon as the meal was consumed, a Chinese
peddler entered under cover of darkness to sell liquor. What follows, the author assured his readers, would be familiar to every soldier who had ever
served in the field:

That night there were several strange scenes that must have given the natives a strange idea of the civilization we wish to foist on them. Drunken
men struck at each other in frenzy and smashed each other's heads on the

ground, with sickening oaths, for no reason whatsoever, except their own
distorted imagination.

The ensuing events took a familiar course. A drunken soldier raped a girl, and
her boyfriend slit the American's throat as he slept off the booze. "With the
natives, down there, their justice is 'an eye for an eye.' Indeed, amongst a civilized mob it is not much further advanced," the author explained needlessly.
When they discovered their dead comrade the next morning, the soldiers
burned the already deserted village and, during the next day's march, gunned
down any native foolish enough to get caught in their gunsights.[34]

Rates of insanity and self-inflicted wounds appear to have been deliberately inflated by anti-imperialist editors for propaganda purposes. The 1900 report of the surgeon general listed 347 cases of mental breakdowns in a period
during which approximately 100,000 soldiers had served in the Philippines, a
figure that makes the rate of insanity infinitesimal. Nevertheless, this report
provoked misleading headlines on the "Awful Rate of Lunacy." Victimized by
his own editor's propaganda, a *Call* reporter was on hand to greet the "thousands of insane soldiers in chains" rumored to be aboard a transport arriving in
San Francisco. To his chagrin, he discovered only sixty-four unmanacled mental
patients.[35]

The *Call* also reported that "self-inflicted wounds are so frequent . . . that
General Otis has been compelled to issue instructions directing that a strong
investigation be made in each case of this character." These instructions have
not been documented, although Otis did at one point protest that most of the
sick filling the hospitals were "malingerers shirking their duty" whom he desperately needed in the field. Wounding oneself and feigning illness are age-old
means of escaping from combat, and undoubtedly they were resorted to in the
Philippines. But since there was so little real combat, in the sense of pitched
battle, in this war, these ruses may also have been the path back to the excite-
ment of Manila, or some other city, from the boredom and isolation of a godforsaken post in the boondocks.[36]

A much more serious indication that American soldiers were unhappy
fighting a war of subjugation and actually sympathized with the political aspirations of the enemy might have been the number of desertions to Aguinaldo's
army. But switching sides has also been a fact of life in every war, and the moti-
vations in these cases were not necessarily political. Some deserted to escape
disciplinary action in their own outfits. Others may have been attracted by the
commissions offered in the Philippine army. At any rate, no more than fifteen
American soldiers switched sides, out of close to 200,000 who served between
1899 and 1902. Nine of these were black, out of the 5,000 Negroes who fought

in the war. Given racist extremism at home, it is a small wonder that there were not more. "Colored" regiments left for the Philippines amidst race riots in Chicago, San Antonio, rural Georgia, and Tennessee. Headlines warned that a "War of the Races Is Threatened," and the anti-imperialist *Call* featured insensitive cartoons depicting "black depravity" and lampooning "Negro Insouciance." When the black Forty-Ninth Volunteer Infantry embarked at San Francisco for the Philippines, a huge minstrel-style, front-page caricature had the Negro soldiers cakewalking up the gangplank. One soldier with ludicrously distended lips and bulging eyes begged of his equally distorted girlfriend, "Jes' one mo' smack at dem cherub lips." Each black officer had "at least two ladies there to bid goodbye," the caption explained, and "when dat coon ban' played de cakewalk," the men "used their guns as walking sticks and their file man as a partner" and "danced away for dear life."[37]

Once in the Philippines, whites refused to salute black officers and jeered instead, "What are you coons doing here?" At higher levels, Otis protested sending black troops, whose loyalty, he felt, would be suspect in fighting other nonwhites. Governor Taft complained to Washington that black soldiers got along "too well with the native women," leading to the latter's "demoralization." He recommended that the "colored" regiments be returned to the United States as soon as it was militarily feasible. The secretary of war ordered that black soldiers who married natives be discharged from the army and sent home.[38]

Apparently "Los Negritos Americanos" did get along better with the native population because, as one black soldier explained it, "they do not push them off the streets, spit at them, [or] call them damn 'niggers.'" Some blacks did confess to feeling uneasy over fighting men of "our own hue and color," but others adopted white prejudices against the "gugus" and insisted that they were "savages" and only "half civilized." Chaplain George W. Prioleau of the Ninth Cavalry accused them of "untruthfulness, idolatry, stealing, and every crime in the decalogue" and vowed that "the indolence and laziness of the Filipino must not and will not retard American progress." Other black soldiers, like so many of their white comrades, felt that the Philippine question was not "for the soldier to decide." As Sergeant M. W. Sadler explained it, his oath of allegiance was colorblind. Another black, Sergeant Michael Robinson, was dismayed that there was not greater enthusiasm for the war back home. In the end, four black infantry and two black cavalry regiments fought in the war with distinction, except for the handful of deserters. These men were both racially and culturally very different from Filipinos, and to assume a mutual attraction based on racial affinity is utterly romantic, possibly even racist.[39]

Contrary to the anti-imperialist argument, it was the lack of combat to in-

terrupt the incessant boredom of garrison duty in remote villages that contributed decisively to low morale. "We haven't done anything but 'wait around.' I
don't like it. The 25th is getting in bad shape," Lyon reported to his wife. He
began almost every letter with the observation that there was "nothing new in
the 'war' today" and closed with the complaint that "another long stupid day is
gone." He catalogued a serious increase in breaches of discipline as the tedium
took its toll on his company's morale: fistfights, drunkenness, sleeping on post,
and pickets imagining attacks and "firing hundreds of rounds at nothing." The
only casualty for months was Lyon's bugler, who suffered a heart attack while
sounding "another false alarm." Above all, Lyon could not stand the constant
"whining" of his bored charges, and was sure that regular soldiers would have
behaved differently under similar circumstances. "I wish you could see these
'volunteers'—the worst yet. I never saw such an undisciplined mob." [40]

A real battle was just the elixir needed for sagging morale. When Lyon's
platoon finally did surround an enemy force and, after a genuine firefight, capture twenty-six Filipinos with their rifles and stockpiles of ammunition and
rice, the men joked, sang, and shouted "Rah for the 25th all the way back" to
their base. Lyon observed that he had never seen them so jubilant and happy.
That evening the heavy drinking was distinctly more festive than escapist. The
lieutenant discreetly retired early and wrote to his wife, "They are kicking up
an awful row. Scared the natives half to death about eight o'clock tonight by
sending up a couple of big rockets from the plaza." Other officers also commented on the galvanic effect that combat had had on the men. It was rehashed
for weeks to come, and suddenly their sojourn in the Philippines took on some
meaning. At least they would be able to bring back some genuine war stories to
tell their grandchildren on some distant winter evening. [41]

Enlisted men also described the boost a real battle was for them. Burr
Ellis of the Californians risked a court-martial by escaping from his hospital bed
to join his regiment fighting in nearby Cavite. "I had lots of fun that morning,"
he explained. Charles Wyland of the Washington Regiment was disturbed over
the degree to which his comrades had grown bloodthirsty and actually enjoyed
the slaughter that they witnessed:

> You see sights you could hardly believe, and life is hardly worth a thought.
> I have seen a shell from our artillery strike a bunch of Filipinos, and then
> they would go scattering through the air, legs, arms, heads, all discon-
> nected. And such sights actually make our boys laugh and yell, "that shot
> was a peach." A white man seems to forget that he is human. [42]

But nowhere is the gung ho spirit of these soldiers revealed more clearly
than in their marching songs, which belie the belief that the Eighth Army

Corps in the Philippines was badly demoralized. In song they immortalized "the raggedy man from Kansas," who achieved "jayhawk glory" with his "Yankee yell" and "fearless charge." Their songs turned maudlin over the flag, mother back on the farm, and "the fallen sons who would never return." They sang the official creed that they were "fighting side by side in the burning Torrid Zone against the right to loot and slaughter burning through the Malay creed" and to bring "liberty and justice . . . leading savage minds to light." Often their songs ended with a lusty "three cheers for the red, white and blue."[43]

In the final analysis, the American soldier who fought in the Philippines differed little from his British counterpart in South Africa or India. It was for both, of course, an era of intense nationalism. But possibly there is another, peculiarly American, explanation for the behavior of the soldiers in the Philippines. Proponents of expansion had hailed the islands as America's "new frontier," and appropriately enough, the men who conquered the Philippines, particularly the volunteers, brought with them a frontier spirit steeped in an individualism that easily degenerated into lawlessness. Virtually every member of the high command had spent most of his career terrorizing Apaches, Comanches, Kiowas, and the Sioux. Some had taken part in the massacre at Wounded Knee. It was easy for such commanders to order similar tactics in the Philippines, particularly when faced with the frustrations of guerrilla warfare. And the men in their command, many of whom were themselves descendants of old Indian fighters, carried out these orders with amazing, if not surprising, alacrity.

11

"Injun Warfare" under Chaffee and Roosevelt

General Adna Chaffee was above all a soldier's soldier, an old, hard-riding cavalryman, who felt more comfortable on a horse than at a desk. He had come up through the ranks in the Civil War and had spent most of his career chasing Indians across the American West. He had commanded the American contingent of an allied expeditionary force in China during the Boxer crisis before being sent to the Philippines as MacArthur's replacement. In his command there would be no mollycoddling of anyone—the enemy, the press, or, least of all, the civilian governor and his commission, with whom the new military commander was ostensibly to share power. Chaffee had little use for civilians and was reported to have pronounced that despised word with an exaggerated initial sibilant. If Otis was a precursor of the modern desk-ridden, publicity-conscious military commander, Chaffee was a throwback to the robust, mud-splattered leader of an earlier era.

At this time, the cavalry was the elite corps of the army, very much the equivalent of today's paratroopers. As soon as he assumed command, Chaffee began to place cavalry officers in key positions. J. Franklin Bell was promoted to brigadier general and given the troublesome southern Luzon province of Batangas to pacify. Chaffee's old buddy from the "Sixth Cav" and the Indian wars, Colonel Jacob Smith, was assigned as Bell's chief of staff. The new commander knew that he could count on this pair for an Indian-style campaign in Batangas, and not the "humanitarian warfare" allegedly conducted prior to his arrival in the Philippines. During one of his rare comments to the press, Chaffee cautioned Joseph Ohl, correspondent for the *Atlanta Constitution*, that "if you should hear of a few Filipinos more or less being put away don't grow too sentimental over it." He curtly informed Governor Taft that he could not trust the commission's native appointments and that it was his intention to give the Filipinos "bayonet rule" for years to come.[1]

Chaffee had been in his new post only two months when President Mc-Kinley was assassinated. As a former Rough Rider, the new commander-in-chief would have no difficulty seeing eye to eye with a cavalryman. In fact, Roosevelt was an unabashed admirer of Chaffee and had urged McKinley to give him command in the Philippines. A few years later, he would reward his martial hero with the army's top post. But Roosevelt was also close to Taft at this time and soon became very upset over the rumors of a sharp rift between the military and civilian governors, which had become impossible to conceal from reporters. On October 8, 1901, he instructed Chaffee:

I am deeply chagrined, to use the mildest possible term, over the trouble between yourself and Taft. I wish you to see him personally, and spare no effort to secure prompt and friendly agreement in regard to the differences between you. Have cabled him also. It is most unfortunate to have any action which produces and which may have a serious effect both in the Philippines *and here at home*. I trust implicitly that you and Taft will come to an agreement.[2]

Chaffee's response, if any, is not recorded, but apparently he did manage to conceal or, at least, control his contempt for Taft and the commission, which not only was comprised of those despised civilians but, even worse, would soon have a few token Filipinos on it.

As for the military situation, Chaffee did not share the optimism of his predecessor. From his point of view, the war was far from over and was not even winding down. Although most of the archipelago was pacified, and even under local self-rule, there were serious trouble spots, particularly in southern Luzon and on some other islands. More ominous was the trouble brewing with the Moros in the Sulu group. The term "Moro," imported by the Spanish from North Africa, blurred the distinctions between about ten different ethnic groups that shared little more than the Islamic faith and a dislike of Christians and Tagalogs. The Moros had always rejected Aguinaldo's claim to sovereignty over their islands, and when insurrectos from Luzon began to recruit suc-cessfully among Christian minorities on these islands, Moslem leaders struck up an alliance of convenience with the Americans. In return for nominal rule, the U.S. Army agreed to continue the Spanish system of governance over their islands, including payoffs to sultans and lesser rulers, and assured the Moros that outside rule would be minimal and in no way interfere with their customs. Actually, the Americans had little choice in the matter as there were too few soldiers to occupy these islands. Hence, only token garrisons under the com-mand of Colonel Sweet were maintained on Jolo and Mindanao.

While this arrangement looked good on paper, the realities of the fierce rivalries among the Moros themselves, and between them and Christian and pagan minorities, meant that the Sulus were a constant irritant for the Americans. Above all, Sweet had to contend with the centuries-old practice of piracy, of which American garrisons proved to be lucrative targets. Each complaint by Sweet elicited little more than polite assurances from Moslem leaders that the piracy would be terminated, but it never was. In May of 1901, Sweet reported to MacArthur that while "relations with the Sultans and Chiefs remain friendly, they will promise anything in the shape of reforms, but these will never be carried out." Finally, he warned MacArthur that there could be "no hope of progress until the United States takes complete control of these islands" and recommended a show of force on Jolo or Mindanao to impress the Moslems that the United States meant business.[3] MacArthur was not about to open up another front on the eve of his departure from the Philippines, however, so he simply left the Moro problem for Chaffee to worry about.

Failure to respond in force merely emboldened the natives, Sweet pleaded with Chaffee. Troops returning to their base on Jolo following training exercises in the summer of 1901 discovered that the natives had taken everything, even the gates to an American cemetery. Sweet's protest to the local sultan produced a charming reply from "your son the Sultan Hadji Mohammed Jamalul, Kirain, to my father the Governor of Tiange" (Jolo):

> Your letter of the 23rd instant received and I understand its contents. I am very sorry indeed that the gates to the cemetery were stolen. It would have been better if the thief had robbed the property belonging to the living, because they have a chance to earn more but the dead have not. Therefore aid me to think how to get rid of stealing in this country. Let us inquire at all places where there are blacksmiths. There are no blacksmiths in Maibun. Above all you must closely examine the blacksmiths in Buz Buz and Moubu as these gates were too heavy to be carried a long distance. Very likely they are in these two places. . . . If we find the thief, let us bury him alive. . . . You are an old man . . . perhaps you have pity on me. As for me I detest thieves.[4]

Chaffee was not amused by the sultan's charm, and when several Americans were killed in a subsequent raid, he dispatched the Twenty-Seventh Infantry Regiment and a battery of mountain artillery to Jolo to keep the natives in line and set an example for other Moslem groups.

At the same time Chaffee further broadened the war by moving one of his favorite regiments, the Ninth Infantry, which had served under him in China, to the islands of Leyte and Samar. The Ninth Infantry had begun its second Philippine tour with two months of drinking and whoring in Manila. Now it was given a dreadful assignment in the backwaters of the Philippine archipelago. Samar, the third largest island after Luzon and Mindanao, had such a rugged interior that only its littoral rim was inhabited to any great extent. The men of the Ninth Regiment labeled it "the heart of googooland." Although the Samarenos were ferocious warriors, they had given Spain surprisingly little trouble, except for two minor uprisings that were largely protests against labor and military conscriptions that had taken their men off the island rather than quests for independence. Their main concern up to the mid–nineteenth century was with Moro raids for rice, women, and slaves. Spanish priests with western skills doubled as military advisers and even leaders, building and organizing defenses against the Moslem pirates, which helped to cement the island's ties to Spain. The defenses also enhanced the isolation and autonomy of each pueblo as a besieged entity, so that Samar never became an integrated community. Possibly the terrain would have militated against such a development, as the best means of transportation between pueblos was by pirate-infested water.

The gradual abatement of Moro raids by the middle of the nineteenth century, along with the boom in the abaca trade for which Samar was an important source, brought the island a little bit closer to the mainstream of Philippine society. But, essentially, it was still primitive and remote when General Vincente Lukban arrived on December 31, 1899, with one hundred riflemen to proclaim that he was the governor of Samar under the Philippine Republic. This Chinese mestizo, scion of a wealthy Luzon family, met with surprisingly little resistance. In part, his success may have been due to Lukban's pragmatic decision to ally himself with a heretical Christian sect, the *Dios-Dios*, or, because of their red garments, the *Pulahanes*. Lukban had a year of grace before elements of the First Infantry landed in January, 1901, under General William Kobbe. They were greeted on the beaches with suicidal bolo charges by Pulahanes, who refused to believe that they could be harmed by flaming rifles. Their conviction gave the Samarenos the reputation in American Army circles of being ferocious, fanatical, and treacherous. Actually, Lukban did not contest the American invasion, but quietly retreated into the interior, leaving behind a well-organized network of Filipino priests and officials loyal to him and to the Republic. Any Samareno suspected of collaborating with the Americans was executed in dramatic fashion as a lesson to others that Lukban still controlled the island. The head of one official who cooperated with the invaders was wrapped in a kerosene-soaked American flag and set on fire.

Shortly before he was succeeded by Chaffee, MacArthur sent Lukban's brother to Samar with an offer of amnesty in return for the surrender of the insurrectos. Lukban turned him down and vowed to fight the Americans to the end. On the eve of his departure, MacArthur recommended "more energetic measures" for Samar, and before the retired commander had landed in San Francisco, Chaffee had the Ninth Infantry on its way to Samar aboard the transport *Liscum*, appropriately named after that regiment's late commander, who had fallen leading his men to the walls of Tientsin. Companies were garrisoned in the principal towns along the coast of Samar. The mayor of one of them, Balangiga, containing about 200 nipa huts and the usual solid monuments to Spanish rule—church, convent, and town hall—had requested of Chaffee American troops to protect his town from "Moro pirates." Had army intelligence done its homework, the troops might have been suspicious, as such raids had become practically nonexistent over the past half-century. The mayor, Presidente Pedro Abayan, warmly greeted Captain Thomas W. Connell and the men of Company C, although it was noted that the other Samarenos seemed very surly. Abayan urged the Americans to use the substantial buildings, and the tribunal became a barracks and arsenal while an empty convent housed the officers and a dispensary.

Connell was a young West Pointer and devout Irish Catholic with a puritanical streak that irritated both his men and the Filipinos. He immediately set about cleaning up Balangiga and working on the morals of its inhabitants. Unable to muster enough volunteers to collect the omnipresent "garbage" and to trim the jungle growth under the huts, which could conceal insurrectos, the captain impressed a work force, forcing them to clean up the "mess" at gunpoint. Abayan suggested that men from the environs could work off back taxes by cleaning up the town. Connell naively agreed, and soon Lukban had inside Balangiga one hundred of his best bolomen disguised as laborers.

Connell then set to work on the local priest and demanded that he ban the immodest clothing and provocative demeanor of the women and the raucous Sunday cockfights. When all he could get out of this priest was a stoic shrug, Connell forbade his men to fraternize with females or attend the cockfights. He decreed that so much as a lewd glance would be a punishable offense. But he could not prevent the inevitable, and soon some drunken soldiers were lured into the bush by seductive females and never seen again. The men learned from this blunder, and the next decoy was dragged under a hut and repeatedly raped. The first woman to complain to Connell of such a gang rape was 65 years old, so he refused to believe her. Then three young girls showed up at his quarters and mortified him by lifting up their skirts to reveal their bruises. Connell seemed as angry over this immodest display as he was over the conduct of his soldiers. He ordered the company into formation and marched the three victims past each soldier standing at attention. When the girls were unable to identify their assailants, he marched them past each sentry on duty, but with no luck. Furious, he issued stricter orders: even touching a native female would be considered the equivalent of rape.

Captain Connell also took seriously his role as diplomat and was concerned that a good impression be made in the colony. To this end, he outlawed the use of such terms as "gugu" and "nigger" by his troops, even when conversing among themselves. To foster a more peaceful atmosphere, he banned the carrying of firearms except while on sentry duty or during official functions. Such rules earned him the title "nigger lover" from his men, his executive officer, Lieutenant E. C. Bumpus, and the surgeon, Major Richard S. Griswold. No one but Connell trusted the natives, least of all those who played "amigo," and with good reason. All of Connell's rules and routines were dutifully reported to Lukban by the mayor of Balangiga, and careful plans were laid to surprise the American garrison there.

Had Connell been kept abreast of what was happening elsewhere on the island of Samar, he might not have left his outpost so vulnerable to attack from within. Before the Ninth Infantry arrived, elements of the First Infantry, landing from Leyte, probed the island. One patrol had stumbled into Lukban's headquarters and captured his family, treasury, supplies, and records. Among the captured documents was a letter from Presidente Abayan of Balangiga informing Lukban that he had petitioned for American troops and would pretend friendship until they let down their guard. The letter was translated into English at the headquarters of General Hughes on Leyte and turned over to Major Edwin F. Glenn, who was in charge of intelligence for the sector. But Hughes interpreted the capture of Lukban's headquarters as the end of the insurrection on Samar and assumed that the Ninth Infantry would have little to do beyond occupying the place. Hughes, in fact, transferred his headquarters from Leyte to Cebu on September 24, 1901, to begin the pacification of that island, and with him went Glenn with Abayan's letter to Lukban safely packed away in his files.

Two days later, on September 26, a mail boat from Manila arrived off Balangiga while making the rounds of the garrisons on Samar. Connell and his men learned for the first time of McKinley's assassination and that Roosevelt was their new president. The captain set about immediately to secure a supply of black crepe and ordered the men into formation as dusk approached to give them instructions on sewing mourning bands on their sleeves. He ordered the flag to be flown at half-mast. Although it was Saturday evening, Connell insisted that the armbands be part of the men's uniform for the eight-o'clock formation the next morning, at which an appropriate eulogy would be read, followed by a memorial mass in the local church.

The planned formation never took place, however, and by Sunday morning the surviving members of Company C had much to mourn about more directly than the death of their president half-way around the globe. The men had broken formation Saturday grumbling over having to use whatever light remained to perform their assigned sartorial task rather than to reread the newly arrived mail. Meanwhile, Connell searched frantically for the local priest to arrange the mass for his late president's Protestant soul. No one had seen the priest all day. He seemed to have vanished. Connell, expecting little from Spanish-trained priests, returned in darkness to his quarters. He decided to retire early in order to get up in time to prepare a substitute service, if necessary, and a eulogy for McKinley.

Unbeknownst to Connell, the church was the scene of unusual activity that night. Beginning about midnight, women carrying small coffins arrived in Balangiga and made their way to the church. Suspicious of this activity, the sentry summoned the sergeant of the guard, who inquired about their purpose. He was told that a cholera epidemic had claimed a great many children in the surrounding area and that the bodies were being brought into the church, where prayers would be said throughout the night. Not satisfied, the sergeant demanded that one coffin be opened, but he quickly ordered it closed and apologized when he spotted a child's body inside. Had he lifted the body he would have discovered bolos hidden underneath, and possibly a living child feigning death. The sergeant was also suspicious of the heavy clothing worn by the women on such a hot night, but he was not going to risk the captain's wrath by taking too close a look. Had he been less cautious he would have uncovered more hidden weapons and discovered that most of the "women" were men. He decided he would report these mysterious proceedings to Lieutenant Bumpus in the morning.

Most of the men were up before reveille that sultry Sunday morning, rereading their mail with the first light while the cooks prepared breakfast. Connell also was up, reading his prayer book and fretting over the missing priest, while the two Protestant officers slept in. The Filipino police chief stopped for a friendly chat with the armed sentry and suddenly seized the soldier's rifle and shot him with it. The church bell immediately pealed and, on that signal, bolomen raced out of their sanctuary; Lukban's planted work crew, armed during the night with the smuggled weapons, charged from another direction, cutting down the remaining sentries before they could get off a shot. Connell's orders had left everyone else unarmed, except for the officers, who kept .45-caliber automatics in their quarters. But bolomen disguised as women had been lounging, waiting for the signal, just outside the old convent. Hearing it, they threw off their disguises, burst into the officers' quarters, murdered Bumpus and the surgeon, Griswold, in their beds and seized their weapons. Connell was surprised while sitting by his window. Armed only with his prayer book, he leaped into the street below and was cut down in full view of his men. With Yankee ingenuity, the remaining men of Company C improvised weapons out of baseball bats, canned goods, tent poles, shovels, and even the water being boiled for their morning coffee. Luckily for them, the natives were confused by the double safety levers on the Krag-Jorgensen rifles and the automatic handguns and were unable to fire them. Nevertheless, the enemy inflicted heavy losses on the Americans with their bolos as the soldiers fought their way to the arsenal. Only a handful reached it and were able to arm themselves.

Since the officers were dead, Sergeant Breton took charge and began to regroup the men and work out a strategy. In addition to the three officers, forty-two men had been slain. Breton had thirty-eight men remaining, eight of whom were too seriously wounded to fight. Formed in a British square, the men cut down hundreds of charging bolomen. But this strategy seriously depleted their supply of ammunition, and Breton knew that their only chance was to escape by water. Continuously moving his square toward the water, the sergeant was able to reach three *barotos*—crude native dugouts—pulled up on shore. Only then did the Americans remember their flag, raised appropriately to half-mast moments before the bloody battle had begun. Six men volunteered to go back for it, but only four returned with the colors. The natives either had been instructed by the police chief or had figured out for themselves how to work the safety system of the Krags. Not without design, the police chief had so ingratiated himself with the Americans that some sentries had taught him the difference between the Krag and the more familiar Springfield.

For an hour and a half the survivors slowly made their way along the shore to Basey, garrisoned by Company G. All the way they were harassed by rifle fire, particularly in the narrow San Juanico Strait that divides Samar and Leyte. Before reaching their destination another seven men were either killed or had succumbed to wounds received in Balangiga. Eight more died in Basey's infirmary. In all, fifty-nine members of Company C were killed and twenty-three wounded. Only six members emerged from the ordeal unscathed.

Captain Bookmiller, the commander at Basey, had little trouble securing fifty-five volunteers to return immediately to Balangiga and avenge their fallen comrades. Indeed, the difficulty was in deciding who would remain behind to guard Basey and the wounded survivors. Virtually every man in his company clamored to go—even the six fit survivors from Company C. Unlike Connell, Bookmiller was adored by his men and not considered a "nigger lover." Bookmiller despised Filipinos and trusted none of them. Those selected to return to Balangiga, including the six men of Company C, expected a good show and Bookmiller did not disappoint them.

The retaliatory force steamed back on the gunboat *Pittsburgh*, whose Gatling guns and Hotchkiss cannon announced their mission and raked the shoreline at any sign of movement. With fixed bayonets, the men charged ashore.

The few Filipinos foolish enough to have remained in Balangiga were cut down immediately with no questions asked. But then the men were stopped in their tracks by the sight of the mutilated bodies of their dead comrades. Connell's head had been chopped off and set on fire; his finger and a West Point ring were missing. Other bodies were slit open and stuffed with flour, jam, coffee, and molasses from the company's mess hall. Even the company's mascot, a dog brought back from China, had not been spared. His eyes had been gouged out and replaced with rocks. "All the dead were mutilated and treated with indescribable indignities," Root later informed the president.

Bookmiller had interrupted a funeral in progress for 250 natives who had lost their lives in Balangiga earlier in the day. Their bodies had been laid out neatly in trenches but had not yet been covered. One of the patrols that Bookmiller had sent to probe the immediate area caught twenty men in hiding, possibly the gravediggers for the occasion. The captain put them to work replacing the dead Filipinos with the mutilated American cadavers. After reading from the Scriptures, Bookmiller ordered the American bodies covered and an appropriate salute fired. In tears of sadness and rage following the sounding of taps by his bugler, Bookmiller ordered the dead natives stacked up and soaked with kerosene. The pleas of two old women, who had emerged from hiding, to give the dead "a Christian burial" were dismissed. As the flames shot up from the funeral pyre, the captain again read from his Bible, "They have sown the wind and they shall reap the whirlwind." Bookmiller himself initiated the whirlwind by turning the twenty prisoners over to the six survivors of Company C. While they were gunning them down, the men of Company G set fire to the town. Back in Basey, Bookmiller reported directly to Manila in language as succinct as Chaffee might have used, "Buried dead, burned town, returned Basey."[5]

No single event in the Philippine war shocked the American people as did the massacre at Balangiga. It was, as so many editors claimed, the worst disaster for the United States Army since Custer's fate at Little Big Horn. Headlines anguished over the "despicable" and "treacherous savagery" of the natives of Samar. The disaster thrust the island of Samar into the American consciousness as dramatically as Dewey's victory at Manila had made Americans conscious of the existence of the Philippine archipelago two and a half years earlier. The effect was intensified by further setbacks on the allegedly pacified islands of Leyte and Luzon. Headlines gave the erroneous impression that subsequent ambushes were on a scale with the Balangiga massacre. "Another Fresh Disaster to American Troops," blared a huge, front-page headline in the *Call*, although only three Americans were killed and five wounded in that ambush on Luzon.[6]

MacArthur became the target of editorial attacks, even in the imperialist press. No better than Otis, he also had "hoodwinked" the American people into believing the war was all but over. MacArthur tried to defend himself, insisting that Balangiga was an isolated incident. Some imperialist editors argued that McKinley's assassination had encouraged already pacified natives to take up arms again. A lengthy, grim headline in the *Call* made it seem that America had returned to square one in the Philippines:

Warlike Spirit Revives Throughout the Philippines
And American Troops Face Hard Fighting
Tribes Regarded As Pacified Taking Up Arms.

A *Call* editorial that day explained that the past "victories" of Otis and MacArthur were nothing more than breathing spells for the natives. Spain had experienced similar lulls, and Americans simply had to learn that "a conquered people" never remain conquered for very long.[7]

General Chaffee was the first to agree with this statement. It was "utterly foolish to pretend that the war was over, or even that the end is in sight," he declared in a rare press conference following the massacre. "The whole Philippine people are now engaged in making war in a manner not in accordance with the recognized laws of war," he warned before making his point that the army was "not to blame for Balangiga." The "murdered men of Company C" were victims of "false humanitarianism" and "the soft mollycoddling of treacherous natives" by Governor Taft and his commission. Who appointed Presidente Abayan, the plot's "mastermind"? Chaffee demanded rhetorically before growling the answer, "the Commission." "The silly talk of benevolence and civilian rule" is interpreted as "weakness." But it would be different from now on, Chaffee assured the press. "The situation calls for shot, shells and bayonets as the natives are not to be trusted."[8]

The press further rationalized the disaster at Balangiga by attributing its success to the scheming of American deserters, who were so familiar with army routines. No one was specifically identified in this case, but the name of David Fagen, "a black renegade from the Colored 24th Infantry," was frequently bandied about as a convenient scapegoat for every American setback, from Lawton's death to the Balangiga massacre. The incidents were much too far apart geographically and chronologically for Fagen to have been involved in all, if any, of them. Indeed, it is unlikely that he ever strayed much beyond the Mount Arayat area, where he had accepted a commission in the Philippine army in November, 1899. Nevertheless, his military exploits and infamy continued to grow in editorial fantasies. When the last of the armed resistance to American rule in Nueva Ecija finally collapsed in the spring of 1901, Captain Fagen fled to the mountains and on to Luzon's east coast with his Filipino wife and a six-hundred-dollar price on his head. In December, a hunter, Anastacio Bartolomé, surprised him on a beach with Negrito companions and carried Fagen's head, finger (sporting a West Point ring), and commission to American authorities to claim the reward. The ring was not Connell's, as many editors continued to claim it was, but belonged to Lieutenant Frederick Alstaetter, once Fagen's prisoner. Army intelligence even suspected that Fagen may have plotted with Bartolomé, a former "insurrectionist" himself, to fake his death with the head and finger of a Negrito.[9]

Rather than blaming Taft's "false humanitarianism" for encouraging Filipinos to renew the struggle in some areas, as it was often charged, a better case might be made for citing the harsh overreaction to often minor incidents by hotheaded junior officers as the leading cause of the armed revival. Communication with Manila was usually poor, and frequently sabotaged, giving the very young commanders of small, remote garrisons awesome power in making local decisions. A case in point is the island of Bohol, where Captain Andrew Rowan had such a command. Because of his fame for having carried "the message to Garcia," the rebel commander in Cuba, years earlier, his action was noted by the press. The *New York Times* buried the story of Rowan's egregious abuse of power, which had caused the war to be resuscitated on Bohol, in a small column on page six:

> Captain Andrew S. Rowan of the 19th Infantry is under investigation for the destruction of a town and thereby causing an active renewal of the insurrection in the island of Bohol. A native who had assassinated a corporal was caught and killed. Captain Rowan then burned an adjacent town and the people, inflamed with rage, rejoined the insurgent chief, Sampson.[10]

What the *Times* omitted from this story was that the corporal had been murdered by the boyfriend of a Filipina he had raped, and that Rowan had actually destroyed two towns. The adjacent town was her village, so that Rowan had punished both her people and those of her boyfriend, as though she were responsible for her own rape! There is no record of any investigation of Rowan, and by then, similar acts of reprisal elsewhere had revived the war on Cebu and Marinduque during the summer of 1901.[11]

The reactions of these junior officers were mild, however, compared with what Chaffee was planning for rebellious areas following the massacre at Balangiga. Actually, President Roosevelt had set the tone by ordering Chaffee to adopt, "in no unmistakable terms," "the most stern measures to pacify Samar." But the general had no intentions of confining such measures to Samar alone. The public outrage over Balangiga seemed to him to be the perfect opportunity to apply extreme tactics to other trouble spots, like the province of Batangas, which continued to struggle under the leadership of General Miguel Malvar when the rest of Luzon was essentially pacified and already under civilian control. Indeed, Chaffee was so sure that the national mood had given him *carte blanche* that he forsook such traditional bureaucratic safeguards as inventing euphemisms to mask his real intentions or relying solely on verbal orders. Hence Chaffee sanctioned orders for Batangas drawn up by General J. Franklin Bell that should never have appeared in writing. Dated December 7, 1901, Bell began with the standard preamble of the day, asserting that

> the United States Government, disregarding many provocations to do otherwise, has for three years exercised an extraordinary forbearance and patiently adhered to a magnanimous and benevolent policy toward the inhabitants of the territory occupied by this brigade.

Bell followed this disclaimer with a long list of Filipino transgressions against the laws of civilized warfare, which read much like a lawyer's brief and related each alleged violation to specific sections of "the well known law and usages of war as announced in General Orders No. 100, Adjutant-General's Office, 1863 (signed by Lincoln)," as though Filipinos could possibly have known of this document. Thus, the general pointed out that the acceptance of offices and the swearing of allegiance to the United States "solely for the purpose of improving their opportunities and facilities for deceiving American officials and treacherously aiding and assisting the cause of the insurrection" clearly violated section 26 of General Orders No. 100. The wearing of civilian clothes with no special markings by the ordinary peasant violated section 63, as did returning home between battles and "divesting themselves of the character and appearance of soldiers . . . concealing their arms . . . posing as peaceful citizens." Bell's orders ticked off scores of such violations by the Filipinos. "They have improvised and secreted in the vicinity of roads and trails rudely constructed infernal machines propelling poisoned arrows or darts." Even the destruction of telegraph wires and bridges violated, in Bell's opinion, some section of Lincoln's General Orders. But the time had come to fight fire with fire, he declared, making clear his intention to "severely punish, in the same or lesser degree, the commission of acts denounced in the aforementioned articles." That is, Bell himself went on record as planning to violate General Orders No. 100 and the accepted tactics of civilized warfare.[12]

Bell elaborated on these orders in a series of circulars, which specifically bestowed on his station commanders the right of retaliation. When an American was "murdered," they were instructed to "by lot select a P.O.W.—preferably one from the village in which the assassination took place—and execute him." Another circular rationalized that "it is an inevitable consequence of war that the innocent must generally suffer with the guilty" and that "a short and severe war creates in the aggregate less loss and suffering than a benevolent war indefinitely prolonged." He warned his commanders that young officers should not be restrained or discouraged without excellent reason. "It is not necessary to seek or wait for authority from headquarters to do anything or take any action which will contribute to the end in view." Since Chaffee received copies of Bell's directive, it had to have been apparent to him that Bell was launching a war of extermination. Indeed, Bell reasoned that since all natives were treacherous, it was impossible to recognize "the actively bad from only the passively so."[13]

The entire population outside of the major cities in Batangas was herded into concentration camps, which were bordered by what Bell called "dead lines." Everything outside of the camps was systematically destroyed—humans, crops, food stores, domestic animals, houses, and boats. Actually, a similar policy had been quietly initiated on the island of Marinduque some months before. When one editor got wind of it, the War Department anxiously inquired of MacArthur if Major Fred A. Smith had ordered the natives into the five principal towns on Marinduque. MacArthur wired back:

> His action effectively suppressing insurrection there which past three months has presented obstinate resistance. Exclusively a military measure carried out without objectionable or offensive features and effected end in view.[14]

Apparently, army officers were unable to perceive anything "objectionable" or "offensive" about being ordered out of one's home while American soldiers burned it to the ground and destroyed one's crops and any food or animal that could not be transported and stored in the larger towns or camps. General Hughes, under whom Bell and Major Smith served, later justified such actions on the grounds that the average native house cost no more than four dollars to build. In the cold parlance of cost-benefit analysis, these tactics were the cheapest means of producing a demoralized and obedient population.[15]

Because Bell's main target was the wealthier and better-educated classes, he singled them out to be impressed into work gangs and particularly chose "the respectable men" who had been appointed to official posts by the commission. Adding insult to injury, Bell made these people carry the petrol used to burn their own country homes. He compared such tactics to those of General Sherman in Georgia during the War Between the States and theorized that once the better elements were miserable enough they would persuade the others to stop fighting.[16]

When Bell's infamous orders were leaked to editors, a shock wave traveled through the anti-imperialist press. The parallels with the notorious Spanish

General Weyler and with Kitchener in South Africa were obvious enough. "Who would have supposed . . . that the same policy would be, only four years later, adopted and pursued as the policy of the United States in the Philippines? Time does truly work wonders; but when or where has it worked a greater wonder than this?" asked the *Philadelphia Ledger*. The editor of the *Baltimore American* declared:

> With what astonishment do we read that a general of our army in the far-off Philippines has actually aped Weyler and Kitchener? Here in this country where we have held our heads so high and so prized the encomiums showered upon us for our ministrations to a suffering humanity, we have actually come to do a thing we went to war to banish. Our good name is dearer than all the islands of the sea.[17]

The editor of the *Detroit Journal* cautioned his readers not to be taken in by any sudden success in the Philippines as a result of these new tactics of Bell and Chaffee. The Spanish had tried them too, with success that proved ephemeral and illusionary in the long run. "When, in short, is the policy of force to win us the respect and affection of a people who are saying almost unanimously that they do not like us and our ways and that they wish to be left to themselves?" he asked.[18]

Imperialist editors responded in predictable fashion. To them, comparing the American army to the Spanish army was inconceivable, if not blasphemous. "General Bell does not propose to starve these people as Weyler did in the Cuban *reconcentrados*. To suppose that he does is an insult to a brave and honorable American soldier," the *Pittsburgh Times* advised angrily. Such criticism of Bell and Chaffee stemmed from pure ignorance, the imperialist editors insisted. "The things which the civilian critics in the United States don't know about military affairs in the Philippines would make a whole library of war history," the *Army and Navy Journal* explained. The editor of the *Boston Journal* saw the problem as essentially a semantic one and predicted that the Filipinos would probably benefit from Bell's plans for them. "The word '*reconcentrado*' has had an ugly sound in American ears," he reasoned. He urged his readers to bear in mind that "the hardship to the Filipinos of Batangas is not the mere leaving of their homes, which are structures of straw and branches, only a little more elaborate than Indian wigwams. They can endure that, and perhaps profit by compulsory removal from abodes that long use and neglect have made unwholesome."[19]

Surprisingly, Bell had the support of correspondents in the Philippines, or, at least, the more conservative ones. The *New York Herald's* Stephen Bonsal cabled his editor that Bell's camps represented a sanitary improvement over the burned-out barrios and were superior to anything these natives had ever experienced before. At the worst these camps were "a temporary inconvenience." Theodore Noyes of the *Washington Evening Star* agreed, while Phelps Whitmarsh was downright enthusiastic over Bell's tactics. For years Whitmarsh had denounced the allegedly "humane tactics" of the army in the Philippines and insisted that the war would go on "until every man caught red-handed" was summarily "executed in the plaza of the nearest town." At long last it appeared America had a general with the stomach to do just this. The silver lining in the Balangiga disaster, Whitmarsh reasoned, was that it had become the catalyst that brought this change about.[20]

Charles Ballantine of the Associated Press came out with a book on the Philippine war that was so bloodthirsty that he published it under a *nom de plume*. "With the firm conviction that the views of the large majority are expressed in this volume," Ballantine dedicated the book to the soldiers serving in the war and in it denounced the "humanitarians" who never understood the Filipino national character:

> Our "little brown brother," the Filipino pure and simple, whom we are so anxious to uplift to his proper plane upon earth and relieve from the burden cast upon him by heredity and a few hundred years of Spanish dominion, is without doubt unreliable, untrustworthy, ignorant, vicious, immoral, and lazy . . . tricky, and, as a race more dishonest than any known race on the face of the earth.

Once these facts were fully understood in the United States, the proper methods of dealing with the Filipinos would become "all too apparent," Ballantine explained. If Otis had fathomed the implications of this reasoning, he had been too much "a silly old woman" to act on them; in MacArthur, America had had a military leader who understood what had to be done, but who had feared that public opinion back home would not permit "what was necessary." Chaffee was a general who didn't give a damn about public opinion but was hog-tied by the Taft Commission, "whose haughty arrogance and insufferable conceit frequently antagonize the natives against the army," Ballantine averred. Indeed, Taft was, in the author's opinion, the real culprit in the drama—even more so than Hoar or any of the anti-imperialists. Taft's opposition to Bell's tactics lent official credence to the propaganda and distortions of the war critics, he charged. In reality, the concentration camps in Batangas were "models of health and sanitation," so much so that the real problem would be getting the people to return to their homes once the area was pacified. Officers such as Chaffee and Bell were ending the war at last, Ballantine exclaimed, and for doing so they were vilified in the press and in Congress:

What is the army's reward? A Congressional investigation! Lives have been cheerfully given up for America's honor and out of chaos and blackness has appeared the dawn of a new era in Philippine history. The result for [*sic*] this has been national ingratitude, partly expressed in the press of the country, but more so in the halls of Congress.[21]

More damning than Bell's orders were the endorsements of them by higher-ranking officers. General Wheaton was a bit more circumspect than Chaffee. Although one of the original hardline generals who conducted the first slaughter of civilians in the Philippines, Wheaton displayed a better instinct for evading any future blame for Bell's tactics by declaring in his endorsement that concentration camps and retaliatory methods were necessary "for the purpose of protecting the natives from guerrilla bands." But Chaffee wrote that "personal contact with the people, a knowledge of their methods and sentiments make [Bell's tactics] necessary," a statement that puts the American military governor on record as fully understanding and approving of the implications of Bell's orders.[22] Chaffee, like Bell, felt no need to cover up or gloss over the new tactics; both believed that Balangiga justified them and that their president and the American people demanded them. As a result, Chaffee permitted stories to go out over the cable that Otis and MacArthur would most certainly have censored. A correspondent covering Bell's campaign filed a story for the front page of the *Philadelphia Ledger* that must have made the citizens of that Quaker city uneasy:

> The present war is no bloodless, fake, opera bouffé engagement. Our men have been relentless; have killed to exterminate men, women, children, prisoners and captives, active insurgents and suspected people, from lads of ten and up, an idea prevailing that the Filipino, as such, was little better than a dog, a noisome reptile in some instances, whose best disposition was the rubbish heap. Our soldiers have pumped salt water into men to "make them talk," have taken prisoner people who held up their hands and peacefully surrendered, and an hour later, without an atom of evidence to show that they were even insurrectos, stood them on a bridge and shot them down one by one, to drop into the water below and float down as an example to those who found their bullet riddled corpses.

This correspondent was not being critical. On the contrary, he stipulated in the article that such tactics were necessary and long overdue. "It is not civilized warfare," he confessed, "but we are not dealing with a civilized people. The only thing they know and fear is force, violence, and brutality, and we give it to them," he concluded approvingly.[23]

The ever-mounting evidence that the army was waging unorthodox warfare made it impossible for the Administration to continue to ignore congressional demands for a thorough investigation. Ironically, it was a casual remark to a reporter by General Jacob Smith that triggered the official inquiry that ultimately led to Smith's own court-martial and conviction. The newly promoted brigadier general told a reporter at the end of 1901 that he intended to set the entire island of Samar ablaze and would probably wipe out most of its population. Hoar picked up the comment and called on the Senate to form a committee for the sole purpose of investigating the war. Forced to respond, the president's apologists countered with the insistence that the standing committee on the Philippines was the legitimate vehicle to conduct such an investigation. This committee was chaired by Senator Lodge, and the anti-imperialists justifiably feared a whitewash. Lodge had been dragging his feet for months on the issue of investigating the war, to the extent that his committee had become inactive. Offering a mock apology for having overlooked Lodge's committee in the first place, Hoar surprised friend and foe alike by agreeing that it should conduct the investigation. For this strategy Hoar was vilified by anti-imperialists, who compared it to Bryan's defection in the treaty fight of 1899. The anticipated travesty would be worse than no investigation at all, they insisted.[24]

In the end, Hoar proved wiser than his critics. Lodge had no choice but to begin the investigation immediately after the recess, in January of 1902. And as Hoar knew, there were too many war critics on Lodge's committee to permit an easy whitewash. Thomas Patterson of Colorado, Edward Carmack of Tennessee, Charles Culbertson of Texas, and crusty Joseph Lafayette Rawlins of Utah were outspoken opponents of the policy of imperialism. Also on the committee was Eugene Hale of Maine, the only Republican who had voted with Hoar against the Treaty of Paris. They would hold their own against any cosmetic efforts by Republicans Lodge, Beveridge, Iowa's William Allison, Nebraska's Charles Dietrich, Vermont's Redfield Proctor, Maryland's Louis McComas, and Michigan's Julius Caesar Burrows.

As was to be expected, Senator Lodge and his Republican colleagues stacked the inquiry with a string of friendly witnesses, men whose conduct in the Philippines itself might have been the subject of the committee's investigation. The war critics on the committee countered by forming a subcommittee that held additional, parallel hearings for witnesses that were less appreciative of the official view of the situation in the Philippines, for the most part veterans of the war. But even before the Democrats and Populists on the committee were able to pressure Lodge to call upon some of their witnesses to testify in the main arena, they were able to wring from the chair's handpicked ones some damaging concessions that proved embarrassing to the Administration. When harmful testimony was elicited, each side jockeyed rather clumsily to introduce leading and loaded questions in order to enhance or to mitigate the damage. Sometimes the hearings degenerated into shouting matches between the committee members. The proceedings might have been more laughable had not the subject been so grim.[25]

Governor Taft occupied the witness stand for almost the entire first month of hearings. As a highly skilled lawyer, Taft should have been a safe witness for the Administration, but he carelessly conceded under questioning that the "so called water cure" had been used "on some occasions to extract information." As though he sensed immediately the enormity of his error, Taft attempted to make light of it by insisting that "there are some amusing instances of Filipinos who came in and said they would not say anything unless tortured; that they must have an excuse for saying what they proposed to say." The opposition on the committee, however, was not amused, and anti-imperialist editors played up Taft's acknowledgment for all it was worth—as though the water cure had never been disclosed before this. Taft's statement was "a most humiliating admission that should strike horror in the mind of every American," declared the *Arena*. The blunder was also poorly timed, in that it almost coincided with the publication of a soldier's letter boasting that the writer had used the water cure on 160 Filipinos, all of whom save twenty-six had died from the ordeal. The army quickly extracted denials from the writer and his superiors. Although the war's critics would never be convinced of it, very few died from this very mild form of torture. Now, however, its widespread use could no longer be denied, thanks to the cheerful concession of Taft and the growing testimony of soldiers and veterans.[26]

Availing themselves of Taft's candor, anti-imperialist senators pressed the witness on other points. Patterson asked him if he thought any war between "superior" and "inferior" races "almost involuntarily" led to "inhuman conduct." Taft agreed that "there is much greater danger in such cases than in dealing with whites." Realizing again that his meaning might be misconstrued, he added that "there never was a war conducted, whether against inferior races or not, in which there were more compassion and more restraint and more generosity" than in this war against the Filipinos. Culbertson promptly asked how he could make such an assertion after reading General Bell's orders. Taft beat a retreat, explaining incongruously that he was talking about war, whereas "war has ended in all these islands except in Batangas and Samar. That which remains is a crime against civilization. It is a crime against the Filipino people to keep up that war under the circumstances." Now Patterson was on his feet, angrily demanding of Taft:

Do you mean by that statement that the army fighting for independence has become so small by captures, by battles, by surrenders, that those who remain fighting for independence are guilty of a crime? Is it a crime because the prospective independence is more remote now than it was two or three years ago?

Taft: It is a crime if they are subjecting their own people in whose interests they profess to be carrying on the war to the greatest privation and suffering.

Patterson: At the hands of the American Army?[27]

Realizing that his testimony often contradicted the Administration's view, Taft at one point pleaded in desperation that "I am here to give my own views." That he was speaking for himself was particularly evident when the Democrats and Populists began to probe into the obvious differences between Taft's assessment of the situation in the Philippines and those of the generals directing the war. "I approach the question from a somewhat different standpoint from the military commanders," he admitted. Carmack pressed on, quoting Chaffee's remark that "history affords us no parallel of a whole people thus practically turning against us and in the genius of no other people was ever found such masterful powers of secrecy and dissimulation." Did the governor agree with this statement? "The charge of treachery against them is unjust I think, in this respect," Taft responded. "They are an Oriental people, and the Oriental believes in saying to the person with whom he is talking what the person would like to hear. That is the tendency of the race," he explained. Carmack then asked if he felt that all the speeches by American leaders declaring the Filipinos to be little better than "treacherous savages" impeded pacification. Taft quietly agreed, despite the fact that Carmack could easily have had President Roosevelt in mind. Lodge understood the possible insinuation and barged into the exchange, shouting, "In this connection, what is the effect of speeches and articles and pamphlets, which have appeared in this country encouraging the Filipinos to resist the authority of the United States?" Naturally, Taft followed Lodge's lead and explained that "all such anti-imperialist utterances were a great obstacle to the success of our efforts there." Rawlins then joined the fray, asking the governor how propaganda that merely asked the American people "to accord the Filipinos justice and gratify their aspirations under proper conditions" could in any way incite them to insurrection. Taft squirmed a bit, conceding that it couldn't, "not put just that way," which provoked Patterson to hold up a speech by Senator Hoar as a perfect example of what Rawlins was talking about. Taft was ignored in the partisan bickering that followed. Armed with the gavel, Lodge restored order and ruled that Taft did not have to comment on Hoar's speech. When Patterson ignored the ruling and continued to press the point, however, Lodge was unable to maintain his own silence and asked Taft, "If anybody circulated that speech in the Philippines, would he not be subject to arrest and imprisonment?" If Taft attempted to answer Lodge, it was lost in the squabble that ensued.[28]

General R. P. Hughes, a key figure who had served under all three military commanders in the Philippine war, followed Taft on the witness stand. He casually conceded that houses were burned indiscriminately as both a deterrent and a tactic to eliminate shelters and hiding places for guerrillas. Senator Dietrich immediately attempted to mitigate the importance of this concession by asking Hughes to estimate the value of these houses. Not assuaged by the general's contention that they cost between $1.50 and $4.00 and took only a few days to construct, Rawlins pressed Hughes on the human consequences of such action and wrung from the witness another damaging admission:

Rawlins: If these shacks were of no consequence what was the utility of their destruction?

Hughes: The destruction was a punishment. They permitted these people to come in there and conceal themselves and they gave no sign. It is always—

Rawlins: The punishment in that case would fall, not upon the men, who could go elsewhere, but mainly upon the women and little children.

Hughes: The women and children are part of the family, and where you wish to inflict a punishment you can punish the man probably worse in that way than in any other.

Rawlins: But is that within the ordinary rules of civilized warfare? Of course you could exterminate the family which would be still worse punishment.

Hughes: These people are not civilized.

Rawlins: But is that within the ordinary rules of civilized warfare?

Hughes: No; I think it is not.

Dietrich: In order to carry on civilized warfare both sides have to engage in such warfare.

Hughes: Yes sir; certainly that is the point. I think that if I am allowed to
go on I will come to a place where I shall have something to say
that will bear directly on this subject.

Hale then observed that the war had become less and less civilized with each
successive commander, and Hughes agreed that "from summer to summer, the
conduct of the war was sterner, stiffer, as you call it."[29]

After two weeks of testimony by Hughes, David P. Barrows was sworn in
as the third witness. He had organized and directed the school system in the
Philippines. As a former university professor, however, he was too accustomed
to delivering lectures to submit to a legalistic style of cross examination.
Hence, he ignored the questions and simply pontificated on a wide range of
topics. Since he supported the official view of conditions in the islands, he was
not disciplined by the chair. The anti-imperialist press had grossly distorted the
situation, he informed the committee. The water cure and concentration camps
were made to seem "more terrible than they are." The former "injured no
one," and the natives in the camps were "there of their own volition," for they
"are pleased with it, because they are permitted to lead an easier life—much
easier than at home." In fact, he said, the natives had, paradoxically, benefitted
from the war. Anticipating Democratic protests, Barrows demurred, "Of
course, I do not wish to assent to the proposition that war is a good thing . . .
but where you have a war existing, it is, I think, better to go ahead and pursue
it rigorously and finish it."[30]

Barrows lasted only three days before General Otis arrived to assert, like a
broken record, that there had been no warfare in the Philippines for the past
two years. "There have been a good many fights since," Senator Hale protested. "By the robbers," Otis shot back. As for American atrocities, "We were
laughed at by Spaniards and European officers for the humanity we exercised,"
Otis contended. The *Call* hooted that once again Otis could have saved himself
some embarrassment by simply glancing at the newspapers before testifying.
Another successful Filipino ambush had been reported that very morning, and
yet another letter from a soldier bragging of torturing and shooting prisoners
was making the journalistic rounds. As though they had little stomach for confronting the general's delusions, anti-imperialist senators asked Otis few questions, and he was dismissed after a few days of testimony.[31]

Meanwhile a worried Secretary Root decided to rush into print a document entitled "Charges of Cruelty, Etc., To the Natives of the Philippines,"[32]
which his staff had compiled to demonstrate that in those "rare instances" when
cruelty had actually been perpetrated by Americans, it did not go unpunished.
Root should have taken time to edit the document more carefully and delete
some painful disclosures, but the secretary had previously indicated a talent for

damaging his own cause with misguided public relations efforts. In a covering letter, Root insisted that "in substantially every case the report [of cruelty] has proved to be either unfounded or grossly exaggerated" after it had been "thoroughly investigated." However, forty-four cases of documented cruelties against the Filipinos were included along with the punishments meted out. Even then, Root felt compelled to rationalize. "That the soldiers fighting against such an enemy with their own eyes witnessing such deeds, should occasionally be regardless of their orders and retaliate by unjustifiable severities is not incredible," he reasoned. But such reasoning hardly lessened the heinousness of the most common crimes listed, rape and looting.[33]

Root's document was not in editorial hands for very long before chortles appeared in the anti-imperialist press over the secretary's conception of "a thorough investigation." In one case, Private T. W. Jones had complained that his company in the Eleventh Cavalry had been ordered to open fire on a native wedding party. When his commanding officer, Captain Scott, was unable to convince Jones to change his story in the initial phase of the "investigation," General Bates sent his inspector general, Major Miller, to look into the matter. The major did not bother to interview Jones, but spoke instead to Scott, who unwittingly added details to Jones's account. A house had been fingered by a native guide as General Cailles's headquarters, and his troopers had been fired on by fleeing Filipinos as they rode up to it. Scott insisted that he had never given an order to fire and that his men only ceased firing at the house after he had threatened them with his pistol. Inside they found two men and one woman killed and three children wounded. But ammunition and twenty "war bolos" were also discovered. Some kind of feast had been in progress, which might have been a wedding party, Scott conceded. On the basis of this interview, Miller dismissed Jones's charges, and Bates in his endorsement commented, "The harrowing account of the killing of a bride and bridegroom seems to be pure fiction." Few reporters reading Root's document could agree with that conclusion.[34]

Another incident documented by Root betrayed the ridiculousness of his claim that careful investigations were made of all charges of cruelty. Peter Pearl, a black civilian working for the Thirty-Eighth Volunteer Infantry, had written directly to President McKinley complaining that the soldiers had murdered prisoners of war and had raped and looted with abandon. By the time an investigation got under way the regiment had already been disbanded. A former officer, however, was still serving in the Philippines, and he was sought out by the investigating officer. Major Anderson's *ad hominem* response to the charges was to insist that all four Negroes who had worked for his former regiment had been "unreliable." "Pete had been sent to prison for stealing from the Colonel," and "Snowball" for striking native women. The major called "Sam" "a crazy preacher type" and could not remember the name of the fourth black, but he was sure it was not "Peter Pearl." But Anderson did agree with Pearl's complaint "that the word 'nigger' was very often used as applied to the natives, probably correctly." He hastened to add, however, that "I never use the word myself." [35]

The ludicrously light sentences given to Americans, particularly to officers, whose crimes could not easily be whitewashed, further damaged Root's claim that justice had been served. Six officers received nothing more than reprimands for shooting and torturing prisoners, assaulting civilians, and looting. In bringing charges of "assaulting prisoners and cruelty" against Lieutenant Bissel Thomas, his commanding officer noted, "Punishment inflicted by Lt. Thomas was 'very severe and amounted to acute torture,' and his actions 'cannot be too much deplored nor too emphatically denounced.'" He was sentenced to pay a three-hundred-dollar fine. But it was the case of Lieutenant Preston Brown that attracted the most editorial attention. Brown had been given a more appropriate punishment of dismissal from the service and five years at hard labor for killing a prisoner. President Roosevelt, however, commuted the sentence to the loss of half his pay for nine months and the forfeiture of thirty-five places on the promotion list. To anti-imperialist editors nothing symbolized better the American contempt for the life of a Filipino than the president's action in the Brown case. [36]

Root's problems did not wane, however, following the editorial uproar that greeted the release of this ill-advised publication. For one thing, the critics on Lodge's committee made clear that they would no longer endure the stream of friendly witnesses without having some of their preferred witnesses called to testify before the whole committee. A subpoena went out to Charles Riley of Northampton, Massachusetts, the first of the famous letter-writing soldiers, just as an embattled Root received word from Chaffee that a major commanding a marine battalion on Samar had executed eleven prisoners without benefit of trial. The case seemed a perfect opportunity for the secretary to demonstrate that wanton killing of natives was not tolerated. A well-publicized trial, conviction, and stiff sentence might displace the embarrassing name of Preston Brown in the anti-imperialist press. Better yet, because the culprit had only been on temporary duty with the army and really belonged to navy, attention might shift from Root's department to the rival Department of the Navy. Root would have been wiser to follow his customary course of pigeonholing such reports. But how could he have anticipated that the court-martial of a Marine Corps officer would open up a horrendous Pandora's box of new embarrassments for his own department?

12

The Last Campaign: Samar Challenges American Innocence

Samar was given first priority by Chaffee following the Balangiga massacre. The victims had served under him in China, and he was eager to avenge them. He created a new military sector that joined Leyte and Samar under a general who would report directly to him. He turned it over to Jacob Smith, along with a shining new brigadier's star. Smith had last served under Bell in Batangas and was directly responsible for much of the slaughter there. His intemperate remarks to the press made clear his disdain for civilized restrictions on the conduct of warfare against "savages." A veteran of the Wounded Knee massacre and well known among Indian campaigners, Smith had been nicknamed "Hell Roaring Jake," allegedly by his men because his voice, disproportionately loud in comparison with his short and slight stature, could be heard all over the battlefield and for decades had filled Indians with fear, as they knew it meant they faced a man who gave no quarter.

Admiral Rodgers, commander of the naval forces in the Philippines, offered Chaffee a battalion of marines for the Samar campaign. To Chaffee, marines were almost as tough as cavalrymen, and he quickly accepted the offer. In the tradition of the Corps, 300 marines, commanded by Major Littleton "Tony" Waller, were under way aboard the U.S.S. *New York* within twenty-four hours. As dapper an officer as ever wore marine green, Waller already boasted a distinguished military career. His latest exploits had been at Tientsin, where he had been breveted a lieutenant colonel. He seemed a sure bet to be a future commandant of the Marine Corps. On reaching Samar, Waller's battalion was temporarily detached from the navy and placed under Smith's command.

Waller was no stranger to human slaughter. As a young officer, he had served in Egypt during the Arabian pasha's rebellion against the khedive and witnessed the display of the heads of captured Bengal Lancers mounted on Arab spears. Following that exhibition, it was ordered that no quarter be given

219

to Arab horsemen, and none was given. In China, Waller saw the brutal and wanton slaughter of the Chinese, largely by German and Russian troops. At one point, steamboat captains complained they could no longer make it up the river with supplies and reinforcements because the floating corpses had clogged the river around Tientsin. But Waller seemed unprepared for the orders he received from General Smith: "I want no prisoners. I wish you to kill and burn, the more you kill and burn the better it will please me. I want all persons killed who are capable of bearing arms in actual hostilities against the United States." Since it was a popular belief among the Americans serving in the Philippines that native males were born with bolos in their hands, Waller demanded "to know the limit of age to respect." He was told "ten years of age." Seeking further clarification, the marine commander asked the general if he really meant that males of ten years and older were to be "designated as capable of bearing arms." Smith confirmed his instructions a second time.[1]

Waller had planned to relieve Bookmiller's Company G of the Ninth Infantry and to make his own headquarters at Basey. Two more companies of marines were to be stationed at Balangiga under Captain Porter. Admiral Rodgers and General Smith accompanied Porter, Waller, and the two companies to Balangiga to witness personally the site of the massacre. There a grim display greeted them. Hogs had dug up the bodies of the American victims that Bookmiller had had buried. The scene proved too much for Smith, who turned to Waller and shouted in an almost uncontrollable rage, "Kill and burn! The more you kill and burn the better you will please me." Waller was a scrupulously professional soldier who disapproved of the slaughter of noncombatants, whether in Egypt, China, or the Philippines. Before taking his departure, he cautioned Porter on Smith's bizarre behavior:

> Porter, I've had instructions to kill everyone over ten years old. But we are not making war on women and children, only on men capable of bearing arms. Keep that in mind no matter what other orders you receive.[2]

One of Waller's first orders was that all native males in the vicinity of Basey and Balangiga report to the marines by October 25, 1901, or "be regarded and treated as enemies." He also warned his men to "place no confidence in the natives and punish treachery immediately with death." For all his professionalism, however, Waller was not above looking for vengeance. The conclusion of his orders set the tone for Waller's operation. "We have also to avenge our late comrades in North China, the murdered men of the Ninth U.S. Infantry."[3] Hence when the marines came across any souvenirs from the Balangiga massacre, such as American foodstuffs, uniforms, or equipment, while on patrol, they gunned down every native in the vicinity regardless of age or sex. Apparently Waller considered such conduct legitimate retaliation.

At first the marines patrolled the more easily traversed coastal border, where they found much evidence of insurgent activity, but no Filipinos. Traveling by the coastal routes denied the marines the element of surprise and gave Filipino soldiers ample time to flee the advancing patrols. Waller began to lead his men deeper and deeper into the never-conquered interior of Samar. Still, success eluded the major until two native prisoners were persuaded to reveal the location of Lukban's headquarters on the Sohoton cliffs along the Caducan River, in the interior. But they warned the Americans that the mountain redoubt was impregnable. Waller had already learned that Spanish maps were woefully inadequate, so he decided to make preliminary probes. Assisted by the navy, the marines constructed a raft to float a three-inch gun and towed it up the river toward Lukban's stronghold. Waller lost two marines to snipers and a gunner's mate on loan from the navy when the raft capsized on the return trip, but he picked up enough intelligence to plan his strategy.

The major led an amphibious assault team up the river with a more stable raft than the first, while Captain Bearss led a group by land from Basey that was to join up with more marines out of Balangiga under Porter's command. The plan was to soften up enemy defenses with the cannon so that a coordinated land- and water-borne assault could trap the insurgents. However, Waller's initial probe had already tipped his hand, and Lukban had rigged cages of huge rocks high above the water approaches to his fort, which kept Waller well out of range. Once Porter realized that Waller's troops could not get past Lukban's trap, he decided to go it alone, without the preliminary barrage and diversionary amphibious attack. Having assigned Sergeant John Quick, already a legend for his heroism in Cuba, to a Colt machine gun on a tripod, Porter and Bearss led a charge on Lukban's headquarters. Lukban's defenders fled the lethal bursts of the machine gun before the charging marines reached the cliffs and, in their haste, left behind scaling ladders for the attacking force. Once they gained the top, the marines slaughtered the fleeing enemy and raised Old Glory to let the frustrated Waller know the redoubt had been taken.

It was a major victory for the marines, who had killed thirty insurgents without suffering a single casualty. If Waller was chagrined that Porter had not waited for him, he did not show it; he recommended brevets or Congressional Medals of Honor for Porter and Bearss and citations for others, including Sergeant Quick, who had already won the nation's highest honors at Guantánamo. General Smith expanded the major's terse report into a glowing eulogy for these "gallant marines," whom he compared to "those barefooted Americans at Valley Forge." More in keeping with the tradition of the Corps, which prefers to consider acts of heroism as routine duty, was the simpler signal from Admiral Rodgers, "Well done, Marines." Root effusively thanked the Secretary of the Navy for the loan of these "brave marines."[4]

More than anyone else, Waller was aware that he had won only a battle and not the island of Samar, whatever Smith and imperialist editors tried to claim. To conquer the island he would have to control its rugged interior. Everywhere there was evidence that Lukban's organization was still active. Waller was unable to prevent his communication line to Porter in Balangiga from being cut. As soon as the marines repaired the line, it was cut again, which so enraged the major that he ordered his men to shoot on the spot any native so much as in its vicinity. Patrols discovered recently evacuated enemy camps and a munitions factory in which the forge was still hot. In one camp they came across mail to the ill-fated members of Connell's company and other mementos of the Balangiga massacre, which spurred them on.

Waller was considering a march across the island in search of a rumored Spanish trail when one of his junior officers, Lieutenant H. A. Day, delivered an unsigned, handwritten message from General Smith declaring that "the interior of Samar must be made a howling wilderness." Whether this bizarre order decided Waller to strike out across the island is impossible to say, but a week later he set out along the coast for the army base at Lanang, on the other side of the island, from which he planned to cross the interior back to Basey. A naval gunboat followed the marines along the coast, and every barrio, hut, and boat they came across was destroyed. The army commander at Lanang, who was junior to Waller, tried politely to dissuade the marine commander from this foolhardy scheme and informed Waller that Bookmiller had tried it but turned back when he was unable to find the trail. But to Waller, Bookmiller's had been simple soldiers, not leathernecks. To make matters worse, the army was short of supplies at Lanang and could provide Waller with no more than four days' worth of field rations. Nevertheless, Waller set out at the end of 1901 after dispatching the gunboat back to Basey with instructions that Captain Dunlop set up a supply base near Lukban's old headquarters on the Sohoton cliffs.

The rivers, heavily swollen by the incessant rain, slowed Waller's march drastically as he had to cross them repeatedly to maintain anything resembling a steady course. The terrain was far steeper than the major had anticipated, the jungle was almost impenetrable, and the leeches kept up a steady assault on the men, which left their faces so swollen their vision was impaired. In addition, the torrential rain returned on the third day out. Unable to meet his scheduled pace under these conditions, Waller was forced to cut the rations in half and then to halve them again. Only the major seemed undaunted by all these hardships. He was in far better shape than his men, most of whom were twenty-five years younger than he. When some of them grew too weak to continue, Waller made the fatal decision of splitting up the group. He would press on to Dunlop's camp with the stronger men, while Porter and Quick would float the weaker ones back to Lanang on rafts.

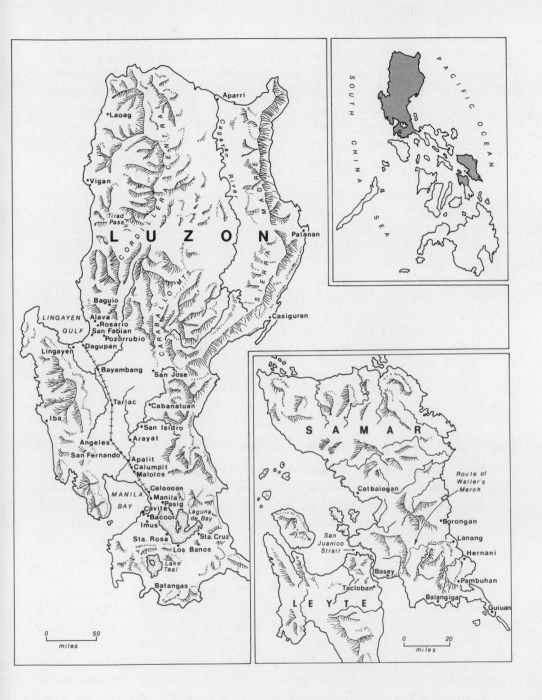

LUZON

Aparri

•Laoag

Cagayan River

•Vigan

Tirad Pass

L U Z O N

Palanan

Baguio

LINGAYEN GULF

Alava•
•Rosario
San Fabian
Pozorrubio
Lingayen •Dagupan

Casiguran

Bayambang

•San Jose

Tarlac

•Cabanatuan

•Iba

•San Isidro
Angeles •Arayat
San Fernando

Apalit
Calumpit
Malolos

MANILA BAY

Caloocan
•Manila
Cavite•Pasig
•Bacoor
Imus
Sta. Rosa•Sta. Cruz
Los Banos
Lake Taal

Batangas

0   50
miles

SOUTH CHINA SEA

PACIFIC OCEAN

S A M A R

Catbalogan

Route of Waller's March

San Juanico Strait

Basey

•Borongan

Lanang

•Hernani

•Pambuhan

Tacloban•

Balangiga

Guiuan

L E Y T E

0   20
miles

Once Waller and the stronger men left, the native bearers remaining with Porter's group became less cooperative. They insisted they could not fell the trees that were needed to construct rafts with bolos. Sergeant Quick grabbed a bolo from one and promptly cut down a tree with it. For good measure he then felled the native with his fist. But the marines were unfamiliar with the vegetation, and the trees that they cut down would not float. Porter suspected that the bearers had known all along that the trees would be useless and were not going to help his group if they could avoid it. His judgment impaired by fever, Porter decided to return to Lanang on foot instead of proceeding to Dunlop's camp in Waller's wake. Floating back to the Pacific side of the island was one thing, but walking back in the condition his men were in was a horrendous proposition. When two messengers from Porter reached Waller with news of the captain's decision, he saw the dangers involved and immediately sent his most trusted guide, Victor, to turn them around. In so doing, the major violated his own dictum never to trust a Filipino. Victor justified Waller's theory by returning to camp with the unlikely story that he had been unable to reach Porter due to heavy insurgent activity. Waller was suspicious, but it was too late to rectify the mistake. His rest site was a clearing planted with sweet potatoes, bananas, and coconuts, which they had discovered not long after leaving Porter's group. He was sure Porter would turn around when he realized that, traveling by foot, he was closer to Dunlop's camp than to Lanang. Porter, too, would discover the planted clearing and rest his men there until they regained their strength. Waller was so sure that Porter would reconsider that he continued his own westward trek toward the Sohoton cliffs rather than wait for Porter.

It was Waller's policy to collect all the bolos from the native bearers at the end of each day. The first night of Victor's return from his abortive attempt to reach Porter's group, the major decided to test the guide and feigned sleep. Sure enough, Victor stole Waller's own bolo that night, and the major had to get it back at gunpoint. Victor was placed under arrest and Waller's men continued. Reaching Dunlop's camp the next day, they returned to Basey by boat. Despite his own high fever, Waller set out immediately with a fresh contingent of marines in search of Porter's group.

Meanwhile Porter struggled to retrace the arduous march from Lanang as the weather worsened and his men grew weaker. The native bearers seemed to fare much better living off the land, but would impart nothing about survival techniques in the terrain so unfamiliar to the Americans. In desperation, Porter split the group again, taking the seven healthiest marines and six natives with him and leaving thirty-three men and eighteen bearers with Lieutenant Williams to follow at a slower pace. Before reaching Lanang, Porter had to leave another four marines along the way. On January 11, 1902, Porter reached his destination and collapsed with a raging fever. The army sent a relief column in search of the remaining marines, but it could do little more than inch its way westward in heavy rains that sent the rivers roaring over their banks. At last the column reached the four marines abandoned by Porter and sent them back to Lanang by boat. But there was no sign yet of the others.

Williams had had his hands full with surly native bearers who would do nothing except at gunpoint. He had trouble collecting the bolos each evening and was aware at one point that three were missing. When he threatened the natives with his pistol for refusing to cut firewood, three bearers attacked him with the missing bolos, took his gun, and fled into the jungle. The other Filipinos had done nothing to intervene on behalf of the young officer, although they did not join in the attack. Even Slim, the one guide who had remained cooperative throughout the march, seemed to acquiesce in the attack on Williams. The wounded officer decided that all the bearers would have to be shot the next morning, while the marines still had sufficient strength to defend themselves. But the army relief column found them before then. As he was being carried out with his men, Williams directed the army to nine men whom he had been forced to abandon along the line of march after he had split from Porter. These marines had not been so lucky; all were dead by the time the relief column reached them. A tenth marine had gone insane and run into the jungle, never to be seen again. The rescuers managed to carry the survivors to boats that would bring them to Lanang. From there they were taken to Smith's headquarters on Leyte, where a convalescent Porter greeted the group, noting that the natives were in better physical condition than the marines. When told of the attack on Williams, the captain ordered all the bearers arrested.[5]

While Waller was in the field, Major Edwin Glenn had arrived in Basey. He and Lieutenant Day, Waller's provost, discovered, through generous use of the water cure, a plot to massacre the marines who had remained in the camp, most of whom were weakened with fever. The plan was identical to the earlier massacre at Balangiga. The church at Basey was to be filled one evening with bolomen disguised as women. The next morning the presidente and padre were to surprise the sentry guarding the camp's three-inch gun and turn it on the barracks and dispensary while the bolomen rushed the other sentries. Day was particularly horrified by this disclosure as he had been so sure of the mayor's loyalty that he had taught him how to operate the artillery piece by inserting the firing pin kept in the sentry's breast pocket. A native merchant who had befriended the Americans was also implicated and after some torture revealed a cache of rifles, most of them Krags taken from Connell's arsenal at Balangiga.

Glenn convened a court-martial, and the mayor and merchant were sentenced to death and the padre to life imprisonment. The condemned were executed that day in the town square by a marine firing squad. Glenn returned to Cebu and Day, using the torture techniques he had perfected under Glenn's supervision, continued the search for more conspirators on his own. He ferreted out one more native allegedly involved in the plot and locked him up to await Waller's return. To the marines who had remained in Basey, the whole town seemed to be seething with treachery, an impression aggravated by the fever that afflicted most of them. Their anger was further roused by a rumor that at least a score of their weakened comrades had been hacked to pieces by native bearers. To this setting, Waller returned from his futile search for Porter's group and collapsed. In a delirium, the bedridden Waller gave Day permission to execute the imprisoned "conspirator" along with Victor, the guide who had plotted to take the marine commander's life. Day and two marines shot the pair and let their bodies lie in the public square as an example to others. The lieutenant was heard to swear that he would like "to kill every Goddam goo goo in town."

To this emotionally charged atmosphere in Basey, the ten arrested bearers arrived in chains, along with Porter's recommendation that they be executed. Day immediately released Slim, his personal protégé in charge of the native constabulary. He then relayed Porter's advice to Waller, who concurred and ordered that all of them be shot, including Slim for not having come to the aid of Williams when he was attacked. It was a bad move. None of these natives had taken part in that attack. Neither had they abandoned the weary, sick, and starved marines on the march back to the camp. While the guilty bearers had fled into the jungle, these ten had returned voluntarily to Lanang in a separate boat provided by the army. An even more serious matter was that the still feverish commander had them executed without benefit of trial. Glenn had at least covered himself with a sham court-martial before executing his prisoners.

Waller's provost lost no time in carrying out his orders. Men hobbled out of sick bay to demand a place on the firing squad to avenge their "murdered" comrades. The ten natives were shot in groups of three (one had been gunned down in the water attempting to make a run for it). Again the bodies were left in the square as an example until one evening, under cover of darkness, some townspeople carried them off for a Christian burial. Waller reported the executions to Smith, as he had scrupulously reported every other event. "It became necessary to expend eleven prisoners. Ten who were implicated in the attack on Lt. Williams and one who plotted against me." Waller had been either too delirious to remember the twelfth native executed, the one that Day had alleged was a conspirator in the plot against Camp Basey, or had never given permission to have him shot. As usual, Smith passed Waller's report on to Chaffee.[6]

For some reason Chaffee decided to investigate these executions. Either he instinctively knew that the political climate back home had been profoundly altered by Root's misfired report, the Senate hearings, and numerous damaging leaks to the press from the War Department, or else he had developed a self-protective reflex. Months earlier, Bell and Smith had carried out similar executions on a much larger scale with no subsequent investigations. But this time Chaffee queried his old comrade in arms, "Smith, have you been having any promiscuous killing in Samar for fun?" His question was probably induced by rumors that Day had had the prisoners shot in stages, wounding them on successive days until they succumbed (possibly a distortion of the lieutenant's decision to let the bodies lie where they fell). Despite Smith's denial, Chaffee decided to pursue the matter. Possibly he expected his "confidential" report to remain safely in Root's desk, but his timing was wrong, and poor Waller, a much more honorable warrior than Generals Wheaton, Young, Bell, Funston, Smith, or Chaffee himself, became a convenient scapegoat. At least Root was eager to cast Waller in that role if the major would only cooperate and play the sacrificial victim.[7]

Waller's outfit on Samar was relieved by army units on February 26, 1902. As they departed for the naval base at Cavite, Smith sent his final signal to them, "You are as fine a group of soldiers as has ever served under my command and I have been an officer for forty years." All the way back to Manila Bay, naval vessels dipped their colors to the transport *Lawton* in honor of the marines on board. Waller led his men ashore amidst formal salutes and wild cheering so loud that even the Marine Corps band could not drown it out. The legend of the Samar battalion was born. For decades to come, marines of any rank would stand when a veteran of the Samar campaign entered a room.

Waller could not have suspected what was in store for him. Reporting smartly to his commanding officer, Marine Corps Colonel James Forney, he was informed that he was under arrest on charges of murder and asked to surrender his sword. A court-martial, composed of both army and Marine Corps officers, convened on March 17, 1902, for Waller's trial. Actually the defendant had more to fear from the officers of his own branch of service, which was then undergoing a fierce internal struggle to name a replacement for the retiring commandant, Major General Charles Heywood. There was the traditional jockeying between staff and line factions for the coveted post, and by the time of Waller's trial it had become a rather nasty intrigue. The leading staff candidate, Colonel C. L. Denny, had raised charges of drunkenness against the top line contender, Colonel Robert Meade. Although he was acquitted, the cloud left by Meade's trial effectively eliminated his candidacy. The line choice had then shifted to Waller as a result of his sensational exploits on Samar. But Waller's conviction would unquestionably remove him from the contest, so Waller was relieved to discover only one staff officer on the court, an old rival, Major William P. Biddle, who had been sent as his replacement when he was arrested. The other two marines, Colonel Forney and Lieutenant Mancell C. Goodrill, were line officers and champions of Waller's candidacy for the post of commandant.

The army officers on the court were strangers to Waller, but in an astute maneuver to win them over he chose as his defense counsel an army officer, Major Edwin Glenn, a West Pointer who had also earned a law degree from the University of Minnesota. Glenn briefed Waller on the army officers sitting in judgment of him. The president of the court was Major General William H. Bisbee, who, as an old Indian-fighter, was deemed friendly, as were Major Edgar B. Robertson, a close friend of the martyred Connell, and three cavalry officers. Waller needed a simple majority for acquittal; he anticipated that Biddle would cast the only vote against him. For this reason, Waller refused to challenge Biddle's position on the court. Biddle's well-known jealousy of Waller, and the professional rivalry between the two officers, would have made such a challenge merely routine; but the accused did not want to create any impression that the court was rigged, since he felt acquittal was a foregone conclusion.

Although Waller lacked formal legal training, he had had considerable experience defending other marines in court-martial proceedings and had once earned the praise of the solicitor general for a brilliant appeal he argued before a circuit court. Indeed, his considerable legal talent did not sit well with Waller's superiors, who rarely appreciate the "sea lawyers" in their outfits. Waller found it necessary to redeem himself on the field of battle in order to save his career. Thus, he fully intended to run his own defense in Manila and to use the formally trained Glenn more as an advisor than as his defense counsel.[8]

For weeks before the trial started, Waller was tried in the press back home, particularly in his adopted city of Philadelphia, whose editors consistently referred to him as the "Butcher of Samar." Anti-imperialist editors sternly warned the Administration that the American people would not tolerate "another Preston Brown." Waller would have to sacrifice a good deal more than half his pay and thirty-five places on a promotion list to satisfy the American public for "such dastardly crimes." Many editors demanded a firing squad, and one even suggested saving the expense of a trial by "hanging the culprit" from the nearest tree, which would, of course, have repeated the crime for which Waller had been indicted.[9]

Anti-imperialist editors refused to give up the rumor that Waller's victims had been shot in stages "for revenge and sport." The *Call* ran this item on its front page for several days, and some editors published artists' conceptions of this fictitious event to lend credence to the lie. So heinous were Waller's alleged actions in the eyes of such editors that he was compared daily to Weyler in Cuba, Kitchener in South Africa, and even to Torquemada in the Spanish Inquisition. William Jennings Bryan insisted that the true analogy was with Adam's consumption of the apple. Instead of the fall of man, however, Waller's vicious acts would bring about the fall of the Grand Old Party, the defeated Democratic candidate predicted. Thus, before he ever stepped into the dock to defend himself, one of the country's finest military officers had become a symbol of infamy and, of course, the goat needed to absolve other Americans of collusion in the slaughter of Filipinos.[10]

Waller was persuaded by Glenn to open his case with a shrewd legal maneuver that caught the judge advocate, Major Henry P. Kingsbury, by surprise. He simply challenged the jurisdiction of the court. Waller's initial orders had stipulated that "you will not regard yourself detached from the First Brigade, Marines." A second set of orders had made clear that Waller would no longer be part of the army's Sixth Separate Brigade commanded by Smith once he returned to Luzon from Samar. Yet it was not until after he had landed at Cavite that he had been informed verbally of the charges against him, and another four days before written ones were preferred. Hence the army, and therefore the court convened by General Chaffee, had no jurisdiction over him. Kingsbury was left sputtering; the best argument he could come up with was that Waller's assertion was correct, but that now "the court had jurisdiction over him simply because he was in its custody at the moment." This argument failed to satisfy General Bisbee, who from the very beginning could scarcely conceal his contempt for Major Kingsbury. Bisbee recessed the court for forty-five minutes in order to ponder Waller's challenge; he returned in complete agreement with it.

The buck was thus passed back to Chaffee as the reviewing authority for Bisbee's decision. He could, of course, pass it on to Root or overturn the decision and order Waller to stand trial. Glenn was positive that Chaffee would be delighted to get rid of this hot potato by sending it off to Washington, where it might bounce from desk to desk until the public forgot the incident or shifted its interest elsewhere. Had Chaffee any inkling of the consequences a trial would produce, he might have done just that. But there was too much pressure from Root not only for a trial, but also for a conviction and severe sentence. Since there had to be a sacrifice, Chaffee, as well as Root, preferred that it be a marine and not an army officer. At any rate, Chaffee ordered Bisbee to reconvene the court and try Waller for murder. Actually, Waller preferred it this way, as a clear acquittal was more desirable to him than escape via a legal technicality, and he had not been happy with Glenn's ploy. Once the trial resumed he rejected Glenn's next suggestion to challenge the prosecutor Kingsbury as a

South Carolina Democrat eager to discredit a Republican Administration. Waller understood that Kingsbury's ineptness, along with the friction between the prosecutor and the president of the court, were in his favor. In Bisbee's eyes, Kingsbury and Biddle, for pushing for the conviction of a gallant fellow officer simply for shooting a few worthless and treacherous natives, were nothing less than traitors.[11]

Waller had intended to base his defense on General Orders No. 100, much in the same manner that Bell had justified his controversial directives months earlier. It was a good legal strategy. This bible for the army, and basic text at West Point, had even been recognized internationally and adopted as the basic code for warfare by the Hague Conference in 1899. Waller was too honorable and too loyal to betray his superior by revealing Smith's orders to him as justification for his actions. Either Kingsbury was unaware of such orders or he was not very wise when he brought General Smith to the stand as a prosecution witness. Smith was not above selling out Waller to save his military career and testified that the major had acted on his own in executing prisoners. This flagrant betrayal not only ended Waller's self-imposed silence, but also permitted the defense to reveal Smith's bizarre orders to the marines without incurring the wrath of General Bisbee. Waller shifted his defense from General Orders No. 100 to the written and verbal directives of Smith, the revelation of which electrified the nation and almost instantly shifted public focus from the major and the marines to the general and the army. One can only guess at the horror felt by Chaffee and Root at this turn of events.

Armed with copies of every written order he had received from Smith and with witnesses to corroborate the verbal ones, Waller informed the court he had been directed to take no prisoners and to kill every male Filipino over age 10. The major's evidence must have given the impression that Smith was a bit demented—sitting on Leyte, apparently brooding over the Balangiga massacre, and impulsively dashing off inflammatory and lawless directives to Waller. This testimony hit the United States like a ricocheting bombshell. In the boldest type imaginable, headlines announced "Waller's Astounding Defense." The *New York Journal* covered much of its front page with giant letters spelling out "KILL ALL." Below, in slightly more restrained type, the headline explained, "Major Waller Ordered To Massacre the Filipinos." Each editor selected a portion of Smith's orders for his front page, so that dailies for April 8, 1902, read "Samar to be Made 'A Howling Wilderness,'" or "To Kill and Burn the More the Better Waller's Instructions." It had to have been a long day for Secretary Root as evening papers vied with their morning rivals to produce more sensational headlines and stories on Waller's testimony. For a short time at least, the line between imperialist and anti-imperialist editors became blurred by the shocking front-page reports, although an eerie silence on the subject of the recent revelations prevailed on the editorial pages of the imperialist press.[12]

Anti-imperialist editors whose patriotism had been impugned so often in the past now demanded that their critics eat crow. "The good imperialists" had once insisted that the "power of the press" would not permit the army to get out of hand, the editor of the *Evening Post* reminded his readers, and then he asked if they had seen any protest in the imperialist press after Waller's startling testimony:

> Well, the Waller-Smith case is now before us, with its terrible revelation that we have been carrying on a warfare in Samar upon men, women and children—above the age of ten—and what is the attitude of the Administration press? With one or two honorable exceptions whose words we print in another column, the whole "incident" is entirely overlooked by our imperialist contemporaries. "Waller accuses Smith" was the headline in one organ over the shocking news from Manila and this in an inconspicuous place. As for editorial comment, why bless you, the trial is not yet concluded; and then, the Filipinos are barbarous and after all every country has to be "stern" in dealing with men who themselves violate the laws of war. In other words since the Filipinos began it (if they did) we must follow and lower ourselves to their level. How eloquent could not our neighbors, the *Sun*, *Times* and *Trib*, be about such atrocities were they reported from Abyssinia, from Armenia, from Kia Chou or from South Africa?[13]

But vindication was too sweet to be tasted in one sitting, so day after day for weeks the editor of the *Evening Post* hammered away at this theme. His imperialist colleagues seemed to have been "struck dumb," he observed. Possibly more pressing news had pushed the Waller-Smith affair off their editorial pages, or did they think Waller's testimony was simply another of those "tall tales" by "a champion liar" designed "to thrill a maiden aunt in Philadelphia"?

> Where be their gibes now? On the one subject which flames highest in the day's news, which most agitates Congress, which even arouses the foreign press, these great leaders of public opinion have not a word to say. What do the *Trib*, the *Times*, the *Sun* think of proved attrocities in the Philippines, or of the suppressed reports which show out of the mouths of our own officers that our whole policy in these islands has been a ghastly failure? They cannot well allege the pressure of more interesting matter. Today's *Tribune* for example has a powerful leader on that thrilling subject,

"Chile's financial plight." The *Times* awakes to a deep interest in Macedonia, and the *Sun* has an eloquent column on a speech concerning Irish home rule . . . but neither of them has a syllable on the burning question of the day. Speak brothers, and let the worst be known. "Speaking will relieve you" as the camp meeting hymn says. We do not care what you say only do say something for the credit of the American press.[14]

Waller was acquitted. If his actions were justified on the basis of Smith's orders, then it was clear to all that the author of those orders would have to stand trial. Chaffee was angered by the verdict that left his old friend so vulnerable, and in his comments to the War Department he called it a "miscarriage of justice." It was reported that Chaffee often found solace on his horse those days following Waller's acquittal. As one writer described it, "For half an hour, as he led his aide in a swift gallop along the sea front, it was '83 again and he was leading his white horse troop of the Sixth Cavalry through the dusty past in Arizona."[15] No doubt Chaffee longed for those good old days when a soldier could shoot a savage or two without having to account for it to some nosey reporter or before a senate committee. But once he dismounted and removed his old black campaign hat with its faded yellow cord, it was the spring of 1902 again, and he had to man a desk and worry about those confounded orders of Smith's. It must have been obvious to the military governor that if Smith were court-martialed and used Waller's defense, his own head would be next on the block.

Additional embarrassments rained down on the Administration that spring, mostly in the form of leaked documents that Root had been sitting on. One was a complaint by Major Cornelius Gardener, a West Point graduate serving as provincial governor of Tabayas, the province next to Batangas. He charged General Bell with making war on the entire population in Batangas, where 100,000 natives had perished. Gardener's motivation was more practical than humane. He argued simply that the "bitter hatred" produced by such tactics was not in the best interests of the United States in the long run. Insisting that the charges were "too general to investigate," Chaffee had forwarded Gardener's report to Root. The secretary promptly lost it in the files, but it was leaked after Roosevelt had congratulated Bell on his campaign to pacify Batangas, and after Root had assured the public that every complaint was "the subject of prompt investigation."[16]

Each revelation renewed the editorial ruckus over Root's "attempts to gild the hideous truth," as the *Springfield Republican* put it. Are these "civil superpatriots in Washington so drunk on this new wine of imperialism that they complacently think they can settle all these things in their own private enclaves and keep Congress and the American people in the dark?" demanded the *Evening Post*. Chaffee chose this inopportune moment to seize a Spanish translation of the American Declaration of Independence as "an incendiary document" and to arrest seven newspapermen in Manila on charges of treason and libel. The charges stuck in only two of the seven cases, and even then the Supreme Court of the Philippines reversed those convictions a year later.[17]

Meanwhile, Sixto Lopez, a key propagandist who operated in Europe and Hong Kong during the war, arrived in Boston in a vain attempt to bring testimony to the Lodge committee. He was immediately deported when he refused to sign a loyalty oath. Apparently the *Boston Herald*'s editor saw nothing incongruous in reporting this episode under the headline, "Sixto Lopez is Back. Returns to Home of Liberty. Boston is Free." But other editors disagreed, finding Lopez's banishment one more example of the government's policy of "silence and suppression," as the *Louisville Courier-Journal* labeled it. "The atmosphere in which such acts are committed is not an American atmosphere. It is the atmosphere of Prussia, Poland, of Siberia and Turkestan," charged the *Republican*. Even more disturbing was the silence on the part of the people. Where were the mass protests that should have followed the exposure of Smith's heinous orders, the demonstrable lying of officials, the continued censorship and suppression of the press in Manila, and the muzzling of Lopez? Almost in anguish, the *Arena* demanded:

> Here we have a startling illustration of the depths of shame to which corporate greed and militarism have already brought the Republic. Is it possible that the conscience of the people has been so anaesthetized by greed for gold that this . . . will fail to awaken them to the deadly peril that threatens the cause of free government and human rights?[18]

As though the Administration did not have enough trouble with its critics, "Fighting Fred" Funston returned to California after an appendectomy and spent his recuperation leave lecturing, writing immodest articles for magazines, and holding frequent press conferences. Billed as "Aguinaldo's Brave Captor," Funston had little trouble attracting audiences with his controversial statements and intemperate attacks on public figures, particularly Governor Taft and his "misguided" policy. "We believe everything and everybody should have a vote, down to cattle and horses," he scoffed. "The Filipino doesn't love us a bit. He doesn't know what gratitude is. He has no sense of appreciation, and I believe he'd like us better if we dealt more severely with him."[19]

Coinciding with Waller's trial in Manila, Funston's cross-country marathon speaking junket was reminiscent of Roosevelt's tour de force in 1900. Wild applause and intoxicating headlines fed the general's escalating self-delusions:

> Bravo! General Funston
> Great Speech by Little Kansan
> Silence While Bullets Fly
> Ignorant Talk at Home Has Slain Our Soldiers
> Got Tremendous Applause and Prolonged Applause
> And Cries of "That's Right." [20]

He told the members of the Lotus Club:

> All of those men who have fallen since December 1900 have been victims
> of a lot of misinformed and misguided people here in the United States. It
> is perfectly proper for us to have all sorts of opinions as to what we should
> do with the Philippines, but for heaven's sake let us keep them to our-
> selves until every square inch of that territory recognizes the sovereignty
> of the United States. [21]

Funston's choicest barbs were directed at the "prattlers" feeding the Senate "tall stories" and "outright lies" in an attempt to discredit the army. "The
whole lot of them" should be "hung for treason," he declared. It was not clear if
Funston was recommending the gallows for some senators on the committee as
well as some witnesses, but anti-imperialist editors interpreted his remark as
such. [22]

One impromptu detour by Funston in New York City further fascinated
and worried the press. As though serving in some plenipotentiary capacity, he
paid a visit to Prince Henry of Prussia aboard the crown prince's yacht. Had
Funston cleared the visit with Washington or was it another impulsive act? demanded the *Call*. Of German stock, Funston did not share the fear and suspicion of his fatherland that so afflicted his superiors. Indeed, he was forever calling for a "Teutonic alliance," rather than only an Anglo-Saxon venture, to
"civilize the world." It is even possible, given his monumental ego, that he may
actually have believed that he could single-handedly alter the decisively pro-
British inertia of American foreign policy. Such behavior, along with his rash
remarks, convinced the editor of the *Call* that "this half cocked hero" was the
most dangerous "man-on-horseback" since Colonel Roosevelt returned from
his celebrated charge up San Juan Hill. [23]

But Funston was not one to heed criticism, particularly from an anti-
imperialist editor. The applause and headlines seemed to impair his judgment
altogether, so that on his return trip to San Francisco, he would emerge from
the train to shout at ecstatic crowds gathered along the route, "Bully for Waller" and "Hooray for Smith." At a banquet in Chicago, he announced he had
personally strung up thirty-five Filipinos without benefit of trial, so why all the

fuss over Waller's "dispatching" a few "treacherous savages?" He assured his listeners that if there had been more Smiths and Wallers—and, by implication, Funstons—in the Philippines, the war would have been over long ago. Egged on by applause, Funston suggested that some impromptu domestic hangings might also hasten the end of the war. For starters, he recommended that all the Americans who had recently petitioned Congress to sue for peace in the Philippines be dragged out of their homes and lynched.[24]

Ensuing headlines in the anti-imperialist press reflected incredulity. "Funston Advises Hanging. Gallows Would Suit Some Americans," announced the *Call*, listing among the candidates for Funston's noose several senators, influential citizens, "the presidents of nearly all American universities, and the leading clergymen of all denominations in the union." The editor advised that "General Funston will do well to repair his inflated condition and sheath his unruly mouth." Instead, Funston arrived in San Francisco a few days later and promptly told a *Call* reporter that his paper's editor and publisher "ought to be strung up to the nearest lamppost." At a banquet in his honor at the posh Palace Hotel, Funston raised the number of prisoners that he had personally executed to fifty, although the *Call*'s reporter noted wryly that he said nothing this time "about hanging Boston's finest citizens." Instead, he lectured the audience on the futility of civilized warfare against "unruly savages."[25]

While Funston continued making fiery speeches, his name came up in another context. Edmund Boltwood, a former captain in the Kansas regiment, appeared before the Lodge committee with corroborating affidavits to testify that the general had personally administered the water cure to numerous suspects and prisoners and on several occasions had ordered his men "to take no prisoners." This report proved too much for the imperialist *New York Times*, which demanded that Funston be court-martialed after Smith. A Massachusetts congressman informed the Harvard Republican Club that he intended to press for Funston's indictment and would not be intimidated "by the threat of some microscopic general who knows as much about the rules of civil government as he does about the rules of civilized warfare." Roosevelt finally defused Funston. When Funston mocked the "overheated conscience" of Hoar in Denver, just before a planned trip to Boston, the president denied his furlough request, and ordered him silenced and officially reprimanded.[26]

Roosevelt did not squelch Funston because he was upset over the use of the water cure. At about the same time he privately assured a friend that the practice was "an old Filipino method of mild torture. Nobody was seriously damaged whereas the Filipinos had inflicted incredible tortures on our people." Roosevelt would never have made this remark publicly, however. Funston's chief sin, in the president's eyes, was that he talked too much. Secondly, he was obviously campaigning for some future office, in uniform, and in a style all too redolent of that Roosevelt had used to upstage McKinley in 1900. Funston was no stranger to national politics, having spent some of his boyhood in Washington while his father, a Civil War hero, had served as a congressman from Kansas for ten years. Already a Roosevelt-Funston ticket was being bandied about in the press, and the president wanted to order this popular general back into the wings while he had the power to do so.[27]

The president did not have the power, however, to prevent Smith's court-martial and the attendant headlines. Chaffee cabled a last-minute appeal on behalf of Smith, and possibly himself, warning Roosevelt that military success was impossible without "severe measures to force disclosure information." He also conceded that "some officers have doubtless failed in exercise due discretion, blood grown hot in their dealings with deceit and lying, hence severity some few occasions. This regretted." But the Administration needed more than regrets from Chaffee to avoid a trial. Chaffee suggested that Smith argue that his orders were never meant to be taken literally. The proud Smith refused and insisted his orders were justified under General Orders No. 100. The latter were vague and contradictory enough to permit such an interpretation. They lumped "part-time guerrillas" together with spies, highway robbers, pirates, and "war rebels," none of whom rated prisoner-of-war status when captured. General Orders No. 100 also gave commanders the right of "retaliation as the sternest feature of war," although they also cautioned that "unjust or inconsiderate retaliation" might degenerate into "wars of savages." On the other hand, the orders advised that "the more vigorously wars are pursued, the better it is for humanity."[28]

Many of Bell's and Smith's orders were either direct quotations or paraphrased portions of General Orders No. 100. But Chaffee himself went beyond them when he ordered his subordinates to obtain information from natives "no matter what measures have to be adopted." Chaffee knew exactly what this order meant and how it was interpreted by Bell and Smith. At the height of the slaughter in southern Luzon, Chaffee wired Washington on Christmas Day, 1901, "Hot time in Batangas." The governor general had to have been aware that his own trial could follow that of Smith.[29]

General Smith's self-righteous candor during his court-martial heated up the headlines needlessly. Dubbed "The Monster" or "Howling Jake," he was compared to Herod even in the imperialist press, which demanded "instant rebuke and repudiation." The *Pioneer Press* in Saint Paul warned the president that Smith's "instant dismissal from the service he has disgraced by the government he has disobeyed will be inadequate atonement for the dishonor he has brought upon the American name." In a rare concession, even Senator Lodge denounced Smith's conduct as "revolting."[30]

Possibly these imperialists hoped that a quick conviction would end the business and leave the nation with the impression that he was a military anomaly. But anti-imperialist cartoonists were already dragging Chaffee, Root, and Roosevelt into the mess, depicting them as dominoes knocking each other over, or pointing to each other over the caption "Who is responsible?" Jacob Gould Schurman joined a number of prominent anti-imperialists to demand that a blue-ribbon committee be appointed to investigate fully the conduct of the army in the Philippines. A senate resolution of May 1, 1902, called upon Root to make available all pertinent information on the orders of Smith, Bell, and Chaffee, with every endorsement from Manila to Washington. Surprisingly, the *New York Times* agreed that it was time "to make a clean breast of it all" and accused the secretary of war of "still trying to hedge." The *Times*'s imperialist editor warned Root that "the stories told recently of torturing and town burning and general license . . . cannot all be dismissed as soldiers' yarns," a remarkable concession from one who had adhered to that explanation throughout the war. [31]

Now it was Roosevelt's turn to leak a story to the press. He revealed an earlier directive dated April 16, 1902—during Waller's trial—in which he demanded that nothing be covered up. "Great as the provocation has been in dealing with foes who habitually resort to treachery, murder, and torture against our men, nothing can justify the use of torture or inhuman conduct of any kind on the part of the American Army," Roosevelt had advised Chaffee. [32]

The leaked directive was just the remedy imperialist editors needed. The *Times* could assure its readers that all the "monsters in uniform of whatever rank" would "be weeded out and punished for their evil deeds. The President is a humane man" and will not "permit anything to be swept under the rug." Roosevelt's ploy even won over some of his sharpest critics, such as the *Call*. That paper found in it "a new direction" and evidence of the "rejuvenation of the Republican Party," which had "strayed from its earlier principles in pursuit of conquest." A few Democratic detractors also gave Roosevelt the benefit of the doubt: "It is indeed gratifying to get this proof that the American conscience has not been wholly seared by this miserable and wicked war of subjugation and extermination." [33]

The *Arena*, however, denied that Roosevelt had had any change of heart. It pointed out that the directive was sent eight days after Waller had revealed Smith's incredible orders, when "the horror and indignation of the nation practically forced the action." Such skepticism was amply justified. On the very day of the leak, Roosevelt directed Root to cable his personal congratulations to General Bell and his command on the successful campaign in Batangas and Laguna provinces. He also assured Root privately that he did not intend "to repeat the folly of which our people were sometimes guilty . . . when they pat-

ted hostile Indians." As though all the embarrassing revelations had never occurred, Roosevelt continued to characterize anti-imperialists as "liars, slanderers and scandalmongers to boot." Clearly, these "startling revelations," as
they were billed in the press, had made little impression on the president, beyond making him feel the necessity to make some cosmetic changes to satisfy
the press.[34]

During Smith's trial in May, an enterprising reporter culled through old
newspaper accounts and official reports on Smith's earlier escapades in the Philippines. The result was possibly the most serious indictment of the army's top
command. Long before being promoted and given a separate command, Smith
had reported routinely of firing on Filipinos carrying white flags. He had constructed cells measuring 15 feet by 30 feet and 6 feet high, out of railroad tracks
torn up by the retreating enemy, into which were crammed up to fifty prisoners
for months at a time, "with no toilet facilities." Colonel Smith was so proud of
these cages that he posed in front of them for a press photographer and gladly
gave out grim statistics on the death rate in his "cattle pen." He had contributed an article to the *Critic* in Manila, in which he blamed the Balangiga massacre on "officers who love 'little brown brother.'" "It seems that General
Smith's method of carrying on civilized warfare was well developed . . . long
before he was sent to wreak vengeance on Samar," noted the *Boston Herald*.[35]

General Wheaton, who had ordered the first mass reprisal in the war three
years earlier, presided over the court that found Smith guilty of "conduct to the
prejudice of good order and military discipline" and sentenced him "to be admonished by the reviewing authority." The court carefully stipulated that it did
not believe Smith meant "everything that his unexplained language implied,"
whereupon Smith turned to the reporters to declare that he meant every word
and that burning and shooting the "treacherous savages" was the only way to
win the war.[36]

Back in Washington, Root concocted a scheme to have Smith declared insane. At worst the convicted general could be declared "temporarily insane,"
he explained to Chaffee and ordered him to convene a medical board for this
purpose. But Chaffee was unable to pressure two of the three appointed medical officers to go along with the ruse. "Board not familiar sufficient circumstances to develop evidence adequate test case," Chaffee frantically cabled Root
and recommended that the insanity ploy be dropped.[37]

While Smith was still en route to San Francisco, a new, sensational revelation of American atrocities in the Philippines pushed him off the news pages
momentarily. The Reverend W. H. Walker, who ran a training school for missionaries in Boston, turned over to the *Boston Journal* a shocking letter from
his son serving in the Philippines. The letter described the systematic execution of 1,300 prisoners in Batangas. A priest had been called in to hear final

confessions, which took days, after which he was hung in full view of the prisoners. Thereafter, prisoners in groups of twenty were forced to dig their own mass graves before being gunned down. It took weeks of working six days and resting on the Sabbath to complete the chore. Walker's letter was not one of protest, however, unless to complain that Waller and Smith had been unfairly singled out for tactics that were not only routine, but necessary to pacify the islands. The victims, at any rate, were members of the "terrible KKK Society [Katipunan]," and would have starved to death, thanks to the efficiency of the army in destroying crops and supplies. Young Walker explained, "To keep them prisoners would necessitate the placing of the soldiers on short rations if not starving them. There was nothing to do but kill them." Securing a retraction from the son was simple enough, since he was still in the army and did not want to be thought of as a war critic, and the father dutifully told reporters that the whole episode had been distorted by the anti-imperialist press.[38]

The damage had already been done by Walker's letter, however, and it was compounded by the concurrent testimony of veterans who had at last been subpoenaed by the Lodge committee. Dismayed over the damaging statements, Lodge and Beveridge tried to intimidate the young witnesses and, failing that, to besmirch their reputations by leaking to the press any unflattering information from their service records, supplied unquestionably by Root. Thus when former Lieutenant Grover Flint, a Harvard graduate working on a biography of his father-in-law, the recently deceased historian John Fiske, refused to be bullied by Lodge and Beveridge, he was asked if he had not been initially turned down for a commission for excessive drinking. Flint insisted that his drinking was no worse than any other soldier's in the Philippines and that he was stone-sober when he had witnessed the atrocities described in his testimony.[39]

Lodge hastily adjourned the hearings while he contemplated another strategy. Twelve days later the "investigation" was reopened with MacArthur, back for a second stint before the committee. The general operated almost like a one-man filibuster, often ignoring questions to embark on endless and tangential soliloquies on just about any subject that entered his head. Thus he "prefaced" his "general remarks":

> As a general proposition, when the command entered Manila Bay everybody was in a totally ignorant but especially sensitive and receptive state of mind. It was apparent, however, that we had entered a new world of various and great resources, teeming with a dense population that was in a paroxysmal state of excitement.

Warming up, the general launched a fascinating discourse on the relationship between climate and decision-making. At least that seems to have been his point:

Under the influence of the far-eastern sun the heated imagination had a
boundless scope for indulgence of the boldest assumptions. Discrimination and sound judgement were taxed to the limit in order to reach anything like a conservative conception of the situation, which was filled with
paradoxical suggestions and apparently hopeless conclusions. Visible indications manifested themselves which were incongruous with each other
and irreconcilable with facts regarded of reliable record and which were
generally accepted as the bases of important deductions in the premises.
In my own behalf I determined not to theorize; but while carrying out the
plain mandates of military duty to allow surrounding circumstances to exert their normal pressure, and thus permit my mind, if it should become
sufficiently permeated, to record such conclusions as its own involuntary
actions should suggest. . . .[40]

Few dared interrupt the general as this merely set him off on another
monologue, or evoked a nonsensical recapitulation of his point, such as:

The existence of the phenomena under the phases herein set forth is an
interesting fact, which in useful effect in respect of the military and political problems now presented for the solution of the United States, is of the
greatest importance.[41]

Without being cued, MacArthur moved on to his pet topic, the "Aryan
race." At least he cautioned the committee that "in opening this branch of my
remarks, I will say this is what I call my ethnological premises. It goes back; it is
perhaps more academical than anything I have yet said." One can only imagine
the effect of such a warning from this witness. MacArthur plowed on, going
from America's "Aryan ancestors" raising cattle to their "imperishable ideas."
Their history was part of a "process of spontaneous evolution," he explained.
"We are now living in a heroic age of human history, from the opening aspect of
which many of our people recoil with misgiving, as though we were of choice
and *de novo* entering upon a questionable enterprise, the remote consequences of which must inevitably prove disastrous to all concerned."[42]

Finally in exasperation, Senator Carmack protested, "You take the one fact
that the witness has been to the Philippines . . . [and] allow him to testify to
anything on earth, to a treatise on political economy if he wants to." Senator
Dietrich came to the general's defense, insisting that MacArthur's "conclusions" were not "hearsay," but drawn from "experience" and from "facts."[43]

The Democrats tried another tack and pressed for direct answers on two
sore points: the end of the war and the discrepancy in the statistical ratios between killed and wounded on'both sides. They refused to endure another "phil-

osophical treatise," and Senator Patterson interrupted MacArthur to shout, "Will you kindly answer the question?" The general told him that the only war in the Philippines had been the short one against Spain. It was not possible to classify the fighting against Filipinos a war because one could not "regard the United States as a foreign people [*sic*] in the Philippines"; it was simply a question of Americans attempting "to govern themselves" in this "tuitionary annex." When asked why then the bulk of the army was bogged down there, MacArthur explained that "the troops are distributed for tactical purposes" and warned that he "would have to go into some shading to give my exact meaning." From MacArthur, this was, indeed, a formidable threat.[44]

Senator McComas attempted to interrupt the questioning on the killed-to-wounded ratios by declaring that "I deny that to begin with. The purpose then is to impute barbarity to the Americans and humanity to the Filipinos." Since these ratios had appeared in MacArthur's own report, he could hardly deny them, however, and simply iterated his standard explanations involving superior marksmanship and genes before concluding that "no war in history has been conducted with as much humanity." He even added, "If Japan should come into our hands in the clean manner, with the clear conscience, with pure morals, and the definite purpose we have in the Philippines, I should say keep it by all means."[45]

The critics began to press Lodge to call as witnesses Emilio Aguinaldo, Sixto Lopez, and Major Cornelius Gardener, but he would have none of that. Instead, he subpoenaed veterans from a "safe" list supplied by Root. But the ploy backfired when these ex-soldiers began to lecture the committee on the necessity of shooting or burning all Filipinos because of their "inability to appreciate human kindness." In a final concession to the Democrats, Lodge agreed to hear from another old "letter writer," ex-Corporal Richard T. O'Brien, who recounted "Stories of Fiendish Cruelty," as they were billed in anti-imperialist headlines. The leading villain was Captain Fred McDonald, dubbed "The Beast of La Nog" for having ravished a peaceful village of that name. O'Brien described how his company had gunned down citizens waving white flags because McDonald had ordered it "to take no prisoners." Only a beautiful mestizo mother was spared to be repeatedly raped by McDonald and several officers and then turned over to the men for their pleasure. Since O'Brien admitted to having not actually witnessed the rapes, Lodge dismissed the charge as "hearsay," a ruling that was not respected by anti-imperialist editors.[46]

The next witness, the army's chief of ordinance, General Crozier, denied that the shell casings presented by O'Brien could have housed dumdum bullets, however possible it was to come to such a conclusion simply by looking at the casings. But no senator challenged him, and he was followed by Bishop James M. Thoburn, a missionary in Asia for forty-three years before his appointment as the leading Methodist prelate in the Philippines. He cautioned the committee that Americans in the Philippines were merely God's pawns, implying at least that the Democratic senators were tampering with divine will. Patterson took up the challenge, only to be gaveled down for "irreverence." Undaunted, the Coloradan tenaciously pursued the point:

Patterson: You think we are there without any design on our part, but through the hand of Providence.

Thoburn: I do. President McKinley once told me in confidence that he tried every possible way to avoid the annexation of the Philippines.

Patterson: God placed us in Cuba, too, didn't he?

Thoburn: Yes, sir.

Patterson: It is your opinion that the hand of God leads great powers to send their armies to the lands of semi-civilized people to subjugate them and bring them under the domination of the great powers?

Thoburn: I would not put it that way . . . I think, if you will allow me to state it in my own terms, that God rules and over rules and verily, as the Good Book teaches us, he so over rules the movements and purposes of bad men as to bring about a result very different than they anticipated.

Patterson: If the British shall in the end subjugate the Boers, will that, in your opinion, be done in the Providence of God.

This time Patterson was shouted down for "irrelevance," since the committee was not investigating South Africa. But the overruled senator bounced back after a tumultuous interruption:

Now it is your theory that if a nation comes to the assistance of a barbarous or a semi-barbarous people . . . they have a right to override against the will of that people, take possession of their country, and kill and burn as much as be necessary for the purpose of that possession and permanent occupancy?

Thoburn: What might be right in one case would be wrong in another.

Patterson: Is God or man doing these things?

> *Beveridge*: I object. This . . . is an irreverent cross examination as to the
> Bishop's interpretation of God and His actions in specific
> events.[47]

Next it was the turn of ex-Captain Fred McDonald, who denied vigorously under oath the charges that O'Brien had raised against him. Lodge then sought really professional help from Colonel Arthur L. Wagner, who was in effect the army's chief public relations officer. His primary function as a witness seems to have been to alter the negative images of General Bell's concentration camps in Batangas. Such camps, he insisted, were created to "protect friendly natives from the insurgents" and to "assure them an adequate food supply," while also teaching them "proper sanitary standards." Under some bitter cross-examination, however, Wagner was forced to concede that in one camp "about two miles long and one mile wide" lived 8,000 Filipinos. By simple calculation, the critics pointed out that there was only a twelve-by-six-foot area for each inhabitant. Wagner confessed that one church housed 127 females, a large house held 270 males, and a simple nipa hut designed for one family sheltered 40 people, but these were only "sleeping arrangements," and during the day they had "complete personal freedom"—that is, up to the "dead line." Beveridge interrupted to inquire why it was not called "a life line" since it served to "protect our friends." Wagner eagerly agreed, wondering, no doubt, why he had not thought of this clever euphemism.[48]

Senator Bacon had remained silent throughout this exchange, awaiting the best moment to produce a letter from the commander of one of Bell's concentration camps, who called them "suburbs of hell." Over loud Republican protests, Bacon began to read the letter for Wagner's reaction. The chair ruled that, unless the senator identified the author, who had asked to remain anonymous, it was "hearsay evidence" and directed the witness not to comment on it. But Bacon had already read part of the letter:

> What a farce it all is . . . this little spot of black sogginess is a recon-
> centrado pen, with a dead line outside, beyond which everything living is
> shot. . . . Upon arrival, I found 30 cases of smallpox, and average fresh
> ones of five a day, which practically have to be turned out to die. At night-
> fall crowds of huge vampire bats softly swirl out of their orgies over the
> dead. Mosquitos work in relays. This corpse-carcass stench wafts in and
> combined with some lovely municipal odors besides makes it slightly un-
> pleasant here.[49]

Critics badgered Wagner on other points until he agreed that some "innocents" had suffered in the Philippines, but he added that the same was true of every war and that it was an injustice as old as man. "The Almighty destroyed

Sodom, notwithstanding the fact there were a few just people in that community." Beveridge chimed in, "How strange: I was thinking of that instance of
Sodom and Gomorrah."[50]

After a two-week recess, the committee reconvened with a carefully
coached former Sergeant Mark Evans on the stand, but Lodge hustled him off
when he insisted that the Filipinos had to be exterminated. Another two-week
hiatus followed before Lodge came up with his final witness, Admiral George
Dewey. Dewey's celebrated victory at Manila Bay was now four years old, and
his clumsy attempts to secure a presidential nomination, along with a recent
marriage to a Catholic in an age of fanatical, antipapist sentiment, had dulled,
to some extent, the luster of this national idol. At any rate, the war critics on
the committee seemed a good deal less intimidated by the admiral's august
presence this time around and pressed him hard with uncomfortable questions,
mostly related to his betrayal of Aguinaldo's trust. "I am not a lawyer; I cannot
debate with you, Senator," Dewey responded angrily on one occasion. "I do not
like your questions a bit. I did not like them yesterday and I do not like them
today," he declared imperiously at another point.[51]

Dewey blithely presented a string of biased opinions as facts, and when
confronted with such objections as, "We have no record of that," he retorted
with a "You may believe me, Gentlemen," or more outrageously, "I think it is a
fact though." Once again, the admiral assassinated the character of his former
friend, Don Emilio. When Carmack protested that there was no evidence that
Aguinaldo was dishonest, Dewey declared, "I could see he was a thief," or,
on another occasion: "I think I will not answer that." In the growing pan-
demonium that marked the last day of the hearings, Patterson managed to ask:

Do you think these innuendoes are just and proper?

Dewey: I do.

Beveridge: I do not know whether any senator objects, but I will frankly
         say that such a question as that the chair will rule is not proper
         and that it is discourteous.

Patterson: I will let the record stand to show that the question is perfectly
         justifiable.

Beveridge: And you will also let the record state what the opinion of the
         chair is upon that subject.

Patterson: I don't care what the opinion of the chair is.

Beveridge: And I will not permit the question to be put.[52]

By this time, the hearing was in shambles, and when the ruffled naval hero stepped down on June 28, Beveridge, on instructions from Lodge, adjourned the committee for good. Apparently, there was no protest from the opposition. A petition from five leading anti-imperialists calling for an *ad hoc* congressional committee to go to the Philippines to interview native leaders and investigate conditions there firsthand was ignored. Beveridge had the last word in the "investigation" by gleaning from the record anything that remotely supported his conclusion that the war was one of the most humane ones in history and then publishing this deceitful cut-and-paste job as a separate senate document. As far as Beveridge was concerned, the Lodge committee had destroyed the malicious fiction of "the slanderers of the Army."[53]

Beveridge's whitewash seems to have been just what many Americans wanted, if a series of tortured editorials is at all reflective of the national mood. One by one, imperialist editors had, at least, accepted the reality of the charges that the recent courts-martial and testimony before the Lodge committee had made so hard to deny. "All Americans have been shocked," conceded the *New York Times*. In Boston, the editor of the *Transcript* described "a great transformation" in the "sentiment of both parties" and predicted that Hoar would no longer stand alone among Republicans. The *Call* prayed that the Grand Old Party would "not only heed but lead this sentiment. Let them declare that the party is not going to be identified with the wholesale murder of children." But this editor worried about those Republicans "afflicted with Funstonism" who were "snubbing as 'sick sentimentality' every expression of humanity which deprecated the universal arson and slaughter." Worse, the *Call* pointed out, "certain smug clerics and smugger laymen were deriding the growing bitterness against military methods." The *Evening Post* was more skeptical about any revolution in public opinion: "There are no blood red 'extras,' no appeals for righteousness, no horrifying pictures of Waller's victims praying for death, no mass meetings, no outburst of historical American sympathy for the downtrodden and suffering peoples." Mass meetings had been called, but only in Boston had the turnout been respectable. It was easier to draw a crowd to protest British atrocities against the Boers, particularly in cities with large German and Irish populations. "Imagine the English reading of our mass protests against the cruelties in South Africa after this!" lamented the *Evening Post* in New York, warning that "only one shame could be greater and that would be for Americans to feel no shame."[54]

Such suspicious pessimism was vindicated as the aroused indignation of imperialist editors over the revelation of American tactics abated. By May, imperialist editors had begun to return, albeit cautiously, to their earlier position justifying the war and imperialism and to attribute all the revealed atrocities to anti-imperialist propaganda. The *New York Tribune* hinted at such a course when, in the middle of the Waller and Smith trials, it cautioned: "'Hear the other side' is sound advice for even anti-imperialists to follow." The *New York Sun* sent up a trial balloon in a letter from A. B. Johnson, the former consul at Amoy, who had been given the standard army tour of the Philippines on his way home from China, to which the entire editorial page was allocated. Johnson defended the army's tactics as necessary to shorten the war:

> In all candor, I say the order to burn and kill or capture the enemy was a humane order, was lawful, and all this sensational testimony is not prompted by a desire to save humanity. . . . I met Captain Glenn, Lt. Conger and Dr. Lyon. They are not demons. Lt. Conger had his old mother in Iloilo with him and a more dutiful son and finer gentleman one would not care to meet.

Two days later, the *Sun*'s editor endorsed Johnson's view and defended Smith's orders to Waller as "a means of protective retribution."[55]

The *Providence Journal*, which only a month earlier had denounced Smith's tactics as "disgraceful" and "unAmerican," suddenly decided they were "the necessities of war which it would be mere sentimentality to blame." All the old clichés of "iron emergencies being met in iron ways" and "fighting fire with fire" were marshalled to justify the use of terror to counter terror. Why were soldiers sent in the first place? asked the *Globe-Democrat* in Saint Louis:

> Was it to try moral persuasion on the infuriated bolomen who were massacring our soldiers daily? How much of this new policy of court-martial is due to the venom of copperheads and the tittle-tattle of shirks? It is strange, indeed, if American soldiers are to be called to the field to fight savages without hurting them.[56]

Suddenly, the whole business was again the fault of the anti-imperialists and war critics who were attacking American soldiers unable to defend themselves in the press. The U.S. Army suddenly replaced the Filipino as victim in this incredible editorial shell game. The *Sun*'s editor worked himself up into a rage on the subject:

> It makes my blood boil with righteous indignation as I realize the fact that such men as Senators Hoar, Tillman, Patterson, Carmack and others of that ilk in the Senate and House are bewildering the minds of the public by their vociferous charges of cruelty and oppression by our brave soldiers in the Philippines against the savages and cannibals over there. There is scarcely a voice raised or a line printed in defense of these men, who are maintaining the honor of our flag on the other side of the globe.[57]

The only time the *Sun* even conceded that a "few transgressions" might have occurred was during this new editorial offensive in May, but then the editor argued that they were little "to stew about" and "water over the dam," and that they would have little bearing on the policy of imperialism:

> Well suppose that the native barbarities have, in some cases, moved our soldiers to transgress the line of gentleness desirable for ordinary warfare? We are confident that, in view of the provocation received and the peculiar nature of the task to be performed, the transgressions were very slight. And at the worst, they have been few. But nothing of what has been reported, admitting it all to be true, has any practical bearing upon the question of American supremacy in the Philippines, its present and future.[58]

In the best American pragmatic tradition, the *Times* in New York soon overcame its agonizing doubts of April to thank effusively the editor of *Harper's Weekly* on May 2 for "a particularly sane view of the situation in the Philippines," which it recommended as "required reading for every thoughtful citizen." Summarizing the article, the *Times* added:

> A choice of cruelties is the best that has been offered in the Philippines. It is not so certain that we at home can afford to shudder at the "water cure" unless we disdain the whole job. The army has obeyed orders. It was sent to subdue Filipinos. Having the devil to fight, it has sometimes used fire.[59]

The next day the *Times* took the offensive again, lashing out at the war's critics as though the Waller and Smith trials had never occurred. The editor attributed "this new business in the press and halls of Congress," this "wallowing in stories of American atrocities," to "a second venture in anti-imperialist politics" after the "humiliating defeat" at the polls in 1900. Now these "anti-everythings were slandering the army." He was particularly incensed over a huge cartoon in the *New York Journal* depicting blindfolded and bedraggled Filipino boys scarcely ten years old lined up before an American firing squad. Old Glory draped an American shield on which a vulture replaced the bald eagle, and General Smith's infamous order was the caption in very large caps, "KILL EVERYONE OVER TEN." "Of all the sins that have been charged against 'yellow journalism,' this is by far the worst," decreed the *Times*.[60]

Since many imperialist editors were also Republicans, they converted this "new criticism" of the war into a partisan issue and warned that this "Democratic slander" would hurt that party more in 1904 than it had in 1900. "The American people say 'No' to the Democratic retirement proposition, with disgust at Democratic slanders on our army," the *Sun* assured its readers. Apparently many Democratic editors took heed, as some who had expressed the greatest shock and indignation over the sensational revelations became increasingly reticent on the war and on imperialism in general. The *New York Journal*, which had once covered its front page with Smith's orders, now buried the latest revelations on inside pages, and simply ignored them on the editorial page. Outrage over the American conduct in the Philippines seemed to have gone out of style.[61]

The Protestant and missionary press continued faithfully to defend the army and the policy of imperialism. In one article, entitled "The 'Water Cure' From a Missionary Point of View," the Reverend Homer Stunz rationalized that "since the victim has it in his own power to stop the process, or prevent it altogether" by divulging what he knows "before the operation has gone far enough to seriously hurt him," it cannot accurately be labeled "torture." Contrary to the impressions created by the press, "the treatment is never given wantonly; or, if so, it was without sanction" and "given only to spies." Stunz even confessed to having personally witnessed the army administering the water cure to several Filipinos. Such an admission must have troubled church leaders, as it followed on the heels of revelations that missionaries in China during the Boxer crisis had accompanied Allied troops demanding revenge and even looting in order to square accounts for the murder of their colleagues and the destruction of missions. Now Stunz was further besmirching the missionary cause with his frankly bloodthirsty justification of Smith's tactics and with a tirade against the general's critics:

> If the violent critics of this method of gaining information could put themselves in the places of soldiers in lonely and remote bamboo jungles, I fancy they would feel differently. . . . The matter would not look as it does here divorced from the stern conditions of warfare with a treacherous enemy.[62]

One medical missionary, Alice B. Condict, published a book in the summer of 1902 with the bristling title, *Old Glory and the Gospel in the Philippines*. Even the editor of the *Missionary Review of the World* felt uneasy over her title, which he called "ill chosen" in his otherwise favorable review of the book. Arthur Judson Brown, a leading spokesman for the Presbyterian Board of Missions, returned from the army's package tour of the islands announcing that all the opposition to the conduct of the war was, in fact, "based on opposition to Protestant missions." The director of all Presbyterian missions, F. F. Ellinwood, penned an appeal to the American people to end all the "bickering" over the war and recognize that the conquest of the Philippines was "a Providential event of the widest reach and of the most momentous consequences and on whole a great step toward the civilization and the evangelization of the world." Bishop Thomas, Indiana's leading Episcopal prelate, also came back from the army tour to tell reporters and Senator Beveridge personally that because the Filipinos were so "treacherous and barbarous," as well as "defective in reasoning," General Smith's tactics were absolutely necessary "to purge the natives of the evil effects that a degenerate form of Christianity has had on them for more than four centuries." It appears that General Smith had as many clerical defenders as he had military ones.[63]

Apologies from the "church militants" should not have come as any surprise at this point, but, nevertheless, anti-imperialists did express shock not only that the religious community failed to condemn Smith's tactics, but that some members tried to justify them. "Especially we would call on the religious press to speak out; it has been rejoicing over the door for the gospel opened by our army in the Philippines. If it holds its peace now it will become partaker in the blood of those murdered Visayans," warned the *Evening Post.* The *Boston Herald's* editor confessed to have been "straining with hand cupped to ear and fervent hope" to hear some clerical denunciation of Smith and Waller:

> The American pulpit, one would naturally suppose would be the most sensitive of all to the outrage on humanity that appears in the torturing of Filipinos, but what may be classed as the political portion of the pulpit, by which we mean that portion which advocates imperialism, is so apprehensive that its peculiar politics may suffer if anything is said against American doings in the east that it is dumb as regards these cruelties.[64]

One small group of Protestant ministers, joined by a rabbi, did hold a meeting at Boston's Tremont Temple on May 22, 1902, to protest the atrocities in the Philippines. The meeting was surprisingly nonpartisan and moderate in tone, in contrast to the strident indignation at most anti-imperialist rallies. The Reverend E. Winchester Donald, who chaired the meeting, stipulated that the group represented neither anti-imperialism nor imperialism, any more than it stood for the Republican or Democratic parties. Three clergymen even expressed the hope that American atrocities were no more than "tall stories" emanating from bored soldiers who had "drawn long bows." The assembly was asked "to support the President and his Secretary of War in their pledges to discover and punish the authors of barbarities . . . upon whose shoulders should rest the responsibility of having disgraced the American flag and Christian America." Only the two speakers who had formal connections with the Anti-Imperialist League, the Reverends A. A. Berle and Robert J. Johnson, refused to give Roosevelt and Root the benefit of the doubt. Rabbi Charles F. Fleisher made some interesting observations on the politics of protest, warning against the highly partisan, self-righteous rhetoric that often accompanies it.[65]

What seems to have stung the imperialists more than any other criticism was that coming from former English supporters, many of whom had grown disillusioned over the atrocities committed by their own soldiers against the Boers. Rudyard Kipling, no less, wrote to the editor of the *Call*:

> All you say about the Philippines, the conflict there between the Americans, military and civil, and the pig headedness of the military and their habits of setting "bulldogs to catch rabbits" is immensely cheering to me, because it is precisely what we are doing in South Africa.[66]

The predicted bipartisan revolt against the Administration's Philippine policies fizzled just as badly in Congress as it did in the press. Republican Congressman Silbey warned in April that "you cannot civilize or conquer any country in the world by first drowning people and then bringing them to life with the butt end of a musket." Once again the *Call* read into the speech evidence that the party of Lincoln was about to become the "conscience of the country." A month later the debate over a new Philippine bill, known as the Organic Act, followed partisan lines. It was full of tired rhetoric about "uplifting savages," as though it were 1898 and the shocking revelations had never occurred. The atrocities were mentioned just once, and then in defense of the army, when Senator Burton cited earlier massacres of Indians at Wounded Knee and Mountain Meadows as precedents before concluding that the slaughter of Filipinos was "entirely within the regulations of civilized warfare." No one even bothered to respond to Burton, and only two Republicans joined Hoar in voting against the Organic Act while a single Democrat favored it. Beveridge hailed this legislative victory as the first step in "the progress of the American people to the mastery of the world."[67]

The press's reaction to the Organic Act was equally partisan. Antiimperialist editors grossly exaggerated its exploitative features, equating it with the economic rape of the archipelago, while their opponents read into it "a magnanimity unsurpassed in human history." In reality, some sharp restrictions were placed over the economic power to exploit, ones that essentially mirrored progressive concerns in the United States. One historian has suggested that imperialists went along with these limitations in order to assuage some guilt they felt over the atrocities and to demonstrate "the nation's purity of motives." But then, many of the imperialists were also progressives, whose attitudes toward the mercantile spirit were ambivalent at best.[68]

President Roosevelt best reflected imperialist amnesia when he declared on July 4, 1902, that not only was the war over, but that it had been the most glorious war in the nation's history. One month earlier, in his Memorial Day address, he had, at least, acknowledged with regret a "few acts of cruelty . . . committed in retaliation" for "the hundreds committed by Filipinos against

American soldiers." Indeed, he outraged the South by adding the mitigating argument that "from time to time, there occurs in our country, to the deep and lasting shame of our people, lynchings, carried out under circumstances of inhuman cruelty and barbarity . . . infinitely worse than any that has ever been committed by our troops in the Philippines." Roosevelt went on to dwell on "the bravery of American soldiers" fighting "for the triumph of civilization over the black chaos of savagery and barbarism."[69] By July, however, the president appears to have forgotten completely even those "few" American transgressions, an oversight that really reflected the American mood. During the height of those dark days of April, 1902, when the "startling disclosures" were impossible to ignore, the *New York World* accurately predicted that the popular reaction to them would be limited, terse, and ephemeral:

> The American public eats its breakfast and reads in its newspapers of our doings in the Philippines.
>
> It sips its coffee and reads of its soldiers administering the "water cure" to rebels; of how water with handfuls of salt thrown in to make it more efficacious, is forced down the throats of the patients until their bodies become distended to the point of bursting; of how our soldiers then jump on the distended bodies . . . so that the treatment can begin all over again. The American public takes another sip of its coffee and remarks, "how very unpleasant!"
>
> It then butters its bread and reads of the ingenious Major Waller who murdered his defenseless victims on the installment plan . . . forgoing until the third day the delight of killing him outright [few critics of the war were able to give up this bit of fiction about Waller].
>
> The American public reaches for another tab of butter and remarks, "how distressing!"
>
> It cracks an egg and reads of the orders of General Smith "to kill and burn"; "to take no prisoners"; "to kill everything [*sic*] over ten," and "to make Samar a howling wilderness."
>
> "Rather extreme" is the comment of the American public, seated at its breakfast, with a feeling of mild disapproval, not unmingled, perhaps, with disgust.
>
> But where is that vast national outburst of astounded horror which an old fashioned America would have predicted at reading such news? Is it lost somewhere in the 8,000 miles that divide us from these abominations? Is it

led astray by the darker skins of the alien race among which these abom-
inations are perpetrated? Or is it rotted away by that inevitable demoralization which the wrongdoing of a great nation must inflict on the con-
sciences of the least of its citizens?[70]

13

The Triumph of American Innocence

American innocence has been historically nurtured and protected by a conveniently selective collective memory. Amnesia over the horrors of the war of conquest in the Philippines set in early, during the summer of 1902. Ironically, anti-imperialists aided the process by insisting that the conflict and its attendant atrocities had been the result of a conspiracy by a handful of leaders who carried out, through deceit and subterfuge, the policy and means of expansion overseas against the will of the majority of their countrymen. By refusing to acknowledge the painful reality that most Americans had been bitten by the same bug that afflicted Roosevelt, Lodge, and Beveridge, the anti-imperialists were letting the people off the hook and in their own way preserving the American sense of innocence. Unfortunately, the man in the street shared the dreams of world-power status, martial glory, and future wealth that would follow expansion. When the dream soured, the American people neither reacted with very much indignation, nor did they seem to retreat to their cherished political principles. If anything, they seemed to take their cues from their leader in the White House by first putting out of mind all the sordid episodes in the conquest, and then forgetting the entire war itself.

Roosevelt tried early to erase the accumulated maculae by directing Root to congratulate the Eighth Army Corps, the fighting force in the Philippines, for its "remarkable restraint" in the face of "savage provocation" and for its perseverence in fighting "a humane war" against such "a treacherous foe." Root's eulogy colored the record and deleted uncomfortable memories:

The enemies by whom they were surrounded were regardless of all obligations of good faith and all limitations which humanity has imposed upon civilized warfare. Bound themselves by the laws of war, our soldiers were called upon to meet every device of unscrupulous treachery and to con-

253

template without reprisal the infliction of barbarous cruelties upon their comrades and friendly natives. They were instructed while punishing armed resistance, to conciliate the friendship of the peaceful, yet had to do this with a population among whom it was impossible to distinguish friend from foe and who in countless instances used a false appearance of friendship for ambush and assassination.

Utilizing the lessons of the Indian wars, it has relentlessly followed the guerrilla bands to their fastness in mountains and jungles and crushed them. It has put an end to the vast system of intimidation and secret assassinations by which the peaceful natives were prevented from taking a general part in government under American authority. . . . It has added honor to the flag which it defended. . . .[1]

Much more dangerous than the fictions of "restraint" and of "humane warfare" in Root's tribute, however, was the assertion once again that the war in the Philippines was over. In fact, with the Tagalogs and Visayans largely subdued, Chaffee was opening a full-scale offensive against the Moros on Mindanao and Jolo. Earlier, he had wired Washington the reassurance that few Moslem leaders supported a lawless chief who had attacked an American garrison on Mindanao. But his "urgent" call to the Moslem leaders for a conference to explore their differences went unanswered. Chaffee then ordered an American brigade to Mindanao on a punitive expedition "in order to prevent war." President Roosevelt had some misgivings and called a halt to the attack after several Moslem villages had been destroyed. After discussing with Chaffee the wisdom of extending the war to Mindanao, Roosevelt agreed to allow the general to use "his own judgment," whereupon the offensive was renewed and even extended to Jolo.[2]

Imperialist editors were as slow as Chaffee was to relinquish the cherished belief that "Asiatics" responded only to force. As though it were still the summer of 1898, instead of 1902, jingoistic editors called for "a sound thrashing" for the "insolent Moros," who had to be made "to heel" just as "the Tagals had been." In an all too familiar tone of outraged innocence, the editor of the *Brooklyn Eagle* declared:

The Moros of Mindanao, without seeming cause and undoubtedly for no other reason than the promptings of religious narrowness and hatred, have arisen against the representatives of this nation who were engaged in peaceful surveys of their country, prosecuted with the sole idea of gaining knowledge of its geography, resources, and people, and of establishing closer and more relations with men whose products we may want and who need our help to raise them in social, mental, and industrial scale and lift them to a better competence. . . .

We cannot recede from the position we have taken in the Philippines. We may better welcome a war that gives us an opportunity to overthrow slavery among the Moros, to punish murder and treachery. These people have carried matters with too high a hand. If they are longing for a fight they shall have it.[3]

Chaffee learned too late that his action had unified the Moslem leaders who had traditionally fought among themselves. Even the Sultan of Bacalod, reputedly friendly to Americans, under whom he had enjoyed many special privileges and rewards, joined the Moro defense against the invaders. In desperation, Chaffee sent an order to this sultan "to cease from troubling the progress of Christianity and make up your mind to be good." Whereupon the sultan curtly informed Chaffee that he intended to maintain the Moslem faith at Bacalod and that he wanted "war not peace." The *Call* observed with resignation, "Of course General Sumner will have to go after him with the Krag-Jorgensen and Gatling guns, and perhaps the 'water cure.'" The same issue of the *Call* warned of "More Trouble on Leyte," and the editor wondered just when it "would all end."[4]

A more immediate problem for the Administration was a decision on the fate of General Smith, who was on his way home with no sentence having yet been determined. Root, in his endorsement, pleaded "extenuating circumstances" for Smith and recommended a light sentence in view of the "conditions of warfare with cruel and barbarous savages." Roosevelt concurred, noting "the well nigh intolerable provocation" on Samar and the general "cruelty, treachery and total disregard of the rules of civilized warfare" by Filipinos. "I also heartily approve of the employment of the sternest measures necessary," the president stipulated in his endorsement before retiring Smith with no additional punishment. Privately, Roosevelt made it clear that Smith's only real sin was his "loose and violent talk," which invariably found its way into the press. By way of illustration, Roosevelt wrote to a friend:

> Inspector General Breckinridge happened to mention quite casually to me with no idea that he was saying anything in Smith's disfavor, that when he met him and asked him what he was doing, he responded "shooting niggers." Breckinridge thought this a joke. I did not.[5]

Unfortunately for the Administration, the loose talk did not end with Smith. During the summer and fall of 1902, the leading American actors in the Philippine drama streamed back home through San Francisco, and few felt shy about defending Smith and his tactics. "It has been necessary to adopt what in other countries would probably be thought harsh measures," the controversial General Bell explained to reporters. He volunteered that one-sixth of the population of Luzon had perished in the struggle. Waller followed Bell a few weeks later, and reporters eagerly awaited some choice remarks from the "Butcher of Samar." The usually taciturn Waller did not disappoint them. He bragged that scarcely a house had been left standing outside the major towns on Samar and cavalierly suggested that rebuilding the island would benefit the natives, who "would rather steal than work." The major defended Smith's orders to him as "proper under the circumstances." Seeming as incensed over the theft of Connell's West Point ring as he was over anything else, Waller reminded reporters of the scene he had witnessed at Balangiga. Generals Young and Wheaton were wiser and more to President Roosevelt's liking. Upon landing at San Francisco, they simply refused to respond to the queries of reporters, except to deny that the "so called 'water cure'" had ever been used by the army in the Philippines.[6]

Soldiers lined the dock in San Francisco on August 1, 1902, to cheer General Smith as he came ashore after more than three years in the islands. For the next few days, Smith granted interviews to fellow officers who came to pay homage to their hero. He met with the press only once—to defend his tactics as necessary to pacify Samar and to blame his troubles on Major Gardener and the "meddlesome" officer in Washington who had leaked the major's report. Gardener had aroused public opinion by distorting conditions in Batangas, thereby creating the need for a scapegoat. Smith's medical officer fired a parting shot as the reporters turned to leave:

> It makes me sick to see what has been said about him [Smith]. If people knew what a thieving, treacherous, worthless bunch of scoundrels those Filipinos are, they would think differently than they do now. You can't treat them the way you do civilized folks. I do not believe that there are half a dozen men in the U.S. Army that don't think Smith is all right.[7]

This last remark was not empty talk. During Smith's trial, a Washington correspondent discovered that officers in the War Department unanimously supported Smith and felt betrayed not only by Gardener, but also by Chaffee and Roosevelt. Newspaperman Henry Loomis Nelson corroborated this impression for the *Boston Herald* after Smith's return: "Almost to a man the Army, both abroad and at home, condemns the punishment of General Smith and insists that any criticism or objection to cruel methods is an assault upon it, an assault which amounts to base ingratitude on the part of the country for which the Army has done so much." After all, they pointed out, Bell and Wheaton had conducted similar campaigns. "But that was before enlisted men and teachers appeared on the scene as 'war correspondents,'" one officer complained. General Hughes was "a hero" for burning "a path 60 miles wide from one end of Panay to the other. . . . Army people seem to think that the purpose of war is to make the enemy uncomfortable," another military spokesman explained.[8]

Root was usually able to silence these officers by demanding explanations for such remarks. But Roosevelt was unable to discipline his inherited chief of staff. The president's enmity for General Miles went back to his days as assistant secretary of the navy, and Roosevelt was not one to forget an old foe. One of his first acts as president was to censure Miles for expressing an opinion on the Battle of Santiago and "opening old wounds" between Admirals Schley and Sampson. Miles badgered Root endlessly to allow him to take personal command in the Philippines. Roosevelt refused, and Miles leaked their exchange to the press. Infuriated, Roosevelt accused him of "playing politics" and "overstepping the bounds of discipline" in search of "public applause."[9]

Roosevelt's charge was not unreasonable, as the general's political ambition was transparent. Miles wanted the Democratic nomination in 1904 and had hoped to cover himself with military glory of more recent vintage before meeting the hero of San Juan Hill in the political arena. Once denied this option, Miles attempted to outflank the "Colonel" by appealing to war critics. Roosevelt informed Root that Miles had actually tried to blackmail him by threatening to expose all the "cruelties" in the Philippines unless he was permitted to take charge of the war. The president pointed out that Miles had once fought the Sioux in a similar fashion and was responsible for the massacre at Wounded Knee, which "had been seized upon at the time by those who wished ill to our government and who desired to discredit the army." Immediately following this encounter with Miles, the Gardener report was leaked to the press and was followed by one embarrassing disclosure after another during 1902, of which it is likely that Miles had been the source.[10]

Miles called a press conference to announce his own plans to end the war swiftly "if he were in a position to do so." With extraordinary pomp and utter simplicity, Miles suggested sending Cuban and Puerto Rican leaders to the Philippines as political missionaries carrying the "glad tydings" of political salvation under benevolent American guidance. Root denounced the plan and press conference as "spectacular and sensational." The anti-imperialist *Call* found the plan "naive" and directed more at the chief of staff's political aspirations than at the war. There had been rumors that Miles would be sacked since Roosevelt had entered the White House. Now the rumors escalated, and one headline that declared "Miles May Go Within Two Weeks" was not referring to the Philippines. But Roosevelt astutely refused to make the general a martyr, and also possibly to open a new can of worms, by firing him. In a letter to his friend, the publisher Herman Kohlsaat, marked "strictly personal," Roosevelt admitted that "it is getting to be a case as to whether I can any longer permit great damage to be done to the Army for the sake of avoiding trouble to myself. Miles is a perfect curse. He has been a detriment to the Army for the last eight years. No man of his rank has ever so purely faked a record as a soldier."[11]

The chief of staff decided that one way to get to the Philippines was to make his own "inspection tour" of the islands in the spring of 1902. Immediately upon his return, he called a press conference to decry American atrocities there. He implied that the soldiers were under orders to murder the enemy wounded. The *New York Times* denounced Miles as "one of those birds which fouls its own nest." Roosevelt was so enraged that he refused to allow France to confer on Miles the Legion d'Honneur, although he had to deny the award to Dewey at the same time in order to be consistent and not appear narrowly vindictive.[12]

The general followed up his tour with an official report to the War Department, which focused in particular on Bell's campaign in Batangas. Not only did Miles confirm the magnitude of death and destruction in that province, but he also called for a complete investigation of the tactics used and started the process by ordering Bell to justify his inflammatory orders to his station commanders. His actions came after the president had singled out Bell and the Batangas campaign for special praise. When Root sat on the report, Miles leaked it to the press. "Do you realize, old man, that about the matter of importance in which I have sacrificed principle to policy has been that of Miles?" Roosevelt lamented to Kohlsaat. "In my judgement he has unquestionably been giving secret information to the foes of the very army of which he is head and has been trying to gain political capital for himself out of the slander upon the officers and men under him. If I could prove this I should remove him." Amazingly, the usually impetuous Roosevelt did refrain from removing Miles in disgrace, but he had good reasons for controlling himself in this case.[13]

Essentially as a result of Miles's efforts, a few more trials were convened in the fall of 1902. Captains Brownell and Ryan and Major Glenn faced judicial action for murder. Glenn had already been fined and admonished for applying the water cure in Igbarras, Panay, and for wantonly burning that town. Now he was charged with the murder of forty-seven prisoners. One witness described how Glenn had ordered his victims to kneel and "repent of their sins" before they were bayoneted and clubbed to death. Glenn did not even attempt to deny this charge, but insisted that such action was in accordance with Chaffee's order to obtain information on the insurrection "no matter what measures have to be adopted." Glenn, Brownell, and Ryan were all acquitted by citing Chaffee's orders as their defense. Indeed, the court decisions in these cases prompted General Smith to consider appealing his conviction on the same grounds. He told reporters that Chaffee's orders to him were "much harsher" than were his orders to Waller. Smith even enlisted the aid of Senator Hanna, McKinley's old chum, who protested on the floor of the Senate that Jake Smith had been singled out as a convenient scapegoat. Hanna was only interested in vindicating Smith and not in bringing Chaffee to trial, which a number of anti-imperialists were demanding as a result of Glenn's acquittal. Had all this commotion occurred five or six months earlier, it might have been stickier for the Administration than it was in the fall of 1902. By then, few editors were calling for Chaffee's head, and, like most Americans, they seemed eager to forget the subject entirely.[14]

In the middle of the turmoil created by Miles's leaks, Chaffee returned to the United States. Taciturn by nature and generally contemptuous of civilians, he avoided press conferences for the most part. He did defend Smith's tactics to one reporter, however, and again in a speech at a testimonial dinner in his honor. "Thanks to Jake Smith, Samar was more peaceful than many parts of the United States," Chaffee declared. He drew guffaws from the banquet audience when he poked fun at the "misguided benevolence" of American civilians in the islands and when he joked about the "severe measures" in store for the Moros of Mindanao. "They are what I call agricultural savages, 150,000 strong," and "of a Mohamedian [sic] faith," he informed them. "They do not wish us to come in contact with them, but we love them and are going to tell them so." His fellow diners clearly enjoyed this jab at Governor Taft and the Philippine Commission.[15]

Miles continued publicly to pressure Root to publish the general's report of his "inspection tour" of the islands, most of which had already been leaked to the press. Finally Root consented, but in order to get even more political mileage out of it, Miles accused the secretary of war of censoring the version that he published. Miles then published the portions of his report left out by Root in an article in the *Army and Navy Journal* in the spring of 1903.[16] In it, he charged, among other things, that many Filipinos had suffocated to death in Bell's concentration camps as the result of cramming more than 600 people into a building measuring seventy feet by twenty feet. But Miles had grossly miscalculated the mood of the American people one year after Smith's trial and the Lodge hearing. The public was, at best, bored with the topic and, at worst, eager to sweep it under the rug. Republican editors either ignored the charges or dismissed them as hearsay designed to serve the fatuous political ambition of Miles. Very few anti-imperialist editors took up the issue again, and planned mass rallies to call for courts-martial for Bell and Chaffee fizzled out, even in Boston. Sam Bowles's *Springfield Republican*, Herbert Welsh's *City and State*, and B. O. Flower of the *Arena* seemed almost alone and somewhat anachronistic in attempting to keep up the demand for the heads of Bell and Chaffee. Such journalistic bastions of anti-imperialism as the *Call* and *Evening Post* on opposite coasts moved on to new and unrelated concerns, such as the "brutal slaughter" of the Yaqui Indians by the Mexican Army and the "lawless methods" of the "meat trust to escalate prices."[17]

When the *Call* did return to the subject of American atrocities in the Philippines, it was to seize upon a convenient rationalization proffered by a former army contract surgeon, Dr. Henry Rowland, who attributed such transgressions to "the tropical and vertical sun impairing the judgement" of men from cooler climates. As a result of this intense heat, "it does not take the American soldier, from private to general, long to conceive of the 'insurrectos' as vermin, only to be ridded by extermination." This explanation was tailor-made to protect American innocence, for which the *Call* was effusively grateful. "Surgeon Rowland's article is timely since it will lead Americans to take a kindlier view of events in which our soldiers have been actors."[18]

On reaching retirement age on August 8, 1903, General Miles quietly left his post without a single word from Roosevelt. Some feeble attempts to make political hay out of the president's failure to deliver a parting eulogy to "this gallant hero of the Civil War" got nowhere, and Miles was essentially ignored at the next Democratic convention. Roosevelt appointed General Samuel Baldwin Marks Young, the incorrigible cavalryman and one of the original hardliners in the Philippines, to the vacant post. The president was enormously biased in favor of the cavalry and even took time from his busy schedule to rehash tactics and training for horse-borne soldiers with his new chief of staff:

> Ought we not sometime to practice our cavalry in charging? If so, would it not be practicable to arrange a row of dummies so that at the culminating moment of the charge the cavalry could actually ride home and hit the dummies? . . . I wish you would see if this dummy idea cannot be worked up.[19]

When General Young reached retirement age a year later, he was replaced by another old cavalryman, General Chaffee. Roosevelt's final choice in 1906 for the army's top post removed any doubts about his sympathies for the hardliners in the Philippines. In that year, he made General Bell his next chief of staff. Even Major Batson called Bell "the real terror of the Philippines," an impressive accolade coming from the commander of Macabebe scouts. Much more than Waller, Bell deserved the epithet "butcher" for his systematic devastation of Batangas. Moreover, as one of the few West Pointers among the leading generals in the Philippine war, Bell lent greater respectability to methods that should have been considered unprofessional.[20]

Roosevelt's appointments to the office of chief of staff were not the only evidence of his contempt for his anti-imperialist critics. In 1903, scarcely a year before he had to stand for reelection, Roosevelt, in effect, seized from Colombia a wide swath across the Isthmus of Panama in order to continue the unsuccessful French effort to link the two oceans at that point. He did so in such a transparent and flagrant manner that he had to have been very confident that anti-imperialism had little political appeal. Indeed, this flagrant imperialist coup actually divided the dwindling ranks of anti-imperialists, rather than breathing new life into their cause. The "purists" refused to be distracted from the cause of Philippine independence and formed a separate organization for that purpose, while those who remained in the Anti-Imperialist League insisted on fighting all manifestations of imperialism.[21]

Once Roosevelt had declared the war in the Philippines officially over, Senator Hoar began to press him even harder to pledge future independence for these islands. The party line had been that the issue could not be discussed until the fighting had stopped. Some Administration supporters had long before lost any illusions that the islands would be profitable and argued that the cessation of hostilities offered the perfect opportunity to withdraw "with honor." The president was rather deceitful in responding to such pressure. He implied that he personally favored an announcement that the Philippines would follow Cuba's path to eventual independence, but that Taft had dissuaded him from doing this. "Will" feared that the announcement would be misconstrued "by the more violent element disposed to agitation" just when American programs were taking hold, Roosevelt explained. He compared his position to that of Lincoln when he delayed emancipating the slaves at the start of the Civil War. "Now it seems to me that Lincoln in these matters showed not abandonment of a high ideal, but great common sense."[22]

Actually, Roosevelt worked very hard to undermine any pressure to pledge eventual independence for the Philippines. When Cardinal Gibbons spoke out in favor of it, Roosevelt cautioned him that such action would play into the hands of the Aglipayans and lead to "the collapse of the Catholic Church in the Philippine Islands." At that very moment, Bishop Hendrick was negotiating with Washington to force the transfer of church properties held by the Aglipayans back to priests recognized by Rome, and any pledge for independence would harm Hendrick's position, Roosevelt warned. He directed Taft to blackmail Cardinal Satolli in a similar fashion by telling him that a pledge for independence would mean a complete victory for the "virtually independent Aglipayan church," which would "speedily sink to about the level of Abyssinian Christianity."[23]

The failure of the newly created Philippine Independence League to collect more than 7,000 signatures on a petition to pledge future independence merely reenforced the president's conviction that the issue had little popular appeal. Senator Schurz rightly predicted that his own party would ignore the petition while the Democrats would only pay it lip service.[24]

Roosevelt got unexpected support from Justice Oliver Wendell Holmes, who confirmed not only "the validity of the title of the United States to the archipeligo," but also the nation's "right to hold the islands in the colonial relation." With some astonishment, Boston's *Evening Transcript* declared of this newest justice of the Supreme Court, "In other words, he will be found to hold the same views as the President on this and cognate subjects."[25]

The coming of the election year of 1904 provoked rumors that the president would soften his position on Philippine independence. A vague reference by Root to "the Philippines following in the footsteps of Cuba" lent credence to the prediction. The Republican convention ignored the issue, however, and the Democrats fudged it by pledging independence in a vaguely distant future, although they did nominate a genuine anti-imperialist in Judge Alton Parker. This nomination helped the remaining anti-imperialists heal the breech caused by Bryan's candidacy. They were convinced that the atrocities, courts-martial, continued fighting, and Roosevelt's "scandalous grab of real estate in Panama" would at last destroy their archenemy. Parker seemed to know better and spent the better part of the campaign on his front porch in Esopus, New York, much in the manner of McKinley in 1900. But Parker was not the incumbent, and he did not have an energetic, young Roosevelt out beating the bushes for him. His running mate was the superannuated Henry Davis, whose 82 years matched the average age of the remaining anti-imperialist supporters.

As an incumbent, Roosevelt could afford to follow McKinley's example, and he sat out the campaign in Sagamore Hill, his summer home on Long Island's Oyster Bay, dashing off letters instead of making speeches. Invariably, these letters involved "Will's insistence" that any pledge for Philippine independence would be "unwise at this time." Indeed, the president was so sure of his opponent's vulnerability on this particular issue that he distorted the Democratic platform by insisting that it did include a plank on "immediate independence." He pointed out that "this would of course mean disaster to the islands and dishonor to ourselves. But on this issue they all, from Cleveland down, seem to be in hearty accord; and mugwumps hail it with hysterical joy." No doubt, anti-imperialists would have preferred such a pledge, and Roosevelt had long cast them as the "Achilles heel of the Democracy." He also characterized them as "professional goo goos" who "bleed for the Filipino," although he was convinced that his party had little to fear from such "virtuous neurotics." To Roosevelt, the entire campaign was a bit of a joke. "Some of the developments of this campaign are too deliciously funny for anything."[26]

Roosevelt's confidence was amply justified by his landslide victory in November. Anti-imperialism had never been a popular issue, although it was impossible to convince the diehards of it. Once again they deceived themselves and attributed Parker's rout to an imperialist conspiracy. "The newspapers were bought up or browbeaten into silence," Bishop Potter charged. "There is not an organ of expression that is not controlled. In private life men are subject to a complete, far-reaching, thorough system of espionage," he explained in almost paranoid fashion. Apparently it was too painful to acknowledge that however wrong the president might have been on this issue, most Americans agreed with him.[27]

Root moved over to the State Department to make room for Taft as secretary of war in Roosevelt's new cabinet. Sweeping economic and political reforms followed Taft's appointment. Taft had more faith in local self-rule than did his predecessor, who insisted that, "in view of the failure of Reconstruction," it would be "foolish" to enfranchise "any non-white people." Taft also understood that one way to quell the rebellion was to make its former leaders government officials, such as the president of a municipality or the governor of a province. Voting restrictions and indirect elections favored the more conservative ilustrado elite, which soon dominated the emerging government as it once had the Philippine Republic under Aguinaldo. By 1908, even Taft found it necessary to assuage his conscience by voicing some concern over the ilustrado oligarchy that he had partially fostered. He reassured himself, however, that the American-sponsored educational system would eventually broaden the base of democracy in the Philippines. Instead, it expanded the oligarchy as it absorbed the newly rich and educated, not only to emasculate any potential challenge, but also to fill the need for an expanding political and economic leadership. Significantly, Rizal emerged as the untarnished national hero, not Aguinaldo, Aglipay, or the radical ilustrado, Mabini, all of whom were relegated to oblivion except for ceremonial occasions or when needed to serve the oligarchy's purposes. The Roman Catholic Church returned to a dominant position, and English replaced Spanish as the nearly universal medium of communication to bind together the many disparate groups in the islands. In short, this ilustrado elite had clearly defeated Mabini's "inner revolution."[28]

Taft also granted civil liberties, which were tested by the emergence of political parties demanding independence and by the acquittal of the Lukban brothers charged with "conspiring to raise rebellion" and of two editors charged with libel for reporting that torture and concentration camps were still being used in Batangas by the constabulary. Such decisions were partially due to a decline in the number of American carpetbaggers on the bench. The days seemed numbered for the likes of Judge Paul W. Linebarger, who once had fortified his court with armed constables, had threatened defense lawyers, and had even been accused of having had a witness murdered. True, the replacements were often just as corrupt, but the new system, at least, was one of Filipino-administered injustice.

The political atmosphere was profoundly altered when American leaders wisely accepted the demand for independence as a legitimate issue. The Federal Party had misread both American intentions and the temper of the Filipino people when it called for statehood. As that party declined, the Americans needed new allies and astutely aligned themselves with the more conservative wing of the newly formed *Partido Nacionalista*, a fragmented coalition of parties that stood for independence. Two conservative *independistas*, Sergio Osmeña and Manuel Quezon, rapidly became provincial governors and then national leaders in control of the newly elected assembly in 1907. Their rapid rise to power was partially due to American support, although one scholar may have overstated the case by labeling them "American-made *caciques*." At any rate, these two dominated the evolving government for decades to come, and Quezon delayed the demand for independence for as long as he could.[29]

Although the back of the "insurrection" had been broken by 1902, a dwindling number of irreconcilables managed to keep it limping along in some places for a few more years in spite of their loss of popular support. The Moros continued the struggle against Manila rule even longer, but the constabulary was able to handle it easily enough, as it did a series of religiopolitical uprisings triggered by peasant unrest over the next few decades. There were even revivals of the pulahanes on Samar and Leyte and of the Katipunan, along the more religious lines of Bonifacio's original organization, on Luzon to harass the Filipino leaders. But not until independence following the Second World War did the Hukbalahap, originally organized to resist Japanese occupation, seriously challenge ilustrado hegemony.[30]

In spite of the eminent success of increased self-rule in the Philippines after 1903, the United States found it difficult to pledge eventual independence. President Taft stuck to the policy of which he was the architect that full economic and political development had to precede even such a pledge. Finally, the Jones Act of 1917 pledged Philippine independence as "soon as a stable government" was formed. The First World War and ensuing peace negotiations probably distracted the Wilson Administration from meeting this pledge. With the return to power of the Republicans in 1920 Philippine independence seemed more remote. Over the next decade, however, the mood of America became increasingly isolationist; army leadership became concerned over its extended and vulnerable position in the face of expanding Japanese power; and farmers, already facing an agrarian depression, wanted greater protection from Philippine produce. All this, plus racial fears over Filipino immigration, helped spur a renewed pledge in 1932 for independence in ten years, which passed over a somewhat peevish veto by outgoing President Hoover. Political rivalry and internal maneuverings in the Philippines caused the Filipinos to reject this offer, only to accept an almost identical one two years later in the Tydings-McDuffie Act signed by a second President Roosevelt. Another world war and the Japanese occupation delayed Philippine independence until July 4, 1946, slightly more than forty-eight years after Dewey's dramatic entrance into Manila Bay.[31]

The major American actors in the conquest of the Philippines went on to reap richer rewards for the most part. Taft became president, and Root went on to represent New York in the U.S. Senate. Generals Young, Chaffee, and Bell all reached the army's top post, although Otis and MacArthur were denied it. Roosevelt shared the average soldier's contempt for Otis, and Taft was not about to appoint his old adversary to the post in 1911 when Bell voluntarily stepped down. The eager young shavetails, Frederick Sladen, William Connor, and Guy Henry, Jr., all became generals. Both Waller and Glenn retired with two stars, although Waller's court-martial did cost him the post of commandant of the Marine Corps in 1910. As the senior colonel and most respected officer in the Corps, he was the obvious choice. No doubt Roosevelt would have had the courage to appoint him, but the more cautious Taft opted for Waller's old staff rival, Colonel Biddle. One final bit of irony in Waller's case is that the army's advocate general later agreed with the major's first plea that the army no longer had jurisdiction over him when the charges were made and decreed the entire proceedings "null and void." Chaffee, Root, and Roosevelt would have been wise to have reached that conclusion in 1902.[32]

Surprisingly, Major Cornelius Gardener's betrayal of General Bell did not wreck his military career. Root had warned Chaffee that his investigation of Gardener's charges "should not give the least color to a claim that there is an attack on him." Nevertheless, Chaffee was so vindictive over the "damnable report" that the major found it necessary to hire a lawyer to protect himself. The general's own staff warned Chaffee that Gardener would "put up a stiff fight if pushed to the corner and that many things will be brought up which never ought to see the light." Possibly such fears continued to work on Gardener's behalf as he finally reached the rank of colonel before retiring.[33]

"Fighting Fred" Funston did not stay out of the national limelight for very long. His bumptious enthusiasm and general lawlessness made him the perennial and quintessential "volunteer." In 1906 he again demonstrated his ability "to be in the right place at the right time," as a sergeant once put it. In temporary command of the Department of the Pacific while his superior, Major General A. W. Greeley, was in Washington, D.C., Funston was thrown from his bed in San Francisco by the earthquake. He "knew at once" that the army was needed "to restore order," he recalled, and attempted to commandeer an automobile, truck, or horse to take him to the Presidio. Fortunately, he had forgotten his sword and his revolver was at headquarters, so he was limited to cursing those who ignored his imperious commands. Once he arrived, he issued severe orders to the hastily assembled troops. Engineers were to create fire lanes by dynamiting buildings. All vehicles were to be pressed into army service. Armed patrols were "to shoot *instantly* any person caught looting or committing any serious misdemeanor." In effect, Funston had declared martial law without having consulted higher authorities on city, state, or national levels.[34]

After Greeley had retired and Funston was named as his successor, Funston used his position to remain in the public eye. He announced to the press that he would use his authority "as commander of the Presidio" to discipline striking workers, but his authority to do so was denied by the War Department.[35] When violent strikes hit the gold mines of California and the governor requested the army's assistance, Funston personally led a strikebreaking force, which he had been training for months, out of the Presidio, and again he had to be reined in by Washington.[36] Roosevelt had no desire to promote his troublesome alter ego, and Taft was certainly not going to reward his old adversary, so it was not until Wilson was president that Funston was awarded his second star after commanding the forces of occupation at Vera Cruz. He died at the age of 52, just as he was hoping to follow "Black Jack" Pershing to Europe and a final battle command. At his own request, he was buried at the Presidio, where the general's medals and uniforms are displayed at the base's museum, while his sword, given to him by the people of Kansas for his capture of Aguinaldo, hangs nearby in the Golden Gate Park's De Young Museum. A grateful San Francisco named a street, school, park, and network of coastal batteries after its adopted son. Today, bathers at Fort Funston or tennis players at Funston Park can be heard to wonder aloud, "Who the devil was Funston, anyway?"

The war of conquest and its atrocities and courts-martial have fared no better than Funston in America's collective memory. The subject is rarely touched upon in history texts, and when it is, this sordid episode is reduced to a bare mention of an "insurrection against American rule." When the war broke out in 1899, an English journalist on the scene scoffed, "Observe, the Filipinos are 'insurgent,' although they never have been subjected to the Yankee domination against which they are fighting, and, therefore, are no more insurgents than were the Spaniards." Six decades later, Secretary of State Christian Herter maintained this myth when he denied a request from his good friend, Ambassador Carlos Romulo, to recognize officially, as a final act of the Eisenhower Administration, that the "insurrection" was, in fact, the Philippine-American War.[37]

The lessons of Batangas and Samar appear to have been lost even on well-educated Americans. In 1970, a Harvard professor decided that one hundred years ago, or even as recently as World War II, "nobody would have raised an issue such as the Song My massacre." Americans *had* raised such issues before, during the war in the Philippines, after Wounded Knee, and as early as the eighteenth century when friendly Indians were slaughtered in a wave of hysteria at Paxton, Pennsylvania. The issue is not that of a new, enlightened generation of sensitive Americans becoming actively concerned over their own country's inhumanity, as this ahistorical psychologist conjectured, but that of *retaining* the lessons from the past. Lieutenant William Calley helped revive memories of earlier and very similar American atrocities in the Philippines. One hoary veteran of the Samar battalion protested to a reporter in Los Angeles that there had been "earlier Mylais" and described his own "search and destroy" mission against a harmless fishing village. "We snuck through the grass as high as a man's head until both platoons had flanked them. We opened fire and killed all but one. They were unarmed."[38]

Epilogue:
The "Gook" and "Gugu" Analogy

The war in Vietnam has rekindled considerable interest in the earlier, almost forgotten, American conquest of the Philippines. Similarities have invited the construction of historical analogies. Both wars were counterinsurgencies intended to deny a racially different people the right of self-determination, fought by American soldiers who expressed a racist contempt for the enemy. The origins of both conflicts remain as murky today as in 1899 and 1964. Even the skipper of the U.S.S. *Maddox*, one of the destroyers allegedly attacked by North Vietnamese gunboats in the Gulf of Tonkin, warned that without actual sightings the entire episode could have been invented by overeager sonar men misinterpreting freak weather effects. The ships were involved in highly provocative maneuvers at the time, inasmuch as the South Vietnamese were at that moment invading an enemy island in the gulf.[1] It is equally apparent that the American military was attempting to draw Filipino fire with provocative actions on the hotly disputed mesa outside Manila in 1899. General Otis chose to interpret local firing, mostly by eager American volunteers, as a full-scale enemy offensive when in fact the only advance that evening had been made by his own troops. There were no serious casualties in the initial encounters on the Tonkin or the mesa, real or manufactured, so the American military could have chosen to interpret both episodes as minor incidents in the sobering light of the following day. Clearly American officers wanted to escalate the fighting, for which they were well prepared, and were highly confident of easy victories. The most discouraging similarity is that in both cases, America grossly underestimated the power of national aspirations and the willingness of the enemy to make enormous, unthinkable sacrifices in the face of awesome odds. In each case, America should have anticipated as much from earlier experiences of the Spanish in the Philippines and of the French in Vietnam. But, again, America's sense of innocence and belief in its own uniqueness make it difficult to learn

268

vicariously, particularly when the lessons come from the "decadent" systems of the "Old World."

Once the American military machines became fully engaged, publicity-conscious generals played games with numbers to convince the American public that the conflicts would be short and sweet, so much so that Congress never declared war and neither one was ever officially labeled a "war." Minor skirmishes were parlayed into major victories, while American setbacks were either played down or concealed altogether. There were also tactical similarities, probably germane to all guerrilla warfare, so that General William Westmoreland sounds almost like a reincarnation of General Arthur MacArthur, complete with a vocabulary designed more to confuse than to enlighten. In essence, there were "protected" areas for concentrated civilian populations, outside of which American patrols engaged in "search and destroy" missions. Civilians bore the brunt of the fighting through the abusive reliance on heavy firepower on the part of Americans and through the more discriminating enemy campaigns against suspected collaborators, particularly as villages changed hands. In both cases the military blamed its failure to achieve the easy victories it had predicted on America's humanistic traditions and on civilians who simply had no heart to do what was necessary to win.

The American interventions both in Vietnam and in the Philippines were motivated in part by good intentions to elevate or to aid the victims, and not simply to conquer and exploit them, an aspect of the conflicts not appreciated always by critics. Writing on "Welfare Imperialism in Vietnam," John McDermott describes how well-intended aid actually produced "a loss of national independence, erratic and imbalanced economic development and growing social chaos," and he concludes that the inspiration for American intervention may have been less to be the world's "policeman" than to be its "social worker." This analysis could be accurately applied to the Philippine venture, in which well-intended, and not exploitative, American economic and political development strategies greatly strengthened a Filipino elite, while making it more dependent on American support, and undermining it at the same time by exporting Jeffersonian ideals that merely exacerbated revolutionary situations.[2]

Historical analogies, however, are invariably misleading and have a tendency to obfuscate more than they reveal. Far too many differences exist to press the analogy between the two episodes in the Philippines and in Vietnam. The most obvious difference is that the United States won the war in the Philippines, whereas it lost the one in Vietnam, in spite of its much greater success in getting the Vietnamese to undertake much of the fighting. Only about 5,000 Filipinos, mostly Macabebes, served as scouts before the war officially ended in 1902, after which America was much more successful in inducing Filipinos to

fight the waning struggle. But more important is that both the international
and the national (that is, American) contexts in which these wars were fought
were vastly different. In 1899, the United States had just emerged as a world
power, and that world was far from being polarized by two military Goliaths
holding it in a nuclear balance of terror. The closest thing to any international
alignment among the many competing powers scrambling for unclaimed real
estate may have been a tacit one between Great Britain and the United States,
both of which viewed Germany with suspicion as a growing challenger. America entered the Philippines to fight colonizers, not to bail out their proxies, as
we more or less did in Vietnam. The Filipinos never received any aid from another power, so the war was an isolated one, rather than part of a global crusade
between conflicting superpowers.[3]

Domestically, the contexts were just as different. The war in the Philippines took place in an era of intense patriotism, greatly enhanced by the immensely popular victory over Spain. The mood of the nation had been greatly
changed by the time the war in Vietnam was fought. Sophisticated nuclear
weaponry had eroded old-fashioned patriotism by challenging the soundness of
the idea of total national autonomy and by questioning the possibility of a military "victory" in the conventional sense. A generation of Americans had been
inculcated by school curricula that stressed the importance of the United Nations, global interdependency, and international cooperation for survival in a
world faced with the rapidly ticking nuclear bomb and the less rapidly ticking
bomb of an expanding population in a world of diminishing natural resources.
Moreover, the conflict in Vietnam followed a series of perceived catastrophes
for America in Asia—first the "loss" of China and a humiliating military stale-
mate in Korea, and then the French defeat in Indochina, which threatened to
topple all the "dominoes" in the area, down to "our" Philippines. It was a more
despairing, cynical, and even narcissistic generation that faced Vietnam, not
the idealistic, naively innocent, and patriotic one that had tackled the
Philippines.

Possibly as a result, the "generation gap" was reversed for the two wars.
Youth enthusiastically embraced imperialism at the turn of the century. An empire presented to these naively optimistic young Americans the vision of a new
"frontier" overseas that would challenge them as the western frontier had once
challenged their ancestors. The cause of anti-imperialism was served by aging,
patrician reformers, which may help to explain the very conservative nature of
the opposition to the war in the Philippines. Precious few protesters in 1900
perceived imperialism as a function of capitalism or as a natural product of the
"American system." On the contrary, most explained it as a deviance from their
national ideals and traditions. Others seemed much more concerned that colo-

nialism violated the free-trade tenets of Adam Smith than that it also denied Locke's principle of self-determination. Some even anticipated the more subtle forms of twentieth-century neocolonialism by insisting that America's growing industrial power would soon control much of the world with neither the expense of invading armies and colonial administration nor the threat of militarism at home. As romantic Anglo-Saxons, these patrician protesters were, like some counterparts in England, often concerned over the potential racial effects of expansion on America's "native stock," which was already being diluted by immigration from southern and eastern Europe. Such radical socialists as Morris J. Swift, who attacked capitalism as the cause of imperialism, were very much the exception in the protests of 1900, however much they may have been the rule by 1968.

The well-established, respectable critics of imperialism in the Philippines were always concerned that their patriotism not be called into question and carried out their dissent with utmost propriety. The same seems to have been true of the early mass protests against American intervention in Vietnam, before 1968, when orderly crowds in a more festive mood filled the streets of American cities, paraded to stadiums, and listened politely to rational attacks on the war. Once younger and more radical protesters succeeded in transforming such peaceful rallies into provocative encounters with agents of authority, most older and more conservative protesters withdrew from the marches. They were no more willing to engage in "trashing" in the streets of Chicago or Berkeley than Moorfield Storey, Erving Winslow, or Thomas Wentworth Higginson would have been decades earlier. Even the few lawless acts during the earlier Philippine protest never came close to resembling the juvenile street and campus scenarios enacted by "Yippies," angry students, and a few aging adolescents on college faculties who found it rejuvenating to play "revolution." The young toughs who hurled clods and epithets at Teddy Roosevelt in 1900 were concerned over labor issues (or they had been hired as props to demonstrate that "Bryanites stood for disorder at home and abroad"). The gentle reformers who gathered at Faneuil Hall or Cooper Union to protest the acquisition of an empire were the last people to hurl objects or vulgar insults at anyone, least of all a fellow patrician such as Roosevelt.[4]

Because the opponents to the war in the Philippines were not able to capture the imagination of youth, they failed both to dissuade young men from enlisting to fight and to attract them to the cause of anti-imperialism upon their return as veterans. Although the enthusiasm to enlist was not what it was during the war with Spain, the government had no trouble raising volunteer regiments to fight in the Philippines; conscription was never seriously considered. Veterans returned shorn of any romantic illusions about combat, particularly in a guerrilla war, but, in sharp contrast with veterans of the later conflict in Vietnam, none organized to oppose the war in the Philippines. Very few had anything to do with the Anti-Imperialist League. John Hall worked for it only after years of being rebuffed in Washington in his attempt to discredit his former commander, General Funston. Most of the veterans who did speak to civilian groups seemed more eager to enlighten their audiences on the realities of warfare in the Philippines than to attack the policy of imperialism. "The repeated stories sent home about the collapse of the insurrection are fanciful dreams of correspondents and military officers who never venture outside of Manila" was the most critical comment that the anti-imperialist *Call* could garner from one such talk in San Francisco. One veteran, John LaWall, prepared a lecture on the war for any audience willing to listen. His chief complaint was that the war was tedious. He said he had looked forward to actual combat "as a possible relief from the monotony of ague, dysentery and outpost duty." As for the much publicized atrocities, LaWall told his audience that such "harsh methods" were necessary because Filipinos are "deceitful and treacherous."[5]

The only trace of bitterness shown by veterans was over their loss of combat and travel pay, and other benefits, because the government refused to acknowledge officially that the conflict had been a "war." A pamphlet prepared for a 1922 reunion of the Minnesota volunteers complained that in "America's first war for humanity"—its longest since the Revolution, with the longest combat service and highest percentage of men killed or wounded—its veterans "Received No Bonus, No War Risk Insurance, No Adjusted Compensation, No Vocational Training and No Hospitalization Until 1922." In that year they were quietly granted veterans' benefits, although the status of the conflict remained an "insurrection."[6]

During the height of the Vietnam protests, some surviving Philippine veterans were sought out to testify, as did Richard Johnson (ideally, a black survivor), that he and his comrades had opposed fighting that war of conquest. In an autobiography written ten years earlier, however, Johnson explained:

My simple mind was too naive at that time to feel any scruples about such principles, for I was filled with the spirit of adventure and also possessed a reasonable share of bigotry. It never occurred to my simple mind that there could be anything wrong, morally or otherwise, with any of our government's undertaking.[7]

Unlike Johnson, however, very few surviving veterans allowed the protest against the war in Vietnam to alter their patriotic perceptions of the one they had fought in the Philippines. A 1968 questionnaire elicited from them all the tired clichés about fighting "Asiatics." One question about the "justice" of their war evoked from Harry Blaine the angry retort that "I was reared to know that one should respect authority. Is patriotism dead?" Joe Bryan answered with the question, "Did you ever see a boy's body after it had been worked on by a bolo man?" Because of failing eyesight, Hugh Clapp, who had been at the controversial post on the mesa the night the war began sixty-nine years earlier, had his daughter write in his dictated answers. They were so fiercely patriotic that she felt compelled to append her own apologetic note: "Father is a flag waver and would not like what is being written about the Philippine Insurrection."

Jesse Peck conceded that he initially had had some qualms about the war, until he was "ordered to bring back two mutilated bodies of American soldiers who had their penises cut off and stuffed in their mouths." After that he knew that no quarter could be given to Filipinos, and in 1968 wrote of them, "My personal opinion is that they were horrid little people, and while time has mellowed my opinion, I can never forgive them for their treatment of some of my buddies." LaWall appended to his questionnaire, "My opinion is that the acquisition of the Philippine Islands, considering the cost in blood and treasure, is no great cause for rejoicing to the American people." Lest that sound too critical, however, he added, "Still I fail to see how any other honorable course could have been pursued except for the one adopted by our country."

When these hoary veterans did make a connection between the war that they had fought and the one raging in Vietnam at the time, it was invariably to give some hardlining advice. Peck volunteered that he "could answer a lot of questions that might have saved many lives in Vietnam. We fought the same guerilla war in the Philippine Islands." Even the milder LaWall insisted that "the insurgents might have been subjugated long before they were had a more vigorous policy been pursued from the beginning," implying that America was repeating this error in Vietnam.[8]

Possibly nothing better illuminates the differences between the two eras than the responses to this questionnaire. The unabashed patriotism of the earlier era helps to explain the failure of the anti-imperialist cause; the temper of the times favored the protest against the war in Vietnam. The latter limited Lyndon Baines Johnson to a single elected term, whereas Teddy Roosevelt won reelection handsomely, and thumbed his nose at the anti-imperialists in the process. Paradoxically, universities were criticized in both eras for undermining the patriotism of American youth. Even the anti-imperialist Senator Hoar, a Harvard trustee, complained of the "gentle hermits of Cambridge," who teach "our youth to be ashamed of their history" and who criticize their country "in excellent English in magazine articles, in orations before literary societies or at the commencements of schools for young ladies."[9] The charge that universities were a subversive influence during the Vietnamese conflict is more easily understood, but even so it is far too easy to exaggerate the actual support that student activists received from college faculties. Only a minority of professors—

a highly visible one, thanks to the advent of television—were actively involved in the protest. Still fewer approved of the puerile excesses of the campus "strikes" (even at San Francisco State). A much smaller number of academics at the turn of the century spoke out against the war in the Philippines. Most of them were older faculty members; their younger colleagues were more apt to use their skills to justify imperialism, if, indeed, they said anything at all on the subject. It would seem that students embraced imperialism, if the hysterical adulation that Roosevelt received on some campuses, including Chicago's, and the eagerness with which college men marched off to war are any indications. Nevertheless, imperialist editors insisted that universities were centers of anti-imperialist dissent. Their accusations reflect a curious cultural paradox that counters an exaggerated American reverence for the efficacy of formal education in molding values with a profoundly anti-intellectual tradition. Possibly this contradiction can be traced historically to the Puritan stress on literacy as the means to salvation and to a romantic frontier suspicion of book learning as impractical, unnatural, and elitist. At any rate, a much better case can be made to indict the literary community that operated outside of academe for lending far greater support to the protests against both wars. In the earlier one, however, novelists and poets, as well as the much smaller number of dissenting professors, carried out their opposition with far greater propriety.

Both interventions appear to have been the responsibility more of political liberals than of conservatives: Kennedy Democrats in 1964 and Progressive Republicans in 1899. The boyhood hero of Lyndon Johnson, architect of the Great Society and military escalation in Vietnam, was Teddy Roosevelt, who gave America the Square Deal and a formal empire. Apparently Johnson never outgrew this adulation, and as president himself allegedly confessed, "Whenever I pictured Teddy Roosevelt, I saw him running or riding, always moving, his fists clenched, his eyes glaring, speaking out against the interests on behalf of the people." Intervention, domestically and overseas, seems to come easier to young reformers, whose frenetically instrumental style precludes any stoic qualities. Convinced that the human condition is perfectable, few such reformers possess a tragic sense of life. In both eras, possibly what was needed most was "the courage to do nothing," as Mary McGrory expressed it, but as she conceded, "this goes against the American grain."[10] Given the knight-errant idealism and missionary thrust in their national character, it is difficult for Americans to stand aside and accept stoically the course of events or to believe that it is outside their power to alter that course, particularly in Asia.

There are other, more tragic parallels between these two American wars in Asia. In retrospect, each one appears to have been so unnecessary. Both Emilio

Aguinaldo and Ho Chi Minh started out with enormous admiration for the United States. The Filipinos, particularly the ilustrado elite that so influenced Aguinaldo, were ready to accept the status of an American protectorate in return for domestic autonomy (which would describe our relationship following the war). Ho was understandably suspicious of China and may have been valuable as a kind of Asian Tito. Lieutenant William Calley and Mylai are now leaving our collective memory as rapidly as General Jacob Smith and Samar once did. This forgetfulness may partially be due to the paucity of popular literature dealing with the two wars, although recent novels and movies are making the war in Vietnam more fertile in this respect. Possibly, a literary lacuna is an unconscious means of forgetting an unpleasant history. In his poem, "On a Soldier Fallen in the Philippines,"[11] William Vaughn Moody hinted at an almost conspiratorial silence about the earlier struggle. With stylistic changes, the poem could almost have been written for one of America's "grunts" returned from Nam in a flag-draped pine box:

> Streets of the roaring town
> Hush for him; hush, be still!
> He comes, who was stricken down
> Doing the word of our will.
> Hush! Let him have his state.
> Give him his soldier's crown,
> The grists of trade can wait
> Their grinding at the mill.
> But he cannot wait for his honor, now that the trumpet has been
>   blown.
> Wreathe pride now for his granite brow, lay love on his
>   breast of stone.
>
> Toll! Let the great bells toll
> Till the clashing air is dim,
> Did we wrong this parted soul?
> We will make it up to him.
> Toll! Let him never guess
> What work we sent him to.
> Laurel, laurel, yes.
> He did what we bade him do.
> Praise, and never a whispered hint but the fight he fought
>   was good;
> Never a word that the blood on his sword was his country's
>   own heart's blood,

A flag for his soldier's bier
Who dies that his land may live;
O banners, banners here,
That he doubt not nor misgive!
That he heed not from the tomb
The evil days draw near
When the nation robed in gloom
With its faithless past shall strive.
Let him never dream that his bullet's scream went wide of
its island mark,
Home to the heart of his darling land where she stumbled
and sinned in the dark.

Notes

CHAPTER 1

1. *San Francisco Call*, Sept. 26, 1900; *Congressional Record*, 57th Cong., 1st Sess., pp. 5071–77.

2. See John Morgan Gates, *Schoolbooks and Krags: The United States Army in the Philippines* for the latest attempt to whitewash the army's conduct. Gates is totally uncritical of the campaigns of such generals as Wheaton and Bell and praises them for conduct that should have resulted in courts-martial for both of them.

3. Archibald Paton Thornton, *Doctrines of Imperialism*, pp. 12–13.

4. Ibid., p. 3; W. L. Langer, "A Critique of Imperialism," *Foreign Affairs* 14 (1935): 103. For the task of defining and developing a theory of imperialism, see A. P. Thornton, *Imperialism in the Twentieth Century*. D. K. Fieldhouse, *Economics and Empire 1830–1914* is the most balanced and objective account. Possibly the most efficient way to sample various schools of thought is to use D. K. Fieldhouse, ed., *The Theory of Capitalist Imperialism* with its contributions by Hobson, Marx, Lenin, Schumpeter, Moon, and Hayes, among others. See Roger Owen and Bob Sutcliffe, eds., *Studies in the Theory of Imperialism* for the mostly neo-Marxist approach, and O. Mannoni, *Prospero and Caliban* for a psychological interpretation.

5. The Cold War and American intervention in Vietnam have stimulated a revival of the historiographic debate on American imperialism, which has produced far too many works to list them all here. Charles S. Campbell, *The Transformation of American Foreign Relations, 1865–1900* best outlines the current state of this debate, as does Marilyn Blatt Young's essay, "The Quest for Empire," in *American–East Asian Relations: A Survey*, edited by James C. Thomson and Ernest R. May. What has been labeled the "new economic determinist" and the "new left" schools may be sampled through William A. Williams, *The Roots of the Modern American Empire*; Gabriel Kolko, *The Roots of American Foreign Policy*; Walter LaFeber and Thomas J. McCormick, *Creation of the American Empire*; Robert L. Beisner, *From the Old Diplomacy to the New, 1865–1900*; Harry Magdoff, *The Age of Imperialism*; and William J. Pomeroy, *American Neo-Colonialism: Its Emergence in the Philippines and Asia*. Some economic historians have begun to snipe at their works. See, for example, William H. Becker, "American Manufacturers and Foreign Markets, 1870–1900: Business Historians and the 'New Economic Determinists,'" *Business History Review* 47 (1973): 466–81, and his

"Foreign Markets for Iron and Steel, 1893–1913: A New Perspective on the Williams School of Diplomatic History," *Pacific Historical Review* 4 (May 1975), 233–48; and Howard Schonberger, "William H. Becker and the New Left Revisionists: A Rebuttal," *Pacific Historical Review* 4 (1975): 249–60.

Frederick Merk, *Manifest Destiny and Mission in American History*; Ernest R. May, *Imperial Democracy: The Emergence of America as a Great Power*; and H. Wayne Morgan, *America's Road to Empire: The War with Spain and Overseas Expansion* are very balanced accounts. Ernest R. May's *American Imperialism: A Speculative Essay* should not be overlooked, and no discussion can ignore the most provocative challenge, James A. Field, "American Imperialism: The Worst Chapter in Almost Any Book," along with replies by Walter LaFeber and Robert Beisner in *American Historical Review* 83 (1978): 644–83.

6. See John K. Fairbank, "'American China Policy' to 1898: A Misperception," *Pacific Historical Review* 39 (1970): 409–20; Thomas J. McCormick, *The China Market: America's Quest for Informal Empire, 1893–1902*; Akira Iriye, *Across the Pacific: An Inner History of American–East Asian Relations*; Stuart Creighton Miller, *The Unwelcome Immigrant: The American Image of the Chinese, 1785–1882*.

7. See George H. Ryder, *The Foreign Policy of the United States in Relation to Samoa*; David M. Pletcher, *The Awkward Years: American Foreign Relations Under Garfield and Arthur*; Milton Plesur, "Rumblings Beneath the Surface: America's Outward Thrust, 1865–1890," in *The Gilded Age: A Reappraisal*, ed. H. Wayne Morgan; Alice Felt Tyler, *The Foreign Policy of James G. Blaine*; Robert Seager, "Ten Years Before Mahan: The Unofficial Case for the New Navy, 1880–90," *The Mississippi Valley Historical Review* 40 (1953): 491–512.

8. See Marilyn Blatt Young, *The Rhetoric of Empire: American China Policy, 1895–1901*; Julius W. Pratt, *The Expansionists of 1898: The Acquisition of Hawaii and the Spanish Islands*.

9. *Congressional Record*, 53rd Cong., 3rd Sess., p. 3109. See William A. Williams, "The Frontier Thesis and American Foreign Policy," *Pacific Historical Review* 24 (1955): 379–95; Morton Rothstein, "The American West and Foreign Markets, 1850–1900," in *The Frontier in American Development: Essays in Honor of Paul Williard Gates*, ed. D. M. Ellis; Frederick Jackson Turner, *The Frontier in American History*.

10. Brooks Adams, "The Spanish War and the Equilibrium of the World," *The Forum* 25 (1898): 641–45; William A. Williams, "Brooks Adams and American Expansion," *New England Quarterly* 25 (1952): 217–32; Brooks Adams, *America's Economic Supremacy*, p. 104; John Fiske, "Manifest Destiny," *Harper's Magazine* 70 (1885): 578–89; Josiah Strong, *Our Country: Its Possible Future and Its Present Crisis*, pp. 161, 165, 186. See Dorothea Muller, "Josiah Strong and American Nationalism," *Journal of American History* 53 (1968): 487–503 for a challenge to the interpretations of Strong. Dunne's statement is in *Literary Digest* 16 (1898): 740.

11. "Empire Can Wait," *Illustrated American* 22 (1897): 713; *San Francisco Call*, Nov. 23, 1897; Fieldhouse, *Economics and Empire*, pp. 59, 61.

12. A. T. Mahan, "The United States Looking Outward," *The Atlantic Monthly* 66 (1890): 816–24. James Field (see next note) argues that Mahan did not stress the expansion of the merchant marine, but he certainly did in this article (p. 817). See also Charles and Elizabeth Livezey, *Mahan on Sea Power*, pp. 79–80, 241–44.

13. Field, "American Imperialism."

14. See Stuart Creighton Miller, "Ends and Means: The Missionary Justification of

Force in Nineteenth Century China," in *The Missionary Enterprise in China and America*, ed. John King Fairbank, pp. 249–82.

15. Richard Hofstadter, "Cuba, the Philippines and Manifest Destiny," in his *Paranoid Style in American Politics*, pp. 145–87.

16. Frederick H. Gillett, *George Frisbee Hoar*, p. 195. See also Joseph Wisan, *The Cuban Crisis as Reflected in the New York Press*; Marcus Wilkerson, *Public Opinion and the Spanish-American War*; George W. Auxier, "The Propaganda Activities of the Cuban Junta in Precipitating the Spanish-American War," *American Historical Review* 19 (1939): 293–98.

17. There are many accounts of the path to empire, but I believe that the most balanced is Morgan's *America's Road to Empire* in that there is no attempt to make Cleveland into a "good guy," or even an anti-imperialist, and McKinley into a "bad guy" and imperialist. Cleveland's attitude toward the rebellion in Hawaii may have been more ambivalent, but he capitulated to pressure from his far more anti-imperialistic secretary of state, Walter Gresham. See Jeffery M. Dorwart, *The Pigtail War: American Involvement in the Sino-Japanese War of 1894–1895*, pp. 4–9; *New York Journal*, Oct. 10, 1897; *New York World*, May 17, 1896.

18. Morgan, *America's Road to Empire*, chap. 2; Claude Feuss, *Carl Schurz: Reformer*, p. 349.

19. Morgan, *America's Road to Empire*, chap. 3; *New York Journal*, Feb. 9, 1898.

20. Howard K. Beale, *Theodore Roosevelt and the Rise of America to World Power*, p. 60; *San Francisco Call*, Feb. 17, 1898.

21. Morgan, *America's Road to Empire*, pp. 52–55; May, *Imperial Democracy*, p. 140; Pratt, *Expansionists of 1898*, pp. 233–78.

22. Morgan, *America's Road to Empire*, pp. 43, 49–56; May, *Imperial Democracy*, p. 143.

23. Morgan, *America's Road to Empire*, pp. 52–55.

24. Margaret Leech, *In the Days of McKinley*, chap. 10.

CHAPTER 2

1. Finley Peter Dunne, "Mr. Dooley on the Philippines," in Edward Atkinson, *The Anti-Imperialist*, no. 2; H. H. Kohlsaat, *From McKinley to Harding: Personal Recollections of Our Presidents*, p. 68. Any basic text repeats this enduring myth that American leaders were ignorant of the Philippines. See, for example, Foster Rhea Dulles, *America in the Pacific: A Century of Expansion*, pp. 201–02; Samuel Flagg Bemis, *A Diplomatic History of the United States*, p. 469. Yet references to the Philippines in the *New York Times Index* grew from 2 in 1895 to 21 in 1896, 24 in 1897, and 18 in 1898 prior to May 1. Eleven of the total were editorials and 30 were front-page stories in which the name of the islands appeared in a headline. The index for the *San Francisco Call* lists slightly more entries for these years. For concern over the threat of Spain's fleet at Manila and over Japan's interest in the Philippines, see *San Francisco Chronicle*, Aug. 24, 1896, Mar. 4, 1898, and *San Francisco Call*, Mar. 5, 1898. The *New York Sun* announced and detailed Dewey's plans on Mar. 3, and on Apr. 27, 1898. See also "Attacking the Philippines," *Providence Journal*, Apr. 26, 1898, and *Congressional Record*, 55th Cong., 2nd Sess., p. 4436. For the press's reaction to Dewey's victory, see *Literary Digest* 16 (1898): 541–42; *Public Opinion* 24 (1898): 579–83.

2. Roosevelt told John Bassett Moore that the entire archipelago was beyond

America's legitimate interest. See David Healy, *U.S. Expansion: The Imperialist Urge in the 1890's*, pp. 80–81. Even anti-imperialists conceded that McKinley entertained "vigorous anti-expansionist ideas" up to the fall of 1898. See George Frisbee Hoar, *Autobiography of Seventy Years*, vol. 2, p. 308, and Henry Parker Willis, *Our Philippine Problem: A Study of American Colonial Policy*, p. 5. Dewey's objections were recorded in the diary of Lt. Frederick Sladen, Oct. 30, Dec. 28, 1898, U.S. Army Military History Research Collection, Carlisle Barracks, Carlisle, Pa. See also Ronald Spector, *Admiral of the New Empire*, pp. 83–92, 98–99.

3. C. S. Olcott, *The Life of William McKinley*, vol. 2, pp. 110–11; Margaret Leech, *In the Days of McKinley*, pp. 327–41; Earl Pomeroy, *Pacific Outpost: American Strategy in Guam and Micronesia*, pp. 3–19; *Literary Digest* 16 (1898): 573, 17 (1898): 307–08; *Public Opinion* 24 (1898): 583. Among the newspapers canvassed in May by these two opinion magazines, only the *Dallas-Galveston News* favored keeping all the islands.

4. *Public Opinion* 24 (1898): 583; *Literary Digest* 16 (1898): 473.

5. *Literary Digest* 17 (1898): 34–38. See *Baltimore American*, June 11, 1898, for an early editorial calling for the annexation of the entire archipelago.

6. *Public Opinion* 24 (1898): 583, 617; *Literary Digest* 16 (1898): 573, 17 (1898): 34–38.

7. *Congressional Record*, 55th Cong., 2nd Sess., pp. 5790, 5967, 6661–65, 6702–07.

8. Andrew Carnegie, *Autobiography*, p. 388; Hay to McKinley, Feb. 20, 1898, as cited in Healy, *U.S. Expansion*, p. 39. See also Ernest R. May, *Imperial Democracy: The Emergence of America as a Great Power*, pp. 251–52.

9. *Literary Digest* 17 (1898): 307–08.

10. Ibid., pp. 332–33, 361–62; *San Francisco Call*, Sept. 10, 17, Dec. 15, 1898; Julius W. Pratt, *The Expansionists of 1898: The Acquisition of Hawaii and the Spanish Islands*, pp. 277 ff.; E. Berkeley Tompkins, *Anti-Imperialism in the United States: The Great Debate, 1890–1920*, p. 178. Tompkins makes it clear that business leaders were far from united on the issue of annexation in 1898. Many agreed with Carnegie that acquiring far-flung, densely populated colonies was to be avoided, whereas the annexation of nearer Caribbean isles was acceptable. H. Wayne Morgan agrees with this interpretation. See his *America's Road to Empire: The War With Spain and Overseas Expansion*, p. 118.

11. *Religious Telescope* 64 (1898): 913; *Christian Evangelist*, July 9, 1898, p. 13; *Woman's Evangel*, Oct. 18, 1898, p. 161; *Interior* 29 (1898): 779, 1040; *Searchlight* 4 (August 1898): 3; *Missionary Record* (Cumberland) 24 (October 1898): 111, 235; *Missionary Review of the World* 11 (1898): 618, 698, 800; *Missionary Woman's Record* 14 (November 1898): 68–69; *American Missionary* 52 (September 1898): 106; *Home Missionary Echoes* 2 (August 1898): 3; *Christian and Missionary Alliance*, Aug. 3, 1898, p. 108; *Literary Digest* 17 (1898): 79. Several missionary conventions in the summer and fall also endorsed American imperialism. See American Board of Commissioners for Foreign Missions, *88th Annual Report*, p. 115; Presbyterian Church, *62nd Annual Report of the Board of Foreign Missions of the Presbyterian Church in the United States*; *Church Standard* 75 (October 1898); *Spirit of Missions* 63 (1898): 523. See also Kenton J. Clymer, "Protestant Missionaries and American Colonialism in the Philippines, 1899–1916: Attitudes, Perceptions and Involvement," forthcoming in a collection edited by Peter W. Stanley.

12. "Presbyterian Imperialism," *Assembly Herald* 1 (1899): 5–6; "The Imperialism of Righteousness," *Standard* (Baptist) 45 (1898): 913; "The Imperialism of Jesus," *Missionary Record* (Cumberland) 25 (December 1899): 147–49, 205; *Foreign Missionary Journal* 49 (1899): 291–93.

13. *Literary Digest* 17 (1898): 79; *Christian and Missionary Alliance*, Aug. 3, 1898, p. 108; *Presbyterian Banner* 29 (1899): 1441–42; *Baptist Home Missionary Monthly* 21 (February 1899): 39–41.

14. *Foreign Missionary Journal* 40 (December 1899): 206; *Searchlight* 4 (August 1898): 3; *Spirit of Missions* 64 (1899): 452; *Missionary Record* (Cumberland) 24 (April 1899): 262–63.

15. *Literary Digest* 17 (1898): 362, 260–261; *Congressional Record*, 55th Cong., 1st Sess., pp. 530–31; *Independent*, Oct. 20, 1898, p. 113; *Monitor* (San Francisco), Aug. 17, 1898; *Ave Maria* 47 (1898): 789.

16. William Langer, *The Diplomacy of Imperialism*, p. 519.

17. *Literary Digest* 17 (1898): 157–58, 519.

18. Whitelaw Reid, *Making Peace with Spain: The Diary of Whitelaw Reid, September to December 1898*, ed. H. Wayne Morgan; Morgan, *America's Road to Empire*, pp. 86 ff.; U.S. Department of State, *Papers Relating to the Foreign Relations of the United States, 1898*, pp. 904–09. There was no opposition to the retention of Puerto Rico, possibly due to its proximity to the United States and its relatively small population.

19. Reid, *Making Peace With Spain*, pp. 54–57; S. Doc. 148, 56th Cong., 1st Sess.

20. *Literary Digest* 17 (1898): 509–10, 511–12.

21. Thomas A. Bailey, *A Diplomatic History of the American People*, pp. 519–20; Henry Pringle, *Theodore Roosevelt: A Biography*, p. 206; L. A. Coolidge, *An Old Fashioned Senator: Orville H. Platt*, pp. 287–88.

22. *Literary Digest* 17 (1898): 157–58, 768–69; Harold Baron, "Anti-Imperialism and the Democrats," *Science and Society* 21 (1957): 222–39.

23. Claude Bowers, *Beveridge and the Progressive Era*, pp. 73–74; *New York Times*, Oct. 6, 1898.

24. Pringle, *Theodore Roosevelt*, p. 206.

25. Baron, "Anti-Imperialism," pp. 224–26; *New York Times*, Oct. 8, 21, 1898; *New York Evening Post*, Oct. 21, 1898; *Literary Digest* 17 (1898): 481; *Century* 56 (1898): 781–88; *Democratic Campaign Book, 1898* (Washington, D.C., 1898), p. 15.

26. Harley Notter, *The Origins of the Foreign Policy of Woodrow Wilson*; Burton J. Hendrick, *The Training of an American*, pp. 256–67; Baron, "Anti-Imperialism," p. 228.

27. *Springfield Republican*, Nov. 10, 1898.

28. William McKinley, *Speeches and Addresses of William McKinley*, pp. 84–85; Morgan, *America's Road to Empire*, pp. 88–89.

29. *Christian Advocate* (New York), Jan. 22, 1903.

30. U.S. Department of State, *Papers Relating to the Foreign Relations of the United States, 1898*, p. 935; S. Doc. 148, p. 31; *Public Opinion* 25 (1898): 583. See also Reid, *Making Peace with Spain*, p. 127, n. 3, and pp. 127–37 ff.

31. *Public Opinion* 25 (1898): 675–77.

32. Olcott, *William McKinley*, vol. 2, pp. 110–11; *Public Opinion* 26 (1898): 675–77; Lodge to Roosevelt, Feb. 9, 1899, in *Selections from the Correspondence of Theodore Roosevelt and Henry Cabot Lodge*, ed. Henry Cabot Lodge (New York, 1922), vol. 1, p. 392.

33. *Congressional Record*, 55th Cong., 3rd Sess., pp. 20, 432–503, 561–62, 1342, 1348, 1445, 1479, 1830, 1845–47.

34. Ibid.

35. Ibid., pp. 433–39, 448–50, 530, 638–42, 924–25, 1532.

36. Ibid.

37. Arthur W. Dunn, *From Harrison to Harding: A Personal Narrative Covering a Third of a Century, 1883–1921*, vol. 1, p. 282; Richard F. Pettigrew, *Imperial Washington*, p. 206; Francis B. Simpkins, *Pitchfork Ben Tillman, South Carolinian*, pp. 8–9; Paolo E. Coletta, "Bryan, McKinley, and the Treaty of Paris," *Pacific Historical Review* 26 (1957): 131–46.

38. *Literary Digest* 17 (1898): 740.

39. Pettigrew, *Imperial Washington*, pp. 270–71; Hoar, *Autobiography*, vol. 2, pp. 321–24; Coletta, "Bryan, McKinley," pp. 135–39.

40. Frederick H. Gillett, *George Frisbee Hoar*, pp. 222–23; Coletta, "Bryan, McKinley," p. 143.

41. S. Doc. 331, 57th Cong., 1st Sess., p. 775; Thomas McD. Patterson, *The Fruits of Imperialism*, p. 9; Tompkins, *Anti-Imperialism in the United States*, pp. 191–95.

42. S. Doc. 331, p. 775; Patterson, *Fruits of Imperialism*, p. 9.

43. *Congressional Record*, 55th Cong., 3rd Sess., pp. 1845–47.

44. *Chicago Journal*, as quoted in the *Literary Digest* 17 (1898): 714.

CHAPTER 3

1. Peter W. Stanley, *A Nation in the Making: The Philippines and the United States, 1899–1921*, pp. 3–48. See also John M. Schumacher, *The Propaganda Movement, 1880–1895*; Eldioro Robles, *The Philippines in the Nineteenth Century*; Cesar Adib Majul, *The Political and Constitutional Ideas of the Philippine Revolution*; Teodoro M. Kalaw, *The Philippine Revolution*; Maximo M. Kalaw, *The Development of Philippine Politics, 1872–1920*.

2. Reynaldo Clemeña Ileto, "*Pasión* and the Interpretation of Change in Tagalog Society," Ph.D. dissertation, Cornell University, 1975, pp. 99, 127, 92–138. See also Gregorio F. Zaide, *History of the Katipunan*; Gregorio F. Zaide, ed., *Documentary History of the Katipunan;* David Joel Steinberg, "An Ambiguous Legacy: Years at War in the Philippines," *Pacific Affairs* 45 (1972): 165–90; Virginia Palma-Bonifacio, ed., *The Trial of Andres Bonifacio*.

3. S. Doc. 62, 55th Cong., 3rd Sess., pt. 2, pp. 338–57; James H. Blount, *The American Occupation of the Philippines, 1898–1912*, chaps. 1 and 2, *passim*.

4. *Literary Digest* 20 (1900): 141, 176.

5. T. M. Anderson, "Our Role in the Philippines," *North American Review* 170 (1900): 272.

6. S. Doc. 331, 57th Cong., 1st Sess., p. 2954.

7. Steinberg, "Ambiguous Legacy," p. 175; Stanley, *Nation in the Making*, pp. 24–54; Majul, *Political and Constitutional Ideas*, chap. 3, *passim*.

8. Stanley, *Nation in the Making*, pp. 53–54; David R. Sturtevant, *Popular Uprisings in the Philippines, 1840–1940*, pp. 96–138.

9. S. Doc. 331, pp. 2954–56; Anderson to Aguinaldo, July 22, 28, 1898, Anderson to Adjutant General, U.S. Army, July 9, 21, 1898, in U.S. Adjutant General's Office, *Correspondence Relating to the War with Spain*, vol. 2, pp. 806, 808–10.

10. Anderson to Adjutant General, July 21, 1898, in *Correspondence*, vol. 2, p. 809.

11. As cited in S. Doc. 66, 56th Cong., 1st Sess., p. 44.

12. The report is in S. Doc. 196, 56th Cong., 1st Sess., pp. 20 ff.; S. Doc. 66, p. 44; *Outlook* 63 (1899): 6–7, 202–03; *Independent*, Sept. 14, 1899.

13. See Dewey's testimony in S. Doc. 331, pp. 2932, 2939, 2978, 2981; Anderson to Adjutant General, July 23, 1898, in *Correspondence*, vol. 2, p. 810; Anderson, "Our Role in the Philippines," pp. 272 ff.; Blount, *American Occupation of the Philippines*, pp. 101–02.

14. S. Doc. 331, pp. 2934–47, 2955, 2958–59.

15. Adjutant General to Merritt, Aug. 10, 1898, in *Correspondence*, vol. 2, p. 812; Elwell S. Otis, *Official Report to the Adjutant General, U.S. Army* (1899), pp. 47–48.

16. Otis, *Official Report* (1899), pp. 47–48; George Dewey, *Autobiography of George Dewey, Admiral of the Navy*, pp. 274–79; Karl Irving Faust, *Campaigning in the Philippines*, p. 96; Oscar K. Davis, "Dewey's Capture of Manila," *McClure's Magazine* 13 (June 1899): 171–83; Dewey's testimony in S. Doc. 331, pp. 2934–43.

17. Anderson to Aguinaldo, all messages Aug. 13, 1898, in *Correspondence*, vol. 2, pp. 813–14; Anderson, "Our Role in the Philippines," pp. 272–73; S. Doc. 208, 56th Cong., 1st Sess., p. 23.

18. Merritt to Adjutant General, Aug. 17, 1898, in *Correspondence*, vol. 2, p. 754.

19. Adjutant General to Merritt, Aug. 17, 1898, ibid.

20. S. Doc. 62, p. 400; S. Doc. 331, pp. 657–58; Otis, *Official Report* (1899), p. 5; Otis to Adjutant General, Sept. 5, 1898, Otis to Aguinaldo, Sept. 8, 1898, in *Correspondence*, vol. 2, pp. 787–92.

21. Whitelaw Reid, *Making Peace with Spain: The Diary of Whitelaw Reid, September to December, 1898*, ed. H. Wayne Morgan, p. 82 and p. 82 nn. 7, 8.

22. S. Doc. 331, pp. 591–93; Otis, *Official Report* (1899), p. 9; S. Doc. 208, 55th Cong., 1st Sess., pp. 25–33; diary of Lt. Frederick Sladen, Oct. 30, Dec. 28, 1898, Jan. 15, 1899, U.S. Army Military History Research Collection, Carlisle Barracks, Carlisle, Pa. (hereafter Carlisle Collection); *Correspondence*, vol. 2, pp. 787–92.

23. Otis, *Official Report* (1899), pp. 10–20; S. Doc. 331, pp. 594, 609, 753; *Correspondence*, vol. 2, pp. 845–47; S. Doc. 208, pp. 34–37.

24. *Correspondence*, vol. 2, pp. 847–50; Otis, *Official Report* (1899), pp. 20–21; S. Doc. 208, pp. 39–40; S. Doc. 331, pp. 591–92, 753; Anderson, "Our Role in the Philippines," pp. 272–73; Francis Millet, *The Expedition to the Philippines*, p. 255.

25. S. Doc. 331, pp. 743–46, 752–62; S. Doc. 208, pp. 37–40.

26. Otis to Aguinaldo, Oct. 14, 27, Nov. 10, 1898, Aguinaldo to Otis, Nov. 4, 1898, in *Correspondence*, vol. 2, pp. 847–50; Otis, *Official Report* (1899), pp. 20–22; S. Doc. 208, p. 40.

27. Otis, *Official Report* (1899), pp. 22–24; S. Doc. 208, pp. 41–44.

28. William Braisted, *The United States Navy in the Pacific, 1897–1909*, pp. 35–38, 49–50; diary of Lt. F. Sladen, Oct. 30, Dec. 28, 1898, Carlisle Collection.

29. Diary of Lt. F. Sladen, Oct. 30, 1898, Carlisle Collection.

30. Ibid.

31. Otis, *Official Report* (1899), pp. 55–65; S. Doc. 208, pp. 50–55 ff.; Otis to Secretary of War, Dec. 30, 1898, in *Correspondence*, vol. 2, p. 864.

32. S. Doc. 331, p. 768; Miller to Otis, Dec. 28, 1898, in Otis, *Official Report*

(1899), p. 62; diary of Lt. F. Sladen, Dec. 28, 1898, Carlisle Collection. See also Agui-naldo's proclamation, Jan. 5, 1899, in *Correspondence*, vol. 2, pp. 910–13.

33. Blount, *American Occupation of the Philippines*, pp. 147–50; S. Doc. 208, pp. 82–83.

34. Adjutant General to Otis, Jan. 1, 1899, Otis to Secretary of War, Dec. 30, 1898, in *Correspondence*, vol. 2, pp. 864–65; diary of Lt. F. Sladen, Dec. 28, 1898, Carlisle Collection; Otis, *Official Report* (1899), pp. 62–64.

35. Otis, *Official Report* (1899), pp. 62–68; S. Doc. 208, pp. 54–55 ff.; S. Doc. 331, p. 785.

36. "Herald of the Revolution," and "Supplement," Jan. 5, 1899, in *Correspondence*, vol. 2, pp. 910–13; Otis, *Official Report* (1899), pp. 76–77, 84.

37. S. Doc. 331, pp. 2709–51, 581–82, 618, 659, 822–23; Otis, *Official Report* (1899), pp. 80–82.

38. S. Doc. 331, p. 527.

39. Ibid.

40. Agoncillo's flight to Canada on the night of February 4, 1899, was also used as evidence that the Filipinos had planned the attack. Because of the time difference, how-ever, some American newspapers had already reported that the war had begun that very evening. See James A. LeRoy, *The Americans in the Philippines*, vol. 2, pp. 16–17, n. 1.

CHAPTER 4

1. Elwell S. Otis, *Official Report to the Adjutant General, U.S. Army* (1899), pp. 90–96; S. Doc. 208, 56th Cong., 1st Sess., p. 2. For the events leading up to the war, see James A. LeRoy, *The Americans in the Philippines*, vol. 2, pp. 1–19, and Herbert Welsh, *The Other Man's Country: An Appeal to Conscience*, pp. 107–28.

2. Letter to Frank Bourne in Otis, *Official Report* (1899), pp. 88–89; Anti-Imperi-alist League, *Mass Meetings of Protest*.

3. Otis, *Official Report* (1899), pp. 90–91; U.S. Adjutant General's Office, *Correspondence Relating to the War with Spain*, vol. 2, pp. 846–48.

4. S. Doc. 331, 57th Cong., 1st Sess., p. 884; Albert G. Robinson, *The Philippines: The War and the People*, pp. 58–60; *Manila Times*, Nov. 17, 1899; James H. Blount, *The American Occupation of the Philippines, 1898–1912*, p. 101.

5. R. B. Sheridan, *The Filipino Martyrs*, pp. 90–92; Pvt. William Christner to his parents, Sept. 22, 1898, Jan. 17, 1899, U.S. Army Military History Research Collec-tion, Carlisle Barracks, Carlisle, Pa. (hereafter Carlisle Collection); S. Doc. 208, p. 25; *Collier's*, Oct. 29, 1898.

6. *San Francisco Call*, Oct. 18, 1899.

7. S. Doc. 331, pp. 789–92; Otis, *Official Report* (1899), pp. 88–93.

8. Otis, *Official Report* (1899), pp. 88–93; S. Doc. 331, pt. 1, pp. 788–90, pt. 2, pp. 898–99, pt. 3, pp. 2709–51; diary of Lt. Frederick Sladen, Feb. 8, 1899, Carlisle Collection; William T. Sexton, *Soldiers in the Sun*, p. 91.

9. Letter of Pvt. Hermann Dittner, Feb. 12, 1899, Carlisle Collection.

10. As cited by Sexton, *Soldiers in the Sun*, p. 91. See also "Report of the War Department, Secretary," House Doc. 2, 56th Cong., 1st Sess., vol. 5, p. 463.

11. As cited in "The Outbreak of Hostilities," Philippine Information Society Pam-phlet no. 6, p. 20.

12. S. Doc. 331, pp. 1392–97.

13. Diary of Lt. F. Sladen, Feb. 7, 1899; William Connor to Sladen, Feb. 11, 1899; William A. Kobbe, "Diary of Field Service in the Philippines, 1898–1901," p. 4; all from the Carlisle Collection.

14. Pvt. H. Dittner to his sister, Feb. 12, 1899, Carlisle Collection; Official Report of the South Dakota Regiment in House Doc. 2, 56th Cong., 1st Sess., pt. 2, pp. 460–61; S. Doc. 331, p. 900.

15. S. Doc. 331, p. 1398.

16. House Doc. 2, pp. 460–61; S. Doc. 331, p. 1394.

17. *San Francisco Call*, Feb. 12, 16, 1899; *Correspondence*, vol. 2, p. 896; S. Doc. 331, pp. 786–88.

18. Diary of Lt. F. Sladen, Feb. 8, 1899, Carlisle Collection; Otis, *Official Report*, p. 92; S. Doc. 331, pp. 508, 625–28, 743–46.

19. S. Doc. 331, pp. 746, 751–52, 766.

20. *San Francisco Call*, Jan. 15, 17, Feb. 12, 16, 1899; *Public Opinion* 26 (1899): 195–98.

21. *Public Opinion* 26 (1899): 195–98; *Literary Digest* 18 (1899): 387; *Boston Evening Transcript*, Feb. 10, 1899.

22. *Public Opinion* 26 (1899): 195–98.

23. *San Francisco Call*, June 2, Oct. 7, 1899.

24. *New York Times*, June 2, 1899; *Public Opinion* 26 (1899): 714.

25. Diary of Lt. F. Sladen, Oct. 9, 1898, Carlisle Collection; Otis, *Official Report* (1899), p. 75; S. Doc. 331, pt. 1, pp. 804–08, 829–31.

26. S. Doc. 331, pp. 804–08.

27. Sladen to Col. O. L. Spaulding, Oct. 16, 1930, Carlisle Collection.

CHAPTER 5

1. Diary of Lt. Frederick Sladen, Feb. 8, 1899, and Pvt. William Christner to his parents, Feb. 11, 1899, U.S. Army Military History Research Collection, Carlisle Barracks, Carlisle, Pa. (hereafter Carlisle Collection).

2. William T. Sexton, *Soldiers in the Sun*, pp. 95–96; William Irwin, "The First Fight with the Insurgents," *The Independent* 51:1 (1899): 886–88.

3. Diary of Lt. F. Sladen, Feb. 8, 1899, Carlisle Collection.

4. Sexton, *Soldiers in the Sun*, pp. 95–98.

5. Ibid.

6. U.S. Adjutant General's Office, *Correspondence Relating to the War with Spain*, vol. 2, pp. 969–90; diary of Lt. F. Sladen, Feb. 8, 1899, Carlisle Collection; James H. Blount, *The American Occupation of the Philippines, 1819–1912*, p. 270; *San Francisco Call*, Feb. 10, 13, 28, Mar. 3, Apr. 14, 18, 30, 1899.

7. *Boston Evening Transcript*, Mar. 22, 1899; *San Francisco Call*, Apr. 14, 1899.

8. *San Francisco Call*, Mar. 26, 28, 31, Apr. 1, 1899.

9. Ibid., June 11, 12, 13, 1899.

10. Ibid., May 12, 1899.

11. Ibid., June 11, 1899; Marrion Wilcox, ed., *Harper's History of the War in the Philippines*, pp. 213–15.

12. *San Francisco Call*, June 12, 1899; Otis to Adjutant General, June 11, 1899, in *Correspondence*, vol. 2, p. 1002.

13. *San Francisco Call*, June 13, 1899; "Report of the War Department, Secretary," House Doc. 2, 56th Cong., 1st Sess., vol. 1, pt. 5, pp. 273–85.

14. *San Francisco Call*, June 16, 1899.

15. Ibid.; *Correspondence*, vol. 2, p. 1012; House Doc. 2, vol. 1, pp. 313–14.

16. *Boston Evening Transcript*, Mar. 22, 1899; *San Francisco Call*, Aug. 28, 1899.

17. *San Francisco Call*, Apr. 14, 24, May 6, 9, 27, 1899; *Literary Digest* 18 (1899): 387.

18. *San Francisco Call*, June 16, 20, 21, 1899.

19. "Filipino Armistice Proposals," *Public Opinion* 26 (1899): 582–83; *Literary Digest* 18 (1899): 381; *San Francisco Call*, May 23, 29, 1899; *Los Gatos Mail*, June 29, 1899.

20. *San Francisco Call*, June 14, 21, 25, 1899; *Public Opinion* 26 (1899): 74.

21. David Joel Steinberg, "An Ambiguous Legacy: Years at War in the Philippines," *Pacific Affairs* 45 (1972): 178; Maximo Kalaw, *The Development of Philippine Politics, 1872–1920*, pp. 214–16; James A. LeRoy, *The Americans in the Philippines*, vol. 2, pp. 88–93, including the notes.

22. *Correspondence*, vol. 2, pp. 1071–78, 1996–97; *San Francisco Call*, Feb. 9, Apr. 29, May 1, 15, 19, 21, 24, 1899; *New York Times*, May 16, 1899.

23. *San Francisco Call*, Oct. 1, 2, 1899.

24. Ibid., May 1, 1899.

25. Philippine Information Society, "The Report of the First Philippine Commission," *Pamphlet Number IV*, pp. 59–61; "Report of the Philippine Commission," S. Doc. 138, 56th Cong., 1st Sess.

26. *Public Opinion* 26 (1899): 582–83; *San Francisco Call*, May 27, 29, June 13, Oct. 7, 1899; *New York Times*, June 27, 29, 1899.

27. *Literary Digest* 18 (1899): 381; *Public Opinion* 26 (1899): 582–83; *New York Criterion*, Feb. 11, 1899.

28. *San Francisco Call*, Apr. 17, 1899; *New York Times*, July 16, 1899; *Correspondence*, vol. 2, pp. 1067–68.

29. *San Francisco Call*, Apr. 14, 1899.

30. Ibid., Mar. 30, Apr. 14, May 14, 28, 1899; letters of Otis and Adjutant General, Apr. 14, 20, 21, May 22, 1899, in *Correspondence*, vol. 2, pp. 964, 970, 993–94.

31. *San Francisco Call*, Aug. 17, 1899; *London Globe*, Aug. 5, 1899.

32. *Public Opinion* 26 (1899): 799–800; *San Francisco Call*, June 18, 19, 20, 26, 1899.

33. See letters of Otis and Adjutant General, Feb. 27, 28, 1899, in *Correspondence*, vol. 2, p. 918; S. Doc. 331, 57th Cong., 1st Sess., p. 674; *San Francisco Call*, Aug. 26, Nov. 22, 1899.

34. *Correspondence*, vol. 2, pp. 1021–53; *San Francisco Call*, Aug. 18, 1899.

35. *Correspondence*, vol. 2, p. 1001; Capt. Matthew Batson to his wife, Sept. 24, 1899, Carlisle Collection.

36. *Literary Digest* 18 (1899): 499.

37. MacArthur reported a total of 5,414 "native scouts" as of June 7, 1902. See *Correspondence*, vol. 2, p. 1277.

38. S. Doc. 331, pt. 1, p. 527.

39. Otis to Adjutant General, Jan. 20, 1899, in *Correspondence*, vol. 2, p. 884; *San Francisco Chronicle*, Nov. 11, 1898.

40. Otis to Adjutant General, Jan. 17, 21, 1899, in *Correspondence*, vol. 2, pp. 881, 1136; Albert G. Robinson, *The Philippines: The War and the People*, pp. 80–83; Harold Martin, "The Manila Censorship," *Forum* 31 (1901): 462–71.

41. *San Francisco Call*, Mar. 29, 1899; *Boston Evening Transcript*, Apr. 3, 1899; *Public Opinion* 26 (1899): 457, 521.

42. *Literary Digest* 19 (1899): 2–4.

43. *San Francisco Call*, July 18, 1899; "History as It Is Made," *Forum* 31 (1900): 595–96.

44. *San Francisco Call*, July 18, 1899; "History as It Is Made," p. 596; *New York Times*, Aug. 5, Sept. 5, 1899; *Public Opinion* 27 (1899): 99–100.

45. Robert Collins to Melville E. Stone, General Manager, Associated Press, July 30, 1899. This letter originally appeared in the *Pittsburgh Post*, Aug. 1, 1899, and then was widely reproduced in the anti-imperialist press. See *San Francisco Call*, Aug. 2, 1899; Robinson, *The Philippines*, pp. 80–84.

46. Robinson, *The Philippines*, pp. 82–84.

47. Ibid.

48. Ibid.

49. *New York Tribune*, June 22, 1899; Otis to Adjutant General, Sept. 9, 1899, in *Correspondence*, vol. 2, p. 1065.

50. *Boston Herald*, Sept. 17, Nov. 16, 1899; *San Francisco Call*, Aug. 23, Sept. 17, 1899.

51. *San Francisco Call*, Aug. 23, Sept. 17, Oct. 25, Dec. 30, 1899; *Literary Digest* 19 (1899): 486, 20 (1900): 344; *Public Opinion* 27 (1899): 484.

52. *San Francisco Call*, Sept. 17, Oct. 25, Dec. 30, 1899.

53. Ibid., July 14, 22, Aug. 9, Sept. 14, 1899.

54. Charles H. King, "In the Blood Stained Trenches at Manila," *San Francisco Call Sunday Magazine*, May 14, 1899, p. 17. See also ibid., July 14, Aug. 9, 17, Sept. 14, 1899.

55. *Kingston* (New York) *Evening Post*, May 8, 1899, as cited in *Literary Digest* 18 (1899): 601; *San Francisco Call*, Apr. 9, 1900.

56. *San Francisco Call*, Apr. 15, 1899.

57. Moorfield Storey and Julian Codman, *Secretary Root's Record: "Marked Severities" in Philippine Warfare*, pp. 12–15.

58. *Omaha Bee*, May 7, 1899; *Literary Digest* 18 (1899): 499, 603; *Public Opinion* 26 (1899): 499; *San Francisco Call*, Apr. 24, June 18, 28, 1899; *New York Times*, July 11, Aug. 16, 1899; *Springfield Republican*, Aug. 15, 1899; S. Doc. 331, pp. 637–39.

CHAPTER 6

1. As cited in the *San Francisco Call*, Nov. 11, 1899. See also S. Doc. 432, 56th Cong., 1st Sess., pp. 26 ff., for a collection of articles written by "friendly" correspondents.

2. *San Francisco Call*, Apr. 1, Sept. 25, Oct. 21, 1899, Jan. 1, 1900; *Literary Digest* 19 (1899): 409–10; *New York Times*, Sept. 16, 1899.

3. *New York Times*, May 15, Aug. 3, 1899; *San Francisco Call*, July 2, Aug. 15, Nov. 15, 16, 1899; *San Francisco Examiner*, Aug. 14, 1899; *Arena* 22 (1899): 568.

4. *San Francisco Call*, Feb. 14, 21, 23, Mar. 30, 31, May 29, June 9, July 17, 1899; *New York Times*, Aug. 7, 1899; *Public Opinion* 27 (1899): 291.

5. Sandiko's order has been widely reproduced. See S. Doc. 331, 57th Cong., 1st Sess., pt. 2, p. 916, Exhibit F, for a photograph of the fragment so often displayed by Otis to illustrate his charge of "Filipino treachery." A translation was published in the *San Francisco Call*, Feb. 23, 1899.

6. *San Francisco Call*, Apr. 3, Sept. 29, 1899; *Literary Digest* 18 (1899): 499.

7. *Literary Digest* 20 (1900): 25; *San Francisco Call*, Dec. 8, 1899, Feb. 16, 1900; *Boston Globe*, June 27, 1900.

8. *San Francisco Call*, Mar. 31, Sept. 1, 1899.

9. *Literary Digest* 19 (1899): 32. General MacArthur repeated this sentiment years later before the Lodge committee. See S. Doc. 331, pt. 2, p. 1926.

10. *New York Times*, Dec. 13, 15, 1899; *San Francisco Call*, Aug. 28, 1899, Jan. 11, 1900; *Boston Evening Transcript*, Jan. 12, 1900.

11. *San Francisco Call*, Nov. 11, 1899.

12. "Is the Philippine War Over?" *Literary Digest* 20 (1900): 523–24.

13. *San Francisco Call*, Aug. 28, 1899; U.S. Adjutant General's Office, *Correspondence Relating to the War with Spain*, vol. 2, pp. 1067–68.

14. *Correspondence*, vol. 2, pp. 1020, 1051–52, 1067–68; *Chicago Tribune*, Oct. 28, 1899, as reproduced in the *San Francisco Call*, Oct. 29, 1899; James A. LeRoy, *The Americans in the Philippines*, vol. 2, chap. 19.

15. *San Francisco Call*, Sept. 8, 1899; LeRoy, *Americans in the Philippines*, vol. 2, chap. 20.

16. *New York Times*, Feb. 22, 1900; *Literary Digest* 19 (1899): 333, 633–34, 20 (1900): 39; *Public Opinion* 27 (1899): 648; *Correspondence*, vol. 2, pp. 1120–23; S. Doc. 432, 56th Cong., 1st Sess., pp. 2–6; *San Francisco Call*, Nov. 11, 14, 18, 20, 22, 26, 27, Dec. 17, 20, 1899, Jan. 26, Feb. 6, 1900.

17. *San Francisco Call*, Feb. 5, 16, Mar. 6, Apr. 10, 1900; *New York Press-Knickerbocker*, as cited in *Public Opinion* 28 (1900): 485.

18. *San Francisco Call*, Mar. 7, Apr. 21, 1900; *Literary Digest* 20 (1900): 523–24.

19. *New York Times*, Feb. 9, 1900; *San Francisco Call*, Apr. 7, 8, 1900; *Public Opinion* 28 (1900): 485–86.

20. *San Francisco Call*, May 9, 1900.

21. Ibid., Apr. 7, 8, 1900; *New York World*, June 3, 1900.

22. *New York World*, June 5, 1900.

23. *San Francisco Call*, June 5, 9, 11, 13, 1900; *New York Sun*, June 11, 1900.

24. *New York World*, June 16, 1900; *San Francisco Call*, June 16, 17, 1900; *Public Opinion* 28 (1900): 775.

25. *New York World*, June 12, 1900; *San Francisco Call*, June 6, 8, 10, 11, 12, 21, 1900.

26. *Nation*, Apr. 26, 1900; *Boston Globe*, June 21, 1900; *Literary Digest* 20 (1900): 779–80; *San Francisco Call*, June 21, 1900.

27. *New York Times*, June 29, 1899; *San Francisco Call*, Oct. 7, 1899; *Literary Digest* 20 (1900): 523–24.

CHAPTER 7

1. *Boston Evening Transcript*, June 2, 1898.

2. Ibid., June 16, 1898; *Boston Herald*, June 16, 1898; Anti-Imperialist League, *Anti-Imperialist Speeches at Faneuil Hall, June 15, 1898*.

3. Robert L. Beisner, *Twelve Against Empire: The Anti-Imperialists, 1898–1900*, pp. 116 ff.; Frederick W. Harrington, "The Anti-Imperialist Movement in the United States, 1898–1900," *Mississippi Valley Historical Review* 22 (1936): 211–30.

4. E. Berkeley Tompkins, *Anti-Imperialism in the United States: The Great Debate, 1890–1920*, pp. 127–28, 150–53. See also Richard E. Welch, *Response to Imperialism: The United States and the Philippine-American War, 1899–1902* for a superb analysis of the anti-imperialist movement, and Daniel B. Schirmer, *Republic or Empire: American Resistance to the Philippine War* for a different interpretation.

5. Anti-Imperialist League, *Report of the Executive Committee of the Anti-Imperialist League, November 25, 1898*, p. 7; *Boston Evening Transcript*, Nov. 26, Dec. 19, 1898; Tompkins, *Anti-Imperialism in the United States*, p. 131.

6. Tompkins, *Anti-Imperialism in the United States*, pp. 127–28, 133, 158–59; *Literary Digest* 19 (1899): 336–37.

7. *Literary Digest* 19 (1899): 336–37; *San Francisco Call*, Oct. 5, 1899; Elting Morison, ed., *The Letters of Theodore Roosevelt*, vol. 3, p. 60; Wallace E. Davis, *Patriotism on Parade: The Story of Veterans and Hereditary Organizations in America, 1783–1900*, p. 335.

8. *San Francisco Call*, Apr. 24, 1899; *Boston Herald*, Apr. 22, 23, 24, 1899; *New York Times*, Apr. 23, 1899.

9. *Literary Digest* 18 (1899): 541–42; *New York Times*, May 2, 1899; *New York Tribune*, May 3, 1899; *San Francisco Call*, May 3, 1899.

10. *Literary Digest* 18 (1899): 541–42; *New York Herald*, May 3, 1899.

11. *Literary Digest* 18 (1899): 541–42; *Boston Evening Transcript*, May 6, 1899; Winslow to Atkinson, Apr. 29, 1899, Atkinson Papers, Massachusetts Historical Society, Boston, Mass. (hereafter Atkinson Papers); Edward Atkinson, *The Anti-Imperialist*, no. 5.

12. Atkinson, *Anti-Imperialist*, no. 5.

13. *New York Times*, Mar. 13, May 1, 1899; *New York Evening Post*, Feb. 23, 1899; *San Francisco Call*, Apr. 11, 1899.

14. As cited in the *San Francisco Call*, Sept. 5, 1899; *Literary Digest* 19 (1899): 336–37.

15. *New York Times*, Sept. 11, 1899; *New Bedford Standard*, as cited in the *Springfield Republican*, Apr. 28, 1902.

16. Letter of Montague Leverson, July 17, 1899, as reprinted in the *San Francisco Call*, Aug. 16, 1900.

17. *San Francisco Call*, Aug. 23, 1899; Morrison I. Swift, *Imperialism and Liberty* and *Advent of Empire*; S. Doc. 208, 56th Cong., 1st Sess., pp. 74–75; Welch, *Response to Imperialism*, pp. 54–55; *Public Opinion* 29 (1900): 7–9; *New York Tribune*, July 3, 1900; *Harper's Weekly*, 44 (1900): 788.

18. Beisner, *Twelve Against Empire*, pp. 193–94.

19. *Nation* 66 (1898): 314; Beisner, *Twelve Against Empire*, pp. 199–211.

20. Beisner, *Twelve Against Empire*, pp. 134–64. The cartoon was in *Literary Digest* 20 (1900): 105. Hoar, Hale and Gorman were denounced as partners in crime who "sowed the wind and now the nation reaps the whirlwind." See *Public Opinion* 26 (1899): 195–98. See also Richard E. Welch, Jr., "Senator George Frisbee Hoar and the Defeat of Anti-Imperialism, 1898–1900," *Historian* 26 (1964): 362–80.

21. Beisner, *Twelve Against Empire*, pp. 203–11; Samuel W. McCall, *The Life of Thomas Brackett Reed*, p. 266.

22. *Literary Digest* 19 (1899): 3; *Public Opinion* 27 (1899): 198–99; *San Francisco Call*, June 24, Nov. 22, 1899.

23. *Public Opinion* 27 (1899): 265, 198–99; *Literary Digest* 19 (1899): 31, 3–4; *New York Times*, June 6, 1899; *San Francisco Call*, Aug. 8, 27, Sept. 6, 1899.

24. See Charles Emory Smith, "McKinley in the Cabinet Room," *Saturday Evening Post*, Oct. 11, 1902.

25. Tompkins, *Anti-Imperialism in the United States*, p. 140.

26. *New York Sun*, June 24, 25, 1900, Feb. 24, 1901.

27. *New York Times*, May 22, 1899; *Literary Digest* 19 (1899): 92–93; *San Francisco Call*, July 15, 1899, Nov. 10, 1900; *Public Opinion* 32 (1902): 406. For the numbers of faculty members, see tables in Samuel Eliot Morison, *The Development of Harvard University Since the Inauguration of President Eliot, 1869–1929* and University of Chicago, *Register, 1900–1901*.

28. *New York Times*, Aug. 18, 1899; Roosevelt to Capt. Mahan, Dec. 13, 1897, in Morison, *Letters of Theodore Roosevelt*, vol. 1, p. 741; Tompkins, *Anti-Imperialism in the United States*, pp. 158–59; Welch, *Response to Imperialism*, pp. 124–32.

29. Henry Codman Potter, "The Problem of the Philippines," *Century Magazine* 61 (1900): 129–35.

30. Potter to Pierce, Apr. 4, 1900, H. C. Potter Papers, Synod House, New York, N.Y.

31. Henry Codman Potter, "China Traits and Western Blunders," *Century Magazine* 60 (1900): 930. For Potter's reconversion to anti-imperialism, see *San Francisco Call*, Feb. 2, Mar. 20, 1901.

32. *New York Journal*, Aug. 31, 1898; Atkinson, *Anti-Imperialist*, no. 1, p. 43; David Starr Jordan, "The Control of the Tropics," *Gunton's Magazine* 8 (1890): 408–10; William Graham Sumner, *The Essays of William Graham Sumner*, vol. 1, pp. 189–92.

33. Beisner, *Twelve Against Empire*, p. 105.

34. John Rollins, "The Anti-Imperialists and Twentieth Century Foreign Policy," plus comments by Harold Baron and Thomas McCormick, *Studies on the Left* 3 (1962): 9–33; Christopher Lasch, "The Anti-Imperialists, The Philippines, and the Inequality of Man," *Journal of Southern History* 24 (1958): 319–31. The debate over the real nature of the anti-imperialist movement is best summarized in Richard E. Welch, Jr., "Motives and Policy Objectives of Anti-Imperialists in 1898," *Mid-America* 51 (1969): 119–29, whether or not one agrees with the author's conclusions. In addition to the above articles, and the works of Tompkins, Beisner, Welch, and Schirmer already cited, see James Shenton, "Imperialism and Racism," in *Essays in American Historiography*, ed. Donald Sheehan and Harold Syrett; J. Roberts Hollingsworth, *The Whirligig of Politics: The Democracy of Cleveland and Bryan*; Richard E. Welch, Jr., "Opponents and Colleagues: George Frisbee Hoar and Henry Cabot Lodge, 1898–1904," *New England Quarterly* 39 (1966): 182–209; Barton Bernstein and Franklin Leib, "Progressive Republican Senators and American Imperialism, 1898–1916: A Reappraisal," *Mid-America* 50 (1968): 163–205; Jerry Israel, *Progressivism and the Open Door*; William Leuchtenburg, "Progressivism and Imperialism: The Progressive Movement and American Foreign Policy, 1898–1916," *Mississippi Valley Historical Review* 39 (1952): 483–504; Robert L. Beisner, "1898 and 1968: The Anti-Imperialists and the Doves," *Political Science Quarterly* 85 (1970): 187–216.

35. Leuchtenburg, "Progressivism and Imperialism," p. 504. See also Sidney Fine,

Laissez Faire and the General Welfare State: A Study of Conflict in American Thought, 1865–1901.

36. Beisner, *Twelve Against Empire*, p. 109, chaps. 1–6, *passim*. See also Geoffery Blodgett, "The Mind of the Boston Mugwump," *Mississippi Valley Historical Review* 48 (1962): 614–34.

37. Beisner, *Twelve Against Empire*, pp. 66, 90, 102; Harold F. Williamson, *Edward Atkinson: The Biography of an American Liberal, 1827–1905*, pp. 268–72; Fine, *Laissez Faire and the General Welfare State*, pp. 64–65; W. R. Thayer, *The Life of John Hay*, vol. 2, p. 199.

38. As cited in William Jennings Bryan, *Republic or Empire? The Philippines Question*, p. 539.

39. Atkinson to Morton, Dec. 19, 1895, Atkinson Papers; Edward Atkinson, "Jingoes and Silverites," *North American Review* 161 (1895): 559; Allan Nevins, *Grover Cleveland: A Study in Courage*, p. 645.

40. Burton J. Hendrick, *The Life of Andrew Carnegie* (New York, 1932), vol. 1, p. 83; Richard Olney, "International Isolation of the United States," *Atlantic Monthly* 81 (1898): 577–78.

41. Roosevelt to Silas McBee, June 23, 1902, and n. 2, in Morison, *Letters of Theodore Roosevelt*, vol. 3, pp. 268–69; Seth M. Scheiner, "Theodore Roosevelt and the Negro, 1901–1908," *Journal of Negro History* 47 (1962): 169–82; Theodore Roosevelt, "The Progressive and the Colored Man," *Outlook* 150 (1912): 909–12; Howard K. Beale, *Theodore Roosevelt and the Rise of America to World Power*, pp. 27–34.

42. George M. Frederickson, *The Black Image in the White Mind*, pp. 200–01; Lasch, "Anti-Imperialists," pp. 319–23. For Carnegie's remarks, see Shenton, "Imperialism and Racism," p. 238. See also Philip Charles Newman, "Democracy and Imperialism in American Political Thought," *Philippine Social Sciences and Humanities Review* 15 (1950): 351–67, and Frederick Merk, *Manifest Destiny and Mission in American History*, pp. 237–47.

43. Frederickson, *Black Image in the White Mind*, pp. 297–306. See also John Spencer Bassett, "Stirring Up the Fires of Racial Antipathy," *South Atlantic Quarterly* 2 (1903): 299 ff.

44. *San Francisco Call*, July 15, Nov. 5, 15, 1899; Albion Tourgée, "The Twentieth Century Peace Makers," *Contemporary Review* 81 (1899): 886–908; S. Doc. 331, 57th Cong., 1st Sess., pt. 3, pp. 2668–2708.

45. Franklin Henry Giddings, *Democracy and Empire: With Studies of Their Psychological, Economic and Moral Foundations*, pp. 4–11, 226, 262–64, 316–29.

46. *Congressional Record*, 55th Cong., 3rd Sess., pp. 838, 1380–89, 1422–32; Mrs. Jefferson Davis, "Why We Do Not Want the Philippines," *Arena* 23 (1900): 1–14.

47. *Nation*, Jan. 13, 1898, p. 23; Frederick Bancroft, ed., *Speeches, Correspondence and Political Papers of Carl Schurz*, vol. 5, pp. 503–06; Charles Francis Adams, *Imperialism and "The Tracks of Our Forefathers," A Paper Read by Charles Francis Adams Before the Lexington, Massachusetts Historical Society, Tuesday, December 20, 1898*, p. 10; *Public Opinion* 25 (1898): 679, 26 (1899): 457; Allan Nevins, ed., *The Letters of Grover Cleveland*, p. 526.

48. *Public Opinion* 25 (1898): 679, 26 (1899): 457; Storey to James Bradley Thayer, Nov. 3, 1899, as cited in Mark A. De Wolfe Howe, *Portrait of an Independent: Moorfield Storey, 1845–1920*, p. 225; *Congressional Record*, 55th Cong., 3rd Sess., p. 838;

Beisner, *Twelve Against Empire*, pp. 23–24, 65, 70–73, and his article, "1898 and 1968," p. 202.

49. *Congressional Record*, 55th Cong., 3rd Sess., pp. 5778, 5790, 5888; *Forum* 26 (1898): 279–81, 650–55; *San Francisco Call*, May 1, 1899.

50. Whitelaw Reid, *The Problems of Expansion*, pp. 13 ff.; *Public Opinion* 26 (1899): 347; *New York Times*, Mar. 3, 1900; *San Francisco Call*, Mar. 3, 1900; "Governing America's Dependencies," *Annals* of the American Academy of Political and Social Sciences, Supplement to 13 (1899): 3–18, 19–46, 46–59.

51. *San Francisco Call*, May 20, July 18, 1899; *Congressional Record*, 55th Cong., 3rd Sess., pp. 958–60.

52. *Congressional Record*, 55th Cong., 3rd Sess., pp. 648–52, 836–40, 2347–49.

53. *San Francisco Call*, July 18, 1899; *Boston Globe*, Oct. 15, 1900.

54. Schirmer, *Republic or Empire*, pp. 214–15; Kelly Miller, "The Effect of Imperialism Upon the Negro Race," *Howard's American Magazine* 5 (October 1900): 87–91 and Frederick L. McGhee, "Another View," pp. 92–96; W. S. Scarborough, "The Negro and Our New Possessions," *Forum* 31 (1901): 341–49. In "Opposition of Negro Newspapers to American Philippine Policy, 1899–1900," *Midwest Journal* 4 (1951): 1–25, George P. Marks made a much stronger case for opposition to imperialism among blacks than in his book on the subject twenty years later, *The Black Press Views American Imperialism (1898–1900)*. As was the case among the white population and press, blacks and their newspapers sometimes changed their positions during the course of events in the Philippines. Marks found in his later study that of the 37 papers he studied, 20 opposed the Philippine venture, 12 supported it, and 5 were neutral or ambivalent. Williard B. Gatewood, *Black Americans and the White Man's Burden, 1898–1903* makes a stronger case for black opposition, but the author seems a bit too intent on doing so, although he was not nearly as affected by the contemporary image of black opposition to the war in Vietnam as was Schirmer in writing *Republic or Empire*. The most balanced discussion on this topic is in Welch, *Response to Imperialism*, pp. 106–11.

55. Welch, *Response to Imperialism*, pp. 111–12, 179, n. 41; Schirmer, *Republic or Empire*, pp. 214–15.

56. New England Anti-Imperialist League, *Second Annual Report*; Lasch, "Anti-Imperialists," pp. 319–31; John Tyler Morgan, "The Future of the Negro," *North American Review* 134 (1884): 83–84; *San Francisco Call*, Aug. 26, Nov. 22, 1899; Joseph O. Baylen and John Hammond Moore, "Senator John Tyler Morgan and Negro Colonization in the Philippines, 1900–1902," *Phylon* 29 (1968): 65–73.

CHAPTER 8

1. *San Francisco Call*, Oct. 13, Dec. 16, 21, 1899.

2. *Congressional Record*, 56th Cong., 1st Sess., pp. 702–30; *San Francisco Call*, Jan. 16, 24, 1900.

3. *Congressional Record*, 56th Cong., 1st Sess., pp. 702–30; *Literary Digest* 20 (1900): 70–72.

4. *Congressional Record*, 56th Cong., 1st Sess., pp. 704–05, 711; *Literary Digest* 20 (1900): 70–72; *San Francisco Call*, Jan. 10, 20, 1900.

5. As cited in the *Literary Digest* 20 (1900): 70–72.

6. *San Francisco Call*, Dec. 29, 1899; Kenneth E. Hendrickson, "Reluctant Ex-

pansionist: Jacob Gould Schurman and the Philippine Question," *Pacific Historical Review* 36 (1967): 414–15.

7. S. Doc. 138, 56th Cong., 1st Sess., vol. 1, pp. 8–88, 121, 416–17.

8. *Literary Digest* 19 (1899): 573.

9. *San Francisco Call*, Jan. 24, 25, 1900; *North American Review* 170 (1900): 54–60; *Literary Digest* 19 (1899): 573, 20 (1900): 176.

10. *Literary Digest* 19 (1899): 573; *San Francisco Call*, Nov. 8, 16, 22, 1899, Jan. 20, Feb. 7, 1900.

11. *San Francisco Call*, Feb. 7, 8, 9, 1900.

12. *Literary Digest* 20 (1900): 203–04; *San Francisco Call*, Feb. 8, 9, 10, 1900; *New York Sun*, Feb. 2, 1900.

13. Ralph E. Minger, "Taft, MacArthur, and the Establishment of Civil Government in the Philippines," *The Ohio Historical Quarterly* 70 (1961): 308–31.

14. Ibid.; S. Doc. 331, 57th Cong., 1st Sess., pt. 1, pp. 65–68.

15. *Boston Evening Transcript*, June 22, 1900; Minger, "Establishment of Civil Government," pp. 318–23.

16. *San Francisco Call*, Feb. 21, 1900; Peter W. Stanley, "The Making of an American Sinologist: William W. Rockhill and the Open Door," *Perspectives in American History* 11 (1977–78): 414–60.

17. *Literary Digest* 21 (1900): 35; *Public Opinion* 29 (1900): 7–9, 103, 168.

18. *Public Opinion* 29 (1900): 7–9, 102, 167–68; *Literary Digest* 21 (1900): 35; Howard K. Beale, *Theodore Roosevelt and the Rise of America to World Power*, p. 76.

19. *San Francisco Call*, Oct. 12, Dec. 25, 1899, Mar. 3, Nov. 20, 1900, Jan. 3, Dec. 12, 1901.

20. Ibid., July 18, 1899.

21. Ibid., July 10, Aug. 11, Oct. 14, 1900; Paul Kleppner, *The Cross of Culture: A Social Analysis of Midwestern Politics, 1850–1890*, pp. 369–75. See also Richard Jensen, *The Winning of the Midwest: Social and Political Conflict, 1888–1896* and Samuel T. McSeveney, *The Politics of Depression. Political Behavior in the Northeast, 1893–1896* for background of the election of 1900.

22. *San Francisco Call*, July 10, Aug. 11, 16, Sept. 14, Oct. 14, 1900; Robert L. Beisner, *Twelve Against Empire: The Anti-Imperialists, 1898–1900*, pp. 121–25.

23. *San Francisco Call*, Aug. 4, 1900; E. Berkeley Tompkins, *Anti-Imperialism in the United States: The Great Debate, 1890–1920*, pp. 226–35; M. A. DeWolfe Howe, *Portrait of an Independent: Moorfield Storey, 1845–1929*, p. 202; Anti-Imperialist League, "Address to the Voters of the United States, Adopted by the National Congress of Anti-Imperialists at Indianapolis, Indiana, August 15–16, 1900," *Liberty Tract No. 13*; *San Francisco Call*, Aug. 16, 17, 1900.

24. Harold Baron, "Anti-Imperialism and the Democrats," *Science and Society* 21 (1957): 222–39; Philip S. Foner, *History of the Labor Movement*, vol. 2, pp. 336–39; *Boston Evening Transcript*, Aug. 21, 1900; *San Francisco Call*, Aug. 24, 1900. See Horace B. Davis, "American Labor and Imperialism Prior to World War I," *Science and Society* 27 (1963): 70–76; Ronald Radosh, "American Labor and the Anti-Imperialist Movement: A Discussion," and Horace Davis's reply, *Science and Society* 28 (1964): 91–104; William George Whitaker, "Samuel Gompers, Anti-Imperialist," *Pacific Historical Review* 38 (1968): 429–45, for the continued debate, largely by "New Left" historians, over the role of labor and to some extent the remarkable reticence of the socialists on the

issue of imperialism and the conquest of the Philippines. See also John C. Appel, "The Relationship of American Labor to United States Imperialism, 1895–1905," Ph.D. dissertation, University of Wisconsin, 1950.

25. *San Francisco Call*, Oct. 20, 1900; *Literary Digest* 21 (1900): 498; *New York Sun*, Mar. 8, Oct. 6, 1900.

26. (Catholic) *Monitor*, Oct. 6, 1900.

27. *San Francisco Call*, Oct. 24, Nov. 17, 22, 1899; Otis to Adjutant General, Feb. 19, 1900, in U.S. Adjutant General's Office, *Correspondence Relating to the War with Spain*, vol. 2, p. 1145; *Woman's Evangel* 19 (1900): 194; *Literary Digest* 21 (1900): 346–47, 499–500; *Home Mission* 73 (1900): 45–46; *Around the World* 1 (1900): 9; *Searchlight* 6 (1900): 8; *San Francisco Call*, Jan. 17, 1900. See also Michael Paul Onorato's review of *Studies in Philippine Church History*, ed. Gerald H. Anderson and Onorato's subsequent exchange with Taft's daughter on the friar issue in *American Historical Review* 76 (1971): 180, 1261–62.

28. *Literary Digest* 18 (1899): 706, 21 (1900): 317–18, 498; *Spirit of Missions* 66 (1901): 559.

29. *Imperialism: A National Temptation, Not An Opportunity* (Washington, D.C., n.d.); *Literary Digest* 21 (1900): 498.

30. Tompkins, *Anti-Imperialism in the United States*, pp. 230–34.

31. Beisner, *Twelve Against Empire*, pp. 191–92; *San Francisco Call*, Aug. 5, 1900.

32. *San Francisco Call*, Oct. 2, 1900. It is even questionable that Governor Poynter actually made the remark that Roosevelt attributed to both him and Bryan. But the Nebraskan governor had vetoed a proposed memorial to soldiers who fought in the Philippines and denounced the war in the process. Nevertheless, Poynter did greet the Nebraska regiment in San Francisco, attempting to board their transport at midnight. See diary of Pvt. Hermann Dittner, July 30, 1899, U.S. Army Military History Research Collection, Carlisle Barracks, Carlisle, Pa. (hereafter Carlisle Collection).

33. *San Francisco Call*, Sept. 25, Oct. 5, 6, 1900.

34. *Public Opinion* 27 (1899): 483.

35. *Republican Campaign Book, 1900*, pp. 343–44; *San Francisco Call*, Oct. 16, 28, 1900; *New York Sun*, Sept. 1, 1900; Mark Sullivan, *Our Times: The United States, 1900–1925*, vol. 1, p. 537.

36. *San Francisco Call*, Sept. 20, 29, Oct. 8, 15, 1900; *Boston Evening Transcript*, Sept. 20, 1900.

37. *Detroit Evening News*, Sept. 7, 1900; *San Francisco Call*, Sept. 8, 21, 1900; *Boston Evening Transcript*, Sept. 20, 1900.

38. *San Francisco Call*, Oct. 7, 1899, Oct. 8, 11, 14, 1900. Senator Hanna came the closest to being seriously hurt when a large block of ice, symbolizing the "ice trust," was dropped through a campaign tent and narrowly missed him. *San Francisco Call*, Oct. 5, 1900.

39. Ibid., Oct. 14, 23, 28, 1900; *New York Sun*, Sept. 24, 27, Nov. 2, 1900.

40. *San Francisco Call*, Oct. 7, 1900.

41. *San Francisco Call*, Oct. 25, 1899, June 3, Aug. 23, Oct. 7, 8, 12, 28, Nov. 2, 1900; *Omaha Bee*, Sept. 28, 1900; *New York Sun*, Sept. 27, Nov. 2, 5, 1900; Beale, *Theodore Roosevelt and the Rise of America*, pp. 70–71.

42. *Literary Digest* 21 (1900): 514; *San Francisco Call*, Sept. 26, 1900.

43. *San Francisco Call*, Oct. 6, 1900; *New York Sun*, Sept. 24, 1900.

44. *San Francisco Call*, Sept. 10, 29, 1900; *Boston Evening Transcript*, Sept. 10, 1900.

45. *San Francisco Call*, Sept. 20, 1900.

46. *New York Tribune*, Oct. 27, 1900; *San Francisco Call*, Oct. 29, 1900; *Harper's Weekly* 44 (1900): 884.

47. *San Francisco Call*, June 21, 1900.

48. Beale, *Theodore Roosevelt and the Rise of America*, pp. 75–76; *New York Sun*, June 24, 1900.

49. "The Cost of the Philippine War," *Public Opinion* 29 (1900): 265–66; *San Francisco Call*, Aug. 14, 1900.

50. *Literary Digest* 21 (1900): 513–14; *Nation* 71 (1900): 124–25; Lt. Samuel Powell Lyon to his wife, Apr. 12, 1900, Carlisle Collection; Sullivan, *Our Times*, vol. 1, p. 537.

51. Anti-Imperialist League, *Report of the Second Annual Meeting of the Anti-Imperialist League* (1900); *Literary Digest* 21 (1900): 514; Beisner, *Twelve Against Empire*, p. 196; *New York Sun*, Nov. 9, 1900. Boutwell's assertion was based on the fact that McKinley's plurality in the eastern states in 1900 was less than it had been in 1896.

52. Beale, *Theodore Roosevelt and the Rise of America*, p. 65, n. 6.

CHAPTER 9

1. *Literary Digest* 21 (1900): 605–06.

2. Ibid.; *Springfield Republican*, Nov. 14, 1900; *San Francisco Call*, Nov. 13, 14, 15, 1900.

3. *Literary Digest* 21 (1900): 605–06.

4. Ibid.; *Boston Herald*, Nov. 16, 1900.

5. *New York Sun*, Jan. 1, 1901; *San Francisco Call*, Jan. 1, 5, 1901; *Springfield Republican*, Jan. 5, 1901; *New York Evening Post*, Jan. 5, 1901; *Boston Post*, Jan. 5, 1901.

6. *New York Times*, Jan. 2, 1901.

7. *Public Opinion* 30 (1901): 326.

8. Ibid., pp. 38–39.

9. Ibid.; *Portland Oregonian*, Jan. 12, 1901, as cited in the *Springfield Republican*, Feb. 13, 1901.

10. Kennan was quoted by the *Springfield Republican*, Mar. 15, 1901, and the *Literary Digest* 31 (1900): 365.

11. *New York Evening Post*, Jan. 28, 1901; *New York Sun*, Feb. 24, 1901.

12. Clipping of Jan. 3, 1901, in Cutter Papers, U.S. Army Military History Research Collection, Carlisle Barracks, Carlisle, Pa. (hereafter Carlisle Collection); *San Francisco Call*, Jan. 5, 1901.

13. *San Francisco Call*, Jan. 11, 1901; *New York Evening Post*, Jan. 11, 14, 1901.

14. *New York Sun*, Jan. 24, 1901.

15. *New York Evening Post*, Jan. 11, 1901; *Springfield Republican*, Jan. 11, 1901.

16. *Springfield Republican*, Jan. 11, 1901.

17. E. Berkeley Tompkins, *Anti-Imperialism in the United States: The Great Debate, 1890–1920*, p. 244; Robert Wiebe, *The Search For Order, 1877–1920*, p. 228; Finley Peter Dunne, *Mr. Dooley's Opinions*, p. 71.

18. *New York Sun*, Feb. 2, 1901; "Political Affairs in the Philippines," S. Doc. 259, 57th Cong., 1st Sess., pp. 32–42. For a more balanced treatment of the Partido Federal,

see Peter W. Stanley, *A Nation in the Making: The Philippines and the United States, 1899–1921*, pp. 68–69, 72–73, 77, 79.

19. *New York Evening Post*, Jan. 30, 1901.

20. *New York Sun*, Dec. 23, 1900; *Boston Evening Transcript*, Mar. 25, 1901. For the society's report, see *Facts About the Filipinos*, vol. 1, nos. 1–12.

21. Schurz is cited in Daniel B. Schirmer, *Republic or Empire: American Resistance to the Philippine War*, p. 243; *New York Times*, Sept. 20, 1900; James LeRoy, *The Americans in the Philippines*, vol. 2, p. 239, n. 1.

22. *New York World*, Feb. 9, 10, 19, 1901.

23. *New York Evening Post*, Feb. 14, 1901.

24. Stanley, *Nation in the Making*, pp. 87–88.

25. David Healy, *U.S. Expansion: The Imperialistic Urge in the 1890's*, p. 173.

26. Stanley, *Nation in the Making*, p. 88.

27. *New York Evening Post*, Feb. 28, 1901; *San Francisco Call*, Feb. 18, 28, 1901; *New York World*, Feb. 17, 1901.

28. S. Doc. 331, 57th Cong., 1st Sess., pt. 2, p. 911.

29. Ralph E. Minger, "Taft, MacArthur, and the Establishment of Civil Government in the Philippines," *The Ohio Historical Quarterly* 70 (1961): 318–20; Taft to Root, July 30, 1900, Root Papers, Library of Congress.

30. Ibid., pp. 320–27; MacArthur to Adjutant General, Aug. 31, 1900, in U.S. Adjutant General's Office, *Correspondence Relating to the War with Spain*, vol. 2, p. 1165; William T. Sexton, *Soldiers in the Sun*, pp. 251–52.

31. *New York Times*, Apr. 28, 1901.

32. *Public Opinion* 30 (1901): 137.

33. S. Doc. 167, 56th Cong., 1st Sess., p. 3.

34. *San Francisco Call*, Feb. 22, 1900, Jan. 4, 1901.

35. *Boston Herald*, Nov. 19, 1900; *San Francisco Call*, Nov. 19, 1900; *New York World*, Dec. 20, 1900.

36. *New York Herald*, Dec. 9, 1900.

37. *San Francisco Call*, Mar. 3, July 1, 1899, Mar. 3, 1900.

38. *New York World*, Jan. 26, 1901; *New York Evening Post*, Feb. 1, 1901; *New York Times*, Mar. 3, 1901.

39. *Chicago Record*, Jan. 29, 1901, as cited in the *Springfield Republican*, Jan. 30, 1901; *Evening Post* and the *World* of New York and the *San Francisco Call*, all Jan. 26, 1901.

40. *New York Evening Post*, Feb. 1, 1901; S. Doc. 331, pt. 3, pp. 2594–95, 2609, 2611–12.

41. *New York Sun*, Feb. 24, 1901.

42. S. Doc. 331, pt. 1, pp. 368–70.

43. Taft to Root, Mar. 17, 1901, as cited in Minger, "Establishment of Civil Government," pp. 326–27; S. Doc. 331, pt. 1, pp. 368–70.

44. S. Doc. 331, pt. 1, pp. 323–45. The song was originally a poem written by Robert F. Morrison in the *Manila Sunday Sun*:

I'm only a common soldier-man in the blasted
   Philippines.
They say I got Brown Brothers here, but I dunno
   what it means.

I like the word Fraternity, but I still draw
the line;
He may be a brother of William H. Taft, but he
ain't no friend of mine.

As cited in Mark Sullivan, *Our Times: The United States, 1900–1925*, vol. 1, p. 7.

45. James H. Blount, *The American Occupation of the Philippines, 1898–1912*, pp. 333–39; *Boston Herald*, Mar. 26, 28, 1901. See also the personal accounts of Funston and Aguinaldo: "The Capture of Aguinaldo," *Scribner's Magazine* 50 (1911): 522–36 and "The Story of My Capture," *Everybody's Magazine* 5 (1901): 131–40. See also the account of the correspondent, O. K. Davis, "The Real Aguinaldo," *Everybody's Magazine* 5 (1901): 141–44. Aguinaldo called Funston "a fictionizer," which should come as no surprise. See also Murat Halstead, *Aguinaldo and His Captor*.

46. *Correspondence*, vol. 2, pp. 1263–68; *San Francisco Call*, Mar. 24, 1901; *Boston Herald*, Mar. 24, 1901; *Literary Digest* 20 (1900): 344.

47. Roosevelt to Funston, Mar. 30, 1901, in *The Letters of Theodore Roosevelt*, ed. Elting Morison, vol. 3, p. 35. Almost a year earlier Roosevelt congratulated William Allen White for an article in *Harper's* on the flamboyant young colonel in command of the Kansas volunteers. "What a perfect corker Funston is!" the governor of New York declared. See Roosevelt to White, May 25, 1899, vol. 2, pp. 1014–15. For Sgt. Daley's comment on Funston, see his letter to his brother, Apr. 11, 1901, Carlisle Collection. See also the *San Francisco Call* for an interview with army officers in the War Department (Mar. 29, 1901), and for Corbin's protest (Apr. 6, 1901).

48. *Springfield Republican*, Mar. 20, 1901; *San Francisco Call*, Mar. 29, Apr. 26, 1901.

49. *San Francisco Call*, Mar. 28, 29, 1901; *Springfield Republican*, Mar. 29, 30, 1901; *Literary Digest* 22 (1901): 467–68. Apparently wearing enemy uniforms was not so uncommon for the Macabebe scouts. In a letter to his wife, Capt. Batson, their commander, described "discarding our uniforms" in order to put on "Amigo clothes" before launching a "surprise attack." See p. 136 of typescript copies of Batson's letters, Carlisle Collection.

50. As cited in *Literary Digest* 22 (1901): 467–68.

51. Ibid., pp. 402–03; *Correspondence*, vol. 2, p. 1263.

52. *Literary Digest* 22 (1901): 433–34, 503–04.

53. Ibid.

54. Ibid., 23 (1901): 3; *Public Opinion* 30 (1901): 805.

55. *San Francisco Call*, Apr. 26, June 25, 1901; Sexton, *Soldiers in the Sun*, pp. 249–50.

56. *San Francisco Call*, Sept. 15, 16, 1899, Jan. 9, Dec. 7, 1900, Apr. 3, 4, 1901; MacArthur to Adjutant General, Apr. 3, 1901, in *Correspondence*, vol. 2, p. 1266.

57. *New York Tribune*, Apr. 2, 5, 8, 16, 1901; *New York Times*, Apr. 1, 16, 1901; *Public Opinion* 30 (1901): 456–59; *San Francisco Call*, Apr. 4, June 25, 1901.

58. Funston as cited in the *San Francisco Call*, Oct. 22, 1899; Maj. William Kobbe, "Diary of Field Service in the Philippines, 1898–1901," p. 42, and Lt. Samuel Lyon to his wife, Apr. 20, 1901, Carlisle Collection. See John Morgan Gates, *Schoolbooks and Krags: The United States Army in the Philippines* for an examination of the army's role in educational, hygienic, and political programs.

59. *Boston Globe*, Mar. 20, 1901; *Springfield Republican*, Mar. 29, 1901; Mark A.

DeWolfe Howe, *Portrait of an Independent: Moorfield Storey, 1845–1929*, p. 177; Robert Beisner, *Twelve Against Empire: The Anti-Imperialists, 1898–1900*, pp. 162, 180, n. 73.

60. *San Francisco Call*, May 7, 11, 1901.

61. Ibid., July 4, 5, 1901; MacArthur's report, July 4, 1901, as cited in Philippine Information Society, *The Philippine Revolution*, pp. 11–12.

62. *San Francisco Call*, Aug. 19, 1901; Philippine Information Society, *Philippine Revolution*, p. 12 (quoting MacArthur's report, pp. 19–20).

CHAPTER 10

1. The most impressive single collection is in the U.S. Army Military History Research Collection at Carlisle Barracks, Carlisle, Pa. (hereafter Carlisle Collection). For impressions of the volunteers in the months before warfare broke out with the Filipinos, see, in particular, the diary of Pvt. Hermann Dittner, letters of Hugh Clapp (both in Nebraska regiment), and letters of Pvt. William Christner (Pennsylvania regiment). In addition to these sources, newspapers and the Anti-Imperialist League published fragments of letters from the Philippines, as well as the comments of veterans upon their return.

2. H. Clapp to his father, Feb. 11, 1899; Pvt. W. Christner to his parents, May 1, 1899; diary of Pvt. H. Dittner, Apr. 29, 1899; Lt. William Connor to Lt. Frederick Sladen, Apr. 1, 1899; all from Carlisle Collection.

3. H. Clapp to his father, Apr. 10, 15, 29, May 27, 1899, Carlisle Collection.

4. The *Pittsburgh Post* survey was reproduced in the *San Francisco Call*, Oct. 27, 1899. Compare the fragments of Burrett's letter published in the *San Francisco Call*, May 26, 1899, and the *New York Sun* as cited in *Literary Digest* 18 (1899): 608.

5. Edward Atkinson, *The Anti-Imperialist*, pp. 32–39.

6. Ibid.; *Eighth Army Corps War Songs* (Manila, 1901), Walter Cutter Papers, Carlisle Collection.

7. Atkinson, *Anti-Imperialist*, pp. 32–39; *New York Evening Post*, May 8, 1899; *Omaha Bee*, May 7, 1899; *San Francisco Call*, Apr. 24, 1899; *Public Opinion* 26 (1899): 499; *Literary Digest* 17 (1899): 499; *Arena* 22 (1899): 568; *Kansas City Times*, n.d., from a clipping collection of Mrs. William James, Widener Library, Harvard University, Cambridge, Mass. (hereafter James Collection).

8. Maj. William Kobbe, "Diary of Field Service in the Philippines, 1898–1901"; Michael J. Lanihan, "I Remember, I Remember"; Pvt. W. Christner to his father, Mar. 19, 1899; all from Carlisle Collection.

9. *Kansas City Times*, n.d., James Collection; *San Francisco Call*, Apr. 4, 8, 1900.

10. Lt. Samuel Powell Lyon, "Notes on the Philippine Insurrection"; Capt. Matthew Batson to his wife, p. 78; both from Carlisle Collection. S. Doc. 331, 57th Cong., 1st Sess., pp. 1443–45.

11. Cutter Papers, Carlisle Collection.

12. Capt. M. Batson to his wife, p. 108, Carlisle Collection; *San Francisco Call*, Dec. 21, 1899.

13. Lt. S. P. Lyon to his wife, May 28–June 18, Oct. 11–Dec. 12, 1899, Jan. 30, 1900; Capt. M. Batson to his wife, May 28–June 18, 1899, p. 59; all from Carlisle Collection.

14. Capt. M. Batson to his wife, Mar. 25–31, 1899, pp. 34–35, Carlisle Collection.

15. Ibid., Apr. 23–May 4, 1899, pp. 47–48.

16. Ibid., pp. 45–47.

17. Ibid., September, October, and November, 1899, pp. 113–14, 120–21.

18. Lt. S. P. Lyon to his wife, Oct. 9, 1899, Mar. 19, Apr. 12, June 17, 1900, Carlisle Collection.

19. Ibid., Jan. 13, 1901.

20. Diary of W. Cutter, pp. 18–19, Carlisle Collection.

21. Ibid.; *Soldier's Banner*, n.d., pp. 10–11, Carlisle Collection.

22. Lt. S. P. Lyon to his wife, Mar. 28, 1900, Carlisle Collection.

23. W. Cutter, "Hank Harkins, Recruit," pp. 46–50, 56–61, and his diary, p. 18, Carlisle Collection.

24. Pvt. Hambleton to his father, Mar. 4, 27, 1900, Carlisle Collection.

25. *Eighth Army Corps War Songs*, Cutter Papers, Carlisle Collection.

26. Letters of Sgt. Beverly Daley, Nov. 16, 1900, Pvt. Hambleton, Mar. 4, 1900, and Capt. M. Batson, Nov. 8, 1900, p. 48, Carlisle Collection.

27. *San Francisco Call*, Aug. 23, Sept. 15, Oct. 25, Dec. 30, 1899; Frederick Funston, *Memories of Two Wars: Cuba and the Philippines*, p. 443. See also *Literary Digest* 19 (1899): 485; *Public Opinion* 27 (1899): 484.

28. Anti-Imperialist League, *Soldiers' Letters, Being Materials for the History of a War of Criminal Aggression*, pp. 3–4, 6–8, 10, 15; *San Francisco Call*, Oct. 18, 1899.

29. Anti-Imperialist League, *Soldiers' Letters*, pp. 3–15; Pvt. Hambleton to his brother, May 26, 1900, Carlisle Collection; *Omaha Bee*, May 7, 1899; *San Francisco Call*, Apr. 24, 1899; *Literary Digest* 18 (1899): 601; *Public Opinion* 26 (1899): 499.

30. *San Francisco Call*, Mar. 6, Apr. 10, 1900, Mar. 12, Apr. 11, 17, 1902; *New York Sun*, Mar. 10, 1902; S. Doc. 331, pp. 881–85; *Kingston* (New York) *Evening Post*, May 8, 1899, as cited in *Literary Digest* 18 (1899): 601; Anti-Imperialist League, *Soldiers' Letters*, pp. 3, 15.

31. S. Doc. 331, pp. 637–39, 894–98.

32. Pvt. W. Christner to his parents, Mar. 13, Apr. 9, 1899; H. Clapp to his father, Apr. 29, 1899; diary of Pvt. H. Dittner, Apr. 29, 1899; all from Carlisle Collection. For the number of volunteers who actually did reenlist, see Otis's reports in U.S. Adjutant General's Office, *Correspondence Relating to the War with Spain*, vol. 2, pp. 1001–02, 1004–05.

33. *Eighth Army Corps War Songs* and *The Jolo Howler*, Jan. 1, 1902, both in Cutter Papers, Carlisle Collection; *Literary Digest* 18 (1899): 601.

34. Pvt. W. Christner to his parents, Sept. 21, 1898; Guy Henry, Jr., "The Life of Guy Henry, Jr.," pp. 26–27; *Soldier's Banner*, n.d., Cutter Papers; all from Carlisle Collection. MacArthur insisted that drunkenness in the islands was no worse than it was among soldiers in the United States. See *Correspondence*, vol. 2, pp. 1150–52. It seems that getting drunk before battle is an old habit. See John Keegan, *The Face of Battle*, pp. 113–14, 181–82, 241, 326.

35. *San Francisco Call*, Mar. 7, Nov. 3, 4, 5, 1900.

36. Ibid., Nov. 23, 1900.

37. Ibid., Aug. 26, Nov. 22, 28, Dec. 3, 1899, Sept. 9, 1900. For a dramatic description of the death of one white deserter to the enemy, Charles Johnson of the Sixth Artillery, see George Shaffer's letter, n.d., 28th Volunteer Infantry, Carlisle Collection. See

Michael C. Robinson and Frank N. Schubert, "David Fagen: An Afro-American Rebel in the Philippines, 1899–1901," *Pacific Historical Review* 44 (1975): 68–83, on this infamous turncoat. However, it is questionable that Fagen was the political rebel these authors have made him out to be. Over 100 soldiers (about 20 black) deserted to the bush, not the enemy, usually with a Filipina, and simply remained in the islands.

38. *Correspondence*, vol. 2, p. 1350; Williard Gatewood, *"Smoked Yankees" and the Struggle for Empire: Letters from Negro Soldiers, 1898–1902*, pp. 243–44; "Race Discrimination in the Philippines," *Independent* 54 (1902): 416–17.

39. Gatewood, *"Smoked Yankees"*, pp. 245–53, 288–308, and his *Black Americans and the White Man's Burden, 1898–1903*, chap. 8; "Negro Sentiment on Imperialism," *San Francisco Call*, Sept. 29, 1899; William T. Sexton, *Soldiers in the Sun*, p. 242; Rienzi B. Lemus, "The Enlisted Man in Action, Or the Colored Soldier in the Philippines," *Colored American Magazine* 5 (May 1902): 46–54. See also Marvin E. Fletcher, *The Black Soldier and Officer in the United States Army, 1891–1917*; George P. Marks, comp. and ed., *The Black Press Views American Imperialism (1898–1900)*. While black soldiers in the Philippines were not prolific writers, their answers to a 1971 questionnaire indicate that they were just as patriotic and gung ho as were their surviving white counterparts. See material on the 24th, 25th, 48th, and 49th Infantry and 9th Cavalry regiments, Carlisle Collection.

40. Lt. S. P. Lyon to his wife, Aug. 16, Nov. 13, 18, 1899, Jan. 7, 1900, and his "Notes on the Philippine Insurrection," and "Philippine Sketches," all from Carlisle Collection.

41. Lt. S. P. Lyon to his wife, Nov. 18, 1901; Kobbe, "Diary," pp. 46–47; diary of William Carey Brown, Jan. 22, 23, 1901; all from Carlisle Collection.

42. Anti-Imperialist League, *Soldiers' Letters*, pp. 7, 13–14.

43. *Eighth Army Corps War Songs*, Cutter Papers, Carlisle Collection.

CHAPTER 11

1. *Nation*, 74 (1902): 61. Chaffee made the comment to Ohl in the fall of 1901.

2. U.S. Adjutant General's Office, *Correspondence Relating to the War with Spain*, vol. 2, p. 1297.

3. William T. Sexton, *Soldiers in the Sun*, pp. 276–77.

4. House Doc. 2, 57th Cong., 1st Sess., vol. 7, pp. 356–57.

5. For Samar's background, see Robert Bruce Cruikshank, "A History of Samar Island, The Philippines, 1768–1898," Ph.D. dissertation, University of Wisconsin, 1975. For highly readable accounts of the Balangiga massacre, see Joseph L. Schott, *The Ordeal of Samar*, pp. 7–55; James O. Taylor, *The Massacre of Balangiga: Being an Authentic Account By Several of the Few Survivers*. For testimony of survivors, see *San Francisco Call*, Sept. 30, 1901; S. Doc. 331, 57th Cong., 1st Sess., pp. 1591–99, 2284–2310; Adolph Gambiss, "Massacre of Company C, 9th U.S. Infantry on the Morning of September 28, 1901, at Balangiga," U.S. Army Military History Research Collection, Carlisle Barracks, Carlisle, Pa.

6. *San Francisco Call*, Sept. 30, Oct. 1, 11, 13, 16, 19, 20, 21, Nov. 16, 1901, Jan. 20, 1902; *Literary Digest* 23 (1901): 422–23; *Public Opinion* 31 (1901): 549. See also Donald Chaput, "The American Press and General Vicente Lukban, Hero of Samar," *Leyte-Samar Studies* 8 (1974): 21–32.

7. *San Francisco Call*, Oct. 21, Nov. 16, 1901.

8. *Public Opinion* 31 (1901): 549; *Nation*, 73 (1901): 2; *San Francisco Call*, Sept. 30, 1901.

9. *San Francisco Call*, Dec. 9, 1901; Michael C. Robinson and Frank N. Schubert, "David Fagen: An Afro-American Rebel in the Philippines, 1899–1901," *Pacific Historical Review* 44 (1975): 68–83.

10. *New York Times*, June 19, 1901.

11. *San Francisco Call*, Oct. 1, 1901.

12. General Bell's orders can be found in a number of sources, e.g., "The Issuance of Certain Orders in the Philippines," S. Doc. 347, 57th Cong., 1st Sess. They were also reproduced in S. Doc. 331, pt. 2, pp. 1606–38.

13. S. Doc. 347.

14. *Correspondence*, vol. 2, p. 1260.

15. *Nation* 72 (1901): 225; S. Doc. 331, pt. 1, pp. 559–62.

16. S. Doc. 331, pt. 3, p. 2625.

17. *Literary Digest* 24 (1902): 24.

18. Ibid.

19. Ibid.

20. *Literary Digest* 24 (1902): 171; S. Doc. 432, 56th Cong., 1st Sess., p. 3; *Outlook* 54 (1900): 913–18.

21. Charles Ballantine [Edgar Bellairs], *As It Is in the Philippines*, pp. 2, 22, 83, 86, 89.

22. S. Doc. 347, 57th Cong., 1st Sess., pp. 2–3.

23. *Philadelphia Ledger*, Nov. 19, 1900, as cited in S. Doc. 166, 57th Cong., 1st Sess., p. 2.

24. General Jake Smith's comments were first published in the *Manila News*, Nov. 4, 1901, as cited in S. Doc. 166, p. 2.

25. The hearings and a great deal of documentation were published in three volumes as S. Doc. 331, 57th Cong., 1st Sess. An abridged version of the oral testimony has been edited by Henry Graff and published in paperback by Little, Brown as *Imperialism and the Philippine Insurrection* (Boston, 1969).

26. S. Doc. 331, pt. 1, pp. 75–76; Benjamin O. Flowers, "Some Dead Sea Fruit of Our War of Subjugation," *Arena* 27 (1902): 647–53; (Philadelphia) *City and State*, Jan. 2, 1902; *San Francisco Call*, Jan. 3, Feb. 19, 20, 1902; *New York Times*, Feb. 25, 1902; S. Doc. 205, 57th Cong., 1st Sess., pp. 3–4.

27. S. Doc. 331, pt. 1, pp. 77–79.

28. Ibid., pp. 80, 88–89, 101–02, 139, 270–73.

29. Ibid., pp. 558–62.

30. Ibid., pp. 679–728.

31. Ibid., pp. 729–848, particularly p. 736; *San Francisco Call*, Mar. 18, 19, 20, 21, 1902. MacArthur followed Otis to the witness stand although a gap of more than two weeks of inactivity on the part of the committee separated their testimony.

32. S. Doc. 331, pt. 2, pp. 1421–84.

33. S. Doc. 205, 57th Cong., 1st Sess., pt. 1, pp. 1–3; *San Francisco Call*, Feb. 20, 1902; *New York Times*, Feb. 20, 1902.

34. S. Doc. 205, pt. 1, pp. 16–18.

35. Ibid., p. 21; *San Francisco Call*, Feb. 20, 1902.

36. S. Doc. 205, pt. 1, pp. 42–44.

CHAPTER 12

1. S. Doc. 213, 57th Cong., 2nd Sess., pp. 3, 6–7, 9–17; Joseph L. Schott, *The Ordeal of Samar*, chap. 3.
2. S. Doc. 213, pp. 3, 6–7, 9–17; Schott, *Ordeal of Samar*, p. 76.
3. S. Doc. 213, pp. 9–17; Schott, *Ordeal of Samar*, pp. 72–73.
4. Schott, *Ordeal of Samar*, chap. 4.
5. Ibid., chap. 5. Waller's marines were not the first group of Americans to cross the island. In June of 1901, two companies of the First U.S. Infantry crossed Samar from Borongan to Catbalogan in five days, according to Andrew Pohlman, *My Army Experience*, pp. 61–63.
6. Schott, *Ordeal of Samar*, chap. 6.
7. *San Francisco Call*, Mar. 16, 17, 1902.
8. Schott, *Ordeal of Samar*, chap. 8.
9. *Philadelphia North American*, Mar. 16, 17, 1902.
10. *San Francisco Call*, Mar. 16, Apr. 24, 1902; Schott, *Ordeal of Samar*, pp. 244–45.
11. Schott, *Ordeal of Samar*, chaps. 8 and 9.
12. See the *Journal, World* and *Evening Post* of New York, *Boston Evening Transcript*, and *San Francisco Call*, all for Apr. 8, 1902.
13. *New York Evening Post*, Apr. 10, 1902.
14. Ibid., Apr. 12, 1902.
15. Schott, *Ordeal of Samar*, p. 169.
16. Gardener's report was widely reproduced in the press as well as in official documents. See S. Doc. 331, 57th Cong., 1st Sess., pt. 2, pp. 881–85; *San Francisco Call*, Apr. 11, 17, 1902; U.S. Adjutant General's Office, *Correspondence Relating to the War with Spain*, vol. 2, pp. 1333–34; Melvin G. Holli, ed., "A View of the American Campaign Against 'Filipino Insurgents': 1900," *Philippine Studies* 17 (1969): 97–111. Holli and other scholars have spelled the major's name "Gardner," but his official records at the U.S. Military Academy at West Point spell it "Gardener."
17. *Springfield Republican, New York Evening Post*, both for Apr. 11, 1902; *Arena* 27 (1902): 538; *San Francisco Call*, Apr. 8, 9, 11, May 27, Aug. 26, 1902, May 21, 1903.
18. *Boston Herald*, Apr. 8, 1902; *Springfield Republican*, Apr. 11, 1902; *Louisville Courier Journal*, May 5, 1902, as cited in *New York Sun*, May 6, 1902; *Arena* 27 (1902): 539.
19. *San Francisco Call*, Jan. 10, 1902; *San Francisco Call Sunday Magazine*, Jan. 26, 1902.
20. *New York Sun*, Mar. 10, 1902.
21. *San Francisco Call*, Mar. 9, 1902.
22. Ibid.
23. Ibid., Mar. 9, 10, 11, 12, 1902.
24. *New York Sun*, Mar. 10, 1902.
25. *San Francisco Call*, Mar. 12, 30, 1902.
26. *New York Times*, Apr. 10, 1902; *Boston Herald* and *San Francisco Call*, both for Apr. 24, 25, 1902. Front-page headlines announced "President Muzzles Funston" and "Funston Silenced. President Orders Him to Cease Talking."

27. Roosevelt to Speck von Sternberg, July 19, 1902, in Elting Morison, ed., *The Letters of Theodore Roosevelt*, vol. 3, p. 298.

28. *San Francisco Call*, Apr. 27, 1902; *New York Sun*, Apr. 26, 1902; *Boston Herald*, Apr. 26, 1902. For Root's order to Chaffee, see Corbin's letter, Apr. 15, 1902, in S. Doc. 331, pt. 2, pp. 1548–49. For General Orders No. 100, see S. Doc. 205, 57th Cong., 1st Sess., pt. 1, pp. 23–34; *Correspondence*, vol. 2, p. 1329.

29. Chaffee to Root, Dec. 25, 1901, in *Correspondence*, vol. 2, p. 1306.

30. *Literary Digest* 24 (1902): 629–30.

31. Ibid.; *Boston Herald*, Apr. 26, 30, 1902; *New York Times*, Apr. 16, May 1, 1902; *San Francisco Call*, Apr. 25, 27, May 1, 7, 1902.

32. *Correspondence*, vol. 2, pp. 1327–28.

33. The *Times* and the *World* in New York and the *Call* and the *Examiner* in San Francisco, all for Apr. 17, 1902.

34. *Arena* 29 (1902): 212–13, 647–65; *Correspondence*, vol. 2, p. 1327; Roosevelt to Root, Feb. 18, 1902, in Morison, *Letters of Theodore Roosevelt*, vol. 3, pp. 232–33.

35. *San Francisco Call* and *Boston Herald*, both for Apr. 24, 1902. For Smith's actual report to MacArthur, Dec. 20, 1899, see House Doc. 2, 56th Cong., 2nd Sess., pt. 4, p. 593. For a picture of Colonel Smith's jails, see clipping (probably from the *Manila News*) in Walter Cutter Papers, U.S. Army Military History Research Collection, Carlisle Barracks, Pa.

36. *San Francisco Call*, Apr. 30, 1902.

37. See the exchange of cables of May 3 and June 18, 1902, in *Correspondence*, vol. 2, pp. 1335, 1347. Roosevelt told Speck von Sternberg that Chaffee had hatched this plot, but the cables make it clear that it was hatched in Washington. See Roosevelt to von Sternberg, July 18, 1902, in Morison, *Letters of Theodore Roosevelt*, vol. 3, p. 298.

38. *Boston Journal*, May 5, 1902; S. Doc. 331, pt. 3, pp. 2262–66.

39. S. Doc. 331, pt. 2, pp. 1527–47, 1726–36, 1765–84.

40. Ibid., pp. 862–66.

41. Ibid., p. 864.

42. Ibid., pp. 867–68.

43. Ibid., pp. 688, 1919–21.

44. Ibid., pp. 1955–57.

45. Ibid., pp. 1926–32 (see pp. 894–98 for another go around with MacArthur on these statistics).

46. Ibid., pt. 3, pp. 1969–85, 2060–69, 2236–51, 2284–2334, 2427–40, 2544–88; *San Francisco Call*, Apr. 18, 22, 28, 29, May 4, 20, 21, 22, 23, 27, 1902. Lodge refused to subpoena Major Gardener on the grounds that his "allegations were not properly sustained," according to the *San Francisco Call*, May 2, 1902.

47. S. Doc. 331, pp. 2668–2708, 2752–87.

48. Ibid., pp. 2846–53.

49. Ibid., pp. 2877–78.

50. Ibid., pp. 2857–59; *San Francisco Call*, May 30, 1902.

51. S. Doc. 331, pp. 2933–41, 2958–70, 2979.

52. Ibid., pp. 2962–73, 2979.

53. S. Doc. 422, 57th Cong., 1st Sess.

54. *Boston Herald*, Apr. 11, 12, 17, 30, 1902; *New York Times*, May 1, 1902; *Boston Evening Transcript*, Apr. 16, 1902; *San Francisco Call*, May 6, 1902; *New York Evening Post*, Apr. 8, 9, 1902.

55. *Boston Herald*, Apr. 17, 1902; *New York Sun*, Apr. 24, 26, 1902; *New York Tribune*, Apr. 12, 1902.

56. *Literary Digest* 24 (1902): 629–30.

57. *New York Sun*, May 4, 1902.

58. As cited in *Literary Digest* 24 (1902): 629; *Public Opinion* 32 (1902): 515.

59. *New York Times*, May 2, 1902.

60. Ibid., May 2, 3, 7, 1902. The cartoon appeared in the *New York Journal*, May 5, 1902.

61. *New York Sun*, May 11, 1902.

62. *Central Christian Advocate*, June 4, 1902.

63. *Missionary Review of the World* 15 (1902): 642; Arthur Judson Brown, *The New Era in the Philippines*, p. 7; F. F. Ellinwood, "The Outlook in the Philippines," *Assembly Herald* 5 (1903): 53; *San Francisco Call*, May 23, 1902; *Spirit of Missions* 67 (March 1902), 165–66.

64. As cited in the *San Francisco Call*, May 6, 1902; *New York Evening Post*, Apr. 9, 1902.

65. Anti-Imperialist League, *Ministers Meeting of Protest Against the Atrocities in the Philippines*, pp. 4–6.

66. *San Francisco Call*, Mar. 9, 1902; *London Daily News*, as cited in *Literary Digest* 24 (1902): 439–40.

67. *San Francisco Call*, Apr. 24, 28, May 9, June 2, 1902.

68. Garel A. Grunder and William E. Livezey, *The Philippines and the United States*, pp. 78–82; Peter W. Stanley, *A Nation in the Making: The Philippines and the United States, 1899–1921*, pp. 88–90; *Literary Digest* 24 (1902): 796–97.

69. *New York Times*, May 31, July 5, 1902; *San Francisco Call*, May 31, June 13, 29, July 5, 1902.

70. *New York World*, Apr. 16, 1902.

CHAPTER 13

1. *San Francisco Call*, July 5, 1902; U.S. Adjutant General's Office, *Correspondence Relating to the War with Spain*, vol. 2, pp. 1352–53.

2. *Correspondence*, vol. 2, pp. 1347, 1349; *San Francisco Call*, Apr. 15, May 4, 12, Aug. 19, 25, Oct. 5, 7, 1902.

3. As cited in *Literary Digest* 24 (1902): 599.

4. *San Francisco Call*, Oct. 4, 1902.

5. Ibid., July 17, 1902; Roosevelt to Speck von Sternberg, July 19, 1902, in Elting Morison, ed., *The Letters of Theodore Roosevelt*, vol. 3, pp. 297–98. Paradoxically, the *Call*'s front-page headline for July 17 announced that the "President Retires Samar Commander With Stern Rebuke."

6. *New York Times*, May 3, 1902; *San Francisco Call*, June 13, 22, July 20, 22, 25, 1902.

7. *San Francisco Call*, Aug. 2, 3, 1902.

8. Ibid., Apr. 27, 1902; *Boston Herald*, Aug. 24, 1902; *New York Times*, July 21, 1902.

9. *San Francisco Call*, Dec. 13, 1901, Feb. 18, Mar. 17, 1902.

10. Roosevelt to Root, Feb. 18, 1902, in Morison, *Letters of Theodore Roosevelt*, vol. 3, pp. 232–33.

11. *San Francisco Call*, Mar. 22, 24, 25, 30, 31, 1902; Roosevelt to Kohlsaat, Mar. 24, 1902, in Morison, *Letters of Theodore Roosevelt*, vol. 3, p. 248.

12. *San Francisco Call*, Apr. 10, May 5, 6, 1902; *New York Times*, Apr. 28, 1902.

13. *San Francisco Call*, Apr. 10, Aug. 26, 1902; Roosevelt to Kohlsaat, June 10, 1902, in Morison, *Letters of Theodore Roosevelt*, vol. 3, p. 271.

14. *San Francisco Call*, July 25, Aug. 19, Dec. 7, 1902, Jan. 13, 1903; *New York Times*, Jan. 9, Mar. 3, 1903. Major Glenn had been suspended from duty for one month and fined $50 for using the "water cure." See *San Francisco Call*, Sept. 23, 1902.

15. *San Francisco Call*, Nov. 11, 13, 1902.

16. Ibid., Apr. 28, 29, May 7, 14, June 23, 1903; *Army and Navy Journal* 40 (1903): 675–76.

17. *Literary Digest* 25 (1903): 100; *Public Opinion* 34 (1903): 584; *San Francisco Call*, June 2, 12, July 24, 1902, Apr. 28, 29, May 7, 14, Aug. 8, 1903; Charles Codman, Henry R. Hardon, and Alton B. Parker, *Anti-Imperialism—The Great Issue*, pp. 13–14.

18. *San Francisco Call*, July 31, 1902.

19. Roosevelt to Lodge, Aug. 6, 1903, and to General Young, Aug. 8, 1903, in Morison, *Letters of Theodore Roosevelt*, vol. 3, pp. 545–46.

20. Letters of M. Batson, p. 133, U.S. Military History Research Collection, Carlisle Barracks, Carlisle, Pa. (hereafter Carlisle Collection). The patterns of resistance and collaboration varied from province to province and according to American tactics. See the collection of articles introduced by Michael H. Hunt in *Pacific Historical Review* 48 (1979), particularly those by Glenn May, "Filipino Resistance to American Occupation: Batangas, 1899–1902," pp. 531–56; Norman G. Owen, "Winding Down the War in Albay, 1900–1903," pp. 557–89; Jorge I. Domínguez, "Response to Occupation by the United States: Caliban's Dilemma," pp. 591–605. See also John A. Larkin, *The Pampangans: Colonial Society in a Philippine Province*.

21. See David McCullough, *The Path Between the Seas: The Creation of the Panama Canal, 1870–1914*, chaps. 9–14; E. Berkeley Tompkins, *Anti-Imperialism in the United States: The Great Debate, 1890–1920*, pp. 257–61.

22. "Republican Attitudes Toward Ultimate Philippine Independence," *Literary Digest* 24 (1902): 791–92; Roosevelt to Hoar, June 16, 1902, in Morison, *Letters of Theodore Roosevelt*, vol. 3, p. 276; Codman, Hardon, and Parker, *Anti-Imperialism*, pp. 10–11.

23. Letters of Roosevelt to Cardinal Gibbons, Apr. 25, 1902, to James Francis Smith, July 11, 1904, and to William Howard Taft, July 29, 1904, in Morison, *Letters of Theodore Roosevelt*, vol. 3, p. 779, vol. 4, pp. 854–55, 869.

24. "Republican Attitudes Toward Ultimate Philippine Independence," *Literary Digest* 24 (1902): pp. 791–92; Frederick Bancroft, ed., *Speeches, Correspondence and Political Papers of Carl Schurz*, vol. 4, p. 349.

25. Unidentified newspaper clipping, Aug. 13, 1903, in collection compiled by Mrs. William James, Widener Library, Harvard University, Cambridge, Mass.

26. Letters of Roosevelt to Joseph Cannon, Sept. 2, 12, 1904, and to John Hay, Aug. 12, 1904, in Morison, *Letters of Theodore Roosevelt*, vol. 4, pp. 938–39, 888–89.

27. Codman, Hardon, and Parker, *Anti-Imperialism*, pp. 13–14. See also Anti-Imperialist League, *Report of the Sixth Annual Meeting of the Anti-Imperialist League* (1904), pp. 16–17.

28. *New York Tribune*, Feb. 7, 1903; Peter W. Stanley, *A Nation in the Making: The*

Philippines and the United States, 1899–1921, pp. 81–138; U.S. War Department, *Special Report January 23, 1908*, vol. 3, p. 238; Bonifacio Salamanca, *The Filipino Reaction to American Rule, 1901–1913*; David Joel Steinberg, "An Ambiguous Legacy: Years at War in the Philippines," *Pacific Affairs* 45 (1972): 165–90. Steinberg argues that Aguinaldo was "relegated to the role of the living dead" because his pact with Spain, oath of allegiance to the U.S., execution of Bonifacio, and probable murder of Luna made him a national idol with enormous feet of clay (pp. 176–77). Of course, Aguinaldo also was not an ilustrado, however much he deferred to that class.

29. Letter of Fiske Warren in *Springfield Republican*, Apr. 9, 1906; Stanley, *Nation in the Making*, pp. 128–38, 142–45, 153–57, 194; Michael Cullinane, "The Politics of Collaboration in Tabayas Province: The Early Political Career of Manuel Quezon, 1903–1906," in a forthcoming collection of articles edited by Peter W. Stanley.

30. The best works on these uprisings are David R. Sturtevant, *Popular Uprisings in the Philippines, 1840–1940*; Reynaldo Clemeña Ileto, "*Pasión* and the Interpretation of Change in Tagalog Society," Ph.D. dissertation, Cornell University, 1975; Robert Bruce Cruikshank, "A History of Samar Island, the Philippines, 1768–1898," Ph.D. dissertation, University of Wisconsin, 1975; and Benedict J. Kirkvliet, *The Huk Rebellion: A Study of Peasant Revolt in the Philippines*. For eyewitness accounts of the Moro campaigns, see "Memoirs of Charles Gerhardt," in the papers of Lt. Horace Hobbs, Carlisle Collection; and John R. White, *Bullets and Bolos*. For the collaboration and its political aftereffects, see David Joel Steinberg, *Philippine Collaboration in World War II* and his "Ambiguous Legacy," pp. 179–90.

31. On the American and Filipino maneuverings toward the attainment of Philippine independence, see Stanley, *Nation in the Making*; Theodore Friend, *Between Two Empires: The Ordeal of the Philippines*.

32. Joseph L. Schott, *The Ordeal of Samar*, p. 281.

33. S. Doc. 331, 57th Cong., 1st Sess., pt. 3, p. 2233; H. T. Allen to Clarence R. Edwards, Apr. 3, 1902, Edwards Papers, Massachusetts Historical Society, Boston, Mass. I am endebted to Glenn May for sharing the last reference with me.

34. Sgt. Beverly C. Daley to his brother, Apr. 11, 1901, Carlisle Collection; Frederick Funston, "How the Army Worked to Save San Francisco," *Cosmopolitan* 41 (July 1906), 239–48.

35. *San Francisco Call*, May 8, 10, 1907.

36. *San Francisco Examiner*, Dec. 6, 7, 13, 14, 21, 1907; *San Francisco Call*, Dec. 6, 11, 13, 14, 16, 21, 29, 1907; Frederick Funston, *Memories of Two Wars: Cuba and the Philippines*, pp. 164–65.

37. *Literary Digest* 18 (1899): 678; *New York Times*, Mar. 20, 1960.

38. *New York Times*, Feb. 15, 1970; *Los Angeles Times*, May 18, 1971.

EPILOGUE

1. This fact was revealed in Senator William Fulbright's foreign relations hearings of Feb. 20, 1968, and was best reported in *I. F. Stone's Weekly*, Mar. 4, 1968, pp. 1–8.

2. John McDermott, "Welfare Imperialism in Vietnam," *The Nation*, July 25, 1966, pp. 76–87. For a similar scenario in the Philippines, see David R. Sturtevant, *Popular Uprisings in the Philippines, 1840–1940*, pp. 47–60.

3. General MacArthur reported "5,414 native scouts, including Philippine cavalry," as of June 7, 1901. U.S. Adjutant General's Office, *Correspondence Relating to the*

War with Spain, vol. 2, p. 1275. The most perceptive comparisons of the two antiwar protests, separated by more than six decades, are found in Richard E. Welch, Jr., *Response to Imperialism: The United States and the Philippine-American War, 1899–1902*, pp. xiii–xvi, and Robert L. Beisner, "1898 and 1968: The Anti-Imperialists and the Doves," *Political Science Quarterly* 85 (1970): 187–216. Welch warns that to explain Vietnam "by means of precedents of the Philippine-American War" is to risk "escalating historical parallelism into historical fiction" (p. xiv). For some examples of this error of reading history backwards, see Stuart Creighton Miller, "Our Mylai of 1900," *Transaction* 7 (September 1970), pp. 19–28; William J. Pomeroy, "Pacification in the Philippines," *France-Asie* 21 (1967): 427–46; Luzviminda Francisco, "The First Vietnam: The U.S.-Philippine War of 1899," *Bulletin of Concerned Asian Scholars* 5 (1973): 2–16; Daniel B. Schirmer, *Republic or Empire: American Resistance to the Philippine War*, especially Howard Zinn's introduction.

    4. Some anti-imperialist editors attempted to read an antiwar protest into the efforts of some soldiers to burn down Fort Stevens, near Astoria, Oregon, but the episode appears to have been provoked solely by a local grievance enhanced by alcohol. See *San Francisco Call*, July 22, 23, 24, 1902.

    5. Ibid., Sept. 14, 1899; LaWall's typed lecture is among the papers at the 27th Infantry, U.S.V., U.S. Army Military History Research Collection, Carlisle Barracks, Carlisle, Pa. (hereafter Carlisle Collection).

    6. *The Flag of Destiny*, among the papers of the Minnesota state volunteer regiment, Carlisle Collection.

    7. See clipping on Johnson's comments to protesters of the war in Vietnam, and his "My Life in the Army, 1899–1922," pp. 20, 58, among the papers of the 48th Infantry, U.S.V., Carlisle Collection.

    8. The U.S. Army Military History Research Institute received approximately 70 answers to the questionnaire, and they are filed in the regimental box for each respondent. For those of Blaine, Bryan, and Clapp, see the boxes for the 35th, 44th, and Nebraska state volunteer infantries, respectively, Carlisle Collection. Peck served in the 32nd Infantry, and LaWall in the 27th.

    9. As cited in Robert L. Beisner, *Twelve Against Empire: The Anti-Imperialists, 1898–1900*, p. 142.

    10. Doris Kearns, *Lyndon Johnson and the American Dream*, p. 37; Mary McGrory's column, *San Francisco Chronicle*, Apr. 14, 1975. This is not to imply that there were not other, more complex motives for intervening in both the Philippines' and Vietnam. For an interesting discussion of the "do-goodness" American impulse, see Luigi Barzani, "The Americans," *Harper's* 263 (December 1981): 29–36.

    11. *Atlantic Monthly* 82 (1901): 288. This poem has also been widely reproduced in anthologies, e.g., in *The New Modern American and British Poetry*, ed. Louis Untermeyer (New York, 1922), pp. 75–76.

Bibliography

Every bibliography must be selective to some extent. For the category of primary sources, I have selected those documents and accounts most relied upon in this study and those most representative of the positions taken by Americans contemporary to the war in the Philippines. I have selected those secondary sources that offer the most recent interpretations of imperialism, the war, and related topics. Occasionally, I found it difficult to assign a category and have labeled "primary" any work written either by an author that had been directly involved in the conquest of the Philippines or by a journalist flagrantly espousing a position on one of the issues involved. Thus I placed two fine histories by William Blount and James LeRoy among the primary sources because both served in the Philippines in one capacity or another. I was less reluctant about placing Katherine Mayo's 1925 muckraking account in the same category.

PRIMARY SOURCES

Manuscript Collections
Harvard University, Houghton Library
    Papers of Gamaliel Bradford
    Papers of William James
    Papers of Charles Eliot Norton
Harvard University, Widener Library
    Anti-Imperialist Broadsides and leaflets
    Anti-Imperialist Speeches at Faneuil Hall
    Scrapbook (compiler unknown) containing broadsides, leaflets, circulars, and letters
        pertaining to anti-imperialism, 1898–1901
    Scrapbook, compiled by Mrs. William James, containing clippings and letters pertaining to anti-imperialism, 1898–1904
    United States Imperialism (pamphlet collection). 7 vols.
Library of Congress
    Papers of William Jennings Bryan
    Papers of Andrew Carnegie
    Papers of George Dewey
    Papers of William McKinley
    Papers of Henry Codman Potter

Papers of Theodore Roosevelt
Papers of Elihu Root
Papers of Carl Schurz
Papers of Moorfield Storey
Papers of William Howard Taft
Massachusetts Historical Society
Papers of Charles Francis Adams
Papers of Edward Atkinson
Papers of George Boutwell
Papers of Clarence R. Edwards
Papers of George Frisbee Hoar
Papers of Henry Cabot Lodge
Papers of Moorfield Storey
Papers of Winslow Warren
United States Army Military History Research Collection, Carlisle Barracks, Carlisle, Pa.
The papers of this collection are arranged by regiment, except for the papers of soldiers who were not assigned to a specific regiment, e.g., aides-de-camp, special units (Philippine Scouts), military journalists, or those who served in more than one regiment. The names of individual soldiers, however, are cross-referenced by regiment.
The Flag of Destiny. Washington, D.C.
Papers of all regiments that served in the Philippines between 1898 and 1908
Papers of Captain (Major) Matthew A. Batson
Papers of Major William Carey Brown
Papers of Private (Corporal) Walter Cutter
Papers of Lieutenant Guy Henry, Jr.
Papers of Lieutenant Horace Hobbs
Papers of Major (Brigadier General) William A. Kobbe
Papers of Private (Sergeant) Michael J. Lanihan
Papers of Major General Samuel Baldwin Marks Young

Newspapers
Only the *New York Times* and the *San Francisco Call* were thoroughly reviewed between 1895 and 1904 via each paper's excellent index. The index of the latter has never been published but is available in the newspaper collection of the main library at the University of California at Berkeley. All other newspapers were spot-checked around key dates during those years.

Atlanta Constitution	*Cleveland Plain Dealer*
Baltimore American	*Detroit Journal*
Baltimore Sun	*Freedom* (Manila)
Boston Evening Transcript	*Freie Zeitung* (Newark)
Boston Globe	*Inter-Ocean* (Chicago)
Boston Herald	*Jolo Howler*
Boston Journal	*Louisville Courier-Journal*
Boston Traveller	*New York Evening Post*
Chicago Record	*New York Herald*
Chicago Tribune	*New York Journal*
City and State (Philadelphia)	*New York Sun*

New York Times   San Francisco Chronicle
New York Tribune   San Francisco Examiner
New York World   Seattle Daily Times
Omaha Bee   Seattle Post-Intelligencer
Philadelphia Ledger   Soldier's Banner (Manila)
Philadelphia North American   Springfield Republican
Portland Oregonian   Volks-Zeitung (New York)
Providence Journal   Wall Street Journal
Railway Age   Washington Evening Star
San Francisco Call   Washington Post

Periodicals
The American Monthly Review of Reviews   The Independent
The Arena   Judge
Army and Navy Journal   Leslie's Weekly
Atlantic Monthly   Literary Digest
Century Magazine   Living Age
Collier's Weekly   McClure's Magazine
The Colored American Magazine   Munsey's Magazine
Contemporary Review   The Nation
Cosmopolitan   The Outlook
Everybody's Magazine   Public Opinion
The Forum   Scribner's Magazine
Gunton's Magazine   The Verdict
Harper's Weekly

Religious and Missionary Newspapers and Periodicals
The American Missionary   The Interior
Around the World   The Missionary Record
The Assembly Herald   The Missionary Record (Cumberland)
The Baptist Home Missionary Monthly The Missionary Review of the World
Catholic World   The Missionary Woman's Record
The Central Christian Advocate   The Monitor (San Francisco)
The Christian Advocate   The Pilot (Boston)
The Christian and Missionary Alliance   The Presbyterian Banner
The Christian Evangelist   The Religious Telescope
The Church Standard   The Searchlight
The Foreign Missionary Journal   The Spirit of Missions
The Home Missionary   The Standard (Baptist)
Home Missionary Echoes   Woman's Evangel

Public Documents
The Congressional Record, 1898–1903.
McKinley, William. *Instructions to the President of the Philippine Commission, April 7, 1900.* Washington, D.C., 1900.
Otis, Elwell S. *Official Report, September, 1899–May 5, 1900.* Washington, D.C., 1900.
———. *Official Report to the Adjutant General, U.S. Army.* Washington, D.C., 1899.

The United States and the Philippine Islands, 1900–1904. Washington, D.C., 1905.

U.S. Adjutant General's Office. *Correspondence Relating to the War with Spain.* 2 vols. Washington, D.C., 1902.

U.S. Congress. 55th Congress. Senate Documents 29, 55, 62, 82, 148, 161, 208, 214. House Document 2.

U.S. Congress. 56th Congress. Senate Documents 66, 134, 138, 148, 167, 179, 196, 208, 218, 221, 387, 426, 432, 435. House Documents 1, 2.

U.S. Congress. 57th Congress. Senate Documents 166, 205, 213, 259, 273, 286, 331, 347, 390, 422. House Documents 2, 596.

U.S. Department of State. *Papers Relating to the Foreign Relations of the United States, 1898–1903.* Washington, D.C., 1899–1904.

U.S. Philippine Commission. *Report, January 31, 1900.* Washington, D.C., 1900.

U.S. War Department. *Reports of the Secretary of War, 1899–1903.* Washington, D.C., 1900–1904.

———. *Special Report of the War Department, January 23, 1908.* Washington, D.C., 1908.

Articles, books, pamphlets, and reports

Abbot, A. R. "The Employment of Negroes in the Philippines." *The Anglo-American Magazine* 6 (September 1901): 196–201.

Adams, Brooks. *America's Economic Supremacy.* New York, 1900.

———. "The Spanish War and the Equilibrium of the World." *The Forum* 25 (1898): 641–45.

Adams, Charles Francis. *Imperialism and "The Tracks of Our Forefathers." A Paper Read by Charles Francis Adams Before the Lexington, Massachusetts, Historical Society, Tuesday, December 20, 1898.* Boston, 1899.

Adams, Charles Kendall. "Colonies and Other Dependencies." *The Forum* 33 (1902): 33–46.

Adams, William Llewellyn. *Exploits and Adventures of a Soldier Ashore and Afloat.* New York, 1911.

Adler, Felix. "The Philippine War: Two Ethical Questions." *The Forum* 33 (1902): 387–99.

Aguinaldo, Emilio. "The Story of My Capture." *Everybody's Magazine* 5 (1901): 131–40.

———. *The True Version of the Philippine Revolution.* Tarlac, 1899.

——— and Pacis, V. A. *A Second Look at America.* New York, 1957.

Algué, Fr. Joseph. "The Philippine Question." *The Independent* 52 (1900): 660–63.

American Board of Commissioners for Foreign Missions. *88th Annual Report.* Grand Rapids, Mich., October 4–7, 1898.

Anderson, Brigadier General Thomas M. "Our Role in the Philippines." *North American Review* 170 (1900): 272–83.

Anonymous ("A Filipino"). "Aguinaldo's Case Against the United States." *North American Review* 169 (1899): 425–32.

Anti-Imperialist League. "Address to the Voters of the United States, Adopted by the National Congress of Anti-Imperialists at Indianapolis, Indiana, August 15–16, 1900." *Liberty Tract No. 13.* Chicago, 1900.

———. *Anti-Imperialist Speeches at Faneuil Hall, June 15, 1898.* Boston, 1898.

———. *Arguments Against a So-Called Imperial Policy.* Washington, D.C., n.d.

———. *Broadsides* and assorted pamphlets. Widener Library, Harvard University, Cambridge, Mass.

———. *Imperialism: A National Temptation, Not an Opportunity*. Washington, D.C., n.d.

———. *In the Name of Liberty: Protest Against the Philippine Policy*. Boston, 1899.

———. *Mass Meetings of Protest*. Boston, 1903.

———. *Ministers Meeting of Protest Against the Atrocities in the Philippines*. Boston, 1902.

———. *The Moral and Religious Aspects of the So-Called Anti-Imperialist Policy*. Washington, D.C., n.d.

———. *Report of the Executive Committee of the Anti-Imperialist League, November 25, 1898*. Boston, 1898.

———. *Reports of the Annual Meetings of the Anti-Imperialist League, 1899–1904*. Widener Library, Harvard University, Cambridge, Mass.

———. *Soldiers' Letters, Being Materials for the History of a War of Criminal Aggression*. Boston, 1899.

Apacible, G. *To the American People*. Boston, 1900.

Atkinson, Edward. *The Anti-Imperialist*, Nos. 1–5. Brookline, Mass., 1899.

———. *"Criminal Aggression: By Whom Committed?"; "The Cost of a National Crime"; "The Hell of War and Its Penalties"*. Brookline, Mass., 1899.

———. *The Imperial Chain*. Brookline, Mass., 1899.

———. "Jingoes and Silverites." *North American Review* 161 (1895): 554–60.

Baldwin, F. Spencer. "Some Gains from Expansion." *The Arena* 22 (1895): 570–75.

Baldwin, Simeon E. "The Constitutional Question Incident to the Acquisition and Government by the United States of Island Territories." *Annual Report of the American Historical Association for the Year 1898*. Washington, D.C., 1899.

Ballantine, Charles [Edgar Bellairs]. *As It Is in the Philippines*. New York, 1902.

Bancroft, Frederick, ed. *Speeches, Correspondence and Political Papers of Carl Schurz*. New York, 1913.

——— and Dunning, William A. *The Reminiscences of Carl Schurz*. 3 vols. New York, 1907–08.

Barrett, John. "The Cuba of the Far East." *North American Review* 164 (1897): 172–80.

———. "The Problem of the Philippines." *North American Review* 167 (1898): 259–67.

———. "The Value of the Philippines." *Munsey's Magazine* 21 (1899): 689–703.

Barrows, David P. *A Decade of American Government in the Philippines*. New York, 1914.

Bass, J. F. "Our New Possessions—The Philippines." *Harper's Weekly* 43 (1899): 245.

Bassett, John Spencer. "Stirring Up the Fires of Racial Antipathy." *South Atlantic Quarterly* 2 (1903): 297–305.

Besant, Walter. "The Future of the Anglo Saxon Race." *North American Review* 163 (1896): 129–43.

Blackburn, The Reverend Alexander. "The Imperialism of Righteousness." *The Standard* (Baptist) 45 (1898): 913.

Blount, James H. *The American Occupation of the Philippines, 1898–1912*. New York, 1912.

Bonsal, Stephen. "The Negro Soldier in War and Peace." *North American Review* 186 (1907): 321–37.

Boutwell, George Sewall. *Anti-Imperialism: Address at a Conference of Anti-Imperialists, Boston, May 16, 1899.* New York, 1900.

———. *The President's Policy: War of Conquest Abroad, Degradation of Labor at Home.* Chicago, 1900.

———. *Reminiscences of Sixty Years in Public Affairs.* 2 vols. New York, 1902.

———. *The War of Despotism in the Philippine Islands: Address at Springfield, Mass., September 5, 1899.* Boston, 1899.

Brent, The Right Reverend Charles H. "With God in the Philippines." *The Spirit of Missions* 68 (February 1903): 77–82.

Bridgeman, Raymond L. *Loyal Traitors: A Story of Friendship For the Filipinos.* Boston, 1903.

Brooks, Francis Augustus. *An Arraignment of President McKinley's Policy of Extending by Force the Sovereignty of the United States Over the Philippine Islands.* Boston, 1899.

———. *The Unauthorized and Unlawful Subjugation of Filipinos in the Island of Luzon by President McKinley.* Cambridge, Mass., 1900.

Brown, Arthur Judson. *Memoirs of a Centenarian.* New York, 1957.

———. *The New Era in the Philippines.* New York, 1903.

———. "Some Filipino Characteristics." *Missionary Review of the World* 15 (1902): 518–24.

Brown, John Clifford. *Diary of a Soldier in the Philippines.* Portland, Maine, 1901.

Bryan, William Jennings. *Republic or Empire? The Philippine Question.* Chicago, 1899.

Bulger, James Joseph. *A Vital Question: Should We Free the Philippines?* San Francisco, 1931.

Burgess, John William. "The Decisions of the Supreme Court in the Insular Cases." *Political Science Quarterly* 16 (1901): 486–504.

———. "How May the United States Govern Its Extra-Continental Territory." *Political Science Quarterly* 14 (1899): 1–18.

Callahan, James Morton. *American Relations in the Pacific.* Baltimore, 1901.

Carnegie, Andrew. "Americanism Versus Imperialism." *North American Review* 167 (1898): 362–72.

———. *Autobiography.* New York, 1930.

———. "Distant Possessions—The Parting of the Ways." *North American Review* 167 (1898): 239–48.

Chamberlain, Fred C. *The Blow From Behind.* Boston, 1903.

Clarke, George Sydenham. "Imperial Responsibilities: A National Gain." *North American Review* 168 (1899): 129–41.

Cleveland, Grover. *The Letters of Grover Cleveland.* Edited by Allan Nevins. Boston, 1933.

Clowes, William L. "American Expansion and the Inheritance of the Race." *The Fortnightly Review* 70 (1898): 884–92.

Codman, Charles; Hardon, Henry R.; and Parker, Alton B. *Anti-Imperialism—The Great Issue.* Boston, 1904.

Coggins, Albert H. "The Menace of Imperialism." *The Arena* 24 (1900): 345–50.

Cohen, Solomon Solis. "The Spectre of Imperialism." *The Arena* 20 (1898): 445–52.

Conant, Charles A. "The Economic Basis of Imperialism." *North American Review* 167 (1898): 326–40.

Condict, Alice Bryan. *Old Glory and the Gospel in the Philippines*. Chicago, 1902.

Crosby, Ernest. *Captain Jinks Hero*. New York, 1902.

———. "The Philippine Question." *The Arena* 25 (1902): 10–11.

Curtis, Mary. *The Black Soldiers, or the Colored Boys in the United States Army*. Washington, D.C., 1915.

Davis, Mrs. Jefferson. "Why We Do Not Want the Philippines." *The Arena* 23 (1900): 1–4.

Davis, Oscar K. "Dewey's Capture of Manila." *McClure's Magazine* 13 (June 1899): 171–83.

———. "The Real Aguinaldo." *Everybody's Magazine* 5 (1901): 141–44.

Davis, William H. "The 'National Dirty' Delusion." *The Arena* 21 (1899): 736–40.

Democratic Campaign Book, 1898. Washington, D.C., 1898.

Denby, Charles. "The Constitution and the Flag." *The Forum* 29 (1900): 257–62.

———. "Criticisms of Our Philippine Policy." *The Independent* 53 (1901): 649–51.

———. "Do We Owe Independence to the Filipinos?" *The Forum* 29 (1900): 401–08.

Dewey, Admiral George W. *Autobiography of George Dewey, Admiral of the Navy*. New York, 1913.

Doster, Frank. "Will the Philippines Pay?" *The Arena* 25 (1901): 465–70.

Dunn, Arthur W. *From Harrison to Harding: A Personal Narrative Covering a Third of a Century, 1883–1921*. New York, 1922.

Dunne, Finley Peter. *Mr. Dooley in Peace and War*. Boston, 1898.

———. *Mr. Dooley in the Hearts of His Countrymen*. Boston, 1899.

———. "Mr. Dooley on the Philippines." *Anti-Imperialist Broadside*, No. 2. Boston, 1898.

———. *Mr. Dooley's Opinions*. Boston, 1901.

Eddy, George Sherwood. *The New Era in Asia*. New York, 1913.

Eighth Army Corps War Songs. Manila, 1901.

Ellinwood, F. F. "The Outlook in the Philippines." *The Assembly Herald* 5 (1903): 53–57.

———. "An Urgent Call From Manila." *The Assembly Herald* 1 (1899): 300–04.

Faust, Karl Irving. *Campaigning in the Philippines*. San Francisco, 1899.

Ferrar, Dean F. W. "Imperialism and Christianity." *North American Review* 171 (1900): 289–95.

Fiske, John. "Manifest Destiny." *Harper's Magazine* 70 (1885): 578–89.

Flowers, Benjamin O. "Some Dead Sea Fruit of Our War of Subjugation." *The Arena* 27 (1902): 647–53.

Forbes, William C.; Worcester, Dean C.; and Carpenter, Frank W. *The Friar Land Inquiry: Philippine Government*. Manila, 1910.

Foreman, John. "The Americans in the Philippines." *Contemporary Review* 86 (1904): 392–404.

———. *The Philippine Islands*. New York, 1899.

———. "Spain and the Philippine Islands." *Contemporary Review* 74 (1898): 20–33.

Foster, Burnside. "Leprosy and the Hawaiian Annexation." *North American Review* 167 (1898): 300–06.

Freeman, Needom N. *A Soldier in the Philippines*. New York, 1901.

Funston, Frederick. "The Capture of Aguinaldo." *Scribner's Magazine* 50 (1911): 522–36.

————. "How the Army Worked to Save San Francisco." *Cosmopolitan* 41 (July 1906): 239–48.

————. *Memories of Two Wars: Cuba and the Philippines.* New York, 1911.

Gantenbein, Brigadier General C. U. *The Official Records of the Oregon Volunteers in the Spanish-American War and the Philippine Insurrection.* Salem, Ore., 1903.

Ganzhorn, John W. *I've Killed Men: An Epic of Early Arizona.* New York, 1959.

George, Jesse. *Our Army and Navy in the Orient.* Manila, 1899.

Giddings, Franklin H. *Democracy and Empire: With Studies of Their Psychological, Economic and Moral Foundations.* New York, 1900.

————. "Destinies of Democracy." *Political Science Quarterly* 11 (1896): 716–31.

————. "Imperialism." *Political Science Quarterly* 13 (1898): 585–605.

————. *The Principles of Sociology.* New York, 1902.

Halstead, Murat. *Aguinaldo and His Captor.* Cincinnati, 1901.

————. "American Annexation and Armament." *The Forum* 24 (1897): 56–66.

————. *The Story of the Philippines: The Eldorado of the Orient.* New York, 1898.

Harrison, Francis Burton. *The Corner-Stone of Philippine Independence.* New York, 1922.

Hawes, H. B. *Philippine Uncertainty, An American Problem.* New York, 1932.

Hibbard, The Reverend D. S. "Missions at the Seat of War." *The Assembly Herald* 1 (1899): 183–84.

Hill, David Jayne. "The War and the Extension of Civilization." *The Forum* 26 (1899): 650–55.

Hoar, George Frisbee. *Autobiography of Seventy Years.* 2 vols. New York, 1903.

————. *No Right Under the Constitution to Hold Subject States.* Boston, 1900.

————. *Our Duty to the Philippines.* Boston, 1900.

Hobbs, Horace. *Kris and Krags: Among the Moros, 1901–1905.* New York, 1962.

Holli, Melvin G., ed. "A View of the American Campaign Against 'Filipino Insurgents': 1900." *Philippine Studies* 17 (1969): 97–111.

Huffcut, Ernest W. *The Philippine Problem in the Light of American International Policy.* Utica, N.Y., 1902.

Irwin, William. "The First Fight with the Insurgents." *The Independent* 51:1 (1899): 886–88.

James, Mrs. William, comp. "Scrapbook Containing Letters and Clippings Pertaining to Anti-Imperialism Between 1898 and 1904." Widener Library, Harvard University, Cambridge, Mass.

Jordan, David Starr. "The Control of the Tropics." *Gunton's Magazine* 8 (1890): 408–10.

————. *Imperial Democracy.* New York, 1899.

————. *The Question of the Philippines.* New York, 1899.

Judson, Henry Pratt. "Our Federal Constitution and the Government of Tropical Territories." *American Monthly Review of Reviews* 19 (1899): 67–75.

Kennan, George. "The Philippines: Present Conditions and Possible Courses." *The Outlook* 67 (1901): 576–84.

Kennon, L. W. V. "The Katipunan of the Philippines." *North American Review* 173 (1901): 208–20.

King, Charles H. "In the Blood Stained Trenches at Manila." *San Francisco Call Sunday Magazine,* May 14, 1899.

King, William Nephew. *The Story of the Spanish American War and Revolt in the Philippines.* New York, 1902.

Kohlsaat, Herman H. *From McKinley to Harding: Personal Recollections of Our Presidents*. New York, 1923.

Laughlin, James Lawrence. *Patriotism and Imperialism*. Chicago, 1899.

Lemus, Rienzi B. "The Enlisted Man in Action, Or the Colored American Soldier in the Philippines." *Colored American Magazine* 5 (May 1902): 46–54.

LeRoy, James A. *The Americans in the Philippines*. 2 vols. Boston, 1914.

Lodge, Henry Cabot. "Our Failure in the Philippines." *Harper's Magazine* 160 (1930): 209–18.

———, ed. *Selections from the Correspondence of Theodore Roosevelt and Henry Cabot Lodge*. 2 vols. New York, 1925.

Mabey, Charles R. *The Utah Batteries, A History*. Salt Lake City, 1900.

Mabini, Apolinario. *Memoirs of the Philippine Revolution*. Translated by Alfredo S. Veloso. Quezon City, 1964.

———. *The Philippine Revolution*. Translated by Leon Guerrero. Manila, 1969.

McClure, Phillips. *Republic Or Empire?* Boston, 1900.

McGhee, Frederick. "Another View." *Howard's American Magazine* 5 (October 1900): 92–96.

McKim, The Reverend Randolph H. "Religious Reconstruction in Our New Possessions." *The Outlook* 63 (1899): 504–06.

McKinley, William. *Speeches and Addresses of William McKinley. From March 1, 1897, to May 30, 1900*. New York, 1900.

McMaster, James Bach. "Annexation and Universal Suffrage." *The Forum* 26 (1898): 393–402.

Mahan, Alfred Thayer. "The Transvaal and the Philippine Islands." *The Independent* 52 (1900): 289–91.

———. "The United States Looking Outward." *Atlantic Monthly* 66 (1890): 816–24.

Markey, Joseph Ignacious. *From Iowa to the Philippines: A History of Company M, Fifty-First Iowa Infantry*. Red Oak, Iowa, 1900.

Martin, Harold. "The Manila Censorship." *The Forum* 31 (1901): 462–71.

Mayo, Katherine. *The Isles of Fear: The Truth About the Philippines*. New York, 1925.

Mayo, W. Hazeltine. "What Shall Be Done with the Philippines?" *North American Review* 167 (1898): 385–92.

Miller, Kelly. "The Effect of Imperialism on the Negro Race." *Howard's American Magazine* 5 (October 1900): 87–91.

Millet, Francis. *The Expedition to the Philippines*. New York, 1899.

Morgan, John Tyler. "The Future of the Negro." *North American Review* 139 (1884): 81–84.

———. "What Shall We Do with the Conquered Islands?" *North American Review* 166 (1898): 641–46.

Morgan, The Reverend T. J. "O America Should Retain the Philippines to Provide Them with Democracy and 'Soul Liberty.'" *Baptist Home Missionary Monthly* 21 (February 1899): 39–41.

Morison, Elting, ed. *The Letters of Theodore Roosevelt*. 8 vols. Cambridge, Mass., 1951–54.

Mott, John R. *Strategic Points in the World's Conquest*. Chicago, 1897.

Neely, F. Tennyson, ed. *Fighting in the Philippines*. New York, 1899.

Neil, Henry. *Exciting Experiences in Our War with Spain and the Filipinos*. Chicago, 1899.

Nevins, Allan, ed. *The Letters of Grover Cleveland*. Boston, 1933.

Olney, Richard. "Growth of Our Foreign Policy." *Atlantic Monthly* 85 (1900): 289–301.

————. "International Isolation of the United States." *Atlantic Monthly* 81 (1898): 577–88.

Palma, Rafael. *My Autobiography*. Manila, 1953.

————. *Our History*. Manila, 1929.

Palmer, Frederick. "White Man and Brown Man in the Philippines." *Scribner's Magazine* 27 (1900): 76–86.

————. *With My Own Eyes*. Indianapolis, 1932.

Parsons, Frank. "The Giant Issue of 1900." *The Arena* 23 (1900): 561–65.

Patterson, Thomas McDonald. *The Fruits of Imperialism*. Boston, 1902.

Peen, Julius A. *A Narrative of the Campaign in Northern Luzon of the Second Battalion, 34th U.S. Volunteer Infantry*. Batavia, Ohio, 1933.

Peffer, William A. *Americanism and the Philippines*. New York, 1900.

Pentecost, The Reverend George. "The Imperialism of Jesus." *The Missionary Record* (Cumberland) 25 (December 1899): 147–49.

Pettigrew, Richard F. *Imperial Washington*. Chicago, 1922.

Philippine Information Society. *Facts About the Filipinos*. Boston, 1900–1901.

————. *The Outbreak of Hostilities*, no. 6. Boston, 1901.

————. *Our Relations with the Insurgents*. Boston, 1901.

————. *The Parting of the Ways*. Boston, 1901.

————. *The Philippine Review*. New York, 1901–1902.

————. *The Philippine Revolution*. Boston, 1901.

————. "The Report of the First Philippine Commission." *Pamphlet Number IV*. Boston, 1900.

Pierce, Edwin C. *Expansion Means Industrial Disaster*. Boston, 1900.

Pohlman, Andrew. *My Army Experience*. New York, 1906.

Potter, Bishop Henry Codman. "China Traits and Western Blunders." *Century Magazine* 60 (1900): 921–30.

————. *The East of To-Day and To-Morrow*. New York, 1902.

————. "National Bigness or Greatness—Which?" *North American Review* 168 (1899): 433–44.

————. "The Problem of the Philippines." *Century Magazine* 61 (1900): 129–35.

Prentiss, A., ed. *The History of the Utah Volunteers in the Spanish-American War and in the Philippine Islands*. Salt Lake City, 1900.

Presbyterian Church. *62nd Annual Report of the Board of Foreign Missions of the Presbyterian Church in the United States*. New York, 1899.

Quezon, Manuel. *The Good Fight*. New York, 1946.

Radcliffe, The Reverend Wallace. "Presbyterian Imperialism." *The Assembly Herald* 1 (1899): 5–6.

Reid, Whitelaw. *Making Peace with Spain: The Diary of Whitelaw Reid, September to December, 1898*. Edited by H. Wayne Morgan. Austin, 1965.

————. *The Problems of Expansion*. New York, 1900.

Reinsch, Paul S. *Colonial Government: An Introduction to the Study of Colonial Institutions*. New York, 1902.

————. "The New Conquest of the World." *World's Work* 21 (1901): 425–31.

————. "Problems of Government in the Philippines." *The Arena* 24 (1900): 281–92.

Republican Campaign Book, 1900. Washington, D.C., 1900.

Ricarte, Artemio. *Memoirs of General Artemio Ricarte*. Manila, 1963.

Richardson, George A. "The Subjugation of Inferior Races." *The Overland Monthly* 35 (January 1900): 49–60.

Robinson, Albert Gardner. *The Philippines: The War and the People*. New York, 1901.

Rodgers, James B. "The Door that Dewey's Cannon Opened." *The Assembly Herald* 1 (1899): 253–55.

———. *The Importance of Time in the Solution of the Negro Problem*. New York, n.d.

Roosevelt, Theodore. "The Progressive and the Colored Man." *The Outlook* 150 (1912): 909–12.

Root, Elihu. *The Military and Colonial Policy of the United States: Addresses and Reports*. Cambridge, Mass., 1916.

Rowland, Dr. Henry. "Fighting Life in the Philippines." *McClure's Magazine* 19 (1902): 241–47.

Russell, Henry B. *The Story of Two Wars: An Illustrated History of Our War with Spain and Our War with the Filipinos*. New York, 1899.

Scanland, J. M. "Our Asiatic Missionary Enterprise." *The Arena* 24 (1900): 258–67.

Scarborough, W. S. *The Educated Negro and His Mission*. Washington, D.C., 1903.

———. "The Negro and Our New Possessions." *The Forum* 31 (1901): 341–49.

Schurz, Carl. "Imperialism." *The Independent* 50 (1898).

———. *The Policy of Imperialism*. Chicago, 1899.

———. "Thoughts on American Expansion." *The Century Illustrated Monthly Magazine* 56 (1898): 781–88.

Sheridan, Richard B. *The Filipino Martyrs*. New York, 1900.

Slavens, T. H. *Scouting in Northern Luzon, Philippine Islands, 1899–1900*. New York, 1947.

Smith, Charles Emory. "McKinley in the Cabinet Room." *Saturday Evening Post*, Oct. 11, 1902, pp. 6–7.

Smith, Goldwyn. "Anglo Saxon Union." *North American Review* 157 (1898): 170–85.

———. "Imperialism in the United States." *The Contemporary Review* 75 (1899): 620–28.

Sonnichsen, Albert. *Ten Months a Captive Among the Filipinos*. New York, 1901.

Spooner, John C. *Imperialism: A Forced and Fictitious Issue*. Washington, D.C., 1900.

Steward, Charles. "Manila and Its Opportunities." *The Colored American Magazine* 31 (August 1901): 255.

Storey, Moorfield, and Codman, Julian. *Secretary Root's Record: "Marked Severities" in Philippine Warfare. An Analysis of the Law and Facts Bearing on the Action and Utterances of President Roosevelt and Secretary Root*. Boston, 1902.

——— and Lichauco, M. P. *The Conquest of the Philippines by the United States, 1898–1925*. New York, 1925.

Strong, Josiah. *Expansion Under New World Conditions*. New York, 1900.

———. *Our Country: Its Possible Future and Its Present Crisis*. New York, 1885.

Stunz, The Reverend Homer C. *The Philippines and the Far East*. New York, 1904.

———. "The 'Water Cure' From a Missionary Point of View." *Central Christian Advocate*, June 4, 1902.

Sumner, William Graham. "The Fallacy of Territorial Expansion." *The Forum* 21 (1896): 414–19.

Swift, Morrison Isaac. *Advent of Empire*. Los Angeles, 1900.

————. *Imperialism and Liberty.* Los Angeles, 1899.

Taylor, James O. *The Massacre of Balangiga: Being an Authentic Account By Several of the Few Survivors.* Joplin, Mo., 1931.

Taylor, John R. M., comp. "The Philippine Insurrection Against the United States." Galley proofs, 5 vols. National Archives, Washington, D.C., 1906.

Thayer, James Bradley. *Our New Possessions.* Cambridge, Mass., 1899. A reprint from the *Harvard Law Review,* March 1899.

Tillman, Benjamin R. "Bryan or McKinley: Causes of Southern Opposition to Imperialism." *North American Review* 171 (1900): 439–46.

Tourgée, Albion. "The Twentieth Century Peace Makers." *Contemporary Review* 81 (1899): 886–908.

Turner, Frederick Jackson. *The Frontier in American History.* New York, 1920.

Twain, Mark. "A Defense of General Funston." *North American Review* 174 (1902): 613–24.

————. "To the Person Sitting in Darkness." *North American Review* 172 (1901): 161-76.

University of Chicago. *Register, 1900–1901.* Chicago, 1901.

Valentine, John Joseph. *Imperial Democracy.* San Francisco, 1899.

Van Bergen, R. "Expansion Unavoidable." *Harper's Weekly Magazine* 44 (1900): 885–86.

Van Dyke, Henry. "The American Birthright and the Philippine Pottage." *The Independent* 50 (1898): 1579–85.

Van Meter, Henry Hooker. *The Truth About the Philippines from Official Records and Authentic Sources.* Chicago, 1900.

Vest, George G. "Objections to Annexing the Philippines." *North American Review* 169 (1899): 564–76.

Von Holst, Hermann E. "Some Expansionist Inconsistencies and False Analogies." *University of Chicago Record* 3 (1899): 339–45.

Villa, Simeon. *Aguinaldo's Odyssey, As Told in the Diaries of Colonel Villa.* Manila, 1963.

Welsh, Herbert. *The Other Man's Country: An Appeal to Conscience.* Philadelphia, 1900.

Wheeler, Benjamin Ide. "The Old World and the New." *Atlantic Monthly* 82 (1898): 145–53.

Whitmarsh, Phelps H. "The Situation in Manila." *The Outlook* 64 (1900): 862–67.

————. "Through Filipino Eyes." *The Outlook* 63 (1899): 835–39.

Wilcox, Marrion, ed. *Harper's Weekly History of the War in the Philippines.* New York, 1900.

Wildman, Edwin. *Aguinaldo: A Narrative of Filipino Ambitions.* Boston, 1901.

Willis, Henry Parker. *Our Philippine Problem: A Study of American Colonial Policy.* New York, 1905.

Wilson, Woodrow. "The Ideals of America." *Atlantic Monthly* 90 (1902): 721–34.

Winslow, Erving. "The Anti-Imperialist League." *The Independent* 51 (1899): 1347–51.

————. "The Anti-Imperialist Position." *North American Review* 171 (1900): 460–68.

Woolsey, Theodore S. "The Government Dependencies." *Supplement to the Annals of the American Academy of Political and Social Sciences* 13 (1899): 6–8.

————. "The Legal Aspects of Aguinaldo's Capture." *The Outlook* 67 (1901): 855–59.

Worcester, Dean C. *The Philippines: Past and Present.* 2 vols. New York, 1951.

Younghusband, G. J. *The Philippines and Round About.* New York, 1899.

SECONDARY SOURCES

Doctoral Dissertations and Unpublished Studies

Appel, John C. "The Relationship of American Labor to United States Imperialism, 1895–1905." Ph.D. dissertation, University of Wisconsin, 1950.

Barnes, Arthur M. "American Intervention in Cuba and the Annexation of the Philippines: An Analysis of Public Discussion." Ph.D. dissertation, Cornell University, 1948.

Clymer, Kenton J. "Protestant Missionaries and American Colonialism in the Philippines, 1899–1919: Attitudes, Perceptions and Involvement." Forthcoming in collection edited by Peter W. Stanley.

Cruikshank, Robert Bruce. "A History of Samar Island, the Philippines, 1768–1898." Ph.D. dissertation, University of Wisconsin, 1975.

Cullinane, Michael. "The Politics of Collaboration in Tabayas Province: The Early Political Career of Manuel Quezon, 1903–1906." Forthcoming in collection edited by Peter W. Stanley.

Dozer, Donald Marquand. "Anti-Imperialism in the United States, 1865–1895: Opposition to Overseas Expansion." Ph.D. dissertation, Harvard University, 1936.

Ileto, Reynaldo Clemeña. "*Pasión* and the Interpretation of Change in Tagalog Society." Ph.D. dissertation, Cornell University, 1975.

Kennedy, Philip W. "The Concept of Racial Superiority and United States Imperialism, 1890–1910." Ph.D. dissertation, St. Louis University, 1962.

King, Peter. "The White Man's Burden." Ph.D. dissertation, University of California at Los Angeles, 1958.

Matré, Richard A. "The Chicago Press and Imperialism, 1899–1902." Ph.D. dissertation, Northwestern University, 1971.

May, Glenn A. "The Pacification of Batangas." In author's possession, n.d.

———. "Private Presher and Sergeant Vergara: The 'Underside' of the Philippine American War." Forthcoming in collection edited by Peter W. Stanley.

Miller, Stuart Creighton. "The American Soldier and the Conquest of the Philippines." Forthcoming in collection edited by Peter W. Stanley.

Mulrooney, Virginia F. "No Victor, No Vanquished: American Military Government in the Philippine Islands, 1899–1901." Ph.D. dissertation, University of California at Los Angeles, 1975.

Owen, Norman G. "Americans in the Abaca Trade: Peele, Hubbard, & Co., 1856–1875." Forthcoming in collection edited by Peter W. Stanley.

Synder, Philip Lyman. "Mission, Empire, or Force of Circumstance? A Study of the American Decision to Annex the Philippine Islands." Ph.D. dissertation, Stanford University, 1972.

Stanley, Peter W. "'The Voice of Worcester is the Voice of God': How One American Found Fulfillment in the Philippines." Forthcoming in collection edited by Peter W. Stanley.

Published Articles and Books

Abaya, Hernando J. *Betrayal in the Philippines.* New York, 1946.

———. "Taft's Views of the Filipinos." *Asian Studies* 6 (1968): 237–47.

Agoncillo, Teodoro. *The Fateful Years.* 2 vols. Quezon City, 1965.

――――. *Malolos: The Crisis of the Republic.* Quezon City, 1960.

――――. *The Revolt of the Masses: The Story of Bonifacio and the Katipunan.* Quezon City, 1956.

Alejandrino, Jose. *The Price of Freedom.* Manila, 1949.

Alfonso, Oscar M. "Taft's early View of the Filipinos." *Solidarity* (Manila) 4 (1969): 52–58.

――――. *Theodore Roosevelt and the Philippines, 1897–1907.* Quezon City, 1970.

Anderson, Gerald H., ed. *Studies in Philippine Church History.* Ithaca, 1969.

Arens, Richard, S.V.D. "The Early Pulahan Movement in Samar and Leyte." *Journal of History* 7 (1959): 303–71.

――――. "Witches and Witchcraft in Leyte and Samar Islands, Philippines." *Philippine Journal of Science* 85 (1956): 451–65.

Armstrong, William M. *E. L. Godkin and American Foreign Policy, 1865–1900.* New York, 1957.

Auxier, George W. "The Propaganda Activities of the Cuban Junta in Precipitating the Spanish American War." *American Historical Review* 19 (1939): 293–98.

Baclagon, Uldarico S. *Philippine Campaigns.* Manila, 1952.

Bailey, Thomas A. "America's Emergence as a World Power: The Myth and the Verity." *Pacific Historical Review* 30 (1961): 1–16.

――――. *A Diplomatic History of the American People.* New York, 1940.

――――. *The Man in the Street.* New York, 1948.

――――. "Was the Election of 1900 a Mandate on Imperialism?" *Mississippi Valley Historical Review* 24 (1937): 43–52.

Baker, George W. "Benjamin Harrison and Hawaiian Annexation: A Reinterpretation." *Pacific Historical Review* 33 (1964): 295–305.

Baron, Harold. "Anti-Imperialism and the Democrats." *Science and Society* 21 (1957): 222–39.

Baylen, Joseph O., and Moore, John Hammond. "Senator John Tyler Morgan and Negro Colonization in the Philippines, 1900–1902." *Phylon* 29 (1968): 65–73.

Beadles, John A. "The Debate in the United States Concerning Philippine Independence, 1912–1916." *Philippine Studies* 16 (1968): 421–41.

Beale, Howard K. *Theodore Roosevelt and the Rise of America to World Power.* New York, 1962.

Becker, William H. "American Manufacturers and Foreign Markets, 1870–1900: Business Historians and the 'New Economic Determinists.'" *Business History Review* 47 (1973): 466–81.

――――. "Foreign Markets for Iron and Steel, 1893–1913: A New Perspective on the Williams School of Diplomatic History." *Pacific Historical Review* 44 (1975): 233–48.

Beisner, Robert L. "1898 and 1968: The Anti-Imperialists and the Doves." *Political Science Quarterly* 85 (1970): 187–216.

――――. *From the Old Diplomacy to the New, 1865–1900.* New York, 1975.

――――. *Twelve Against Empire: The Anti-Imperialists, 1898–1900.* New York, 1968.

Bemis, Samuel Flagg. *A Diplomatic History of the United States.* New York, 1955.

Bernstein, Barton J., and Leib, Franklin A. "Progressive Republican Senators and American Imperialism, 1898–1916: A Reappraisal." *Mid-America* 50 (1968): 163–205.

Bernstein, David. *The Philippine Story.* New York, 1947.

Bertoff, Rowland Tappan. "Taft and MacArthur, 1900: A Study in Civil-Military Relations." *World Politics* 5 (1953): 196–213.

Blodgett, Geoffery T. "The Mind of the Boston Mugwump." *The Mississippi Valley Historical Review* 48 (1962): 614–34.

Bowers, Claude. *Beveridge and the Progressive Era.* Boston, 1932.

Braisted, William R. *The United States Navy in the Pacific, 1897–1909.* Austin, Tex., 1958.

Campbell, Charles S. *Anglo-American Understanding, 1893–1903.* Baltimore, 1957.

———. *Special Business Interests and the Open Door Policy.* New Haven, 1961.

———. *The Transformation of American Foreign Relations, 1865–1900.* New York, 1976.

Chaput, Donald. "The American Press and General Vincente Lukban, Hero of Samar." *Leyte-Samar Studies* 8 (1974): 21–32.

Cherny, Robert W. *Populism, Progressivism, and the Transformation of Nebraska Politics.* Lincoln, Neb., 1981.

Clariño, José V. *General Aguinaldo and Philippine Politics.* Manila, 1928.

Coffman, Edward M. *The Hilt of the Sword: The Career of Peyton C. March.* Madison, 1966.

Cole, Wayne S. *An Interpretive History of American Foreign Relations.* Homewood, Ill., 1968.

Coletta, Paolo E. "Bryan, McKinley, and the Treaty of Paris." *Pacific Historical Review* 26 (1957): 131–46.

———. "McKinley, the Peace Negotiations, and the Acquisition of the Philippines." *Pacific Historical Review* 30 (1961): 341–50.

———. *William Jennings Bryan: Political Evangelist.* Lincoln, Neb., 1964.

Coolidge, L. A. *An Old Fashioned Senator: Orville H. Platt.* New York, 1910.

Corpuz, Onofre. *The Philippines.* New York, 1966.

Crippen, Harlan R. "Philippine Agrarian Unrest: Historical Backgrounds." *Science and Society* 10 (1964): 337–60.

Cropp, Richard. *"The Coyotes": A History of the South Dakota National Guard.* Mitchell, S.D., 1962.

Cullinane, Michael. "Implementing the New Order: The Structure and Supervision of Local Government During the Taft Era." In *Compadre Colonialism,* edited by Norman Owen. Ann Arbor, 1971.

Davis, Horace B. "American Labor and Imperialism Prior to World War I." *Science and Society* 27 (1963): 70–76.

Davis, Wallace E. *Patriotism on Parade: The Story of Veterans and Hereditary Organizations in America, 1783–1900.* Cambridge, Mass., 1955.

Dixon, Thomas. *The Leopard's Spots: A Romance of the White Man's Burden.* New York, 1962.

Domínguez, Jorge I. "Response to Occupation by the United States: Caliban's Dilemma." *Pacific Historical Review* 48 (1979): 591–605.

Dorwart, Jeffery M. *The Pigtail War: American Involvement in the Sino-Japanese War of 1894–1895.* Amherst, Mass., 1975.

Ducay, Bernardo. *The Struggle of the Filipinos for Liberty.* Manila, 1929.

Dulles, Foster Rhea. *America in the Pacific: A Century of Expansion.* New York, 1932.

Eggert, Gerald G. *Richard Olney: Evolution of a Statesman.* University Park, Pa., 1974.

Epistola, S. V. "The Hong Kong Junta." *Philippine Social Science and Humanities* 26 (1961): 3–65.

Fairbank, John King. "'American China Policy' to 1898: A Misperception." *Pacific Historical Review* 39 (1970): 409–20.

———, ed. *The Missionary Enterprise in China and America.* Cambridge, Mass., 1974.

Farrell, John T. "Archbishop Ireland and Manifest Destiny." *Catholic Historical Review* 33 (1947): 269–301.

———. "Background of the 1902 Taft Mission to Rome." *Catholic Historical Review* 36 (1950): 1–32.

Fernandez, Leandro H. *The Philippine Republic.* New York, 1926.

Feuss, Claude. *Carl Schurz: Reformer.* New York, 1932.

Field, James A. "American Imperialism: The Worst Chapter in Almost Any Book." *American Historical Review* 83 (1978): 644–83.

Fieldhouse, D. K. *Economics and Empire 1830–1914.* Ithaca, 1973.

———, ed. *The Theory of Capitalist Imperialism.* New York, 1967.

Fine, Sidney. *Laissez Faire and the General Welfare State: A Study of Conflict in American Thought, 1865–1901.* Ann Arbor, 1956.

Fletcher, Marvin E. *The Black Soldier and Officer in the United States Army, 1891–1917.* Columbus, Mo., 1974.

Foner, Philip S. *History of the Labor Movement.* 2 vols. New York, 1955.

Foronda, Marcelino. "The Canonization of Rizal." *Journal of History* 7 (1950): 1–48.

———. *Cults Honoring Rizal.* Manila, 1961.

Francisco, Luzviminda. "The First Vietnam: The U.S.-Philippine War of 1899." *Bulletin of Concerned Asian Scholars* 5 (1973): 2–16.

Frederickson, George M. *The Black Image in the White Mind.* New York, 1971.

Friedel, Frank. *The Splendid Little War.* Boston, 1958.

Friend, Theodore. *Between Two Empires: The Ordeal of the Philippines.* New Haven, 1965.

Garraty, John A. *Henry Cabot Lodge.* New York, 1953.

Garrett, Shirley Stone. "China Missions and the Perils of Benevolence." *Worldview* 15 (1972): 15–19.

Gates, John Morgan. *Schoolbooks and Krags: The United States Army in the Philippines.* Westport, Conn., 1973.

Gatewood, Williard B. "Black Americans and the Quest for Empire." *Journal of Southern History* 38 (1972): 545–66.

———. *Black Americans and the White Man's Burden, 1898–1903.* Urbana, Ill., 1975.

———. *"Smoked Yankees" and the Struggle for Empire: Letters from Negro Soldiers, 1898–1902.* Urbana, Ill., 1971.

Gibson, William M. "Mark Twain and Howells: Anti-Imperialists." *New England Quarterly* 20 (1947): 435–70.

Gillett, Frederick H. *George Frisbee Hoar.* Boston, 1934.

Glad, Paul W. *The Trumpet Soundeth: William Jennings Bryan and His Democracy, 1896–1912.* Lincoln, Neb., 1960.

Golay, Frank H. *The Philippines: Public Policies and National Development.* Ithaca, 1962.

Goodman, Grant K. "General Artemio Ricarte and Japan." *Journal of Southeast Asian History* 7 (1960): 48–60.

Graebner, Norman A. "The Year of Transition—1898." In *An Uncertain Tradition: American Secretaries of State in the Twentieth Century*, edited by Norman A. Graebner. New York, 1961.

Graff, Henry, ed. *Imperialism and the Philippine Insurrection*. Boston, 1969.

Grunder, Garel A., and Livezey, William E. *The Philippines and the United States*. Norman, Okla., 1951.

Harbaugh, William Henry. *Power and Responsibility: The Life and Times of Theodore Roosevelt*. New York, 1961.

Harrington, Frederick W. "The Anti-Imperialist Movement in the United States, 1898–1900." *Mississippi Valley Historical Review* 22 (1936): 211–30.

Healy, David. *U.S. Expansion: The Imperialistic Urge in the 1890's*. Madison, Wis., 1970.

Hendrick, Burton J. *The Life of Andrew Carnegie*. 2 vols. New York, 1932.

———. *The Training of an American*. Boston, 1928.

Hendrickson, Kenneth E., Jr., "Reluctant Expansionist: Jacob Gould Schurman and the Philippine Question." *Pacific Historical Review* 36 (1967): 405–21.

Hobson, John Atkinson. *Imperialism*. Ann Arbor, 1965.

Hofstadter, Richard. *The Paranoid Style in American Politics*. New York, 1965.

Holbo, Paul S. "Presidential Leadership in Foreign Affairs: William McKinley and the Turpie-Foraker Amendment." *American Historical Review* 72 (1967): 1321–35.

Hollingsworth, J. Rogers. *The Whirligig of Politics: The Democracy of Cleveland and Bryan*. Chicago, 1963.

Howe, M. A. DeWolfe. *Portrait of an Independent: Moorfield Storey, 1845–1929*. Boston, 1932.

Hunt, Michael H. "Resistance and Collaboration in the American Empire, 1898–1903: An Overview." *Pacific Historical Review* 48 (1979): 467–71.

Hurley, Victor. *Jungle Patrol: The Story of the Philippine Constabulary*. New York, 1939.

Iriye, Akira. *Across the Pacific: An Inner History of American–East Asian Relations*. New York, 1967.

Israel, Jerry. *Progressivism and the Open Door*. Pittsburgh, 1971.

Johnson, J. R. "Imperialism in Nebraska, 1898–1904." *Nebraska History* 44 (1963): 141–66.

Jensen, Richard. *The Winning of the Midwest: Social and Political Conflict, 1888–1896*. Chicago, 1971.

Kalaw, Maximo M. *The Case for the Filipinos*. New York, 1916.

———. *The Development of Philippine Politics, 1872–1920*. Quezon City, 1928.

Kalaw, Teodoro M. *Gregorio H. Del Pilar: El Hero de Tirad*. Manila, 1930.

———. *The Philippine Revolution*. Manila, 1969.

Karsten, Peter. "The Nature of 'Influence': Roosevelt, Mahan, and the Concept of Sea Power." *American Quarterly* 23 (1971): 585–600.

Kearns, Doris. *Lyndon Johnson and the American Dream*. New York, 1976.

Keegan, John. *The Face of Battle*. New York, 1976.

Keesing, Felix M. *The Philippines: A Nation in the Making*. New York, 1937.

Kirk, Grayson. *Philippine Independence: Motives, Problems, and Prospects*. New York, 1936.

Kirkvliet, Benedict J. *The Huk Rebellion: A Study of Peasant Revolt in the Philippines*. Berkeley, 1977.

Kleppner, Paul. *The Cross of Culture: A Social Analysis of Midwestern Politics, 1850–1890*. New York, 1970.

Koebner, Richard, and Schmitt, Helmut. *Imperialism: The Story and Significance of a Political Word, 1840–1960*. Cambridge, 1964.

Kolko, Gabriel. *The Roots of American Foreign Policy*. Boston, 1969.

LaFeber, Walter, and McCormick, Thomas J. *Creation of the American Empire*. Chicago, 1973.

———. *The New Empire: An Interpretation of American Empire*. Ithaca, 1968.

———. "A Note on the 'Mercantilistic Imperialism' of Alfred Thayer Mahan." *The Mississippi Valley Historical Review* 48 (1962): 674–85.

Langer, William L. "A Critique of Imperialism." *Foreign Affairs* 14 (1935): 102–19.

———. *The Diplomacy of Imperialism, 1890–1902*. New York, 1956.

Lansang, J. A. "Philippine-American Experience: A Filipino View." *Foreign Affairs* 25 (1952): 226–34.

Lantenari, Vittorio. *The Religions of the Oppressed: A Study of Modern Messianic Cults*. New York, 1963.

Lanzar-Carpio, Maria C. "Anti-Imperialist Activities Between 1900 and the Election of 1904." *Philippine Social Science Review* 4 (1932): 239–54.

Larkin, John A. *The Pampangans: Colonial Society in a Philippine Province*. Berkeley, 1972.

Lasch, Christopher. "The Anti-Imperialists, the Philippines and the Inequality of Man." *Journal of Southern History* 24 (1958): 319–31.

Leech, Margaret. *In the Days of McKinley*. New York, 1959.

Lens, Sidney. *The Forging of the American Empire*. New York, 1971.

Leopold, Richard W. "The Emergence of America as a World Power: Some Second Thoughts." In *Change and Continuity in Twentieth Century America*, edited by John Braeman, Robert H. Bremmer, and Everett Walters. Columbus, Ohio, 1964.

Leuchtenburg, William E. "The Needless War with Spain." In *Times of Trial*, edited by Allan Nevins. New York, 1958.

———. "Progressivism and Imperialism: The Progressive Movement and American Foreign Policy, 1898–1916." *The Mississippi Valley Historical Review* 39 (1952): 483–504.

Linderman, Gerald F. *The Mirror of War: American Society and the Spanish American War*. Ann Arbor, 1974.

Lininger, Clarence. *The Best War at the Time*. New York, 1964.

Link, Arthur. *Woodrow Wilson: The Road to the White House*. Princeton, 1947.

Livermore, Seward W. "American Strategy Diplomacy in the South Pacific, 1890–1914." *Pacific Historical Review* 12 (1943): 35–51.

Livezey, Charles and Elizabeth. *Mahan on Sea Power*. Norman, Okla., 1947.

Loy, Edward H. "Editorial Opinion and American Imperialism: Two Northwest Newspapers." *Oregon Historical Quarterly* 72 (1971): 209–24.

McCall, Samuel W. *The Life of Thomas Brackett Reed*. Boston, 1914.

McCormick, Thomas J. *The China Market: America's Quest for Informal Empire, 1893–1901*. Chicago, 1967.

———. "Insular Imperialism and the Open Door: The China Market and the Spanish American War." *Pacific Historical Review* 32 (1963): 155–69.

McCullough, David. *The Path Between the Seas: The Creation of the Panama Canal, 1870–1914*. New York, 1977.

McDermott, John. "Welfare Imperialism in Vietnam." *The Nation* 203 (1966): 76–88.

McDonald, Timothy G. "McKinley and the Coming of the War with Spain." *Midwest Quarterly* 7 (1966): 225–39.

McGurrin, James. *Bourke Cockran: A Free Lance in American Politics*. New York, 1948.

McKee, Delber L. "Samuel Gompers, the A.F. of L., and Imperialism, 1895–1900." *Historian* 21 (1959): 187–99.

McSeveney, Samuel T. *The Politics of Depression. Political Behavior in the Northeast, 1893–1896*. New York, 1972.

Magdoff, Harry. *The Age of Imperialism*. New York, 1969.

Majul, Cesar A. "Aguinaldo and Mabini." *Historical Bulletin* (Manila) 3 (1959): 19–26.

———. *Mabini and the Philippine Revolution*. Quezon City, 1960.

———. *The Political and Constitutional Ideas of the Philippine Revolution*. Quezon City, 1957.

Mannoni, O. *Prospero and Caliban*. New York, 1964.

Marks, George P., comp. and ed. *The Black Press Views American Imperialism (1898–1900)*. New York, 1971.

———. "Opposition of Negro Newspapers to American Philippine Policy, 1899–1900." *Midwest Journal* 4 (1951): 1–25.

Mason, Gregory. *Remember the Maine*. New York, 1939.

May, Ernest R. *American Imperialism: A Speculative Essay*. New York, 1968.

———. *Imperial Democracy: The Emergence of America as a Great Power*. New York, 1961.

May, Glenn. "Filipino Resistance to American Occupation: Batangas, 1899–1902." *Pacific Historical Review* 48 (1979): 531–56.

Merk, Frederick. *Manifest Destiny and Mission in American History*. New York, 1963.

Miller, Richard H. *American Imperialism in 1898: The Quest for National Fulfillment*. New York, 1970.

Miller, Stuart Creighton. "Ends and Means: The Missionary Justification of Force in Nineteenth Century China." In *The Missionary Enterprise in China and America*, edited by John King Fairbank. Cambridge, Mass., 1974.

———. "Our Mylai of 1900." *Trans-action* 7 (1970): 19–28.

———. *The Unwelcome Immigrant: The American Image of the Chinese, 1785–1882*. Berkeley, 1969.

Millis, Walter. *The Martial Spirit*. New York, 1931.

Minger, Ralph E. "Taft, MacArthur, and the Establishment of Civil Government in the Philippines." *The Ohio Historical Quarterly* 70 (1961): 308–31.

Morgan, H. Wayne. *America's Road to Empire: The War with Spain and Overseas Expansion*. New York, 1965.

———, ed. *The Gilded Age: A Reappraisal*. Syracuse, 1963.

———. *William McKinley and His America*. Syracuse, 1963.

Morison, Samuel Eliot. *The Development of Harvard University Since the Inauguration of President Eliot, 1869–1929*. Cambridge, Mass., 1930.

———; Merk, Frederick; and Friedel, Frank, eds. *Dissent in Three American Wars*. Cambridge, Mass., 1970.

Mott, Frank Luther. *A History of American Magazines*. 5 vols. Cambridge, Mass., 1938–68.

Muller, Dorothea. "Josiah Strong and American Nationalism." *Journal of American History* 53 (1968): 487–503.

Neale, R. G. *Great Britain and United States Expansion, 1898–1900.* East Lansing, Mich., 1966.

Nelson, Raymond. *The Philippines.* London, 1968.

Nevins, Allan. *Grover Cleveland: A Study in Courage.* New York, 1932.

Newman, Philip Charles. "Democracy and Imperialism in American Political Thought." *Philippine Social Sciences and Humanities Review* 15 (1950): 351–67.

Nichols, Jeannette P. "The United States Congress and Imperialism, 1861–1897." *The Journal of Economic History* 21 (1961): 526–38.

Notter, Harley. *The Origins of the Foreign Policy of Woodrow Wilson.* Baltimore, 1937.

Olcott, Charles S. *The Life of William McKinley.* 2 vols. Boston, 1916.

Onorato, Michael P., ed. *Philippine Bibliography, 1894–1946.* Santa Barbara, 1969.

———. "The United States and the Philippine Independence Movement." *Solidarity* 5 (1970): 2–15.

Osgood, Robert Endicott. *Ideals and Self-Interest in America's Foreign Relations.* Chicago, 1953.

Owen, Norman G., ed. *Compadre Colonialism: Studies on the Philippines Under American Rule.* Ann Arbor, 1971.

———. "Winding Down the War in Albay, 1900–1903." *Pacific Historical Review* 48 (1979): 557–89.

Owen, Roger, and Sutcliffe, Bob, eds. *Studies in the Theory of Imperialism.* London, 1972.

Palma-Bonifacio, Virginia, ed. *The Trial of Andres Bonifacio.* Manila, 1963.

Plesur, Milton. *America's Outward Thrust: Approaches to Foreign Affairs, 1865–1890.* DeKalb, Ill., 1971.

Pletcher, David M. *The Awkward Years: American Foreign Relations Under Garfield and Arthur.* Columbia, Mo., 1962.

Pomeroy, Earl. *Pacific Outpost: American Strategy in Guam and Micronesia.* Palo Alto, 1951.

Pomeroy, William J. *American Neo-Colonialism: Its Emergence in the Philippines and Asia.* New York, 1971.

———. *An American-Made Tragedy: Neo-Colonialism and Dictatorship in the Philippines.* New York, 1974.

———. "Pacification in the Philippines." *France-Asie* 21 (1967): 427–46.

Pratt, Julius W. *America's Colonial Experiment: How the United States Gained, Governed, and in Part Gave Away an Empire.* New York, 1951.

———. *The Expansionists of 1898: The Acquisition of Hawaii and the Spanish Islands.* Baltimore, 1936.

Pringle, Henry F. *Theodore Roosevelt: A Biography.* New York, 1931.

Radosh, Ronald, and Davies, Horace B. "American Labor and the Anti-Imperialist Movement: A Discussion." *Science and Society* 28 (1964): 91–104.

Reuter, Frank T. *Catholic Influence on American Colonial Policies, 1898–1904.* Austin, Tex., 1967.

Rickover, Hyman G. *How the Battleship Maine Was Destroyed.* Washington, D.C., 1976.

Robinson, Michael C., and Schubert, Frank N. "David Fagen: An Afro-American Rebel in the Philippines, 1899–1901." *Pacific Historical Review* 44 (1975): 68–83.

Robles, Eldioro. *The Philippines in the Nineteenth Century.* Quezon City, 1969.

Rollins, John. "The Anti-Imperialists and Twentieth Century American Foreign Policy." *Studies on the Left* 3 (1962): 9–24.

Rothstein, Morton. "The American West and Foreign Markets." In *The Frontier in American Development: Essays in Honor of Paul Williard Gates*. Edited by D. M. Ellis. Ithaca, 1969.

Ryder, George H. *The Foreign Policy of the United States in Relation to Samoa*. New Haven, 1933.

Rystad, Göran. *Ambiguous Imperialism: American Foreign Policy and Domestic Politics at the Turn of the Century*. Stockholm, 1975.

Salamanca, Bonifacio S. *The Filipino Reaction to American Rule, 1901–1913*. Hamden, Conn., 1968.

Saum, Lewis. "The Western Volunteers and the 'New Empire.'" *Pacific Northwestern Quarterly* 57 (1966): 18–27.

Scheiner, Seth M. "Theodore Roosevelt and the Negro, 1901–1908." *Journal of Negro History* 47 (1962): 169–82.

Schirmer, Daniel B. *Republic or Empire: American Resistance to the Philippine War*. Cambridge, Mass., 1972.

Schonberger, Howard. "William H. Becker and the New Left Revisionists: A Rebuttal." *Pacific Historical Review* 44 (1975): 249–61.

Schott, Joseph L. *The Ordeal of Samar*. Indianapolis, 1964.

Schumacher, John M. *The Propaganda Movement, 1880–1895*. Manila, 1973.

Schumpeter, Joseph. *Imperialism*. New York, 1955.

Seager, Robert. "Ten Years Before Mahan: The Unofficial Case for the New Navy, 1880–1890." *The Mississippi Valley Historical Review* 40 (1953): 491–512.

Seed, Geoffrey. "British Views of American Policy in the Philippines Reflected in Journals of Opinion, 1898–1907." *Journal of American Studies* 2 (1968): 49–64.

Semmel, Bernard. *Imperialism and Social Reform: English Social-Imperial Thought, 1895–1914*. Cambridge, Mass., 1960.

Sexton, William Thaddeus. *Soldiers in the Sun*. Harrisburg, Pa., 1939.

Shenton, James. "Imperialism and Racism." In *Essays in American Historiography*, edited by Donald Sheehan and Harold Syrett. New York, 1960.

Simpkins, Francis B. *Pitchfork Ben Tillman, South Carolinian*. New York, 1944.

Spector, Ronald. *Admiral of the New Empire*. Baton Rouge, 1974.

Stanley, Peter W. "The Making of an American Sinologist: William W. Rockhill and the Open Door." *Perspectives in American History* 11 (1977–78): 414–60.

———. *A Nation in the Making: The Philippines and the United States, 1899–1921*. Cambridge, Mass., 1974.

———. "William Cameron Forbes: Proconsul in the Philippines." *Pacific Historical Review* 35 (1966): 285–302.

Steinberg, David Joel. "An Ambiguous Legacy: Years at War in the Philippines." *Pacific Affairs* 45 (1972): 165–90.

———. *Philippine Collaboration in World War II*. Ann Arbor, 1967.

Sturtevant, David R. "Guardia de Honor: Revitalization Within the Revolution." *Asian Studies* 4 (1966): 342–52.

———. *Popular Uprisings in the Philippines, 1840–1940*. Ithaca, 1976.

———. "Sakdalism and Philippine Radicalism." *Journal of Asian Studies* 21 (1962): 199–215.

Sullivan, Mark. *Our Times: The United States, 1900–1925*, vol. 1. New York, 1926.

Sumner, William Graham. *The Essays of William Graham Sumner*. New Haven, 1934.

Taylor, George E. *The Philippines and the United States: Problems of Partnership*. New York, 1964.

Thayer, W. R. *The Life of John Hay*. Boston, 1915.

Thomson, James C., and May, Ernest R., eds. *American–East Asian Relations: A Survey*. Cambridge, Mass., 1972.

———; Stanley, Peter W.; and Perry, John Curtis. *Sentimental Imperialists: The American Experience in East Asia*. New York, 1981.

Thornton, Archibald Paton. *Doctrines of Imperialism*. New York, 1965.

———. *Imperialism in the Twentieth Century*. Minneapolis, 1977.

Tompkins, E. Berkeley. *Anti-Imperialism in the United States: The Great Debate, 1890–1920*. Philadelphia, 1970.

Turner, Frederick Jackson. *The Frontier in American History*. New York, 1920.

Tyler, Alice Felt. *The Foreign Policy of James G. Blaine*. Minneapolis, 1927.

Van Alstyne, Richard W. *The Rising American Empire*. New York, 1960.

Veeder, Russell. "The Philippine Question in the Red River Valley Press, 1898–1901." *North Dakota Quarterly* 42 (1974): 96–112.

Vevier, Charles. "American Continentalism: An Idea of Expansion, 1845–1910." *American Historical Review* 65 (1960): 323–35.

———. "Brooks Adams and the Ambivalence of American Foreign Policy." *World Affairs Quarterly* 30 (1930): 3–18.

Wall, Joseph Frazier. *Andrew Carnegie*. New York, 1970.

Wallace, Anthony. "Revitalization Movements." *American Anthropologist* 58 (1956): 264–81.

Weinberg, Albert K. *Manifest Destiny*. Baltimore, 1933.

Weinert, Richard P. "The Massacre at Balangiga." *American History Illustrated* 1 (1966): 37–40.

Welch, Richard E. "American Atrocities in the Philippines: The Indictment and the Response." *Pacific Historical Review* 43 (1974): 233–55.

———. *Imperialists Versus Anti-Imperialists: The Debate Over Expansion in the 1890's*. Itasca, Ill., 1972.

———. "Motives and Policy Objectives of Anti-Imperialists in 1898." *Mid-America* 51 (1969): 119–29.

———. "Opponents and Colleagues: George Frisbee Hoar and Henry Cabot Lodge, 1898–1904." *New England Quarterly* 39 (1966): 182–209.

———. "Organized Religion and the Philippine-American War." *Mid-America* 55 (1973): 184–206.

———. "'The Philippine Insurrection' and the American Press." *The Historian* 36 (1973): 34–51.

———. *Response to Imperialism: The United States and the Philippine-American War, 1899–1902*. Chapel Hill, 1979.

———. "Senator George Frisbee Hoar and the Defeat of Anti-Imperialism, 1898–1900." *The Historian* 26 (1964): 362–80.

———. *Senator George Frisbee Hoar and the Half-Breed Republicans*. Cambridge, Mass., 1971.

Whitaker, William George. "Samuel Gompers, Anti-Imperialist." *Pacific Historical Review* 38 (1968): 429–45.

White, John R. *Bullets and Bolos*. New York, 1928.

Wickberg, Edgar. *The Chinese in Philippine Life, 1850–1898.* New Haven, 1965.

———. "The Chinese Mestizo in Philippine History." *Journal of Southeast Asian History* 5 (1964): 62–110.

Wiebe, Robert. *The Search For Order, 1877–1920.* New York, 1957.

Wilkerson, Marcus. *Public Opinion and the Spanish-American War.* Baton Rouge, 1932.

Williams, William Appleman. "Brooks Adams and American Expansion." *New England Quarterly* 25 (1952): 217–32.

———. "The Frontier Thesis and American Foreign Policy." *Pacific Historical Review* 24 (1955): 379–95.

———. *The Roots of the Modern American Empire.* New York, 1969.

———. *The Tragedy of American Diplomacy.* New York, 1962.

Williamson, Harold F. *Edward Atkinson: The Biography of an American Liberal, 1827–1905.* Boston, 1934.

Wisan, J. E. *The Cuban Crisis as Reflected in the New York Press.* New York, 1934.

Wolff, Leon. *Little Brown Brother. How the United States Purchased and Pacified the Philippine Islands at the Century's Turn.* Garden City, N.Y., 1961.

Young, Marilyn Blatt. "The Quest for Empire." In *American–East Asian Relations: A Survey,* edited by James C. Thomson and Ernest R. May. Cambridge, Mass., 1972.

———. *The Rhetoric of Empire: American China Policy, 1895–1901.* Cambridge, Mass., 1968.

Zaide, Gregorio F. *A Documentary History of the Katipunan.* Manila, 1941.

———. *A History of the Katipunan.* Manila, 1939.

———. *Philippine Political and Cultural History.* 2 vols. Manila, 1949.

———. *The Philippine Revolution.* Manila, 1954.

Index

Abbott, Lyman, 123, 139
Adams, Brooks, 6, 8, 117
Adams, Charles Francis, 105, 120, 124, 140, 158
Adams, Henry, 8, 105
Aglipayan Church, 139, 171, 261
Agoncillo, Felipe, 46, 55, 92, 284n40
Aguinaldo, 167, 171
Aguinaldo, Emilio, 20, 25, 30, 31; and insurrection of 1896, 33–35; and Bonifacio's execution, 34; in exile, 35–36; early relations
  of, with Americans, 35–37, 40–56; admiration of, for U.S., 37–38, 275; ilustrado influence over, 38–39, 275; Dewey's betrayal of,
  42–43, 244; peace offers of, 63, 69, 76–78;
  and murder of Luna, 75–76; denies atrocities, 93–94; flees Lawton, 96–97; published
  view of war of, 132–33, 184; and Democrats,
  142–43, 145–46; praised by ilustrados, 155;
  portrayed as "outlaw," 157, 158, 160, 244;
  capture of, 167–70; cooperation of, following
  capture, 170–71; as potential witness, 241; as
  tarnished hero, 263
Alejandrino, Jose, 76, 78, 171
Alger, Russell, 12, 80–81, 83
Allen, William, 15, 26
Altgeld, John, 106, 107, 142, 144
Anderson, T. M., 37, 40–44 passim
Anglo-Saxon romanticism: and imperialism, 6,
  125, 134, 162; and missionaries, 7, 18–19;
  and anti-imperialists, 121–25, 136; and Mac-
  Arthur, 189, 240
Anti-Imperialist League: and annexation,
  29; formation and membership of, 105–06;
  conservative nature of, 106–10; accused of
  treason, 107–10; organizes protests, 109,

114, 140, 154, 245; fails to enlist key anti-
imperialists, 110–11; quality of leadership
of, 113–14; and Negroes, 127; becomes divided, 261
Anti-imperialists: racial fears of, 15, 26, 122–
  28 passim, 271; oppose annexation, 25–27,
  29–30; and Bryan, 28, 137–38; as "traitors,"
  65, 107–10, 142–43, 145–46, 155; oppose
  war with Spain, 104; as aging patricians, 114,
  117; as neocolonialists, 118–20; as elitist
  Anglo-Saxons, 120–22; and Boer War, 136;
  attempt to form third party, 137–38; accused
  of slandering the army, 141, 246–47; attempt
  to negotiate with Aguinaldo, 141–42; rationalize political defeats, 148–49, 263; and
  Spooner bill, 159–60; and soldiers, 176,
  185–87; waning enthusiasm of, 259
Arena, quoted, 213, 233, 237, 259
Argüelles, Manuel, 75, 76–77
Army and Navy Journal, quoted, 209, 259
Atkinson, Edward: and neocolonialism, 4, 119;
  and formation of Anti-Imperialist League,
  105; branded a "traitor," 107–08, 142; personal propagandizing of, 107–09; elitist
  Anglo-Saxonism of, 120–22; loses interest in
  anti-imperialism, 140
Atrocities: Spanish, 9; American, 88–90, 118,
  154, 183, 187–88, 211, 216, 217–18, 238–39,
  243; and correspondents, 91, 209–11; Filipino, 92–94; as issue in elections, 129, 262;
  denounced by Hoar, 155–56; worldwide,
  164. See also "Water cure"

Bacon, Augustus, 26, 28, 29, 30, 243
Balangiga: occupation of, 200–01; massacre at,

331